JN415099

CRIMINOLOGY

범죄학

제대로 알기(2판)

양원규 · 배철효 · 정우열 · 장철영 공저

본서의 특 · 장점

- 경비지도사 추천도서
- 범죄학개론의 종결서
- 최근 법령과 기출문제의 분석과 반영
- 해설주(解說註)와 인용주(引用註)의 정확한 표기(表記)

백산출판사

머리말

범죄학은 범죄현상에 대한 체계화된 지식이다. 범죄학 과목은 현재 경비지도사의 시험과목일 뿐만 아니라 고시 등 각종 시험과목의 하나로 이미 자리매김하고 있으며, 수사학을 대체하는 과목으로 경찰행정학과에 개설되어 있고, 대학 교양과목으로도 이미 많은 대학교에서 수강되고 있다. 이는 작금(昨今)의 범죄의 심각성에 따른 생활치안·체감치안의 확보라는 시대적 요청이 분출된 결과라 할 것이다.

본서의 특·장점은 다음과 같다.

첫째, 범죄학에 대한 이해를 도모하기 위해 관련 형법, 형사소송법, 범죄심리학, 조직범죄론, 범죄피해자학, 교정학, 형사정책학의 내용을 반영하여, 관련 분야의 자료를 찾아야 하는 독자들의 수고를 덜도록 하였다.

둘째, 경비지도사의 주요 과목인 범죄학개론의 기출문제를 분석하고 관련된 내용에 대한 상세한 설명과 함께 각종 시험의 수험서로써 부족함이 없도록 하였다.

셋째, 범죄학의 주요 용어(用語) 중 한글로써 그 정확한 의미를 알 수 없는 것은 한자(漢字)와 영어(英語)를 병기(併記)하여 용어에 대한 정확한 이해를 도모하였다.

넷째, 독자 중심의 one stop service란 concept하에 관련된 법조문을 반영하여, 법전을 다시 찾아야 하는 수고를 덜도록 하였다.

다섯째, 각주(脚註)는 실제 기출문제의 내용과 이에 따른 보충설명을 하였고, 추가적인 심화학습이 필요한 경우를 고려하여 내용의 출처를 명확히 하였다.

본서는 경찰학을 공부하는 많은 후학들을 위해 『민간경비론 제대로 알기』(백산출판사, 2013년), 『경찰학총론 제대로 알기』(백산출판사, 2013년, 2판), 『조직이론 제대로 알기』(대왕사, 2012년), 『경찰관리론 제대로 알기』(백산출판사, 2012년, 2판), 『행정학 제대로 알기』(백산출판사, 2011년, 6판), 『경찰학총론 I 제대로 알기』(백산출판사, 2009년), 『경찰학총론 II 제대로 알기』(백산출판사, 2009년), 『경찰행정법 제대로 알기』(한올출판사, 2009년, 2판), 『경찰조직관리론 제대로 알기』(백산출판사, 2010년)와 함께 시리즈로 집필되었다.

『범죄학 제대로 알기』를 출간함에 앞서, 먼저 범죄학 분야에 선구적인 역할을 하신 많은 선배 교수님의 노고에 감사드리고자 한다. 특히 이윤호 교수님, 이상현 교수님, 전대양 교수님, 송병호 교수님, 조병인 교수님, 이만종 교수님, 김용준 교수님, 임상곤 교수님, 공정식 교수님의 연구에 많은 도움을 받았기에 이에 그 고마운 마음을 표시하고자 한다.

졸저를 탈고(脫稿)할 수 있었던 것은 공저자(共著者)인 대경대학교 양원규 교수, 수성대학교 배철효 교수, 경운대학교 정우열 교수, 대구외국어대학교 장철영 교수의 헌신적인 노력과 연구의 결과이며, 미흡하고 부족한 책임 또한 모두의 천학비재(淺學菲才)로 돌리며, 앞으로 더욱 분발(奮發)하고자 한다.

또한 본서의 출판을 위해 수고해 주신 백산출판사 진욱상 사장님, 진성원 상무님, 금병수 부장님 그리고 편집부 및 관계자분들의 노고에 감사한 마음을 전한다.

머리 숙여 독자 제위에게 감사드린다.

2014년 1월

양원규 · 배철효 · 정우열 · 장철영

공저자 일동

차례

제 1 편 범죄일반론

제 3 편 범죄원인론

제16장 심리학적 범죄원인론 / 242

제17장 사회학적 범죄원인론 / 258

제 4 편 범죄대책론

표 차례

그림 차례

Criminological Theory Summaries

Theory	Main Points	Theorists/Researchers
Classical	Crime occurs when the benefite outweigh the costs—when people pursue self-interest in the absence of effective punishments. Crime is a free-willed choice. See also deterrence, rational choice.	Beccaria
Positivist	Crime is caused or determined. Lombroso placed more emphasis on biological deficiencies, whereas later scholars would emphasize psychological and sociological factors. Use science to determine the factors associated with crime.	Lombroso Guerry Quetelet
Individual Trait	Criminals differ from noncriminals on a number of biological and psychological traits. These traits cause crime in interaction with the social environment	Glueck & Glueck Mednick Caspi Moffitt
Social Disorganization	Disorganized communities cause crime because informal social controls break down and criminal cultures emerge. They lack collective efficacy to fight crime and disorder.	Shaw & McKay Sampson Bursik & Grasmick
Differential Association Social Learning Subcultural	Crime is learned through associations with criminal definitions. These definitions might be generally approving of criminal conduct or be neutralizations that justify crime only under certain circumstances. Interacting with antisocial peers is a major cause of crime. Criminal behavior will be repeated and become chronic if reinforced. When criminal subcultures exist, then many individuals can learn to commit crime in one location and crime rate—including violence—may become very high.	Sutherland & Cressey Sykes & Matza Akers Wolfgang & Ferracuti Anderson
Anomie Institutional-Anomie	The gap between the American Dream's goal of economic success and the opportunity to obtain this goal creates structural strain. Norms weaken and 'anomie' ensues, thus creating high crime rates. When other social institutions (such as the family) are weak to begin with or also weakened by the American Dream, the economic institution is dominant. When such an institutional imbalance exists—as in the United States—then crime rates are very high.	Merton Messner & Rosenfeld

Strain General Strain	When individuals cannot obtain success goals (money, status in school), they experience strain or pressure. Under certain conditions, they are likely to respond to this stain through crime. The strains leading to crime, however, may not only be linked to goal blockage (or deprivation of valued stimuli) but also to the presentation of noxious stimuli and the taking away of valued stimuli. Crime is a more likely response to strain when it results in negative affect (anger and frustration).	Cohen Cloward & Ohlin Agnew
Control General Theory of Crime Control Balance Power Control	Asks the question, "Why don't people commit crime?" They assume that criminal motivation is widespread. They key factor in crime causation is thus the presence or absence of control. These controls or containment might be rooted in relationship (e.g., social bonds) or be internal (e.g., self-control). Exposure to control also might differ by social location and by the historical period, such as the changing level and type of control given to males and females.	Hirschi Reckless Gottfredson Hagan
Rational Choice Deterrence	Building on classical theory, crime is seen as a choice that is influenced by its costs and benefits—that is, by its "rationality." Crime will be more likely to be deterred if its costs are raised (e.g., more effort required, more punishment applied), especially if the costs and immediate. Information about the costs and benefits of crime can be obtained by direct experiences with punishment and punishment avoidance, and indirectly by observing whether others who offend are punished or avoid punishment.	Stafford & Warr Patternoster Cornish & Clarke Matsueda
Routine Activities	Crime occurs when there is an intersection in time and space of a motivated offender, an attractive target, and a lack of capable guardianship. People's daily routine activities affect the likelihood they will be an attractive target who encounters an offender in a situation where no effective guardianship is present. Changes in routine activities in society (e.g., women working) can affect crime rates.	Cohen & Felson

Labeling Reintegrative Shaming	People become stabilized in criminal roles when they are labeled as criminal, are stigmatized, develop criminal identities, are sent to prison, and are excluded from conventional roles. Reintegrative responses are less likely to create defiance and a commitment to crime.	Lemert Matsueda Braithwaite Sherman
Critical	Inequality in power and material well-being create conditions that lead to street crime and corporate crime. Capitalism and its market economy are especially criminogenic because they create vast inequality that impoverishes many and provides opportunities for exploitation for the powerful.	Bonger Quinney Greenberg Currie Colvin
Peacemaking	Crime is caused by suffering, which is linked to injustice rooted in inequality and daily personal acts of harm. Making "war on crime" will not work. Making peace is the solution to crime.	Quinney
Feminism	Crime cannot be understood without considering gender. Crime is shaped by the different social experiences of and power is exercised by men and women. Patriarchy is a broad structure that shapes gender-related experiences and power. Men may use crime to exert control over women and to demonstrate masculinity—that is, to show that they are "men" in a way consistent with societal ideals of masculinity.	Adler Daly Chesney-Lind Messerschmidt
Developmental Life Course	Crime causation is a developmental process that starts before birth and continues throughout the life course. Individual factors interact with social factors to determine the onset, length, and end of criminal careers. They key theoretical issues involve continuity and change in crime. Some theories predict continuity across the life course; others predict continuity for some offenders and change for other offenders; and some predict continuity and change for the same offenders.	Moffitt Sampson & Laub
Integrated	These theories use components from other theories—usually strain, control, and social learning—to create a new theory that explains crime. They often are life-course theories, arguing that causes of crime occur in a sequence across time.	Elliott Thornberry Tittle Cullen

Adapted from: Cullen & Agnew (2002). Criminological Theoy: Past to Present (Essential Readings). Los Angeles, CA: Roxbury.

범죄학의 주요 용어(Glossary)

A

acquaintance rape Rape characterized by a prior social, though not necessarily intimate or familial, relationship between the victim and the perpetrator.

administrative law Law that regulates many daily business activities. Violations of these regulations generally result in warnings or fines, depending on their adjudged severity.

Age of Reason See **Enlightenment.**

aggravated assault (UCR) An unlawful attack by one person upon another for the purpose of inflicting severe or aggravated bodily injury. See also **simple assault.**

alloplastic adaptation A form of adjustment that results from changes in the environment surrounding an individual.

androcentricity A single-sex perspective, as in the case of criminologists wso study only the criminality of males.

anomie A social condition in which norms are uncertain or lacking.

anomie theory See **strain theory.**

Anti-Drug Abuse Act A federal law (Public Law 99-570) enacted in 1986 that established new federal mandatory minimum sentences for drug offenses.

antisocial (asocial) personality A term used to describe individuals who are basically unsocialized and whose behavior pattern brings them repeatedly into conflict with society.

antisocial personality disorder A psychological condition exhibited by individuals who are basically unsocialized and whose behavior pattern brings them repeatedly into conflicts with society.

applied research Scientific inquiry that is desingned and carried out with practical applications in mind.

Arrestee Drug Abuse Monitoring (ADAM) Program A National Institute of Justice program, that tracks trends in the prevalence and types of drug use among booked arrestees in urban areas.

arson The willful or malicious burning or attempt to burn, with or without intent to defraud, of a dwelling house, public building, motor vehicle or aircraft, personal property of another, and so on.

asocial personality See **antisocial personality**.

assault See **aggravated assault; simple assault**.

asset forfeiture The authorized seizure of money, negotiable instruments, securities, or other things of value. In federal antidrug laws, the authorization of judicial representatives to seize all monies, negotiable instruments, securities, or other things of value furnished or intended to be furnished by any person in exchange for a controlled substance, and all proceeds traceable to such an exchange.

atavism A term used by Cesare Lombroso to

suggest that criminals are physiological throwbacks to earlier stages of human evolution. The term is derived from the Latin term *atavus*, which means "ancestor."

attachment theory A social-psychological perspective on delinquent and criminal behavior that holds that the successful development of secure attachment between a child and his or her primary caregiver provides the basic foundation for all future psychological development.

audit trail A sequential record of computer system activities that enables auditors to reconstruct, review, and examine the sequence of states and activities surrounding each event in one or more related transactions from inception to output of final results back to inception.

autoplastic adaptation A form of adjustment that results from changes within an individual.

B

bank fraud Fraud or embezzlement that occurs within or against financial institutions that are insured or regulated by the U.S. government. Financial institution fraud includes commercial loan fraud, check fraud, counterfeit negotiable instruments, mortgage fraud, check kiting, and false credit applications.

behavior theory A psychological perspective that posits that individual behavior that is rewarded will increase in frequency, while that which is punished will decrease.

behavioral genetics The study of genetic and environmental contributions to individual variations in human behavior.

bias crime See **hate crime**.

biological theory A theory that maintains that the basic determinants of human behavior, including criminality, are constitutionally or physiologically based and often inherited.

booster A frequent shoplifter.

born criminal An individual who is born with a genetic predilection toward criminality.

bourgeoisie In Marxist treory, the class of people who own the means of production.

Brady Handgun Violence Prevention Act A federal law (Public Law 103-159) enacted in 1993 that initiated a national background checking system for all potential gun purchasers.

Brawner rule A somewhat vague rule for determining insanity that was created in the 1972 federal court case of *United States v. Brawner* (471 F.2d 969), since superseded by statute, and asks the jury to decide whether the defendant could be *justly* held responsible for the criminal act with which he or she stands charged, in the face of any claims of insanity or mental incapacity.

broken windows thesis A perspective on crime causation that holds that physical deterioration in an area leads to increased concerns for personal safety among area residents and to higher crime rates in that area.

bulletin board system (BBS) A computer accessible by telephone and used like a bulletin board to leave messages and files for other users. Also called *computer bulletin board*.

burglary By the narrowest and oldest definition, the trespassory breaking and entering of the dwelling house of another in the nighttime with the intent to commit a felony. Also, the unlawful entry of a structure to commit a felony or a theft.

burglary (UCR) The unlawful entry of any fixed structure, vehicle, or vessel used for regular residence, industry, or business, with or without force, with intent to commit a felony or a larceny.

| C |

Cambridge Study in Delinquent Development A longitudinal (life-course) study of crime and delinquency tracking a cohort of 411 boys born in London in 1953.

capable guardian One who effectively discourages crime.

capital punishment The legal imposition of a sentence of death upon a convicted offender. Also called *death penalty*.

carjacking The stealing of a car while it is occupied.

Chicago Area Project A program focusing on urban ecology and originating at the University of Chicago during the 1930s, which attempted to reduce delinquency, crime, and social disorganization in transitional neighborhoods.

Chicago School of criminology See **ecological theory.**

child sexual abuse (CSA) A term encompassing a variety of criminal and civil offenses in which an adult engages in sexual activity with a minor, exploits a minor for purposes of sexual gratification, or exploits a minor sexually for purposes of profit.

civil law The body of law that regulates arrangements between indviduals, such as contracts and claims to property.

Classical School A criminological perspective of the late 1700s and early 1800s that had its roots in the Enlightenment and that held that hmans are rational beings, that crime is the result of the exercise of free will, and that punishment can be effective in reducing the incidence of crime, as it negates the pleasure to be derived from crime commission.

clearance rate The proportion of reported or discovered crimes within a given offense category that are solved.

Code of Hammurabi An early set of laws established by the Babylonian king Hammurabi, who ruled the ancient city from 1792 to 1750 B.C.

cohort A group of individuals having certain significant social characteristics in common, such as gender and date and place of birth.

cohort analysis A social scientific technique that studies over time a population with common characteristics. Cohort analysis usually begins at birth and traces the development of cohort members until they reach a certain age.

Commission on Law Observance and Enforcement See **Wickersham Commission.**

common law Law originating from usage and custom rather than from written statutes. The term refers to nonstatutory customs, traditions, and precedents that help guide judicial decision making.

Communications Dencency Act A federal statute signed into law in 1996, the CDA is Title 5 of the federal Telecommunications Act of 1996 (Public Law 104-104, 110 Stat. 56). The law sought to protect minors from harmful material on the Intenet, and a portion of the CDA criminalized the knowing transmission of obscene or indecent messages to any recipient under 18 years of age. In 1997, however, in the case of *Reno v. ACLU* (521 U.S. 844), the U.S. Supreme Court found the bulk of the CDA to be unconstitutional, ruling that it contravenes First Amendment free speech guarantees.

comparative criminologist A criminologist involed in the cross-national study of crime.

comparative criminology AThe crossnational study of crime.

Comprehensive Crime Control Act A far-reaching federal law (Public Law 98-473) enacted in 1984 that mandated new federal sentencing guidelines, eliminated parole at the federal level, limited the use of the insanity defense in federal criminal courts, and increased federal penalties associated with drug dealing.

computer abuse Any unlawful incident associated with computer technology in which a victim suffered or could have suffered loss or in which a perpetrator by intention made or could have made gain.

computer bulletin board See **bulletin board system (BBS).**

computer crime Any violation of a federal or state computer crime statute. See also **Cybercrime.**

computer-related crime Any illegal act for which knowledge of computer technology is involved in its perpetration, investigation, or prosecution.

computer virus A set of computer instructions that propagates copies or versions of itself into computer programs or data when it is executed.

conditioning A psychological principle that holds that the frequency of any behavior can be increased or decreased through reward, punishment, or association with other stimuli.

conduct norms Shared expectations of a social group relative to personal conduct.

confidentiality See **data confidentiality.**

conflict perspective An analytical perspective on social organization that holds that conflict is a fundamental aspect of social life itself and can never be fully resolved.

confounding effects A rival explanation, or competing hypothesis, that is a threat to the internal or external vaidity of a research design.

consensus model An analytical perspective on social organization that holds that most members of society agree about what is right and what is wrong and that the various elements of society work together in unison toward a common vision of the greater good.

constitutional theory A theory that explains criminality by reference to offenders' body types, inheritance, genetics, or external observable physical characteristics.

constitutive criminology The study of the process by which human beings create an ideology of crime that sustains the notion of crime as a concrete reality.

containment Aspects of the social bond that act to prevent individuals from committing crimes and that keep them from engaging in deviance.

containment theory A from of control theory that suggests that a series of both internal and external factors contributes to law-abiding behavior.

control group A group of experimental subjects that, although the subject of measurement and observation, is not exposed to the experimental intervention.

control ratio The amount of control to which a person is subject versus the amount of control that person exerts over others.

control theory See **social control theory.**

controlled experiment An experiment that attempts to hold conditions (other than the intentionally introduced experimental intervention) constant.

convict criminology A new analytical paradigm consisting of writings on the subject matter of criminology by convicted felons and ex-inmates who have acquired academic credentials, or who are associated with credentialled others.

corporate crime A violation of a criminal statute either by a corporate entity or by its executives, employees, or agents acting on behalf of and for the benefit of the corporation, partnership, or other form of business entity.

correctional psychology The branch of forensic psychology concerned with the diagnosis and classification of offenders, the treatment of correctional populations, and the rehabilitation of inmates and other law violators.

correlation A causal, complementary, or reciprocal relationship between two measurable variables. See also **statistical correlation.**

Cosa Nostra Literally, "our thing." A criminal organization of Sicilian origin. Also called *the Mafia*, *the Outfit*, *the Mob*, *the syndicate*, or simply the *organization*.

crime Human conduct in violation of the criminal laws of a state, the federal government, or a local jurisdiction that has the power to make such laws.

crime typology A classification of crimes along a particular dimension, such as legal categories, offender motivation, victim behavior, or the characteristics of individual offenders.

Crime Victims' Rights Act A 2004 federal law that establishes statutory rights for victims of federal crimes, and gives victims the necessary legal authority to assert those rights in federal courts.

criminal anthropology The scientific study of the relationship between human physical characteristics and criminality.

criminal career The longitudinal sequence of crimes committed by an individual offender.

criminal homicide The illegal killing of one human being by another.

criminal homicide (UCR) The UCR category that includes and is limited to all offenses of causing the death of another person without justification or excuse.

criminal justice system The various agencies of justice, especially the police, courts, and corrections, whose goal it is to apprehend, convict, punish, and rehabilitate law violators.

criminal justice The scientific study of crime, the criminal law, and components of the criminal justice system, including the police, courts, and corrections.

criminal law The body of law that regulates actions that have the potential to harm the interests of the state or the federal government.

criminal psychology See **forensic psychology.**

criminal receiver See **fence.**

criminalist A specialist in the collection and examination of the physical evidence of crime.

criminality A behavioral predisposition that disproportionately favors criminal activity.

criminality index The actual extent of the crime problem in a society. The criminality index is computed by adding the actual crime rate and the latent crime rate.

criminalize To make illegal.

criminaloids A term used by Cesare Lombroso to describe occasional criminals who were pulled into criminality primarily by environmental influences.

criminologist One who is trained in the field of criminology. Aloso, one who studies crime, criminals, and criminal behavior.

criminology An interdisciplinary profession built around the scientific study of crime and criminal behavior, including their forms, causes, legal aspects, and control.

criminology of place See **environmental criminology.**

critical criminology See **radical criminology.**

cross-impact analysis A technique of futures research that attempts to analyze one trend or event in light of the occurrence or nonoccurrence of a series of related events.

cultural transmission The transmission of delinquency through successive generations of people living in the same area through a process of social communication.

culture conflict theory A sociological perspective on crime that suggests that the root cause of criminality can be found in a clash of values between variously socialized groups over what is acceptable or proper behavior.

Cyber Security Enhancement Act Part of the Homeland Security Act of 2002, this federal law directed the U.S. sentencing commission to take several specific factors into account in creating new sentencing guidelines for computer criminals.

cybercrime Crime committed with the use of computers or via the manipulation of digital forms of data. See also **computer crime.**

cyberspace The computer-created matrix of virtual possibilities, including online services, wherein human beings interact with one another and with the technology itself.

cyberstalking An array of hightechnology related activities in which an offender may engage to harass or "follow" individuals, including e-mail and the Internet.

cyberterrorism A form of terrorism that makes use of high technology, especially computer technology and the Internet, in the planning and carrying out of terrorist attacks.

cycloid A term developed by Ernst Kretschmer to describe a particular relationship between body build and personality type. The cycloid personality, which was associated with a heavyset, soft type of body, was said to vacillate between normality and abnormality.

D

dangerous drug A term used by the Drug Enforcement Administration to refer to "broad categories or classes of controlled substances other than cocaine, opiates, and cannabis products." Amphetamines, methamphetamines, PCP (phencyclidine), LSD, methcathinone, and "designer drugs" are all considered to be dangerous drugs.

dangerousness The likelihood that a given individual will later harm society or others. Dangerousness is often measured in terms of recidivism, or the likelihood of new crime commission or rearrest for a mew crime within a fiveyear period following arrest or release from confinement.

dark figure of crime The numerical total of unreported crimes that are not refleced in official crime statistics.

data confidentiality The ethical requirement of social scientific research to protect the confidentiality of individusal research participants, while simultaneously preserving justified research access to the information participants provide.

data encryption The process by which information is encoded, making it unreadable to all but its intended recipients.

date rape Unlawful forced sexual intercourse with a woman against her will that occurs within the context of a dating relationship.

Daubert stándard A test of scientific acceptability applicable to the gathering evidence in criminal cases.

DCS-1000 A network diagnostic tool that is capable of assisting in criminal investigations by monitoring and capturing large amounts of Internet traffic. Previously called Carnivore.

death penalty See **capital punishment.**

deconstructionist theory A postmodern perspective that challenges existing criminological theories in order to debunk them and that works toward replacing traditional ideas with concepts seen as more appropriate to the postmodern era.

decriminalization The redefinition of certain previously criminal behaviors into regulated activities that become "ticketable" rather than "arrestable."

defensible space The range of mechanisms that combine to bring an enviroment under the control of its residents.

Delphi Method A technique of futures research that uses repetitive questioning of experts to refine predictions.

demographics The characteristics of population groups, usually expressed in statistical fashion.

demography The study of the characteristics of population groups.

descriptive statistics Statistics that describe, summarize, or highlight the relationships within data that have been gathered.

designer drugs "New substances designed by slightly altering the chemical makeup of other illegal or tightly controlled drugs."

desistance The cessation of criminal activity or the termination of a period of involvement in offending behavior.

desistance phenomenon The observable decrease in crime rates that is invariably associated with age.

determinate sentencing A criminal punishment strategy that mandates a specified and fixed amount of time to be served for every offense category. Under the strategy, for example, all offenders convicted of the same degree of burglary would be sentenced to the same length of time behind bars. Also called *fixed sentencing*.

deterrence The prevention of crime. See also **general deterrence; specific deterrence**.

deterrence strategy A crime-control strategy that attempts "to diminish motivation for crime by increasing the perceived certainty, severity, or celerity of penalties."

deviant behavior Human activity that violates social norms.

differential association The sociological thesis that criminality, like any other form of behavior, is learned through a process of association with others who communicate criminal values.

differential identification theory An explanation for crime and deviance that holds that people pursue criminal or deviant behavior to the extent that they identify themselves with real or imaginary people from whose perspective their criminal or deviant behavior seems acceptable.

Digital Theft Deterrence and Copyright Damages Improvement Act Passed in 1999, this federal law (Public Law 106-160) attempted to combat software piracy and other forms of digital theft by amending Section 504(c) of the Copyright Act, thereby increasing the amount of damages that could potentially be awarded in cases of copyright infringement.

disclosure (of research methods) The provision of information to potential subjects informing them of the nature of the research methods to be used by the social scientific study in which their involvement is planned.

discrediting information Information that is inconsistent with the managed impressions being communicated in a given situation.

displacement A shift of criminal activity from one location to another.

displastic A mixed group of offenders described by constitutional theorist Ernst Kretschmer as highly emotional and often unablle to control themselves. They were thought to commit mostly sexual offenses and other crimes of passion. The term is largely of historical interest.

distributive justice The rightful, equitable, and just diatribution of rewards within a society.

dizygotic (DZ) twins Twins that develop from separate ova, and that carry the genetic material shared by siblings.

DNA fingerprinting See **DNA profiling**.

DNA profiling The use of biological residue

found at the scene of a crime for genetic comparisons in aiding the identification of criminal suspects.

domestic terrorism The unlawful use of force or violence by a group or an individual who is based and operates entirely within the United States and its territories without foreign direction and whose acts are directed at elements of the U.S. government or population.

dramaturgical perspective A theoretical point of view that depicts human behavior as centered around the purposeful management of interpersonal impressions. Also called *dramaturgy*.

dramaturgy See **dramaturgical perspective**.

drug-defined crime A violation of the laws prohibiting or regulating the possession, use, or distribution of illegal drugs.

drugs-related crime A crime in which drugs contribute to the offense (excluding violations of drug laws.)

drug trafficking Manufacturing, distributing, dispensing, importing, and exporting (or possession with intent to do the same) a controlled substance or a counterfeit substance.

Durham rule A srandard for judging legal insanity that holds that an accused is not criminally responsible if his or her unlawful act was the product of mental disease or mental defect.

E

ecological theory A type of sociological approach that emphasizes demographics (the characteristics of population groups) and geographics (the mapped location of such groups relative to one another) and that sees the social disorganization that characterizes delinquency areas as a major cause of criminality and victimization. Also called *Chicago School of criminology*.

ectomorph A body type originally described as thin and fragile, with long, slender, poorly muscled extremities and delicate bones.

ego The reality-testing part of the personality. Also called the *reality principle*. More formally, the personality component that is conscious, most immediately controls behavior, and is most in touch with external reality.

electroencephalogram (EEG) The electrical measurement of brain wave activity.

encryption See **data encryption**.

endomorph A body type originally described as soft and round or overweight.

Enlightenment A social movement that arose during the eighteenth century and that built upon ideas like empiricism, rationality, free will, humanism, and natural law. Also called *Age of Reason*.

environmental crime A violation of the criminal law that, although typically committed by businesses or by business officials, may also be committed by other people or by organizational entities and that damages some protected or otherwise significant aspect of the natural environment.

environmental criminology An emerging perspective that emphasizes the importance of geographic location and architectural features as they are associated with the prevalence of criminal victimization. (*Note*: As the term has been understood to date, environmental criminology is not the study of environmental crime but, rather, a perspective that stresses how crime varies from place to place.) Also called *criminology of place*.

environmental scanning "A systematic effort to identify in an elemental way future developments (trends or events) that could plausibly occur over the time horizon of interest" and that might affect one's area of concern.

ethnic succession The continuing process whereby one immigrant or ethnic group succeeds another by assuming its position in society.

ethnocentrism The phenomenon of "culture-centeredness" by which one uses one's own culture as a benchmark against which to judge all other patterns of behavior.

eugenic criminology A perspective that holds that the root causes of criminality are passed from generation to generation in the form of "bad genes."

eugenics The study of hereditary improvenment by genetic control.

evidence-based That which is built on scientific findings; and especially practices and policies founded upon the results of randomized controlled experiments.

evolutionary ecology An approach to understanding crime that draws attention to the ways people develop over the course of their lives.

experiment See **controlled experiment; quasi-experimental design**.

experimental criminology A form of contemporary criminology that makes use of rigorous social scientific techniques, especially randomized controlled experiments and the systematic review of research results.

expert systems Computer hardware and software that attempt to duplicate the decision-making processes used by skilled investigators in the analysis of evidence and in the recogniton of patterns that such evidence might represent.

exposure-reduction theory A theory of intimate homicide that claims that a decline in domesticity, accompanied by an improvement in the economic status of women and a growth in domestic violence resources, explains observed decreases in intimate-partner homicide.

expressive crime A criminal offense that results from acts of interpersonal hostility, such as jealousy, revenge, romantic triangles, and quarrels.

external validity The ability to generalize research findings to other settings.

F

felony A serious criminal offense, specifically one punishable by death or by incarceration in a prison facility for a year or more.

felony murder A special class of criminal homicide in which an offender may be charged with first-degree murder when that person's criminal activity results in another person's death.

feminist criminology A self-conscious corrective model intended to redirect the thinking of mainstream criminologists to include gender awareness.

fence An individual or a group involved in the buying, selling, and distribution of stolen goods. Also called **criminal receiver.**

first-degree murder Criminal homicide that is planned or involves premeditation.

focal concerns Key values of any culture, especially the key values of a delinquent subculture.

folkways Time-honored customs. Although folkways carry the force of tradition, their violation is unlikely to threaten the survival of the group. See also **mores.**

forcible rape (UCR) The carnal knowledge of a female forcibly and against her will. Assaults or attempts to commit rape by force or threat of force are also included in the UCR definition; however, statutory rape (without force) and other sex offenses are excluded.

foreign terrorist organization (FTO) A foreign organization that engages in terrorist activity that threatens the security of U.S. nationals or the national security of the United States and that is so designated by the U.S. secretary of state.

forensic psychiatry A branch of psychiatry having to do with the study of crime and criminality.

forensic psychology The application of the science and profession of psychology to questions and issues relating to law and legal system.

forfeiture See **asset forfeiture.**

frustration-aggression theory A theory that holds that frustration, which is a natural consequence of living, is a root cause of crime. Criminal behavior can be a form of adaptation when it results in stress reduction.

future criminology The study of likely futures as they impinge on crime and its control.

futures research "A multidisciplinary branch of operations reserch" whose principal aim "is to facilitate long-range planning based on (1) forecasting from the past supported by mathematical models, (2) crossdisciplinary treatment of its subject matter, (3) systematic use of expert judgment, and (4) a systems-analytical approach to its problems."

futurist One who studies the future.

G

gateway offense An offense, usually fairly minor in nature, that leads to more serious offenses. Shoplifting, for example, may be a gateway offense to more serious property crimes.

gender gap The observed differences between male and female rates of criminal offending in a given society, such as the United States.

general deterrence A goal of criminal sentencing that seeks to prevent others from committing crimes similar to the one for which a particular offender is being sentenced.

general strain theory (GST) a perspective that suggests that lawbreaking behavior is a coping mechanism that enables those who engage in it to deal with the socioemotional problems generated by negative social relations.

general theory A theory that attempts to explain all (or at least most) forms of criminal conduct through a single, overarching approach.

general theory of crime A perspective on crime, developed by Travis Hirschi and Michael Gottfredson, that asserts "that the operation of a single mechanism, low self-control, accounts for 'all crime, at all times'; [including] acts ranging from vandalism to homicide, from rape to white-collar-crime."

genetic determinism The belief that genes are the major determining factor in human behavior.

globalization A process of social homogenization by which the experiences of everyday life, marked by the diffusion of commodities and ideas, can foster a standardizaton of cultural expressions around the world.

guilty but mentally ill (GBMI) A finding that offenders are guilty of the criminal offense with which they are charged, but because of their prevailing mental condition, they are generally sent to psychiatric hospitals for treatment rather than to prison. Once they have been declared cured, however, such offenders can be transferred to correctional facilities to serve out their sentences.

H

habitual offender statute A law intended to keep repeat criminal offenders behind bars. These laws sometimes come under the "three strikes and you're out" rubric.

hacker A person who uses computers for exploration and exploitation.

hard determinism The belief that crime results from forces that are beyond the control of the individual.

hate crime A criminal offense in which the motive is hatred, bias, or prejudice based on the actual or perceived race, color, religion national origin, ethnicity, gender, or sexual orientation of another individual or group of individuals. Also called *bias crime*.

Hate Crimes Sentencing Enhancement Act A federal law (28 U.S.C. Section 994) enacted in 1994 as part of the Violent Crime Control and Law Enforcement Act that required the U.S. Sentencing Commission to increase the penalties for crimes in which the viction was selected "because of [his or her] actual or perceived race, color, religion, national origin, ethnicity, gender, disability, or sexual orientation."

hedonistic calculus The belief, first proposed by Jeremy Bentham, that behavior holds value to any individual undertaking it according to the amount of pleasure or pain that it can be expected to produce for that person. Also called *utilitarianism*.

heritability A statistical construct that estimates the amount of variation in a population that is attributable to genetic factors.

heroin signature program (HSP) A Drug Enforcement Administration program that identifies the geographic source of a heroin sample through the detection of specific chemical characteristics in the sample peculiar to the source area.

homicide The killing of one human being by another.

household crime (NCVS) An attempted or completed crime that does not involve confrontation, such as burglary, motor vehicle theft, and household larceny.

human agency The active role that people take in their lives; the fact that people are not merely subject to social and structural constraints but actively make choices and decisions based on the alternatives that they see before them.

human development The relationship between the maturing individual and his or her changing environment, as well as the social processes that the relationship entails.

human smuggling Illegal immigration in which an agent is involved for payment to help a person cross a border clandestinely.

human trafficking See **trafficking in persons**.

hypoglycemia A medical condition characterized by low blood sugar.

hypothesis An explanation that accounts for a set of facts and that can be tested by further investigation. Also, something that is taken to be true for the purpose of argument or investigation.

I

id The aspect of the personality from which drives, wishes, urges, and desires emanate. More formally, the division of the psyche associated with instinctual impulses and demands for immediate satisfaction of primitive needs.

identity theft The unauthorized use of another individual's personal identity to fraudulently obtain money, goods, or services; to avoid the payment of debt; or to avoid criminal prosecution.

illegitimate opportunity structure Subcultural pathways to success that the wider society disapproves of.

impression management The intentional enactment of practiced behavior that is intended to convey to others one's desirable personal characteristics and social qualities.

incapacitation The use of imprisonment or other means to reduce the likelihood that an offender will be capable of committing future offenses.

individual rights advocate One who seeks to protect personal freedoms in the face of criminal prosecution.

inferential statistics Statistics that specify how likely findings are to be true for other populations or in other locales.

informed consent The ethical requirement of social scientific research that research subjects be informed as to the nature of the research about to be conducted, their anticipated role in it, and the uses to which the data they provide will be put.

infrastructure The basic facilities, services, and installations needed for the functioning of a community or society, such as transportation and communications systems, water and power lines, and public institutions, including schools, post offices, and prisons.

insanity (legal) A legally established inability to understand right from wrong or to conform one's behavior to the requirements of the law.

insanity (psychological) Persistent mental disorder or derangement.

insider trading Equity trading based on confidential information about important events that may affect the price of the issue being traded.

institutional robbery Robbery that occurs in commercial settings, such as convenience stores, gas stations, and banks.

instrumental crime A goal-directed offense that involves some degree of planning by the offender.

instrumental Marxism A perspective that holds that those in power intentionally create laws and social institutions that serve their own interests and that keep others from becoming powerful.

integrated theory An explanatory perspective that merges (or attempts to merge) concepts drawn from different sources.

interactional theory A theoretical approach to exploring crime and delinquency that blends social control and social learning perspectives.

interactionist perspective See **social process theory.**

interdiction An international drug control policy that aims to stop drugs from entering the country illegally.

internal validity The certainty that experimental interventions did indeed cause the changes observed in the study group. Also, the control over confounding factors, which tend to invalidate the results of an experiment

international terrorism The unlawful use of force or violence by a group or an individual who has a connection to a foreign power or whose activities transcend national boundaries against people or property to intimidate or coerce a government, the civilian population, or any segment thereof in furtherance of political or social objectives.

Internet The world's largest computer network.

intersubjectivity A scientific principle that requires that independent observers see the same thing under the same circumstances for observations to be regarded as valid.

intimate-partner assault A genderneutral term used to characterize assaultive behavior that takes place between individuals involved in an intimate relationship.

irresistible-impulse test A standard for judging legal insanity that holds that a defendant is not guilty of a criminal offense if the person, by virtue of his or her mental state or psychological condition, was not able to resist committing the crime.

| J |

jockey A professional car thief involved regularly in calculated, steal-to-order car thefts.

joyriding An opportunistic car theft, often committed by a teenager seeking fun or thrills.

Juke family A well-known "criminal family" studied by Richard L. Dugdale.

just deserts model The notion that criminal offenders deserve the punishment they receive at the hands of the law and that punishments should be appropriate to the type and severity of crime committed.

justice model A contemporary model of imprisonment in which the principle of just deserts forms the underlying social philosophy.

K

Kallikak family A well-known "criminal family" studied by Henry H. Goddard.

Kefauver Committee The popular name for the federal Special Committee to Investigate Organized Crime in Interstate Commerce, formed in 1951.

Kriminalpolitik The political handling of crime. Also, a criminology-based social policy.

L

labeling An interactionist perspective that sees continued crime as a consequence of limited opportunities for acceptable behavior that follow from the negative responses of society to those defined as offenders. Also, the process by which a negative or deviant label is imposed.

La Cosa Nostra See **Cosa Nostra.**

larceny The unlawful taking or attempted taking of property (other than a motor vehicle) from the possession of another, by stealth, without force or deceit, with intent to permanently deprive the owner of the property.

larceny-theft (UCR) The unlawful taking, carrying, leading, or riding away of property (other than a motor vehicle) from the possession or constructive possession of another. Attempts are included.

latent crime rate A rate of crime calculated on the basis of crimes that would likely be committed by those who are in prison or jail or who are otherwise incapacitated by the justice system.

law and order advocate One who suggests that under certain circumstances involving criminal threats to public safety, the interests of society should take precedence over individual rights.

Law Enforcement Assistance Administration (LEAA) A federal program, established under Title 1 of the Omnibus Crime Control and Safe Streets Act of 1967, designed to provide assistance to police agencies.

learning theory A perspective that places primary emphasis upon the role of communication and socialization in the acquisition of learned patterns of criminal behavior and the values that support that behavior.

left realism A conflict perspective that insists on a pragmatic assessment of crime and its associated problems. Also called *realist criminology*.

left-realist criminology An approach to the subject matter of criminology based on ideas inherent in the perspective of left realism.

legalization Elimination of the laws and criminal penalties associated with certain behaviors—usually the production, sale, distribution, and possession of a controlled substance.

liberal feminism A perspective that holds that the concerns of women can be incorporated within existing social institutions through conventional means and without the need to drastically restructure society. Criminal laws, such as the Violence against Women

Act, for example, have been enacted in order to change the legal structure in such a way that it becomes responsive to women's issues.

life course Pathways through the age-differentiated life span. Also, the couse of a person's life over time.

life course criminology A developmental perspective that draws attention to the fact that criminal behavior tends to follow a distinct pattern across the life cycle.

lifestyle theory Another term for the routine activities approach of Lawrence Cohen and Marcus Felson. See **routine activities theory**.

M

Mafia See **Cosa Nostra**.

mala in se Acts that are thought to be wrong in and of themselves.

mala prohibita Acts that are wrong only because they are prohibited.

Marxist criminology A perspective on crime and crime causation based on the writings of Karl Marx.

masculinity hypothesis (1) A belief (from the late 1800s) that criminal women typically exhibited masculine features and mannerisms. (2) In the late 1990s, the belief that, over time, men and women will commit crimes that are increasingly similar in nature, seriousness, and frequency. Increasing similarity in crime commission was predicted to result from changes in the social status of women (for example, better economic position, gender role convergence, socialization practices that are increasingly similar for both males and females, and so on).

mass murder The illegal killing of four or more victims at one location within one event.

mesomorph A body type described as athletic and muscular.

meta-analysis A study of other studies about a particular topic of interest.

metatheory A theory about theories and the theorizing process.

misdemeanor A criminal offense that is less serious than a felony and is punishable by incarceration, usually in a local confinement facility, typically for a year or less.

M'Naughten rule A standard for judging legal insanity that requires that offenders not know what they were doing, or if they did, that they not know it was wrong.

modeling theory A form of social learning theory that asserts that people learn how to act by observing others.

money laundering The process of converting illegally earned assets, originating as cash, to one or more alternative forms to conceal such incriminating factors as illegal origin and true ownership.

Monitoring the Future A national self-report survey on drug use that has been conducted since 1975.

monozygotic (MZ) twins Twins that develop from the same egg and that carry virtually the same genetic material.

moral enterprise The efforts made by an interest group to have its sense of moral or ethical propriety enacted into law.

mores Behavioral proscriptions covering potentially serious violations of a group's values. Examples include strictures against murder, rape, and robbery. See also **folkways.**

motor vehicle theft (UCR) The theft or attempted theft of a motor vehicle. According to the Federal Bureau of Investigation, this offense category includes the stealing of automobiles, trucks, buses, motorcycles, motorscooters, and snowmobiles.

murder An unlawful homicide.

N

National Advisory Commission on Criminal Justice Standards and Goals A federal body commissioned in 1971 by President Richard Nixon to examine the nation's criminal justice system and to set standards and goals to direct the development of the nation's criminal justice agencies.

National Crime Victimization Survey (NCVS) A survey conducted annually by the Bureau of Justice Statistics that provides data on surveyed households that report they were affected by crime.

National Incident-Based Reporting System (NIBRS) A new and enhanced statistical reporting system that will collect data on each single incident and arrest within 22 crime categories.

National Survey on Drug Use and Health (NSDUH) A national survey of illicit drug use among people 12 years of age and older that is conducted annually by the Substance Abuse and Mental Health Services Administration.

National Violence against Women (NVAW) Survey A national survey of the extent and nature of violence against women conducted between November 1995 and May 1996 and funded through grants from the National Institute of Justice and the U.S. Department of Health and Human Services' National Center for Injury Prevention and Control.

National Youth Survey (NYS) A longitudinal panel study of a national sample of 1,725 individuals that measured self-reports of delinquency and other types of behavior.

natural law The philosophical perspective that certain immutable laws are fundamental to human nature and can be readily ascertained through reason. Human-made laws, in contrast, are said to derive from human experience and history—both of which are subject to continual change.

natural rights The rights that, according to natural law theorists, individuals retain in the face of government action and interests.

negative affective states Adverse emotions that derive from the experience of strain, such as anger, fear, depression, and disappointment.

negligent homicide The act of causing the death of another person by recklessness or gross negligence.

neoclassical criminology A contemporary version of classical criminology that emphasizes deterrence and retribution, with reduced emphasis on rehabilitation.

neurosis A functional disorder of the mind or of the emotions involving anxiety, phobia, or other abnormal behavior.

No Electronic Theft Act A 1997 federal law (Public Law 105-147) that criminalizes the willful infringement of copyrighted works, including by electronic means, even when the infringing party derives no direct financial benefit from the infringement (such as when pirated software is freely distributed online). In keeping with requirements of the NETA, the U.S. Sentencing Commission enacted amendments to its guidelines on April 6, 2000, to increase penalties associated with electronic theft.

nonprimary homicide Murder that involves victims and offenders who have no prior relationship and that usually occurs during the course of another crime such as robbery.

nothing-works doctrine The belief popularized by Robert Martinson in the 1970s that correctional treatment programs have little success in rehabilitating offenders.

nurturant strategy A crime control strategy that attempts "to forestall development of criminality by improving early life experiences and channeling child and adolescent development" in desirable directions.

| O |

occasional offender A criminal offender whose offending patterns are guided primarily by opportunity.

occupational crime Any act punishable by law that is committed through opportunity created in the course of an occupation that is legal.

offense A violation of the criminal law or, in some jurisdictions, a minor crime, such as jaywalking, sometimes described as "ticketable."

offense specialization A preference for engaging in a certain type of offense to the exclusion of others.

Office of Juvenile Justice and Delinquency Prevention (OJJDP) A national office that provides monetary assistance and direct victim-service programs for juvenile courts.

Office of National Drug Control Policy (ONDCP) A national office charged by Congress with establishing policies, priorities, and objectives for the nation's drug-control program. ONDCP is responsible for developing and disseminating the *National Drug-Control Strategy*.

omertà The informal, unwritten code of organized crime, which demands silence and loyalty, among other things, of family members.

Omnibus Anti-Drug Abuse Act A federal law (Public Law 100-690) enacted in 1988 that substantially increased federal penalties for recreational drug users and created a new cabinet-level position (known unofficially as the drug czar) to coordinate the drug-fighting efforts of the federal government.

Omnibus Crime Control and Safe Streets Act A federal law enacted in 1967 to eliminate the social conditions that create crime and to fund many anticrime initiatives nationwide.

operant behavior Behavior that affects the environment in such a way as to produce responses or further behavioral cues.

operationalization The process by which concepts

are made measurable.

opportunity structure A path to success. Opportunity structures may be of two types: legitimate and illegitimate.

organized crime The unlawful activities of the members of a highly organized, disciplined association engaged in supplying illegal goods and services, including gambling, prostitution, loan-sharking, narcotics, and labor racketeering.

P

Panopticon A prison designed by Jeremy Bentham that was to be a circular building with cells along the circumference, each clearly visible from a central location staffed by guards.

paradigm An example, a model, or a theory.

paranoid schizophrenic A schizophrenic individual who suffers from delusions and hallucinations.

Part Ⅰ offenses The crimes of murder, rape, robbery, aggravated assault, burglary, larceny, and motor vehicle theft, as defined under the FBI's Uniform Crime Reporting Program. Also called *major crimes*.

Part Ⅱ offenses Less serious offenses as identified by the FBI for the purpose of reporting arrest data.

participant observation A strategy in data gathering in which the researcher observes a group by participating, to varying degrees, in the activities of the group.

participatory justice A relatively informal type of criminal justice case processing that makes use of local community resources rather than requiring traditional forms of official intervention

patriarchy The tradition of male dominance.

peace model An approach to crime control that focuses on effective ways for developing a shared consensus on critical issues that could seriously affect the quality of life.

peacemaking criminology A perspective that holds that crime control agencies and the citizens they serve should work together to alleviate social problems and human suffering and thus reduce crime.

penal couple A term that describes the relationship between offender and victim. Also, the two individuals most involved in the criminal act: the offender and the victim.

persistence Continuity in crime. Also, continual involvement in offending.

persistent thief One who continues in common-law property crimes despite no better than an ordinary level of success.

personal robbery Robbery that occurs on the highway or street or in a public place (and that is often referred to as "mugging") and robbery that occurs in residences.

pharmaceutical diversion The process by which legitimately manufactured controlled substances are diverted for illicit use.

phenomenological criminology The study of crime as a social phenomenon that is created through a process of social interaction.

phenomenology The study of the contents of human consciousness without regard to external conventions or prior assumptions.

phishing Pronounced "fishing." An Internet-based scam to steal valuable information such as credit card numbers, social security numbers, user IDs, and passwords.

phone phreak A person who uses switched, dialed-access telephone services for exploration and exploitation.

phrenology The study of the shape of the head to determine anatomical correlates of human behavior.

piracy See **software piracy**.

pluralist perspective An analytical approach to social organization that holds that a multiplicity of values and beliefs exists in any complex society but that most social actors agree on the usefulness of law as a formal means of dispute resolution.

positivism The application of scientific techniques to the study of crime and criminals.

postcrime victimization Problems that tend to follow from initial victimization, Also called *secondary victimization*.

postmodern criminology A brand of criminology that developed following World War II and that builds on the tenets inherent in postmodern social thought.

power-control theory A perspective that holds that the distribution of crime and delinquency within society is to some degree founded upon the consequences that power relationships within the wider society hold for domestic settings and for the everyday relationships among men, women, and children within the context of family life.

primary deviance Initial deviance often undertaken to deal with transient problems in living.

primary homicide Murder involving family members, friends, and acquaintances.

primary research Research characterized by original and direct investigation.

professional criminal A criminal offender who makes a living from criminal pursuits, is recognized by other offenders as professional, and engages in offending that is planned and calculated.

Project on Human Development in Chicago Neighborhoods (PHDCN) An intensive study of Chicago neighborhoods employing longitudinal evaluations to examine the changing circumstances of people's lives in an effort to identify personal characteristics that may lead toward or away from antisocial behavior.

proletariat In Marxist theory, the working class.

prosocial bonds Bonds between the individual and the social group that strengthen the likelihood of conformity. Prosocial bonds are characterized by attachment to conventional social institutions, values, and beliefs.

prostitution The offering of one's self for hire for the purpose of engaging in sexual relations, or the act or practice of engaging in sexual activity for money or its equivalent.

protection/avoidance strategy A crime-control strategy that attempts to reduce criminal opportunities by changing people's routine activities, by increasing guardianship, or by incapacitating convicted offenders.

psychiatric criminology Theories that are derived from the medical sciences, including neurology, and that, like other psychological theories, focus on the individual as the unit of analysis. Psychiatric theories from the basis of psychiatric criminology. See also **forensic psychiatry**.

psychiatric theory A theory derived from the medical sciences, including neurology, and that, like other psychological theories, focuses on the individual as the unit of analysis.

psychoactive substance A substance that affects the mind, mental processes, or emotions.

psychoanalysis The theory of human psychology founded by Sigmund Freud on the concepts of the unconscious, resistance, repression, sexuality, and the Oedipus complex.

psychoanalytic criminology A psychiatric approach developed by Sigmund Freud that emphasizes the role of personality in human behavior and which sees deviant behavior as the result of dysfunctional personalities.

psychological profiling The attempt to categorize, understand, and predict the behavior of certain types of offenders based on behavioral clues they provide.

psychological theory A theory derived from the behavioral sciences that focuses on the individual as the unit of analysis. Psychological theories place the locus of crime causation within the personality of the individual offender.

psychopath An individual who has a personality disorder, especially one manifested in aggressively antisocial behavior, and who is lacking in empathy. Also called *sociopath*.

psychopathology Any psychological disorder that causes distress, either for the individual or for those in the individual's life. Also, the study of pathological mental conditions—that is mental illness.

psychopathy A personality disorder characterized by antisocial behavior and lack of affect.

psychosis A form of mental illness in which sufferers are said to be out of touch with reality.

psychotherapy A form of psychiatric treatment based on psychoanalytical principles and techniques.

public policy A course of action that government takes in an effort to solve a problem or to achieve an end.

punishment An undesirable behavioral consequence likely to decrease the frequency of occurrence of that behavior.

pure research Research undertaken simply for the sake of advancing scientific knowledge.

Q

qualitative method A research technique that produces subjective results, or results that are difficult to quantify.

quantitative method A research technique that produces measurable results.

quasi-experimental design An approach to research that, although less powerful than experimental designs, is deemed worthy of use when better designs are not feasible.

R

Racketeer Influenced and Corrupt Organizations (RICO) A statute that was part of the federal Organized Crime Control Act of 1970 and that is intended to combat criminal conspiracies.

radical criminology A perspective that holds that the causes of crime are rooted in social conditions that empower the wealthy and the politically well organized but disenfranchise the less fortunate. Also called *critical criminology; Marxist criminology*.

radical feminism A perspective that holds that any significant change in the social status of women can be accomplished only through substantial changes in social institutions such as the family, law, and medicine. Radical feminism argues, for example, that the structure of current legal thinking involves what is fundamentally a male perspective, which should be changed to incorporate women's social experiences and points of view.

randomization The process whereby individuals are assigned to study groups without biases or differences resulting from selection.

rape (NCVS) Carnal knowledge through the use of force or the threat of force, including attempts. Statutory rape (without force) is excluded. Both heterosexual and homosexual rape are included.

rape (UCR) See **forcible rape**.

rape myth A false assumption about rape such as "When a woman sats no, she really means yes." Rape myths characterize much of the discourse surrounding sexual violence.

rape shield law A statute providing for the protection of rape victims by ensuring that defendants do not introduce irrelevant facts about the victim's sexual history into evidence.

rational choice theory A perspective that holds that criminality is the result of conscious choice and that predicts that individuals choose to commit crime when the benefits outweigh the costs of disobeying the law.

reaction formation The process by which a person openly rejects that which he or she wants or aspires to but cannot obtain or achieve.

realist criminology See **left realism**.

recidivism The repetition of criminal behavior.

recidivism rate The percentage of convicted offenders who have been released from prison and who are later rearrested for a new crime, generally within five years following release. See also **dangerousness**.

reintegrative shaming A form of shaming, imposed as a sanction by the criminal justice system, that is thought to strengthen the moral bond between the offendar and the community.

relative deprivation A sense of social or economic inequality experienced by those who are unable, for whatever reason, to achieve legitimate success within the surrounding society.

replicability A scientific principle that holds that valid observations made at one time can be made again later if all other conditions are the same.

research The use of standardized, systematic procedures in the search for knowledge.

research design The logic and structure inherent in an approach to data gathering.

restitution A criminal sanction—in particular, the payment of compensation by the offender to the victim.

restorative justice A postmodern perspective that stresses "remedies and restoration rather than prison, punishment and victim neglect."

retribution The act of taking revenge upon a criminal perpetrator.

reward A desirable behavioral consequence likely to increase the frequency of occurrence of that behavior.

risk analysis See **threat analysis.**

robbery (UCR) The taking of or attempting to take anything of value from the care, custody, or control of a person or persons by force or threat of force or violence or by putting the victim in fear.

routine activities theory A brand of rational choice theory that suggests that lifestyles contribute significantly to both the volume and the type of crime found in any society. Also called *lifestyle theory*.

| S |

scenario writing A technique intended to predict future outcomes, that builds upon environmental scanning by attempting to assess the likelihood of a variety of possible outcomes once important trends have been indentified.

schizoid A person characterized by schizoid personality disorder. Such disordered personalities appear to be aloof, withdrawn, unresponsive, humorless, dull, and solitary to an abnormal degree.

schizophrenic A mentally ill individual who is out of touch with reality and who suffers from disjointed thinking.

secondary deviance Deviant behavior that results from official labeling and from association with others who have been so labeled.

secondary research New evaluations of existing information that had been collected by other researchers.

secondary victimization See **Postcrime victimization**.

second-degree murder Criminal homicide that is unplanned and that is often described as "a crime of passion."

securities fraud The theft of money resulting from intentional manipulation of the value of equities, including stocks and bonds. Securities fraud also includes theft from securities accounts and wire fraud.

selective disinhibition A loss of self-control due to the characteristics of the social setting, drugs or alcohol, or a combination of both.

selective incapacitation A social policy that seeks to protect society by incarcerating the individuals deemed to be the most dangerous.

self-control A person's ability to alter his or her own states and responses.

self-report survey A survey in which anonymous respondents, without fear of disclosure or arrest, are asked to confidentially report any violations of the criminal law that they have committed.

separation assault Violence inflicted by partners on significant others who attempt to leave an intimate relationship.

serial murder Criminal homicide that involves the killing of several victims in three or more separate events.

sex trafficking The recruitment, harboring, transportation, provision, or obtaining of a person for the purpose of a commercial sex act.

sibling offense An offense or incident that culminates in homicide. The offense or incident may be a crime, such as robbery, or an incident that meets a less stringent criminal definition, such as a lover's quarrel involving assault or battery.

simple assault (NCVS) An attack without a weapon, resulting either in minor injury or in undetermined injury requiring less than two days of hospitalization. See also **aggravated assault.**

situational choice theory A brand of rational choice theory that views criminal behavior "as a function of choices and decisions made within a context of situational constraints and opportunities."

situational crime prevention A social policy approach that looks to develop greater understanding of crime and more effective crime prevention strategies through concern with the physical, organizational, and social environments that make crime possible.

snitch An amateur shoplifter.

social bond The link, created through socialization, between individuals and the society of which they are a part.

social capital The degree of positive relationships with others and with social institutions that individuals build up over the course of their lives.

social class Distinctions made between individuals on the basis of important defining social characteristics.

social contract The Enlightenmentera concept that human beings abandon their natural state of individual freedom to join together and form society. In the process of forming a social contract, individuals surrender some freedoms to society as a whole, and government, once formed, is obligated to assume responsibilities toward its citizens and to provide for their protection and welfare.

social control theory A perspective that predicts that when social constraints on antisocial behavior are weakened or absent, delinquent behavior emerges. Rather than stressing causative factors in criminal behavior, control theory asks why people actually obey rules instead of breaking them.

social development perspective An integrated view of human development that examines multiple levels of maturation simultaneously, including the psychological, biological, familial, interpersonal, cultural, societal, and ecological levels.

social disorganization A condition said to exist when a group is faced with social change, uneven development of culture, maladaptiveness, disharmony, conflict, and lack of consensus.

social disorganization theory A perspective on crime and deviance that sees society as a kind of organism and crime and deviance as a kind of disease or social pathology. Theories of social disorganization are often associated with the perspective of social ecology and with the Chicago School of criminology, which developed during the 1920s and 1930s.

social ecology An approach to criminological theorizing that attempts to link the structure and organization of a human community to interactions with ist localized environment.

social epidemiology The study of social epidemics and diseases of the social order.

social learning theory A psychological perspective that says that people learn how to behave by modeling themselves after others whom they have the opportunity to observe.

social life The ongoing and (typically) structured interaction that occurs between persons in a society, including socialization and social behavior in general.

social pathology A concept that compares society to a physical organism and that sees criminality as an illness.

social policy A government initiative, program, or plan intended to address problems in society. The "war on crime," for example, is a kind of generic (large-scale) social policy—one consisting of many smaller programs.

social problems perspective The belief that crime is a manifestation of underlying social problems, such as poverty, discrimination, pervasive family violence, inadequate socialization practices, and the breakdown of traditional social institutions.

social process The interaction between and among social institutions individuals, and groups.

social process theory A theory that asserts that criminal behavior is learned in interaction with others and that socialization processes that occur as the result of group membership are the primary route through which learning occurs. Also called the *interactionist perspective*.

social relativity The notion that social events are differently interpreted according to the cultural experiences and personal interests of the initiator, the observer, or the recipient of that behavior.

social responsibility perspective The belief that individuals are fundamentally responsible for their own behavior and that they choose crime over other, more law-abiding courses of action.

social structure The pattern of social organization and the interrelationships among institutions characteristic of a society.

social structure theory A theory that explains crime by reference to some aspect of the social fabric. These theories emphasize relationships among social institutions and describe the types of behavior that tend to characterize groups of people rather than individuals.

socialist feminism A perspective that examines social roles and the gender-based division of labor within the family, seeing both as a significant source of women's subordination within society. This perspective calls for a redefinition of gender-related job status, compensation for women who work within the home, and equal pay for equal work regardless of gender.

socialization The lifelong process of social experience whereby individuals acquire the cultural patterns of their society.

sociobiology "The systematic study of the biological basis of all social behavior."

sociological theory A perspective that focuses on the nature of the power relationships that exist between social groups and on the influences that various social phenomena bring to bear on the types of behaviors that tend to characterize groups of people.

sociopath See **psychopath**.

soft determinism The belief that human behavior is the result of choices and decisions made within a context of situational constraints and opportunities.

software piracy The unauthorized and illegal copying of software programs.

somatotyping The classification of human beings into types according to body build and other physical characteristics.

specific deterrence A goal of criminal sentencing that seeks to prevent a particular offender from engaging in repeat criminality.

spousal rape The rape of one spouse by the other. The term usually refers to the rape of a woman by her husband.

stalking A course of conduct directed at a specific person that involves repeated visual or physical proximity; nonconsensual communication; verbal, written, or implied threats; or a combination thereof that would cause a reasonable person fear. Also, a constellation of behaviors involving repeated and persistent attempts to impose on another person unwanted communication and/or contact.

state-organized crime Acts defined by law as criminal and committed by state officials in the pursuit of their work as representatives of the state.

statistical correlation The simultaneous increase or decrease in value of two numerically valued random variables.

statistical school A criminological perspective with roots in the early 1800s that seeks to uncover correlations between crime rates and other types of demographic data.

statute A formal, written enactment of a legislative body.

statutory law Law in the form of statutes or formal, written strictures made by a legislature or governing body with the power to make law.

stigmatic shaming A form of shaming, imposed as a sanction by the criminal justice system, that is thought to destroy the moral bond between the offender and the community.

strain theory A sociological approach that posits a disjuncture between socially and subculturally sanctioned means and goals as the cause of criminal behavior. Also called *anomie theory*.

strategic assessment A technique that assesses the risks and opportunities facing those who plan for the future.

structural Marxism A perspective that holds that the structural institutions of society influence the behavior of individuals and groups by virtue of the type of relationships created. The criminal law, for example, reflects class relationships and serves to reinforce those relationships.

subcultural theory A sociological perspective that emphasizes the contribution made by variously socialized cultural groups to the phenomenon of crime.

subculture A collection of values and preferences that is communicated to subcultural participants through a process of socialization.

sublimation The psychological process whereby one aspect of consciousness comes to be symbolically substituted for another.

substantial-capacity test A standard for judging legal insanity that requires that a person lack the mental capacity needed to understand the wrongfulness of his or her act or to conform his or her behavior to the requirements of the law.

superego The moral aspect of the personality; much like the conscience. More formally, the division of the psyche that develops by the incorporation of the perceived moral standards of the community, is mainly unconscious, and includes the conscience.

supermale A male individual displaying the XYY chromosome structure.

superpredator One of a new generation of juveniles "who are coming of age in actual and 'moral poverty' without the benefits of parents, teachers, coaches and clergy to teach them right from wrong and show them 'unconditional love.'" The term is often applied to inner-city youths who meet the criteria it sets forth.

survey research A social science data-gathering technique that involves the use of questionnaires.

T

tagging The process whereby an individual is negatively defined by agencies of justice. Also called *labeling*.

target hardening The reduction in criminal opportunity for a particular location, generally through the use of physical barriers, architectural design, and enhanced security measures.

techniques of neutralization Culturally available justifications that can provide criminal offenders with the means to disavow responsibility for their behavior.

TEMPEST A standard developed by the U.S. government that requires that electromagnetic emanations from computers designated as "secure" be below levels that would allow radio receiving equipment to "read" the data being computed.

terrorism Premeditated, politically motivated violence perpetrated against noncombatant targets by subnational groups or clandestine agents, usually intended to influence an audience.

test of significance A statistical technique intended to provide researchers with confidence that their results are, in fact, true and not the result of sampling error.

testosterone The primary male sex hormone. Produced in the testes, its function is to control secondary sex characteristics and sexual drive.

Thanatos A death wish.

theory A series of interrelated propositions that attempt to describe, explain, predict, and ultimately control some class of events. A theory gains explanatory power from inherent logical consistency and is “tested” by how well it describes and predicts reality.

threat analysis A complete and thorough assessment of the kinds of perils facing an organization. Also called *risk analysis*.

three-strikes legislation Criminal statutes that mandate life impirsonment for criminals convicted of three violent felonies or serious drug offenses.

total institution A facility from which individuals can rarely come and go and in which communal life is intense and circumscribed. Individuals in total institutions tend to eat, sleep, play, learn, and worship (if at all) together.

trafficking in persons (TIP) The exploitation of unwilling or unwitting people through force, coercion, threat, or deception.

transnational organized crime Unlawful activity undertaken and supported by organized criminal groups operating across national boundaries.

trend extrapolation A technique of futures research that makes future predictions based on the projection of existing trends.

trephination A form of surgery typically involving bone, especially the skull. Early instances of cranial trephination have been taken as evidence for primitive beliefs in spirit possession.

truth in sentencing A close correspondence between the sentence imposed upon those sent to prison and the time actually served prior to prison release.

Twelve Tables Early Roman laws written crica 450 B.C., which regulated family, religious, and economic life.

U

unicausal Having one cause. Unicausal theories posit only one source for all that they attempt to explain.

Uniform Crime Reporting Program (UCR) A Federal Bureau of Investigation summation of crime statistics tallied annually and consisting primarily of data on crimes reported to the police and on arrests.

utilitarianism See **hedonistic calculus**.

V

variable A concept that can undergo measurable changes.

verstehen The kind of subjective understanding that can be achieved by criminologists who immerse themselves in the everyday world of the criminals they study.

victim-impact statement A written document that describes the losses, suffering, and trauma experienced by the crime victim or by the vicrim’s survivors. In jurisdictions where victim-impact statements are used, judges are expected to consider them in arriving at an appropriate sentence for the offender.

victimization rate (NCVS) A measure of the occurrence of victimizations among a specified population group. For personal crimes, the rate is based on the number of victimizations per 1,000 residents aged 12 or older. For household crimes, the victimization rates are calculated using the number of incidents per 1,000 households.

victimogenesis The contributory background of a victim as a result of which he or she becomes prone to victimization.

victimology The study of victims and their contributory role, if any, in crime causation.

victim-precipitated homicide A killing in which the victim was the first to commence the interaction or was the first to resort to physical violence.

victim precipitation Contributions made by the victim to the criminal event, especially those that led to its initiation.

victim proneness An individual's likelihood of victimization.

Victims of Crime Act (VOCA) A federal law enacted in 1984 that established the federal Crime Victims Fund. The fund uses monies from fines and forfeitures collected from federal offenders to supplement state support of local victims' assistance programs and state victim compensation programs.

victim-witness assistance program A program that counsels victims, orients them to the justice process, and provides a variety of other services, such as transportation to court, child care during court appearances, and referrals to social service agencies.

Violence against Women Act (VAWA) A federal law enacted as a component of the 1994 Violent Crime Control and Law Enforcement Act and intended to address concerns about violence against women. The law focused on improving the interstate enforcement of protection orders, providing effective training for court personnel involved with women's issues, improving the training and collaboration of police and prosecutors with victim service providers, strengthening law enforcement efforts to reduce violence against women, and increasing services to victims of violence. President Clinton signed the reauthorization of this legislation, known as the Violence against Women Act 2000, into law on October 28, 2000.

Violent Crime Control and Law Enforcement Act A federal law (Public Law 103-322) enacted in 1994 that authorized spending billions of dollars on crime prevention, law enforcement, and prison construction. It also outlawed the sale of certain types of assault weapons and enhanced federal death penalty provisions.

Violent Criminal Apprehension Program (VICAP) The program of the Federal Bureau of Investigation focusing on serial murder investigation and the apprehension of serial killers.

virus See **computer virus.**

W

white-collar crime Violations of the criminal law committed by persons of respectability and high social status in the course of their occupation.

Wickersham Commission Created by President Herbert Hoover in 1931, and officially known as the *Commission on Law Observance and Enforcement*, the mandate of this commission was to develop "objectives to improve justice system practices and to reinstate law's role in civilized governance." The commission made recommendations concerning the nation's police forces and described how to improve policing throughout America.

workplace violence The crimes of murder, rape, robbery, and assault committed against persons who are at work or on duty.

제1편

범죄일반론

제 01 장 범죄의 의의

제1절 범죄의 개념[1)]

1. 범죄의 개념

범죄(crime)의 개념은 절대적 개념이 아니라 시대와 국가에 따라 달리 규정되는 상대적 개념이며 다의적 개념이다.[2)]

1) 절대적 범죄개념과 상대적 범죄개념

절대적 범죄개념	시대와 국가를 초월해서 절대적으로 적용되는 범죄의 기준은 존재하지 않는다.
상대적 범죄개념	• 일정한 국가의 법질서를 통해서 규정된 범죄형식을 기준으로 하는 범죄개념으로 시대와 국가에 따라 다르다. • 예 우리나라는 과거에 혼인빙자간음죄를 형법에 규정하고 처벌하였으나, 2012년 헌법재판소 위헌결정으로 폐지하였다. • 예 간통죄는 우리나라에서는 범죄이지만 일부 국가에서는 범죄가 아니다.

1) 양원규, 범죄학 제대로 알기, 백산출판사, 2012; 임상곤, 범죄심리학원론, 백산출판사, 2004:21-23. ; 이상현, 범죄심리학, 박영사, 2004(3판):8; 1990.9.10. 89헌마82 전원합의부, 2010.10.25. 2000헌바60 전원합의부, 2008.10.30. 2007헌가17・21, 2008헌가7・26, 2008헌바21・47(병합) 전원합의부, 네이버 백과사전 참조 ; 공정식, 살아있는 범죄학, 교육과학사, 2011:17-18.

2) 어떤 일탈행위에 대해 범죄라고 규정하는 것은 시대와 국가에 따라 다르다. 즉, 특정 국가에 있어서 시대에 따라 어떤 행위가 범죄로 새로이 규정되기도 하고, 또한 범죄로 규정되었던 어떤 행위가 시대의 변화에 따라 비(非)범죄화되기도 한다.

*혼인빙자간음죄(婚姻憑藉姦淫罪)

1) 개요

혼인을 빙자하거나 기타 위계(僞計)로서 음행(淫行)의 상습(常習) 없는 부녀를 기망(欺罔)하여 간음함으로써 성립하는 범죄이다.

구(舊) 「형법」 제304조는 개인의 성적(性的) 자기결정권을 제한할 뿐만 아니라 헌법이 보장하는 사생활의 비밀과 자유를 제한하고 있고, 또 여성을 보호한다는 미명(美名) 아래 사실상 국가가 여성의 성적 자기결정권을 부인해왔다며, 여성의 존엄과 가치에 역행하는 법조항으로, 헌법재판소는 혼인빙자간음죄가 위헌(違憲)이라는 결정을 내렸다. 이에 따라 해당 조항이 폐지(2012.12.18 법률 제11574호, 2013.6.19 시행)되었다.

2) 형법규정 폐지

형법 제304조 삭제 〈2012.12.18〉

3) 헌법재판소 위헌결정

- 형법 제304조 위헌소원 (2009.11.26. 2008 헌바 58, 2009 헌바 191(병합) 전원재판부)

【판시사항】

형법 제304조 중 "혼인을 빙자하여 음행의 상습없는 부녀를 기망하여 간음한 자" 부분이 헌법 제37조 제2항의 과잉금지원칙을 위반하여 남성의 성적(性的) 자기결정권 및 사생활의 비밀과 자유를 침해하는지 여부(적극)

【결정요지】

이 사건 법률조항의 경우 입법목적에 정당성이 인정되지 않는다. 첫째, 남성이 위력이나 폭력 등 해악적 방법을 수반하지 않고서 여성을 애정행위의 상대방으로 선택하는 문제는 그 행위의 성질상 국가의 개입이 자제되어야 할 사적인 내밀한 영역인데다 또 그 속성상 과장이 수반되게 마련이어서 우리 형법이 혼전 성관계를 처벌대상으로 하지 않고 있으므로 혼전 성관계의 과정에서 이루어지는 통상적 유도행위 또한 처벌해야 할 이유가 없다.

다음 여성이 혼전 성관계를 요구하는 상대방 남자와 성관계를 가질 것인가의 여부를 스스로 결정한 후 자신의 결정이 착오에 의한 것이라고 주장하면서 상대방 남성의 처벌을 요구하는 것은 여성 스스로가 자신의 성적 자기결정권을 부인하는 행위이다.

또한 혼인빙자간음죄가 다수의 남성과 성관계를 맺는 여성 일체를 '음행의 상습 있는 부녀'로 낙인찍어 보호의 대상에서 제외시키고 보호대상을 '음행의 상습없는 부녀'로 한정함으로써 여성에 대한 남성우월적 정조관념에 기초한 가부장적·도덕주의적 성 이데올로기를 강요하는 셈이 된다.

결국 이 사건 법률조항은 남녀 평등의 사회를 지향하고 실현해야 할 국가의 헌법적 의무(헌법 제36조 제1항)에 반(反)하는 것이자, 여성을 유아시(幼兒視)함으로써 여성을 보호한다는 미명 아래 사실상 국가 스스로가 여성의 성적 자기결정권을 부인하는 것이 되므로, 이 사건 법률조항이 보호하고자 하는 여성의 성적 자기결정권은 여성의 존엄과 가치에 역행하는 것이다.

결혼과 성에 관한 국민의 법의식에 많은 변화가 생겨나 여성의 착오에 의한 혼전 성관계를 형사법률이 적극적으로 보호해야 할 필요성은 이미 미미해졌고, 성인이 어떤 종류의 성행위와 사랑을 하건, 그것은 원칙적으로 개인의 자유 영역에 속하고, 다만 그것이 외부에 표출되어 명백히 사회에 해악을 끼칠 때에만 법률이 이를 규제하면 충분하며, 사생활에 대한 비범죄화 경향이 현대 형법의 추세이고, 세계적으로도 혼인빙자간음죄를 폐지해 가는 추세이며 일본, 독일, 프랑스 등에도 혼인빙자간음죄에 대한 처벌규정이 없는 점, 기타 국가형벌로서의 처단기능의 약화, 형사처벌로 인한 부작용 대두의 점 등을 고려하면, 그 목적을 달성하기 위하여 혼인빙자간음행위를 형사처벌하는 것은 수단의 적절성과 피해의 최소성을 갖추지 못하였다.

이 사건 법률조항은 개인의 내밀한 성생활의 영역을 형사처벌의 대상으로 삼음으로써 남성의 성적 자기결정권과 사생활의 비밀과 자유라는 기본권을 지나치게 제한하는 것인 반면, 이로 인하여 추구되는 공익은 오늘날 보호의 실효성이 현격히 저하된 음행의 상습없는 부녀들만의 '성행위 동기의 착오의 보호'로서 그것이 침해되는 기본권보다 중대하다고는 볼 수 없으므로, 법익의 균형성도 상실하였다.

결국 이 사건 법률조항은 목적의 정당성, 수단의 적절성 및 피해최소성을 갖추지 못하였고 법익의 균형성도 이루지 못하였으므로, 헌법 제37조 제2항의 과잉금지원칙을 위반하여 남성의 성적 자기결정권 및 사생활의 비밀과 자유를 과잉제한하는 것으로 헌법에 위반된다.

간통죄

1) 간통죄 논란

우리나라에서 간통죄는 1953년 10월 이전까지 유부녀에게만 적용됐었다. 그러나 유부녀만을 간통죄의 처벌대상으로 한 것은 평등권에 위배되는 것으로 위헌여부를 따져 유부남과 유부녀 모두 처벌받도록 1954년에 법을 개정하여 현재는 남녀 쌍방을 처벌하는 쌍벌죄를 채용하여 간통한 유부남도 처벌대상(헌법 11조 1항)이 됐다.

우리나라에서도 간통죄에 대한 존폐시비가 꾸준히 일었으나, 헌법 제17조 '사생활의 비밀과 자유' 조항을 들어 간통죄의 위헌을 제기한 제소사건에 대해, 1990년 9월 헌법재판소는 "간통죄의 규정은 헌법규정에 의하여 국가에서 부과된 개인의 존엄과 양성(兩性)의 평등을 기초한 혼인과 가정생활의 유지·보장의무이행에 부합하는 법률이다"라는 결정을 내린 바 있다.

헌법재판소는 2001년 10월 25일에도 "개인의 성적(性的) 자기결정권보다 가정을 보호하는 법적 장치가 필요하다"는 합헌결정을 내렸다. 또 2008년 10월 30일에도 "간통죄는 과잉금지원칙에 위배하여 성적 자기결정권, 사생활의 비밀과 자유를 침해하지 아니하고, 또한 그 법정형이 책임과 형벌간 비례원칙 등에 위배하여 과중한 것으로 볼 수 없다"며 합헌결정을 내렸다.

그러나 합헌결정을 내면서도 성 개방에 대한 사회적 수용분위기를 감안, 이례적으로 "입법자는 간통죄 폐지론에 대해 진지한 접근이 필요하다"고 언급하였다.

2) 외국의 간통죄

노르웨이는 1972년, 덴마크 1930년, 스웨덴 1937년, 일본 1947년, 옛 서독 1969년, 프랑스가 1975년에 폐지했고, 미국도 10여 개 주를 제외하고 대부분 폐지됐다. 간통죄가 남아 있는 나라는 우리나라와 스위스, 그리스, 이슬람국가 등이다.[3)]

3) 헌재 1990.9.1. 89헌마82 전원합의부, 2010.10.25. 2000헌바60 전원합의부, 2008.10.30. 2007헌가17·21, 2008헌가7·26, 2008헌바21·47(병합) 전원합의부, 네이버 백과사전 참조.

2) 형식적 범죄개념과 실질적 범죄개념

형식적 범죄개념	• 법률적 의미의 범죄를 말하며, 형법상의 범죄개념을 말한다. 즉, 범죄를 형식적으로 파악하여 범죄란 형벌법규에 의하여 형벌이 과하여지는 행위 즉, 구성요건에 해당하는 위법·유책한 행위를 말한다. • "법률이 없으면 범죄도 없고 형벌도 없다(죄형법정주의)"는 입장이다.[4]
실질적 범죄개념	• 범죄란 사회에 유해하거나 법익을 침해하는 반(反)사회적 행위를 말한다. 그러나 반(反)사회적 행위가 모두 범죄는 아니다. • 실질적 범죄개념은 어떤 행위를 범죄로 할 것인가에 대한 입법의 기준과 한계를 제시한다는 점에서 "범죄의 형사정책적 의의"라고도 한다. • 실질적 범죄개념도 해당 국가의 헌법의 구속을 받으며, 시대와 국가에 따라 변한다.

2. 일탈 및 비행

1) 일탈행위(일탈행동: deviant)

- 특정 사회에서 요구하는 사회규범 · 가치 등의 기준에 따르지 않거나 상반(相反)되는 행위를 말한다.
- 범죄의 개념과 마찬가지로 일탈행위의 개념도 시대와 국가에 따라 달라지는 상대적 개념이다.

  일탈행위의 예 범죄 · 비행 · 마약 · 폭행, 속어 · 비어 · 은어의 사용, 신에 대한 모독, 정치 · 경제에 대한 과격한 언동 등
- 범죄와 일탈행위 및 비도덕성이 반드시 일치하는 것은 아니다.

  예 도박은 범죄(카지노 제외)이나 가족 간의 오락으로서의 화투 · 카드놀이는 범죄가 아니며 비도덕적이지도 않다.[5] 지나친 이기주의는 비도덕적 행위이나 범죄는 아니다.

---

4) "법률이 없으면 범죄도 없고 형벌도 없다"는 주장에 부합하는 범죄의 개념은 "형식적 의미의 범죄"이다. 2008, 2010 기출

5) 술값내기로 3만원 상당의 판돈을 걸고 속칭 '고스톱'을 했다면 도박이 아닌 단순한 오락행위로 볼 수 있다. 2011.9.14. 전주지법 무죄선고.

일탈과 범죄 2010 기출

- 일탈(deviant)이란 개념 안에 범죄의 개념이 포섭되어 있는 것이고, 일탈의 개념이 범죄의 개념보다 더 크다. 즉, 일탈의 범주 안에 범죄가 포함되고, 범죄의 범주 안에는 일탈이 당연히 포함되어 있는 것이다.
- 일탈과 범죄의 관계에서, 일탈이란 개념은 형법상의 범죄의 개념보다 넓어서, 일탈에는 범죄뿐만 아니라 범죄로 규정되지는 않았지만 비난의 대상이 되는 행위도 포함된다.
  예 알코올 중독, 자살기도, 가출, 부부 사이의 불화, 불손한 행위 등은 일탈이지만 범죄는 아니다.
- 형법상의 범죄란 범죄의 개념을 형식적으로 파악하여, 범죄란 형벌법규에 의하여 형벌이 과하여지는 행위 즉, 구성요건에 해당하는 위법·유책한 행위를 말한다. 따라서 "법률이 없으면 범죄도 없고 형벌도 없다"는 입장이다.
- 법이 제정되면서 어떤 일탈행위가 범죄로 규정되기도 하고, 법이 개정되면서 어떤 범죄가 비범죄화되기도 하기에, 범죄는 법의 제정과 개정에 따라 새로이 규정되는 밀접한 관계에 있다.

[그림 1-1] 일탈과 범죄 간의 중첩

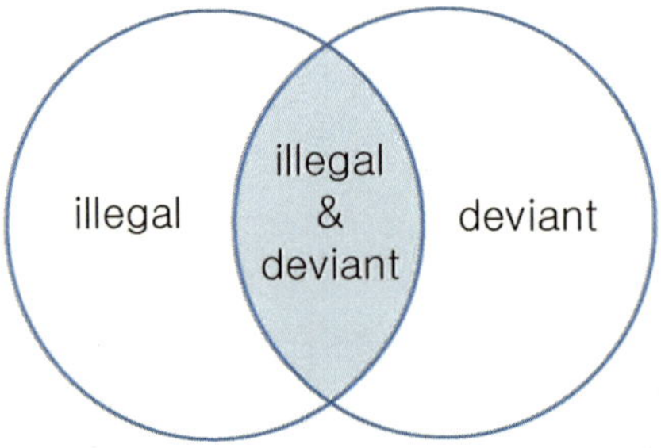

2) 비행(delinquency)[6]

- 비행(非行)은 사회규범에서 벗어난 행위를 말한다.

6) 임상곤, 범죄심리학원론, 백산출판사, 2004:21-23; 이상현, 범죄심리학, 박영사, 2004(3판):8.

광의(廣義)의 비행	• 폭력적인 범죄로부터 일반적인 사회규범까지 포함한다. 즉, 모든 반(反)사회적 행위를 포함하는 개념이다. • P. V. Young은 비행을 "사회적으로 붕괴의 위험성이 있는 행상(行狀) 내지 인격적 태도"로 보았다.
협의(狹義)의 비행	• 소년비행(juvenile deliquency)을 말하며, 일반적으로 비행이라고 할 때는 협의의 비행을 말한다. • S. Gluck는 비행을 "특정한 시간과 장소에 있어서의 법규범 및 법률에 위반되는 청소년의 행위"라고 정의하고 있다.

• 범죄와 비행의 관계는 모든 범죄가 비행인 것은 아니며 모든 비행이 범죄인 것은 아니다. 따라서 비행행위가 바로 범죄로 되지 않는 것도 있다.

예 교통사고를 당한 사람을 보고 도움을 주지 않고 지나친 경우, 많은 사람들이 구조하지 않은 사람의 행위를 냉담하고 비도덕적이라고 비난할지는 몰라도, 법은 일반인에게 구조의 의무를 부과하고 있지 않으므로 그 사람을 법적으로 처벌하지는 못한다.

• 현재 범죄로 간주되는 많은 행위가 한때에는 이상한 행동 또는 비행으로만 인정된 적도 있다.

예 대마초의 소지와 판매는 미국의 경우 1937년 연방법에 의하여 금지되기 전까지는 합법적인 것이었다.

• 범죄 또는 비합법적인 행위가 상황요건이나 시대상황의 변동에 따라 사회규범에 적합한 것으로 인정되는 경우 비(非)범죄화가 되거나 형(刑)이 감형된다.

예 낙태죄와 간통죄, 혼인빙자간음죄

〈청소년비행 지위비행〉7)

1) 청소년비행 2012 기출

• 각종 법령을 위반하는 범법적인 반(反)사회적 행위를 비롯하여 현행 형법에는 저촉되지 않으나 사회적·도덕적 윤리규범에 어긋나는 비(非)도덕적인 행위, 미성년자에게 금지하고 있는 행위, 사회와 집단생활에 부적응 행동 등, 과거나 현재의 객관적인 행위뿐만 아니라 앞으로의 잠재적 행위까지 포함하고 있다.

• 공공의 가치체계를 침범하거나 그 위험성이 충분히 예측되는 것으로, 흔히 범죄라 불리는 행위를 비롯하여 부모가 어찌할 수 없는 일, 정당한 사유 없는 가정 이탈, 불량 교우

7) 남재성, 가정폭력 경험이 청소년의 지위비행에 미치는 영향 ― 강원지역 청소년을 중심으로 ― 한국범죄학, 2011 5권 1호:199-226.

의 교제, 유해한 장소 출입, 상습적 타락, 도박, 성행위, 기타 자기 또는 타인의 적성을 해하는 행위 등과 같이 청소년에게 금지되어 있는 일련의 행위이다.

- 성인범죄와는 구별되는 개념으로 청소년에 대해서만 사용되는 개념이다. 비행의 개념 정의에 있어 청소년을 성인과 구별하는 이유는 청소년은 성인과 같은 판단능력 및 책임능력이 부족하고 인격적 미성숙이 있는 반면 개선 가능성이 많기 때문이다.

2) 지위비행 2011 기출

- 청소년들에게 위반되는 행위로서 성인이 했을 때는 그다지 문제가 되지 않으나 청소년이 했을 때에는 청소년이라는 사회적 지위 때문에 일탈행동으로 간주될 수 있는 것이 지위비행이다. 예 음주, 흡연, 유흥업소 출입, 성(性)과 관련된 활동, 음란물에의 접촉 등
- 청소년의 지위비행은 행위 자체가 경미하여 형법으로 처벌하기에는 무리가 있는 행위이나, 이를 방치하였을 경우 청소년이 성인이 되어 범죄행동으로 발전할 가능성이 많은 행위를 말하며, 지위비행이 지속될 경우 만성적 범죄자로 성장할 수 있는 가능성도 크다.

제2절 범죄의 법률적 정의와 비법률적 정의

1. 범죄의 법률적 정의

법률적으로 범죄란 법이 요구하는 행위를 고의적으로 하지 않거나, 법이 금지하고 있는 행위를 고의적으로 한 행위이다. 이는 합의론적 관점과 갈등론적 관점에 따라 차이가 있다.

합의론적 관점	법은 사회의 가치·신념·의견의 주류를 반영한 것이며, 범죄는 법의 위반이자 사회의 전체요소에 모순되는 행위이다.	
갈등론적 관점	• 범죄는 피(被)지배집단을 대상으로 지배집단의 지위와 권한을 보호하기 위해 고안된 정치적 산물이다. 예 흑인을 살해하거나 강간한 백인보다, 백인을 살해하거나 강간한 흑인이 훨씬 무거운 처벌을 받는 경우가 많음.	
	• A.T. Turk	– 법이란 영향력 있는 집단의 이익을 보호하기 위한 하나의 무기이다.
	• W. Chambliss & R. Seidman	– 법은 지배집단이 자신들의 우월성을 보장하기 위한 행위규범이다.

	• E. Doleschal & H. Klapmults	– 범죄는 실제 행위의 위해여부와는 아무런 관계도 없는 사회세력에 의해서 유지된다.
	• R. Quinney	– 범죄는 정치적으로 조직된 사회에서 지배계층에 의해 만들어지기 때문에, 범죄의 정의도 지배계층의 이익과 갈등을 초래하는 행위로 이루어진다.

2. 범죄의 비법률적 정의

1) 필요성

- 모든 행위를 법률적으로 규정할 수 없으며, 규정할 경우 과잉범죄화(over-criminalization) 되어 범죄자를 양산하게 된다.
- 법률적 정의는 암수범죄(dark figure crime: 暗數犯罪)가 제외되며, 범죄로 규정되지 않은 수많은 사회의 위해 초래행위가 간과될 우려가 많기에, 범죄학의 연구는 편파적 · 부분적 연구에 불과하게 된다.

2) 접근방법

사회-법률적 접근(socio-legal approach), 비교문화적 접근, 통계적 접근, 낙인적 접근, 인권적 접근, 이상향적-무정부주의적 접근(utopian-anarchist approach) 등이 있다.

제 02 장 범죄학의 의의

제1절 범죄학의 의의

1. 범죄학의 개념과 연구범위

1) Garofalo

Garofalo는 범죄학(Criminology)을 "범죄의 현상과 원인규명을 주된 내용으로 하는 사실학 · 경험과학"이라고 하였다.[1)]

2) Sutherland

Sutherland는 범죄학을 "사회현상으로서의 비행 또는 범죄에 관한 지식의 총체"라 하고, 범죄학은 법 제정과정과 범법과정 및 범법에 대한 반응이라 하면서, 범죄원인학과 행형학(行刑學: Penology)으로 구성된다고 주장하였다."[2)]

3) 서덜랜드(Sutherland)와 크레시(Cressey) 2011 기출

- Sutherland와 Cressey는 범죄학이란 "범죄를 사회적인 현상으로 간주하는 지식체계"이며, 범죄학의 연구범위에는 법 제정의 과정, 제정된 법의 위반과정, 법 위반행위에 대한 대응과정 등이 포함되며, 범죄학의 궁극적인 목적은 이러한 법, 범죄, 범죄에 대

1) • 범죄학(Criminology)이란 용어는 1879년 프랑스의 '또미나르'에 의해 최초로 사용되었고, 1885년 이탈리아의 가로팔로가 본격적으로 사용하였다.
  • 가로팔로는 자연범(自然犯)의 개념을 인정하여, 범죄학을 국가마다 다른 법체계로부터 독립시켰다. 또한 Garofalo의 범죄학 개념은 규범학인 형법학과 정책학인 형사정책을 구별하게 하는 기초를 마련하였다.

2) 지광준, 형사정책, 경인, 1998:6–8.

한 조치와 관련된 여러 가지 과정들에 대한 일반적이고 신뢰할 수 있는 원칙들을 확립하는 데 있다고 하였다.[3)]

- 범죄학은 법의 기원과 발달에 관한 "법사회학", 범죄의 원인을 규명하는 "범죄병리학", 범죄에 대한 사회학적 반응인 "행형학(行刑學)"으로 구성된다고 보았다.

4) 윌리암스(Williams)

Williams는 범죄학이란 "사회현상으로서의 비행과 범죄에 대한 지식의 체계"로서, 범죄행위와 그에 대한 사회의 반응에 대한 과학적인 접근을 말한다고 하였다.[4)]

5) 기번스(Gibbons)

기번스(Gibbons)는 범죄학을 형법의 제정과정과 범법행위에 대한 대응체제인 형사사법제도, 법의 기원, 범죄량과 그 분포, 범죄의 원인을 연구하는 학문이라고 정의하였다.

6) 천정환

천정환은 범죄학을 범죄원인론, 현상론, 대책론을 연구과제로 하는 학문이라는 광의의 입장을 취하고 있다.[5)]

---

3) Edwin Sutherland and Donald Cressey, Principle of Criminology, 6th ed., Philadelphia : Lippincott, 1960:3.

4) J. E. Williams, Criminology and Criminal Justice, London, 1982:4.

5) • 천정환, 신범죄학, 백산출판사, 2006:45-46.
   • Taft는 범죄학을 범죄인의 처우에 필요한 모든 항목을 포함하는 '광의의 범죄학'과 범죄의 원인만을 언급하는 '협의의 범죄학'으로 나누었다. '협의의 범죄학'은 범죄원인론과 범죄현상이론만을 포함하는 개념이며, '광의의 범죄학'은 범죄원인론 외에 범죄대책과 예방론까지도 포함한다. D. R. Taft, Criminology, 3rd ed., p. 3.
   • 김보환은 범죄학을 협의, 광의, 최광의로 나누어, '협의의 범죄학'은 범죄원인론만을 의미하고, '광의의 범죄학'은 범죄원인론뿐만 아니라 형벌론과 교정론이 포함되는 범죄대책론까지 포함하고, '최광의의 범죄학'은 광의의 개념에다 범죄수사학까지 포함시키고, 범죄학은 최광의로 해석하되, 범죄학은 서덜랜드가 주장하는 법사회학과 피해자학, 그로스(H. Gross)가 주장하는 범죄수사론, 범죄예방과 대책에 관한 형사사법제도론이 포함되어야 한다고 주장한다. 김보환, 교정학, 교학사, 2005:15-16.

7) 이만종

- 이만종은 범죄학을 형사학의 한 분야로 규정하고, 범죄학의 주요 테마를 범죄현상론, 범죄원인론, 범죄학이론으로 한정시켜 범죄원인론에 중점을 두고 있다.[6]
- 범죄학이란 사회현상으로서의 비행과 범죄에 대한 지식의 체계로서 범죄행위와 그에 대한 사회의 반응에 관한 연구의 과학적 접근이라고 할 수 있으며, 종합과학으로써 사회학 · 생물학 · 의학 · 심리학 · 역사학 · 정치경제학 · 교육학 · 자연과학 등의 지식을 요구한다고 할 것이다.

〈표 1-1〉 범죄학의 대상: 이만종의 견해

<table>
<tr><td rowspan="8">형사법학</td><td>형법학</td><td>–</td><td>–</td></tr>
<tr><td>형사소송법학</td><td>–</td><td>–</td></tr>
<tr><td rowspan="6">형사학</td><td rowspan="3">범죄학</td><td>범죄현상론</td></tr>
<tr><td>범죄원인론</td></tr>
<tr><td>범죄학이론</td></tr>
<tr><td rowspan="3">형사정책</td><td>형사사법정책론</td></tr>
<tr><td>형벌보안처분론</td></tr>
<tr><td>범죄자처우론</td></tr>
</table>

출처: 이만종, 범죄학개론, 학현사, 2005:5.

2. 범죄학 연구의 필요성

1) 범죄현상의 파악

- 범죄가 사회계층별, 연령별, 성별, 지역별 등 각 기준에 따라 사회적으로 어떻게 분포되고 있는지 그 실태를 연구하는 것이 필요하다.
- 어떤 유형의 사람이 무슨 범죄에 대하여 어떠한 조건하에서 어느 정도의 공포를 느끼는지를 파악하는 것이 필요하다.

6) 이만종, 범죄학개론, 학현사, 2002:2.

2) 범죄원인의 분석과 통제방안의 수립

- 범죄는 유형별로 범행의 동기, 성격, 수법, 범죄자의 속성 등 거의 모든 면에서 많은 차이가 있기 때문에, 범죄의 원인을 규명함에 있어서도 일반론뿐만 아니라 특정범죄자의 특정범행을 규명할 수 있는 개별적인 범죄원인의 규명도 필요하다.
- 범죄통제를 위한 사회적 대책은 범죄문제의 발생을 사전에 예방하는 것과 이미 발생한 범죄사건에 대한 사후대응으로 나눌 수 있다. 범죄피해에 따른 과다한 비용, 피해회복의 불가능, 범죄자의 처리와 개선의 비용과 어려움 등을 고려할 때 범죄의 통제는 사전예방이 우선시되어야 한다.

3) 범죄자 교정과 피해자 부조

- 범죄의 악순환을 벗어나기 위해서는 범죄자 자신의 각오와 노력, 경찰에서의 검거율의 증진, 검찰의 적정한 기소권의 행사, 재판단계에서의 양형의 합리화, 교정단계에서의 철저한 교정교화활동 및 사회의 따뜻한 포용력이 필요하다.
- 최근에는 범죄행위를 가해자와 피해자가 상호작용하여 만들어낸 것으로 보는 범죄피해자학이 강조되고 있다.

제2절 범죄학의 연구방법

1. 의의

범죄학에 대한 사회과학적·사실학적 연구방법에 있어서 질적(qualitative) 연구방법에는 개별조사법이, 양적(quantitative) 연구방법에는 표본집단조사법, 대량관찰법, 실험법 등이 있다.

2. 질적(qualitative) 연구방법 2012 기출

질적(qualitative) 연구방법인 개별조사법에는 사례·생애사 연구, 추적조사, 참여적 관찰법 등이 있다.

1) 사례 · 생애사 연구(case, life history studies)

- 미시 범죄학적(micro criminological) 관점이며, 하나 또는 몇 개의 대상에 대한 깊이 있는 정밀조사를 목표로 하고, 일기, 편지, 자서전, 전기(傳記) 등을 분석한다.
- 깊이 있는 질적 자료의 수집이나, 분석을 위해 선택된 사례의 부정형성(不定型性)이나 연구자의 편견이 개입될 우려가 있다.

> •사례연구의 예 Sutherland의 직업절도범(The Professional Thief, 1937), Thraser의 갱(The Gang: A Study of 1313 Gangs in Chicago, 1927), Shaw의 잭 롤러(The Jack Roller, 1930)
> 생애사 연구의 예 Mass의 발라치 페이퍼(The Valachi Papers, 1968), Teresa와 Renner의 마피아에서의 내 인생(My Life in the Mafia, 1973)

2) 참여적 관찰법(participant observation)

- 연구자가 스스로 범죄 또는 비행집단 내에 그들과 똑같은 지위 및 자격을 가지고 들어가 그들과 똑같은 조건으로 생활하면서 그들의 범죄동기와 제반 활동상을 직접적으로 관찰 · 기록하는 방법이다.
- 장점은 그 배경이나 지속적 활동이라는 살아 있는 자료를 얻을 수 있는 것이다.
- 단점은 연구자 자신이 범죄행위를 실제로 행하는 경우가 발생할 위험이 있으며, 객관적인 관찰방법의 적용이 어려워 주관적인 편견이 개입될 소지가 많으며 사실이 왜곡될 소지가 많으며, 연구자의 윤리성 문제가 제기될 수 있는 것이다.

> 예 Lanni의 조직범죄에 대한 연구(Study of Organized Crimes, 1972), Polsky의 사기꾼(Con Artists, 1967), Klockars의 전문적 장물아비(Professional Fences, 1974), Yablonsky의 약물중독자(Drug Addicts, 1965)

3. 양적(quantitative) 연구방법

양적(quantitative) 연구방법에는 표본집단조사법, 대량관찰법, 실험연구 등이 있다. 표본집단조사법에는 자기보고식 조사, 피해자 조사, 정보제공자 조사 등이 있다.

〈실험연구〉[7)]

1. 실험연구의 의의 2012 기출

– 실험연구(experimental research)란 실험(experiment)을 통하여 자료를 수집하고 분석하는 연구를 말한다.

– 실험연구는 복잡한 사회(정책)현상 중에서 연구의 목적상 관심이 있는 요소(변수)들만을 선별하여 그들 간의 관계, 특히 인과관계(cause & effect relationship)를 집중적으로 관찰하고 분석하는 방법으로 매우 유용하다.

2. 실험연구의 장·단점

장점	• 실험연구는 변수 간의 인과관계를 명확히 규명할 수 있다. • 실험조건을 연구자가 임의로 조작하여 그가 원하는 방향으로 연구를 진행시킬 수 있다. • 실험상황의 재조성(再造成)을 통하여 반복적 연구가 가능하여 연구의 보편성과 일반성을 높일 수 있다.
단점	• 실험연구는 현실성의 결여로 인하여 연구결과를 일반화시키기는 다소 애매한 점이 있다. • 인간의 가치와 윤리적인 측면에서도 실험이 용인될 수 없는 점이 있을 수 있다. • 복잡다단한 사회현상을 단순한 실험이라는 방법을 통해 규명해 보려는 데에 실험연구의 근본적인 한계가 있다.

3. 실험연구의 종류

실험상황	현지 실험연구(field experimental study)	현실적인 사회상황이나 정책환경 속에서 실제로 실험조건을 통제하고 변수를 조작하여 그 효과를 보고자 하는 경우
	실험실 실험연구(laboratory experimental study)	실험자가 원하는 조건을 갖춘 연구상황을 만들어 변수를 조작하여 그 효과를 관찰하는 경우
실험조작이나 통제의 정도	전실험연구(pre–experimental study)	연구자의 실험변수의 조작이나 실험상황에 대한 통제가 거의 불가능한 경우
	진실험연구(true experimental study)	연구자의 의도에 맞게 실험변수의 조작이나 통제가 충분히 행해지는 경우
	준실험연구(quasiexperimental study)	어느 정도 통제가 가능하나 연구자의 임의대로 충분히 이루어지지 않는 경우

7) 김렬, 사회과학 조사방법론, 박영사, 1999:146–151.

코호트 분석

- 코호트(cohort)는 원래 로마의 군대조직을 가리키는 말로써 '한 무리의 전사(戰士) 또는 군인'을 의미하는 용어였다.
- 코호트(cohort)란 용어가 학문적으로 널리 사용되게 된 것은 인구학의 발전과 관련이 깊다. 인구학에서 코호트는 일정한 지리적 공간에 존재하는 인구 가운데 특정한 기간 동안 유의미한 생애(生涯) 경험을 공유하는 사람들을 지칭한다. 공통의 생애 경험 가운데 가장 대표적인 형태가 출생(出生)인데, 특정한 기간 내에 태어난 사람을 출생 코호트(birth cohort)라 한다.
- 오늘날 코호트란 용어는 사회과학은 물론이고 의학을 비롯한 자연과학에서도 널리 사용되고 있는데, 공통의 생애 경험을 중시하는 일련의 분석기법을 코호트 분석이라고 한다.

제 03 장 범죄현상의 파악

제1절 공식적 범죄통계자료(Official Crime Statistics)

1. 의의

경찰·검찰·법원·교정기관 등 형사사법기관의 공식적 통계를 이용하여, 범죄와 범죄자 및 범죄피해와 피해자에 대한 제반사항을 조사·연구하는 데 이용되는 자료이다.[1)]

2. 유형

〈표 1-2〉 범죄통계 2010 기출

미국	• 형사사법통계국 (Bureau of Justice Statistics)	• 형사사법통계자료집 (Sourcebook of Criminal Justice Statistics)
	• 연방수사국(FBI)	• 종합범죄보고서(Uniform Crime Report)
독일	• 독일연방수사국	• 경찰범죄통계
일본	• 법무총합연구소	• 범죄백서
한국	• 경찰청	• 범죄분석, 경찰백서, 경찰통계연보, 교통사고통계
	• 대검찰청	• 범죄분석[2)], 마약류범죄백서, 심사분석, 검찰연감
	• 법무연수원	• 범죄백서
	• 법무부	• 검찰연감

1) • 범죄학자들의 연구목표는 i) 범죄현상을 정확히 파악함으로써 범법자의 특성을 이해하고 ii) 형사사법 프로그램의 효과를 평가하고 iii) 형사사법기관의 의사결정을 돕는 데 있다.
• 범죄율은 인구 10만 명당 범죄발생건수를 말한다. 2007 기출

2) "범죄분석"은 대검찰청에서 발행하는 공식적 범죄통계자료이다. 2007 기출

	• 법무부 교정본부	• 교정수용통계연보
	• 법무부 범죄예방정책국	• 비행소년통계
	• 법원행정처	• 사법연감
	• 문화체육관광부	• 청소년백서
	• 교육부	• 청소년백서
	• 통계청	• 한국의 사회지표, 한국통계연감
	• 국립과학수사연구소	• 국립과학수사연구소보

3. 장 · 단점[3)]

1) 장점

• 범죄자료를 매년 정기적으로 취합함으로써 연도별, 지역별, 성별, 연령별 등의 비교를 가능하게 한다.

• 공식통계가 특정한 범죄에 대한 다양한 정보를 수집하기 때문에, 범죄와 범죄자에 대한 유형과 추세를 파악하는 데 매우 유용하다.[4)]

2) 단점

• 공식통계는 발각되고 신고되고 기록된 범행에 국한되며 제한적이다.

• 공식통계는 통계를 작성하는 형사사법기관의 한계와 편견, 능력과 열의에 따라 달라진다.

• 범죄수치를 범죄율과 관련된 생태적 변화나 요소와 연계시키지 않는다. 즉, 범죄의 인지건수는 실제 범죄수의 증감 이외에 다른 요소로부터도 영향을 받는다.

• 범죄에 대하여 법률적 분류를 활용하기 때문에, 범죄학적 분류에 따라 다소 동질적 범주로 재분류되지 않는 한 사회과학자들에게는 큰 도움이 되지 않는다.[5)]

3) 김용준, 범죄피해자학, 백산출판사, 2009:15-16; 이만종, 범죄학개론, 학현사, 2005:13-18.
4) W. G. Doener and S. P. Lab, Victimology, 2nd ed., Cincinnati, OH : Anderson Publishing Co., 1998:24.
5) Fattah, op. cit., pp. 27-28.

- 범죄자와 피해자에 대한 정보와 자료가 부족하다.
- 인지건수는 유죄자의 수가 아니다. 인지건수 안에는 나중에 경범죄처분으로 처리되어 검찰에 송치되지 않은 것, 검찰에 의해 기소가 유예된 것, 재판단계에서 정당방위나 심신상실로 인정되어 무죄가 된 것도 포함되어 있다.
- 범죄를 기록함에 있어서 일정한 계상(計上)처리가 이루어지는 경우가 있다. 피의자의 행위 수에 따라 '건수'를 계산하는 경우이다. 단, 범죄가 경합한 경우(한 사람이 동시에 복수의 구성요건에 해당되는 행위를 한 경우) 통계에는 이 중에서 가장 무거운 죄만이 기록된다. '인원'에 대해서도 마찬가지이다. 동일인물이 복수범죄를 저지른 경우에는 법정형의 가장 무거운 범죄(법정형이 동일한 경우에는 주된 범죄)를 한 사람이 실행한 것으로 계상된다. 그리고 예비·미수나 결과적 가중범이 처벌되는 경우의 범죄는 각 범죄의 인지건수에 포함된다.

〈표 1-3〉 공식적 범죄통계의 한계[6)]

구분	내용
부분성	• 범죄통계는 부분성을 지닐 따름이다.
수량성	• 범죄통계는 수사기관에 적발된 범죄사건의 수와 양을 나타내줄 뿐이다.
왜곡성	• 범죄통계는 수사기관에 적발된 범죄의 발생규모와 피해규모를 축소 또는 확대시켜 보여주는 측면을 지닌다.

4. 암수(暗數)범죄

1) 의의

암수(dark figures)범죄란 경찰에서 인지하지 못한 범죄를 말한다. 즉, 실제로 범죄가 발생하였으나 수사기관에 인지되지 않았거나 인지되기는 하였으나 해명되지 않아 공식적인 범죄통계에 나타나지 않는 범죄행위의 총체이다.

---

6) • 공식적 범죄통계는 숨은 범죄(암수범죄)를 파악하지 못하며, 형사사법기관에 의해 왜곡될 수 있으며, 단속을 많이 하면 범죄건수가 많아진다는 문제점이 있다. 그러나 범죄현상을 파악하는 데 여러 가지 의미 있는 자료가 된다. 2007 기출
• 조병인, 현대사회와 범죄, 법문사, 2000:48-50.

〈표 1-4〉 암수(暗數)범죄의 구분

절대적 암수범죄	• 실제로 범죄는 발생하였으나 고소・고발 등 신고가 이루어지지 않아 수사기관에서 인지하지 않았거나, 피해자가 범죄인지조차도 알지 못하는 범죄. • 피해자 없는 범죄 즉, 피해자가 없거나 피해자와 가해자의 구별이 어려운 범죄에서 많이 발생함.[7]
상대적 암수범죄	• 수사기관에 인지되었지만 해결하지 못함으로 인해 공식통계에 기록되지 않은 범죄(수사기관의 검거율과 증거 채취력의 정도와 밀접하게 관련됨). • 법집행기관의 자의 내지 재량도 상대적 암수범죄와 관련됨.
범죄경력의 암수	• 어떤 범죄로 유죄판결을 받았으나, 실은 형사소추기관에 의해 입증된 것보다 많은 범죄를 범함으로써 나머지는 공식통계에서 누락된 범죄로, 여죄(餘罪)조사에 의해 알 수 있음.
규범적 암수	• 실질적인 범죄개념에 포함되면서 형식적 범죄개념에서 제외되는 행위.

출처: 이만종, 범죄학개론, 학현사, 2005:14. 일부 수정.

2) 암수가 발생원인

- 완전범죄로 인한 범죄의 미인지 내지 미검거
- 피해자의 신고기피 사항으로 ⅰ) 범죄가 완료되지 않고 미수에 그친 경우, ⅱ) 경제적 또는 신체적으로 피해가 없는 경우, ⅲ) 경미한 범죄로 범죄피해가 심각하지 않은 경우, ⅳ) 무기류가 사용되지 않은 경우, ⅴ) 범죄피해에 대한 보상을 받기가 어렵다고 여기는 경우, ⅵ) 피해자가 범죄자의 보복이 두려워 통보하지 않은 경우(조직범죄 등), ⅶ) 성범죄와 같이 범죄가 개인비밀을 누설할 우려가 있는 경우, ⅷ) 형사사법절차에 대한 부담감으로 경찰에 불신감을 갖고 있거나 적대감정을 지니고 있는 경우
- 법집행기관의 선별화 과정에서의 자의적 처리에 의한 누락
- 형사사법기관의 활동의 소극성 및 무능

7) • 피해자가 없는 범죄(Victimless Crime)란 마약이나 대마초・마리화나 복용, 도박, 음주와 주정(酒酊), 매춘, 동성연애 및 공중 앞에서의 노출행위와 같이 그 불법적인 사용이나 불법적인 행위로서 공공질서에 위배되는 범죄를 말한다. 즉, 타인에게 해를 끼치지 않으나, 사회적으로 받아들여지지 않고, 법적으로 금지된 상품이나 서비스를 비밀리에 필요로 하는 당사자 간에 교환하는 행위를 말한다.
• 슈어(E. Schur)는 금지된 행위의 주체자나 금지된 물품의 상호당사자를 제외하고는 타인에게 어떠한 해를 끼치지 않는다는 의미에서 피해자 없는 범죄(Victimless Crime)라고 이름 붙였다.

- 형사사법기관의 이념 즉, 응보이념을 취하면 인지된 대부분의 사건이 공식적으로 처리되지만, 갈등해소 서비스가 중심이 되면 대부분의 사건들이 비공식적으로 처리되기 때문이다.
- 소추하였으나 증거불충분 등으로 무죄판결을 받는 경우, 사법기관들의 통계행정체계의 미비로 인한 탈루, 정치적 이유로 인한 통계조작 등이 있다.

3) 암수조사의 장점

- 공식범죄통계는 주로 실무적 관점에서 중대한 범죄를 파악하지만, 암수조사는 범죄학적 관점에서 경미한 일탈행위 등을 잘 파악한다.
- 범죄로 인한 물질적 · 신체적 · 정신적 피해에 대한 자료를 제공함으로써 범죄피해의 위험성에 대한 정보를 제공하며, 형사입법과 형사적용에 관한 주민들의 인식과 기대, 가치관 등을 조사할 수 있다.
- 암수조사의 결과와 법집행기관의 통계를 비교함으로써 공식적 사회통제기관의 역할수행의 효율성을 확인할 수 있으며, 조사방법상의 왜곡이 거의 없기 때문에 국제적인 범죄비교를 용이하게 한다.

4) 암수조사의 한계

- 설문조사는 현실에 대한 간접적 파악이므로 그 자체로 왜곡의 가능성을 가지고 있다. 즉, 질문의 양식, 순서, 강조 등에 따라 응답에 영향을 미칠 수 있어 신빙성과 유용성에 의문이 제기된다.
- 마약범죄, 경제범죄, 정치범죄, 조직범죄와 가정 내에서의 범죄에 대한 자료를 거의 제공하지 못한다.
- 일부 범죄는 대상자의 개인적인 망각이나 잊고 싶은 기억 등으로 경찰에 신고되지도 않으며 암수조사에서도 밝혀지지 않는다. 또한 조사자와 피조사자의 태도에 따라 조사결과가 왜곡될 수도 있다.
- 암수를 추정하는 주요 방법으로는 자연적 관찰, 인위적 관찰(실험)식 피해자 조사, 실제 범죄를 범한 범죄자에 대한 자기보고식 조사(self report survey), 정보제공자 조사(제3자를 통한 조사), 형사사법기관의 재량연구 등이 있다.

제2절 비공식적 조사자료

1. 자기보고식 조사(self-report survey) 2011 기출

1) 의의

특정 인구집단을 대상으로 면접이나 설문지를 통해 수집하는 조사방법이다. 이는 범죄의 암수(dark figure)에 대한 올바른 분석의 필요성에 의한 대안으로 등장하게 된 것이다.[8)]

2) 장점

- 공식통계에서 얻을 수 없는 범죄피해자의 성격, 태도, 행동습관에 관한 자료를 구할 수 있어 범죄피해원인, 범죄피해 실태 및 피해발생 과정을 연구할 수 있다.
- 형사사법기관의 선별적인 사건 처리과정에 영향을 받지 않은 범죄피해발생의 분포를 알 수 있다.

3) 단점

- 특정한 시기에 특정한 지역에서 특정한 표본을 추출하여 조사하는 것이 대부분이어서, 전국적인 조사와 계획적인 조사가 되지 못한다. 즉, 대표성이 없어서 연구결과의 일반화가 곤란하다.
- 조사대상자들의 기억력과 정확성의 문제, 조사별 상이한 기억기간의 설정, 조사항목의 중복, 애매모호한 응답지[9)], 범죄피해에 대한 과다 또는 과소보고 등의 문제점을 가진다.
- 자기보고식 조사 그 자체가 가지고 있는 내적 한계 즉, 연구대상자들이 불성실하게 응답할 경우 올바른 자료를 구할 수 없으며, 다양한 종류의 범죄피해 실태를 포착할 수 없다.

---

8) • "귀하는 지난 6개월 동안 몇 건의 비행을 하였습니까?"의 질문이 사용되는 연구방법은 "자기보고식 조사"이다. 2007 기출
 • 공식범죄통계 자료와 비교할 때 자기보고식 자료의 특징은 범죄자의 태도, 가치, 행동에 대한 정보를 얻을 수 있다는 것이다. 2008 기출

9) 여러 번, 가끔, 종종 등의 애매하고 불분명한 표현 등.

2. 피해자 조사(victim survey) 2011, 2012 기출

1) 의의

• 피해자를 통해 범죄를 파악하는 방법으로써, 공식통계가 암수범죄(暗數犯罪)의 문제를 지니기에, 실제 범죄의 피해자는 공식적으로 보고되고 기록된 것보다 많을 것으로 가정하고 있다.10)

• 적정수의 가구(家口)를 임의로 추출하여 조사원이 직접 방문하여 가족들의 범죄피해에 관하여 면접조사하는 것이다.

• 범죄피해자조사는 가해자와 피해자가 동시에 존재하는 범죄라는 동전의 양면을 모두 살펴볼 수 있는 기회를 제공함으로써, 암수범죄(dark figure)를 밝혀내고 범죄피해 실태를 보다 정확하게 판단하는 데 기여한다.

• 범죄피해자조사는 과거의 일정기간 동안에 특정범죄피해에 대한 경험유무를 응답자에게 묻거나, 경험하였다면 피해는 어느 정도이며 그 상황에 대해 어떻게 대응했는지에 대한 조사이다.

• 범죄피해조사에 의한 통계는 사회의 삶의 질이나 안전을 측정할 수 있는 사회지표로 사용된다.11)

• 우리나라의 경우 1990년 한국형사정책연구원에서 서울지역의 범죄실태에 대한 조사를 한 것이 최초이다. 현재, 3년마다 범죄피해조사를 실시하여『한국의 범죄피해에 대한 연구』라는 책자를 발간하고 있다.

2) 장점

• 대개의 경우 전국규모의 조사이기 때문에, 공식통계나 자기보고식 조사보다 대표성 있는 자료수집이 가능하다.

• 형사사법기관에서 수집한 공식통계보다 더 좋고 자세한 정보를 제공할 수 있다.

• 범죄피해의 위험성이 높고 낮음에 관련된 다수 요인에 관한 자료와 다양한 집단의 위험성의 분포에 관한 자료를 제공해 준다.

---

10) 공식범죄통계에서 파악되지 않은 숨은 범죄에 관련된 정보를 얻을 수 있는 방법은 "피해자조사"이다. 2008, 2010 기출

11) 김용준, 범죄피해자학, 백산출판사, 2009:17-24; 김준호 외, 청소년비행론, 청목출판사, 2003:32.

- 범죄피해 이후 피해자가 겪는 영향, 피해의 결과, 다양한 형사사법기관과 그들의 업무수행결과, 각 기관이 고객에게 제공하는 서비스의 질 등을 평가할 수 있게 하며, 이웃감시와 같은 특정한 범행사건의 감소와 예방에 관한 프로그램의 효과성을 평가하게 해줄 수도 있다.
- 피해자는 형사사법기관과 피해자의 상호작용의 정도나 상호작용의 부족함에 대한 정보를 제공하며, 형사사법기관의 업무수행과 그들의 피해자에 대한 만족도를 측정할 수 있게 해주어서 결국 사법제도에 대한 공공의 태도를 측정할 수 있게 해준다.
- 시민들의 범죄피해에 대한 두려움과 실제 피해위험성이나 피해경험과의 관계도 측정할 수 있게 해준다.
- 자신의 피해사실을 경찰에 보고하지 않는 피해자 수와 그들의 특성 및 피해사실을 신고하는 피해자와의 차이점에 대한 가치 있는 정보를 제공해 주며 이는 특정한 범죄피해를 신고하지 않는 이유를 알 수 있게 해준다.[12)]

3) 단점

- 범죄의 피해가 발생했을지 모르는 범죄피해에 대한 추정일 뿐이지 실제로 그 범죄가 반드시 발생했다는 것을 의미하는 것은 아니다.
- 조사내용상의 한계로써, 전체 범죄를 파악하는 데 불충분하여, 조직범죄나 조직을 대상으로 하는 범죄피해를 파악하기 곤란하며, 피해자 없는 범죄(victimless crime)나 화이트칼라 범죄는 조사되기 어려우며, 살인 · 강간 등은 조사되기 어렵다.[13)]
- 비교기준의 차이로 공식통계와 직접 비교할 수 없으며, 과소보고(under-reporting)와 과대보고(over-reporting)가 있다.
- 망각(妄覺)이나 잘못된 기억으로 인해 조사대상자의 응답이 잘못될 수 있으며, 조사대상자의 수치심과 명예보호 등의 문제가 있다.[14)]

---

12) 이윤호, 범죄학, 박영사, 2007:23-41.
13) '범죄피해조사'에서 가장 조사하기 어려운 범죄유형은 '살인'이다. 2007 기출
14) • 고의적 오류는 의도적으로 면접자에게 정보를 잘못 전하거나 판단을 그르치게 하는 것으로써, 자기 자신의 피해사실을 여러 가지 이유로 면접자에게 제대로 말하지 않는 경우를 말한다.
  • 비의도적 오류는 피해사실을 모르거나 잊었거나, 질문을 잘못 이해하거나, 사건을 잘못 알고 있는 데 따른 오류이다.

- 전국단위로 이루어지는 피해자조사의 경우, 표본의 대표성을 확보하기가 더욱 어려우며, 가구를 표집대상으로 하고, 18세 이상 거주자만을 면접하기 때문에, 기업이나 18세 이하 시민의 피해조사는 제외되기 마련이다.
- 면접자가 주로 주간에 가정을 방문하여 면접하기 때문에 표본의 크기가 충분하지 않으면 사례의 수가 불충분해지고 통계적 분석이 어려우며, 표본의 모든 구성원을 다 면접할 수도 없다.15)
- 대체로 지나치게 큰 전국규모의 표본과 면접자가 가구를 방문하여 대면면접(face-to-face interview)을 하기에 비용이 많이 든다.
- 사람들의 기억력과 참여의지 또는 비용의 문제로 대부분 쉽게 기억될 수 있는 중요범죄로 한정되고, 모든 유형의 범죄피해를 다 조사할 수는 없다.

3. 정보제공자 조사

법집행기관에 알려지지 않은 범죄나 비행을 인지하고 있는 자로 하여금 이를 보고케 하는 것으로서, 피해자조사에 의하여 밝혀지지 않는 범죄를 밝히기 위한 보조수단으로 사용되고 있다.

15) 지정된 사람이 이사를 가고 추적이 불가능하거나, 표출된 가구가 빈집일 수도 있고 또 모든 면접대상자가 다 면접에 응하지 않을 수도 있으며 면접에 응하더라도 모든 질문에 성실하게 응답하지 않을 수도 있기 때문이다. Fattah, op. cit., p. 35.

제 04 장 범죄의 사회인구학적 특성

제1절 성별 · 연령

1. 성별(gender)과 범죄

1) 의의

거의 모든 범죄에서 남성이 여성보다 높은 범죄율을 보여주고 있다.[1] 여성범죄가 증가하고 있지만, 남성범죄 또한 증가하고 있다.

2) 여성범죄의 원인

(1) 롬브로조(Lombroso)

- 여성은 남성에 비해 수동적이며, 남성보다 진화가 덜 되었으며, 보다 어린이 같으며, 덜 감성적이며, 지능이 낮아서 범죄성이 약하지만, 경건함 · 모성애 · 저지능 · 약함 등 여성의 전형적인 특질이 부족한 소수의 여성범죄집단이 있다고 주장하였다.
- 범죄여성은 몸에 털이 많이 나는 등의 신체적 특성으로 정상적인 여성과 구별될 수 있으며, 감정적인 면에서도 비행여성은 남성과 더 가까운 것으로 보인다는 '남성적 가설'을 주장하였다.[2]

1) 예외적으로 여성이 남성보다 높은 범죄율을 보여주고 있는 것은 여성범죄인 매춘이다.
2) '남성적 가설(masculinity hypothesis)'은 Lombroso가 "The Female Offender(1895)"에서 주장한 것으로써, 여성범죄자들은 신체적으로 몸에 털이 많으며 감성적으로는 범죄적 또는 비범죄적 남성과 더 가깝다는 것이다.

(2) 프로이드(Freud)

여성은 일반적으로 수동적이지만, 범죄여성은 남성에 대한 자연적인 시기심을 억제할 수 없어서 규범으로부터 일탈하는 것으로 간주하고 있다.

(3) 폴락(O. Pollak)

- 여성은 자연적으로 범죄지향적인 성향이 있다고 보고 있다. 여성이 남성보다 더 일탈적이고, 약으며, 생리적이고, 사회적으로 어떤 유형의 범죄에 대해서는 더 용이하다는 것이다.
- 여성이 남성에 못지않은 범죄를 저지르지만 단지 여성의 범죄는 은폐되거나 편견적인 선처를 받기 때문에 공식적 통계상 적은 것으로 보일 뿐이라는 것이다. 2011 기출
- 여성이 남성에 의해 이용되기보다는 남성을 범죄에 이용한다는 '기사도정신 가설(chivalry hypothesis)'을 주장하였다.

(4) 아들러(F. Adler)

F. Adler는 1970년대, '신여성범죄자(new female criminal)'의 개념을 주장하면서, 전통적으로 여성범죄율이 낮은 이유는 여성의 사회・경제적 지위가 낮기 때문이었고, 여성의 사회적 역할이 변하고 생활행태가 남성의 생활상과 유사해지면서 여성의 범죄활동도 남성과 닮아간다고 주장하였다.

3) 여성범죄의 특징[3)]

- 은폐된 범죄성(masked criminality) 즉, 여성이 주로 범하는 범죄의 유형이 가시적이지 않아서 인지되기 힘들고, 자신을 은폐하기도 쉽다.[4)]

---

3) 전대양, 현대사회와 범죄, 형설출판사, 2002:76; 이윤호, 범죄학, 박영사, 2007:42-81.

4) • 여성범죄는 자신의 신체적 매력을 이용하여 범행을 하는 경우도 있으며, 범행수법은 독살・유기・미신의 활용 등 비신체적 수법을 선택하는 경우가 많으며, 남성을 부추기거나 끌어들여 범행을 하는 경우도 있다. 2003 기출

• 여성범죄는 남성범죄에 비하여 은폐적 특성을 가지며, 정범(正犯)으로 범죄를 행하는 경우보다 배후에서 공범으로 가담하는 경우가 많다. 또한 남성과 비교할 때 대부분 우발적이고 상황적으로 발생하는 범죄가 많으며, 범행수법을 살펴보면 잘 아는 대상을 범행대상으로 삼고, 비신체적 수법을 활용하며, 경미한 범죄를 반복하는 특성이 있다. 2004, 2008 기출

- 우발적 · 상황적 범죄와 배후에서의 교사범, 공범, 종범(從犯)으로 가담하는 경우가 많다.
- 대개 자신이 잘 아는 사람을 주로 범죄의 대상으로 삼는다.
- 독살, 유기(遺棄), 미신 활용 등 비신체적 범행수법을 택하는 경우가 많다.
- 경미한 범행을 반복해서 자주 행한다.
- 범죄의 동기가 여성의 성적 위기감과 모성애의 발로에서 기인하는 경우가 많다.
- 주변 남성의 암시나 유혹에 따라 그 남성을 위하여 범행하게 되는 경우가 많다.
- 여성범죄자의 반수 가까이가 누범자이며, 일반적으로 지능이 낮고 정신박약자 내지 정신병질자가 많다.
- 여성의 사회적 지위가 낮은 나라에서는 여성에게 개방된 사회적 활동범위가 현저히 좁기 때문에 범죄를 범할 기회가 적지만, 여성의 사회적 진출이 많이 이루어짐에 따라 여성의 범죄도 증가한다.
- 남성의 경우 미혼범죄자의 범죄율이 기혼자보다 높은 것에 비해서, 여성의 경우는 기혼자의 범죄율이 높다.
- 자신의 육체를 무기로 삼아 범행하는 경우가 많으며, 큰 사기꾼 중에는 의외로 여성이 많다.

2. 연령과 범죄

1) 의의

- 서덜랜드(Sutherland)와 크레시(Cressey)는 여러 나라의 범죄통계를 분석한 결과, 대체로 범죄성이 최고인 시기(The Ago of Maximum Criminality)는 사춘기 또는 그 직전의 시기이며, 이를 정점으로 꾸준히 감소한다는 사실을 발견하였다.
- 허쉬(Hirschi)와 갓프레드슨(Gottfredson)은 사회 · 경제적 지위, 결혼관계, 성별 등에 관계없이 젊은 사람이 나이든 사람보다 많은 범행을 한다고 주장하고 있다.[5)]

---

5) • 범죄자의 특성으로서, 남성이 여성보다 폭력범죄를 더 저지르며, 하층일수록 폭력범죄를 더 저지를 가능성이 높으며, 미혼일수록 범죄를 저지를 가능성이 높다. 또한 노인일수록 폭력범죄를 덜 저지른다. 2007 기출
• Riedl은 범죄행위가 30세 이전에 나타나는 것을 '조발(早發)범죄', 30세 이후에 나타나는 것을

- 로우(Rowe)와 타이틀(Tittle)은 범죄행위에 참여할 가능성에 대한 스스로의 추정인 '범죄적 성향(Criminal Propensity)'을 연구한 결과, 이 범죄적 성향이 연령에 따라 점차적으로 감소한다고 하였다.

2) 연령과 범죄의 상관관계

- 변화하는 사회적 역할과 사회화의 결과로 나이가 들어갈수록 범죄율이 감소한다는 것이다.

Matza의 성장효과 (maturation effect)이론	사회에 대한 책임감 등의 사회학적 연령이 증가하여 30대 이후 범죄가 감소한다.
Sigel의 노쇠화 (aging out)이론	시설수용의 기간이 길어져 나이가 들수록 범행에 대한 동기와 기회가 줄어든다.
Reckless의 정착과정 (settling down process)이론	과거 시설수용의 경험이 재범의 동기를 억제하여 재범을 방지한다.

- 양적 특징은 범죄유형에 따라 다르게 나타나지만, 질적 특징을 보면 일반적으로 청년기에는 폭력적인 범죄유형이 많고, 갱년기와 노년기에는 지능적인 범죄가 많다.

제2절 계층 · 가정 · 교육

1. 계층과 범죄

1) 의의

- 하류계층이 범인성 요인이 많다는 논리는 범행에 대한 유인요인을 많이 가지고 있다는 것이다.
- 하류계층은 원하는 물품과 봉사를 관습적인 방법을 통해 얻을 수 없을 경우, 결국에는 불법적인 방법에 호소하여 획득하게 된다는 '도구적 · 제도적 범죄(instrumental crimes)'를 저지른다.

'지발(遲發)범죄'라고 하였다.

- 가난하게 사는 사람들은 자신을 강인하고 나쁜 사람으로 인식함으로써 긍정적인 자아상을 개발할 수 없기 때문에 자신의 분노와 좌절감을 표현하는 수단으로써 폭력이나 강간과 같은 폭력성의 '표출적 범죄(expressive crimes)'를 많이 범한다는 것이다.
- 풍속범죄는 주로 하류계층에 속하는 사람들에 의해 범해지나 경제범죄 등의 지능범죄는 중상류 계층에 의해 범해지고 있다.

2) 연구결과

Tittle 등은 35개의 자기보고식 연구를 분석한 결과, 사회・경제적 지위와 범죄는 직접적인 관계가 없다고 주장하였다. Elliott 등의 연구에서는 가벼운 비행의 경우 사회・경제적 지위와는 무관하나 강력범죄에 있어서는 하류계층의 범행이 더 많다고 분석하였다.

2. 가정과 범죄

결손가정, 훈육과 통제, 상호작용과 응집도, 가족 내의 범죄성과 부도덕성 등이 범죄에 영향을 미치는 요인으로 보고 있다.

1) 결손가정

- 결손가정(broken home)이란 양친 모두 또는 어느 일방이 없는 가정을 말하며, 그 원인은 사별, 이혼, 별거, 유기(遺棄), 실종, 수형(受刑), 장기부재 등이다.[6)]
- 결손의 결과 자녀에 대한 훈육・통제・보호에 차질이 생기게 되고, 경제적 빈곤, 감정적 상실, 사회화에 필요한 역할모형의 상실, 통제의 약화와 그에 따른 비행적 교우관계의 발전 등에 기인하여 결손가정이 비행을 유발하는 한 요인으로 작용한다고 본다.
- 다수설은 학령기 전에는 어머니가 없는 경우가 더 위험하고, 학령기 후에는 아버지가 없는 경우가 더 위험하다고 한다. 또한 대체로 결손을 어린 나이에 일찍 경험할수록

6) • 양친이 모두 있더라도 가정의 본질적 기능인 생활의 상호보장이 결여되어 있는 가정은 '형태적 결손가정'이라고 하며, 자녀에 대한 심리적 및 신체적 양육이 결여된 가정은 '기능적 결손가정'이라고 한다.
• 소년비행에 있어서 가정의 기능적 결함은 비행유발에 있어 중요한 요인이 될 수 있으며, 부모의 일관성 있는 훈육방식이 소년비행의 억제에 있어 중요하며, 갈등가정은 가족 간의 갈등으로 인하여 가출의 원인이 될 수 있다. 2004 기출

더 큰 영향을 받게 되며, 소년보다는 소녀가 더 큰 영향을 받으며, 어머니보다는 아버지의 결손이, 미혼부모나 유기(遺棄), 수형(受刑), 별거 등으로 인한 결손이 사별(死別), 이혼, 질병 등에 의한 결손보다 더 많은 영향을 미치며, 경미범죄보다는 강력범죄와 더 큰 관계가 있다고 본다.

〈표 1-5〉 가정결함의 형태

구분	내용
비행가정	• 사회적 부적응자가 가족의 구성원으로 되어 있는 가정, 기능적 결손가정
갈등가정	• 가족 간에 감정·이해·가치관 등 심리적 갈등이 존재하여 인간관계의 융화가 결여된 가정
시설가정	• 고아원 등 기타 아동양육시설이 가정의 역할을 하는 경우

2) 훈육과 통제(discipline & control)

- 훈육은 훈육의 일관성·강도·질에 의해 결정되며, 훈육의 유형보다는 훈육의 일관성이 비행에 있어서 더 중요한 원인이 된다고 본다.
- '훈육결함'이란 자녀에 대한 부모의 무관심, 부모의 신체적·도덕적·지적 결함으로 인한 훈육의 불가, 훈육에 대한 부모의 의견 불일치, 지나치게 엄격하거나 부족한 훈육 등을 말한다.

(1) 버트(Burt)

훈육의 결함을 소년비행의 가장 중요한 요인 중 하나로 지목하였다.

(2) 글뤽(Glueck)부부

- 훈육을 소년비행에 있어서 중요한 요인으로 보았으며, 느슨하거나 일관적이지 못한 훈육이 매우 엄격한 훈육방법보다는 비행과 더 높은 관계가 있었으며, 확고하지만 친절한 훈육방법은 비(非)비행소년과 더 많은 관련이 있다는 것이다.
- 훈육방법으로서의 체벌은 비(非)비행소년보다 비행소년의 부모에 의해서 더 자주 사용된다는 것을 발견하였다.

(3) 나이(Nye)

- 극단적으로 권위주의적인 훈육은 청소년의 이동성(mobility)을 방해하게 되어 동료집단과 자유롭게 상호작용할 수 없게 되어, 청소년의 동료집단관계에 지장을 초래하게 된다.
- 지나치게 관대한 훈육은 청소년의 행동을 지도할 준거점(reference point)이 될 수 있는 통제와 한계를 마련해 주지 못한다.

(4) 매코드(McCord)부부와 졸라(Zola)

McCord부부와 Zola는 청소년에 대한 훈육의 방법을 6가지로 구분하였다. 무원칙한 훈육이 비행을 유발하는 중요한 요인이며, 훈육의 유형보다는 훈육의 일관성이 비행에 있어서 더 중요한 요인이 된다고 보는 것이다.

〈McCord부부와 Zola의 청소년 훈육의 6가지 방법〉

구분	내용
1) 사랑지향적 훈육 (love-oriented discipline)	합리성이 동원되고 특권과 보상을 보류하는 등의 방법으로 처벌
2) 처벌적 훈육	체벌을 이용하여 분노, 공격성, 위험이 내재되는 훈육
3) 느슨한 훈육 (lax discipline)	부모의 어느 한쪽도 충분한 통제하지 않는 훈육
4) 무원칙적인 훈육 (erratic discipline) 1	부모의 어느 한쪽이 사랑지향적인 데 반하여, 다른 한쪽에서는 느슨하거나 2가지 유형을 왔다 갔다 하는 훈육
5) 무원칙적인 훈육 (erratic discipline) 2	부모 모두가 사랑지향적 훈육과 느슨한 훈육 및 처벌적 훈육을 모두 활용하는 훈육
6) 무원칙적인 훈육 (erratic discipline) 3	한쪽 부모는 처벌적이고, 다른 부모는 느슨한 경우 또는 양쪽 부모가 모두가 왔다 갔다 하는 훈육

3) 가정의 결집성과 상호작용

- 쇼(Saw)와 매케이(McKay)는 비행유발요인으로 작용하는 것은 가족구성원의 공식적 결손이 아니라 오히려 내적인 긴장과 부조화라고 주장하였다.

• 태판(Tappan)도 가정에서의 갈등, 부조화, 긴장이 비행소년에게서 종종 발견되고 있음을 지적하고, 이것은 가정의 공식적 결손보다 아동의 부적응에 있어서 중요한 과정이라고 주장하였다.

• 나이(Nye)는 비행의 정도가 부모와 자식 간의 수용(acceptance)과 거부(rejection) 정도에 비례하며, 부모가 자식을 거부하는 것은 직접적으로 비행과 관련되고 있으나 부모자식 간의 수용은 낮은 비행의 확률과 관계된다. 또한 부모가 자식을 거부하는 것은 자식이 부모를 거부하는 것보다 더 중요한 것으로 이해되고 있다.

• 디보스(DeVoss)는 일본과 이탈리아 연구에서, 가족의 응집력이 부족한 가정일수록 많은 비행소년이 발생한다고 하였다.

4) 가족의 부도덕성과 범인성

• 지나친 음주의 문제, 마약의 복용, 가족 간의 폭력성, 법・제도와의 충돌 등 부모와 형제자매를 비롯한 가족구성원이 겪고 있는 이들 문제가 다른 가족의 비행성과 범인성에 상당한 영향을 미치는 것으로 밝혀지고 있다.

• 가정의 범죄성, 무규범성, 문제성 등이 자녀의 비행에 상당한 영향을 미치는 것으로 보고 있다.

3. 교육과 범죄

• 범죄인의 학력은 평균적으로 일반국민보다 낮고, 학교에의 적응성 여부는 직접 비행과 관련되는 것이며 특히 성적불량, 학습무기력, 학습태만 등은 범죄 내지 비행의 원인이 된다고 볼 수 있다.

• 다만 화이트칼라 범죄는 오히려 교육의 역기능을 보여주고 있다.

제3절 경제 · 직업 · 매스컴

1. 경제와 범죄

1) 빈곤과 범죄

토비(J. Toby)는 절대적 빈곤에서 느끼는 박탈감보다 경제사정이 좋아지면서 개개인의 기대수준의 차이에 따라 발생하는 심리적 빈곤현상인 상대적 박탈감(relative deprivation)이 복지적 범죄와 관련된다고 주장하였다.

2) 경기변동과 범죄

- 경제환경은 직 · 간접적으로 범죄의 정도와 종류에 영향을 미치며, 특히 재산범죄에서 두드러지게 나타난다.
- 대체로 호황기에는 주로 사치성 범죄, 종업원 및 젊은 층의 범죄가 증가하고, 불황기에는 여성보다 남성범죄율이 높고, 미혼보다 기혼자의 범죄율이 높으며, 기업주, 고연령층의 범죄, 절도 등 일반범죄가 증가한다고 분석되고 있다.
- 유엔 사회방위연구소는 자동차절도 등은 범행기회의 증대로 인하여 오히려 호경기에 많이 일어나는 반면 대부분의 경제범죄와 음주 등은 경제적 공황기에 증가하는 것으로 보고 있다.

3) 실업과 범죄

실업이 범죄에 영향을 미치며, 범행에 가장 많이 노출된 범죄지향적인 사람에게 가장 큰 영향을 미친다. 실업이 범죄를 확산시키는 사회조건을 결정하는 주요 요인이나, 실업의 해결이 바로 범죄의 해결을 의미하지는 않는다.

2. 직업과 범죄

경리직원이나 은행원 등은 횡령, 배임 등의 재산범죄를 범하기 쉽고, 기업가들은 세법, 노동법 등 특별법위반, 공무원은 뇌물죄, 변호사 · 의사 · 목사 등은 명예와 관련된 범죄, 농수산업자는 절도 등 재산범죄를 범하기 쉬운 환경적 요인이 많다.

3. 매스컴과 범죄

• 매스컴은 범죄유발적 측면과 범죄억제적 측면을 모두 가지고 있다.

정화(淨化)가설	Feshbach는 매스컴을 통한 음란·폭력성의 간접적 경험은 대리만족과 함께 공격에너지를 일시적으로 감소시킨다.
억제가설	매스컴은 시청자로 하여금 폭력피해에 대한 책임감과 보복에 대한 공포심을 일으켜 그의 공격적 성향을 억제한다.
자극성 가설(모방효과)	범죄와 관련된다는 입장으로는 매스컴이 범죄 실행의 장면을 노골적으로 묘사함으로써 사회적 암시효과가 생겨 범행수법을 배우고 새로운 모방범행을 한다.[7]
습관성 가설	폭력장면을 장기적으로 보면 범죄행위에 대해 무감각해지고 범죄를 미화하는 가치관이 형성되어 장기적으로 범죄를 유발한다.

• 일반적인 연구들은 TV의 폭력성이 상당수의 성인과 어린이들의 공격적 행동의 빈도와 종류에 영향을 미친다고 보고 있다.

제4절 범죄현황의 평가

1. 1990년대의 범죄동향[8]

• 고용구조가 불안해진 결과로 보복성 폭력범죄 및 생계비 마련을 위한 강·절도범죄가 증가하였다.

• 사기·횡령·배임행위 및 외국인을 상대로 한 범죄가 증가하였다.

• 자동차절도 및 빽소니 범죄가 증가하였다.

• 신용카드범죄, 매점매석행위, 자살 및 알코올중독, 마약투약, 매춘, 도박, 투기 등에 탐닉하는 인구가 증가하였다.

7) 1999년 개봉된 영화 '주유소 습격사건'을 보고 모방범죄가 발생하였고 범인들이 체포되었다.

8) 1990년대는 국내경기의 침체와 이로 인한 실업증가로 치안상황이 매우 불안하였다. 조병인, 현대사회와 범죄, 법문사, 2000:22-24.

2. 2000년의 범죄동향[9)]

- 각종 범죄가 폭발적으로 증가하였고, 매년 범죄가 증가하였다.
- 범죄의 질적 변화로 직무와 전문지식인 범죄와 범죄의 흉악화 추세가 나타났다.
- 배금풍조의 심화로 재산범죄인 사기, 횡령, 배임죄와 자동차절도가 급증하였다.[10)]
- 지적재산권의 위기로 타인의 무형재산을 무단으로 침해하는 행위가 급증하고 있다.
- 절도·폭력 등 형법범죄가 크게 늘어났으며, 여성범죄와 청소년 범죄자 수가 범죄자 100명 중 22명인 22.6%이며, 검거된 범죄자의 절반 이상이 재범자로 2000년 검거된 범죄자의 61.2%는 재범자로 같은 범죄를 저지른 경우도 19.4%가 되었다.[11)]

3. 2005년의 범죄동향

- 범죄의 흉악화·폭력화[12)]와 새로운 범죄현상이 출현하였다.
- 비공식적인 사회통제가 약화되었으며, 국제화로 외국인의 불법입국, 체류가 증가하고 체류외국인의 각종 범죄가 증가하였으며 그 범죄양상도 충동·우발적인 수준을 벗어나 조직화·지능화되는 경향을 보여 사회적 트러블을 일으킬 가능성이 높아졌다.
- 총기를 사용한 범죄가 확산되고 있으며, IMF 등을 거치면서 나타난 거품경제의 붕괴에 의한 경제범죄와 화이트칼라 범죄 등이 증가하였다.

---

9) • 이만종, 범죄학개론, 학현사, 2005:42-45.
 • 조병인, 현대사회와 범죄, 법문사, 2000:12-21.

10) 2000년도 이후 공식범죄통계에서 가장 많이 발생한 형법범죄의 유형은 '재산범죄'이다. 2008 기출

11) 미국에서는 FBI가 "통일범죄보고서(Uniform Crime Report : UCR)"의 자료를 근거로 하여 각 범죄가 어떠한 비율로 발생하고 있는가를 종합하여 보고하고 있으며, 이를 범죄시계(Crime clock)라 부르며, 미국 내의 범죄현황을 나타내는 잣대의 하나로 범죄학에서 종종 사용되고 있다.

12) 우리나라의 범죄가 서구 경제선진국의 범죄와 다른 이유는 ⅰ) 비공식적인 사회통제가 여전히 심하다. ⅱ) 커다란 사회적인 트러블이 적다. ⅲ) 총기통제가 잘 이루어지고 있다. ⅳ) 중류의식을 지닌 사람의 비율이 높다. ⅴ) 교육수준·식자율(識者率)이 높다. ⅵ) 지구대, 치안센터, 파출소 등 지역경찰제도가 치안유지에 효과를 거두고 있다. 이만종, 범죄학개론, 학현사, 2005:45-48.

제2편

범죄유형론

제 05 장 범죄유형의 의의

제1절 범죄의 유형

1. 형법적 논의

1) 결과범과 거동범

(1) 결과범(실질범)

- 결과의 발생을 요건으로 하는 범죄를 말한다. 예 살인죄, 상해죄 등
- 결과적 가중범도 결과범의 특수한 형태에 속한다.

(2) 거동범(형식범)

결과의 발생을 요하지 않고 법에 규정된 행위를 함으로써 성립하는 범죄를 말한다.

예 주거침입죄, 무고죄, 위증죄, 폭행죄 등

2) 침해범과 위험범

(1) 침해범

구성요건이 법익의 현실적 침해를 요하는 범죄를 말한다. 예 살인죄, 상해죄 등

(2) 위험범

구분	추상적 위험범	구체적 위험범
의의	• 일반적인 위험성만 있으면 가벌성을 인정하는 범죄	• 현실적인 위험의 발생을 구성요건에 명시하고 있는 범죄

위험의 발생	• 구성요건표지가 아님	• 위험을 발생시킨 구성요건표지
위험의 인식	• 고의의 인식내용이 아님	• 고의의 인식내용
범죄의 성질	• 형식범	• 실질범
위험발생입증	• 불요	• 필요
해당 범죄	• 현주건조물 방화죄, 공용건조물 방화죄, 타인소유 일반건조물 방화죄, 연소죄, 위증죄, 무고죄, 유기죄(제271조 제1항, 제2항), 낙태죄, 명예훼손죄, 신용훼손죄, 업무방해죄	• 자기소유 일반건조물 방화죄, 일반물건 방화죄, 자기소유 일반건조물·일반물건 실화죄, 가스 등 공작물 손괴죄, 유기죄(제271조 제3항, 제4항)[1]

3) 즉시범, 상태범, 계속범

(1) 즉시범

시간적 계속을 필요로 하지 않고 행위객체를 침해 또는 위태시킴으로써 범죄가 기수(旣遂)에 이름과 동시에 완수에 이르는 범죄를 말한다. 예 살인죄, 상해죄 등

(2) 상태범

실행행위로 구성요건결과가 발생하여 기수에 이르고 종료되었지만, 기수 이후에도 실행행위로 야기된 위법상태가 계속되는 범죄를 말한다. 예 절도죄, 강도죄, 사기죄, 공갈죄, 횡령죄, 배임죄 등

(3) 계속범

구성요건적 행위 내지 법익침해상태가 기수에 이르고 기수 이후에도 위법상태가 계속되고 종료되지 않는 범죄를 말한다. 예 체포·감금죄, 다중불해산죄, 주거침입죄, 퇴거불응죄, 약취·유인죄, 직무유기죄

4) 일반범, 신분범, 자수범

(1) 일반범

'~한 자'라고 규정되어 있어 누구나 정범이 될 수 있는 범죄를 말한다.

1) '중'자가 붙은 범죄 즉, 중상해죄, 중유기죄 등은 구체적 위험범이나 다만 중체포·감금죄는 아니다.

(2) 신분범

- 진정신분범은 일정한 신분 있는 자에 의하여만 성립되는 범죄이다. 예 직무유기죄(제122조), 수뢰죄(제129조), 도주죄(제145조), 위증죄(제152조), 허위진단서작성죄(제233조), 간통죄(제241조), 유기죄(제271조), 업무상비밀누설죄(제317조), 횡령죄(제355조 제1항), 배임죄(제355조 제2항)
- 부진정신분범은 신분 없는 자에 의하여도 범죄가 성립할 수 있지만 신분 있는 자가 죄를 범한 때에는 형이 가중되거나 감경되는 범죄이다. 예 존속살해죄(제250조 제2항), 영아살해죄(제251조), 업무상과실치사죄(제268조), 업무상낙태죄(제270조), 영아유기죄(제272조), 업무상횡령죄(제356조), 업무상배임죄(제356조)

(3) 자수범

- 행위자가 자신이 직접 실행해야 범할 수 있는 범죄를 말한다.
- 구성요건의 자수에 의한 직접적 실현에 의하여서만 범죄의 특수한 행위 위반가치가 실현될 수 있는 범죄를 말한다. 예 위증죄, 간통죄 등

5) 목적범, 경향범, 표현범

(1) 목적범

- 진정목적범은 목적의 존재가 범죄의 성립요건인 범죄이다. 예 내란죄, 강제집행면탈죄, 다중불해산죄, 허위공문서작성죄(허위진단서작성죄×), 통화 · 유가증권 · 문서 등의 각종 위조 · 변조죄, 음행매개죄, 영리약취 · 유인죄, 준강도죄, 각종 예비 · 음모죄
- 부진정목적범은 목적의 존재가 형의 가중 · 감경사유인 범죄이다. 예 내란목적살인죄, 모해위증죄, 모해증거인멸죄, 출판물에 의한 명예훼손죄, 판매목적 아편 등 소지죄, 결혼 · 국외이송목적 약취 · 유인죄

(2) 경향범

행위자의 주관적 경향이 구성요건요소로 되어 있거나 범죄유형을 함께 규정하고 있어, 이러한 행위자의 내적 경향의 표출에 의해서 구성요건이 충족되는 범죄를 말한다. 예 공연음란죄, 학대죄 · 가혹행위죄, 영업 · 상습성을 지닌 범죄 등

(3) 표현범

행위자의 내면적인 지식상태와 모순되는 표현으로서 행위가 행해졌을 때 범죄가 되는 경우를 말한다. 예 위증죄, 무고죄, 허위감정·통역·번역죄, 불고지죄 등

2. 범죄학적 논의

1) 형사범과 행정범[2)]

- 형사범은 그 성질이 사회윤리에 반하는 범죄를 가리키며, 자연범이라고도 한다.
- 행정범은 원래는 사회윤리에 반하지 않는 행위를 행정의 단속목적을 위해서 범죄화한 것이다.[3)]

2) 동기에 의한 유형

① 이욕범	범죄자가 자신의 경제적인 이익을 위해서 행한 범죄 예 절도, 횡령, 배임, 통화위조 등
② 곤궁범	범죄자가 경제적인 곤궁으로부터 벗어나기 위하여 실행한 범죄 예 절도, 영아살인, 유기 등
③ 격정범	증오, 질투, 복수심, 성욕 등의 격정에 휩싸여 저지른 범죄 예 폭행, 상해, 살인, 강간 등
④ 유쾌범	경제적인 목적이나 격정에 의한 충동 없이 스릴이나 흥분을 얻고자 하는 목적으로 저지른 범죄 예 가게물건 절도, 과속질주 등
⑤ 정치범	정치적인 목적으로 저지른 범죄 예 내란(內亂), 소요(騷擾) 등

3) 행위양태의 성질에 의한 유형

① 폭력범	피해자의 신체에 대해 공격을 가하는 범죄 예 살인, 상해, 강도, 강간
② 지능범	피해자에게 물리적 공격을 가하지 않고, 기망(欺罔), 사기행위로 남을 속여 넘기는 일이나 임무위반 등의 방법으로 저지른 범죄 예 사기, 횡령 등
③ 무력범	범죄자의 무력한 태도에 의해 실행되는 범죄 예 절도, 영아살인 등

2) 이만종, 범죄학개론, 학현사, 2005:18, 참조.
3) 기본적으로 형사범의 대다수는 법전에 의해 규정되어 있으며, 행정범의 대부분은 형법전 이외의 법규(특별법)에 의해 규정되어 있다.

제2절 5대 범죄와 범죄지표

1. 5대 범죄

- '5대 범죄'는 '주요범죄'를 통칭하는 개념으로서, '살인 · 강도 · 강간 · 절도 · 폭력'을 말하며[4], 1991년 범죄와의 전쟁 1주년 성과분석을 위해 도입되었다.
- 경찰청 수사국은 1987년 '주요범죄'라는 용어를 사용하지 않고, 형법범 · 특별법범 · 강력범 · 절도범 · 폭력범으로 구분하여 사용하였으며, 1988년에는 '중요범죄'라는 용어를 사용하였으며, '중요범죄' 유형에는 강력범, 절도범 및 폭력범이 포함되었다. 1999년 이후부터는 '5대 범죄'에 마약, 방화를 추가한 '7대 범죄' 개념이 사용되기도 한다.

2. 범죄지표

구분	내용
범죄지표	매년 전국 각급 경찰관서에서 취급한 형사사건의 범죄통계원표(발생통계원표 · 검거통계원표 · 피의자통계원표)를 토대로 산출한 통계를 의미한다.
범죄율	인구 10만 명당 범죄발생건수를 계산한 것으로, 인구대비 범죄발생건수를 비교할 수 있다는 점에서 유용한 자료이지만, 중요 범죄와 상대적으로 가벼운 범죄가 동등한 범위로 취급되어 통계화된다는 문제가 있다.[5]
범죄시계	미국의 범죄통계에서 나오는 것으로 매시간 범죄발생현황을 표시한 것인데, 일반인에게는 범죄예방기능을 한다.[6]
피해자시계	매시간 피해자 발생현황을 표시하며 범죄시계보다 더 빨리 움직인다. 범죄유형과 범죄특성에 따라 피해자시계의 속도도 달라진다.
천정환의 "교정시계"	교정국에서 발간하는 각종 통계표의 방향을 제시해 주며, 재사회화의 속도를 나타내는 것으로써, 이미 의식이 고착화된 노인의 교정시계는 잘 가지 않으나 상대적으로 소년수형자의 교정시계는 빨리 갈 수 있어 자원배분의 기준이 될 수 있다. 교정시계는 수용자 개인의 교정시계, 각 교도소의 교정시계, 한국의 교정시계가 있다.

4) 5대 강력범죄는 살인, 강도, 강간, 폭력, 절도를 말한다. 2008 기출
5) 천정환, 신범죄학, 백산출판사, 2006:57-59.
6) 정신교, 범죄학개론, 형설, 2005:36.

범죄농담	한 지역사회에서 일정기간에 발생한 총범죄를 강도, 살인과 같은 중한 범죄로 나눈 것을 말하여, 범죄농담률이 높을수록 그 지역사회는 중범죄가 많이 발생한다고 추론할 수 있다. 범죄농담을 한 지역사회에서 일정기간 동안에 발생한 총범죄를 매춘 등 피해자 없는 범죄로 나눈 개념으로 정의한다면 범죄농담이 높은 지역은 그 지역범죄인들의 특수한 욕구를 추론할 수 있다.
범죄농담지도	각 지역들의 범죄농도를 전국적으로 표시한 것으로써, 범죄학적 의의는 국가가 범죄예방정책을 세울 때 그 준거기준과 방향을 제시해 주는데 있다.

제 06 장 살인범죄

제1절 형법적 논의

1. 살인죄(criminal homicide)의 의의

- 살인죄란 사람을 살해함으로써 그 생명을 침해하는 것을 내용으로 하는 범죄이다.

제250조(살인, 존속살해) ① 사람을 살해한 자는 사형, 무기 또는 5년 이상의 징역에 처한다.
② 자기 또는 배우자의 직계존속을 살해한 자는 사형, 무기 또는 7년 이상의 징역에 처한다.

- 보호법익은 사람의 생명이며, 보호의 정도는 침해범이다.

2. 구성요건

1) 주체

피해자 이외의 모든 자연인을 말하며, 범인은 본죄의 주체가 될 수 없다.

2) 객체

사람이란 자연인이며[1], 시기(始期)는 자연분만인 경우는 진통설, 제왕절개수술에 의한 분만인 경우는 자궁절개시가 통설이다. 종기(終期)는 맥박정지설이 종래의 통설이며, 뇌사설은 유력설이다.

1) 행위자 이외의 타인을 의미하며, 자살은 구성요건해당성이 없으므로 불가벌이다.

3) 행위

- 사람을 살해하는 것으로서, 고의로 사람의 생명을 자연적인 사기(死期)에 앞서서 인위적으로 단절시키는 것을 말한다.
- 기본적인 구성요건은 보통살인죄(제250조 제1항)이며, 가중적 구성요건으로는 존속살인죄(제250조 제2항), 감경적 구성요건으로는 영아살인죄(제251조), 촉탁・승낙에 의한 살인죄(제252조 제1항)가 있다.[2)]
- 사람을 살해한다는 인식과 의사 즉, 고의가 있어야 하며, 미필적 고의로도 족하다.

4) 살해의 수단

살해의 수단, 방법에는 제한이 없다. 살해의 수단은 작위 또는 부작위 모두 가능하다.

3. 살인죄의 종류

■ 보통살인죄

> **제250조(살인, 존속살해)** ① 사람을 살해한 자는 사형, 무기 또는 5년 이상의 징역에 처한다.
> **제254조(미수범)** 전4조의 미수범은 처벌한다.
> **제256조(자격정지의 병과)** 제250조, 제252조 또는 제253조의 경우에 유기징역에 처할 때에는 10년 이하의 자격정지를 병과할 수 있다.

■ 존속살인죄

> **제250조(살인, 존속살해)** ② 자기 또는 배우자의 직계존속을 살해한 자는 사형, 무기 또는 7년 이상의 징역에 처한다. 〈개정 1995.12.29〉

2) 자살교사・방조(제252조 제2항)와 위계・위력에 의한 살인죄(제253조) 및 내란목적살인(제88조) 등은 제3의 독자적 범죄형태이다.

- 직계존속은 법률상의 개념이며, 혼인 외의 출생자의 경우 생부(生父)는 인지시(認知時)에만 법률상의 직계존속이 되나, 생모(生母)는 자(子)의 출생으로 당연히 직계존속이 된다. 입양의 경우는 타인 사이라 할지라도 합법절차에 따라 입양관계가 성립하면 법률상 직계존속이 된다.
- 배우자도 법률상의 배우자를 의미하며, 현재의 생존배우자이며, 사실혼관계에 있는 자는 제외된다.

■ 영아살인죄

> **제251조(영아살해)** 직계존속이 치욕을 은폐하기 위하거나 양육할 수 없음을 예상하거나 특히 참작할 만한 동기로 인하여 분만 중 또는 분만직후의 영아를 살해한 때에는 10년 이하의 징역에 처한다.

■ 촉탁 · 승낙에 의한 살인죄

> **제252조(촉탁, 승낙에 의한 살인등)** ① 사람의 촉탁 또는 승낙을 받아 그를 살해한 자는 1년 이상 10년 이하의 징역에 처한다.

■ 자살교사 · 방조죄

> **제252조(촉탁, 승낙에 의한 살인등)** ② 사람을 교사 또는 방조하여 자살하게 한 자도 전항의 형과 같다.

- 자살교사란 자살의 결의가 없는 자에게 자살을 결의하게 하는 것을 말하며, 자살방조란 이미 자살을 결의하고 있는 자를 원조하여 자살을 용이하게 하는 것을 말한다.[3)]

■ 위계 등에 의한 촉탁살인죄

> **제253조(위계등에 의한 촉탁살인등)** 전조의 경우에 위계 또는 위력으로써 촉탁 또는 승낙하게 하거나 자살을 결의하게 한 때에는 제250조의 예에 의한다.

3) 진정으로 같이 죽을 의사로 죽을 약속을 하고 정사를 기도한 경우에도 타인의 자살에 방조한 사실이 인정되면 당연히 자살방조죄가 성립한다.

■ 살인예비 · 음모죄

제255조(예비, 음모) 제250조와 제253조의 죄를 범할 목적으로 예비 또는 음모한 자는 10년 이하의 징역에 처한다.

〈살인의 유형〉[4]

구분	내용
교살	끈으로 목을 매어 질식하게 하여 살해하는 방법
총살	권총, 소총, 사냥총 등을 이용하여 살해하는 방법
액살	손이나 발로 목 부위를 눌러 질식하도록 하는 방법
절자살	예리한 칼이나 송곳 같은 것으로 자르거나 찔러서 치명적인 상처를 주어 살해하는 방법
폭살	폭발물질인 다이너마이트나 기타 화약 등을 이용하여 살해하는 방법
박살	박살 또는 타살이라 함은 둔탁한 망치, 곤봉, 몽둥이, 철주 등의 둔기로 때려서 살해하는 방법
독살	취약, 제초제, 싸이나 등 독극물을 음식물이나 음료수 등에 타서 복용하도록 하여 살해하는 방법
소살	휘발유, 신나, 석유 등 인화성 물질을 이용하여 태워서 살해하는 방법
기타 방법	부작위에 의한 살해방법과 실수사(失手死)로 위장하는 경우 등

〈살인의 동기〉

구분	내용
물욕살인	재물이나 이익을 목적으로 하는 살인행위
원한살인	남녀관계, 경제관계, 고용관계, 치욕적 관계 등으로 상호 간에 관계가 악화되어 살인행위로 발전하는 것
치정살인	남녀의 애정관계에 문제가 발생하여 살해하는 것
정신이상 살인	정신적 병중에 있는 자가 순간적으로 발작을 일으켜 사람을 살해하는 경우
미신적 살인	과학적으로 증명되지 않은 방법에 의하여 불치의 병을 치료할 수 있다고 믿고 몸의 장기를 약으로 사용하기 위하여 살해하는 경우와 안수기도, 광신적 종교의 교리에 의하여 단식토록 하여 죽게 한 경우 등의 살인
쾌락살인	자신의 성충동을 정상적인 성행위로는 만족하지 못하고 살인행위의 방법으로써 성적 욕구를 충족하기 위하여 살인행위를 함과 동시에 성교를 함으로써 성적 욕구를 충족하는 행위
이유 없는 살인	살인의 원인을 찾을 수 없는 완전히 돌발적으로 발생한 살인

4) 임상곤, 범죄심리학원론, 백산출판사, 2004:354-361, 참조.

제2절 범죄학적 논의

1. 살인의 개념

범죄적 살인(criminal homicides)은 특정인에 대한 타인에 의한 불법적 죽음을 말한다.[5]

2. 살인의 특징[6] 2009, 2010 기출

- 살인은 낯선 사람에 의해 가해지는 경우는 매우 적으며, 오히려 면식범(面識犯)에 의해 저질러지는 경우가 많다.
- 피해자 유발살인(victim-precipitated homicides)도 발생하고 있다.[7]
- 살인의 동기는 의외로 매우 사사로운 것에 지나지 않는다.[8] 예 부부・친구・동료 간 등의 말다툼이 살인으로
- 범죄피해조사를 통한 실태파악이 불가능하다.
- 살인은 도구를 사용하는 경향이 많으며[9], 음주나 약물사용과 관련이 많다.
- 살인의 피해는 원상회복될 수 없으며, 주로 하층집단에 의해서 행해지며, 우발적 동기에 의한 경우가 많다.[10]

---

5) 강력범죄란 살인, 강도, 강간 등을 말한다. 2008 기출

6) • 살인범죄자의 연령분포를 볼 때 30~40대 남성이 가장 많으며, 도검류에 의한 피해가 가장 많으며, 전통적 범죄유형에 속하며, 피해자와 가해자가 면식관계가 있는 경우가 대부분이다. 2008 기출
• 이상현, 범죄심리학, 박영사, 2004:289-290, 참조.

7) 특히 남녀 모두 가해자와 피해자와의 관계에 있어서는 반드시 가해자의 일방적인 공격에 의하여 살인이 발생하는 것이 아니고 오히려 피해자 측에서 책임이 있는 살인이 많다는 것이다. 이에 대하여 볼프강(M. E. Wolfgang)은 피해자에 의하여 유발되는 살인이 26%가 된다고 발표하였다. 이상현, 범죄심리학, 박영사, 2004:289.

8) 살인의 일반적인 경향은 남성의 경우 격정이나 싸움・말다툼에 의한 기회적인 살인이 많아 면식이 있는 사람, 친구, 면식이 없는 사람이 피해자가 되기 쉽다. 이에 반하여 여성의 살인은 그 장소에서 일시적인 감정의 폭발로 범행에 이르는 것은 적고, 어느 정도의 계획성이나 피해자와 가까운 관계에 있는 가족 간의 불화나 원한・분노에 의해서 보다 많이 발생하고 있기 때문에 남편, 자녀, 애인 등의 피해자가 많다. Kaare Svalastoga, "Homicide and Social Contact in Denmark," American Journal of Sociology, Vol. 62, 1966:37-41.

9) 살인수단으로서 일반적으로 도검이나 독극물, 줄(끈), 총기 등의 순으로 사용되고 있으며, 특히 남성의 경우 도검이나 도끼 등 날이 있는 도구가 48.2%이고, 여성의 경우 끈(줄)을 사용하는 것이 32.0%라고 한다. 대검찰청, 범죄분석, 1983(1/4-4/4).

10) 살인은 격정범(激情犯)이 많다. 즉, 계산된 행동의 산물이 아니라 폭발전인 감정의 압박에 의해

- 연령별로는 살인범은 일반적으로 남녀가 20~25세에서 가장 많고, 평균연령은 여성이 높고 분산폭도 넓다. 남성의 경우는 피해자의 평균연령이 가해자보다 높지만 여성은 여성에게 특유한 살인이 많고 특히 여성범죄의 하나인 영아유기는 영아살인과도 관련되는 것으로 피해자의 평균연령이 낮다.
- 성별의 경우 여성에 비해서 남성의 살인이 높은 것은 일반범죄와 같다.
- 직업의 경우 살인발생률이 높은 것은 무직, 농공업, 상업, 종업원 순이고 특히 여성의 경우 무직, 주부, 서비스업 등이 많다.
- 전과별로는 살인자는 초범자가 가장 많고 다음으로 2범, 3범의 순으로 나타난다.[11]

3. 살인범죄의 원인

1) 생물학적 원인

(1) 인종학적(ethological) 이론

인간은 생물학적으로 다른 동물보다 살인본능이 강하다.

(2) 유전학적(genetic) 이론

XYY염색체를 가진 남성은 살인과 같은 범죄를 범할 우려가 있다. 즉, Y염색체가 남성을 강인하고 공격적으로 만들기 때문에 XYY염색체를 가진 남성은 통상적으로 공격적인 경향을 가질 확률이 높다는 것이다.

2) 심리학적 · 심리분석학적 이론

ego가 역할을 제대로 하지 못하여 즉, id를 만족시켜 주지 못하거나 superego를 거역했을 때, 불행해지거나 죄의식을 갖게 되고, 나아가 정신적 질병을 앓게 되어, 결국 살인과 같은 폭력으로 이끌리게 된다.

저질러지는 경우가 많다.

11) 대검찰청, 범죄분석, 1983(1/4–4/4).

3) 좌절-공격성(frustration-aggression)에 관한 이론

• Henry & Short는 자살은 자신을 향한 내부지향적 공격성이나, 살인은 타인을 향한 외부지향적 공격성이라고 한다.

• 세력이론(power theory)은 하류계층의 빈곤한 사람들이 부유한 사람에 비해 살인범죄에 더 많이 연루된다. 이는 부유한 사람들이 자신의 폭력성을 보다 문명적 · 비공격적으로 표출할 수 있는 여러 가지 방법과 대안이 있는 반면에, 하류계층은 방법과 대안들을 박탈당했기 때문이다.

4. 연쇄살인

1) 의의

• 연쇄살인은 연속적으로 살인행위를 저지르는 범죄를 말한다.[12)]

• 범인은 주로 계획적으로 범행을 저지르며 일정한 간격으로 살인을 저지르는 공통점을 갖고 있다.

2) 연쇄살인의 특징

• 순간적인 충동이 아닌 철저한 계획하에 행해진다.

• 다른 살인범죄와 달리 살인의 과정에서 자신이 했다는 일종의 표시를 남기기도 하는 자기과시적 범죄가 많다.

• 사건의 횟수를 거듭할수록 더 발전된 범행수법을 연구 · 개발하여 실행하는 것이 일반적이다. 범인이 대부분의 시간을 살인에 대한 공상, 계획, 준비 등에 보낸다.

• 범인이 잡히지 않는 이상, 사회에 극심한 공포심을 유발한다.

• 동기가 분명하지 않아 범인을 색출하는 데 있어 어려움이 크다.

---

12) '연쇄살인'이란 말을 처음 사용한 것은 미국 FBI 요원 '로버트 레슬리'인데, 70년대에 영국에서 열린 국제회의에 참석하였다가 거기서 깊은 인상을 받고 반복적으로 살인을 저지르는 사람을 연쇄살인범이라 부르기 시작했다. 김용준, 범죄피해자학, 백산출판사, 2009:68.

3) 우리나라에서 일어난 연쇄살인범죄[13]

김대두	1975년, 수원과 평택 등에서 17명을 살해하였다.
순경 우범곤	1982년, 경남 의령에서 총기를 난사해 주민 56명이 숨졌다.
지존파	1994년, 사업가 부부 등 5명을 잔인하게 살해하고 암매장하거나 불태웠다.
온보현	1994년, 부녀자 6명을 연쇄납치하고 살해하였다.
정두영	1999년 6월부터 2000년 4월까지 부산과 울산 지역에서 부유층 9명을 살해하였다.
유영철	2003년 9월부터 불과 10개월 만에 21명을 살해하고 시신 11구는 토막 내 암매장하였다.
정남규	2004년 1월부터 2년 동안 13명을 숨지게 하고 강도상해사건만 25건을 저질렀다.
강호순	2006년 12월부터 2008년 12월까지 2년간 경기 서남부지역에서 실종된 부녀자 7명을 모두 살해해서 암매장하였다.
화성 연쇄살인사건	1986년부터 91년까지 경기도 화성 일대에서 부녀자 10명이 성폭행당하고 숨진 미제사건이다.

13) 김용준, 범죄피해자학, 백산출판사, 2009:70-71.

제 07 장 강도범죄

제1절 형법적 논의

1. 강도죄의 의의

- 강도죄는 폭행 또는 협박으로 타인의 재물을 강취하거나 기타 재산상 이익을 취득하거나 제3자로 하여금 취득하게 함으로써 성립하는 범죄이다.
- 보호법익은 소유권 또는 재산권을 보호하는 외에 자유권 즉, 의사결정과 의사활동의 자유도 보호법익이 된다. 보호받는 정도는 침해범이다.
- 가중적 구성요건으로는 특수강도죄, 강도상해 · 치상죄, 강도살인 · 치사죄, 해상강도죄 및 상습강도죄가 있다.

1) 요건

- 폭행 또는 협박으로 타인의 재물을 강취하거나 재산상의 이익을 취득한다는 인식이 있어야 한다. 미필적 고의로도 족하다.
- 고의 이외에 재물을 강취한 때에는 불법영득의 의사가 재산상의 이득을 취득하는 때에는 불법이득의 의사가 있어야 한다.
- 객체는 타인의 재물[1] 또는 재산상의 이익[2]이다.

2) 행위

- 강취란 폭행 · 협박으로 상대방의 반항을 억압해서 그의 의사에 반하여 자기 또는 제3

1) 타인소유 · 타인점유의 재물이어야 한다.
2) 재물 이외에 일체의 재산적 가치가 있는 이익을 말한다.

자의 점유로 옮기는 것을 말한다.

- 폭행 또는 협박은 상대방의 의사를 억압하여 반항을 억압할 정도의 상태에 이를 것이 필요하다.
- 착수 시기는 강도의 의사로 폭행 또는 협박을 개시한 때이고, 기수 시기는 재물 또는 재산상의 이익을 취득한 때이다.

2. 강도죄의 유형

■ 강도죄

제333조(강도) 폭행 또는 협박으로 타인의 재물을 강취하거나 기타 재산상의 이익을 취득하거나 제삼자로 하여금 이를 취득하게 한 자는 3년 이상의 유기징역에 처한다.

제342조(미수범) 제329조 내지 제341조의 미수범은 처벌한다. [전문개정 1995.12.29]

■ 특수강도죄

제334조(특수강도) ① 야간에 사람의 주거, 관리하는 건조물, 선박이나 항공기 또는 점유하는 방실에 침입하여 제333조의 죄를 범한 자는 무기 또는 5년 이상의 징역에 처한다. 〈개정 1995.12.29〉

② 흉기를 휴대하거나 2인 이상이 합동하여 전조의 죄를 범한 자도 전항의 형과 같다.

제342조(미수범) 제329조 내지 제341조의 미수범은 처벌한다. [전문개정 1995.12.29]

■ 준강도죄

제335조(준강도) 절도가 재물의 탈환을 항거하거나 체포를 면탈하거나 죄적을 인멸할 목적으로 폭행 또는 협박을 가한 때에는 전2조의 예에 의한다.

제342조(미수범) 제329조 내지 제341조의 미수범은 처벌한다. [전문개정 1995.12.29]

■ 인질강도죄

> **제336조(인질강도)** 사람을 체포·감금·약취 또는 유인하여 이를 인질로 삼아 재물 또는 재산상의 이익을 취득하거나 제3자로 하여금 이를 취득하게 한 자는 3년 이상의 유기징역에 처한다. [전문개정 1995.12.29]
>
> **제342조(미수범)** 제329조 내지 제341조의 미수범은 처벌한다. [전문개정 1995.12.29]

■ 강도상해·치상죄

> **제337조(강도상해, 치상)** 강도가 사람을 상해하거나 상해에 이르게 한 때에는 무기 또는 7년 이상의 징역에 처한다. 〈개정 1995.12.29〉
>
> **제342조(미수범)** 제329조 내지 제341조의 미수범은 처벌한다. [전문개정 1995.12.29]

- 강도상해죄는 강도죄와 상해죄의 결합범이고, 강도치상죄는 강도죄와 과실치상죄의 결합범이며 결과적 가중범이다.

■ 강도살인·치사죄

> **제338조(강도살인·치사)** 강도가 사람을 살해한 때에는 사형 또는 무기징역에 처한다. 사망에 이르게 한 때에는 무기 또는 10년 이상의 징역에 처한다. [전문개정 1995.12.29]
>
> **제342조(미수범)** 제329조 내지 제341조의 미수범은 처벌한다. [전문개정 1995.12.29]

- 강도살인죄는 강도죄와 살인죄의 결합범이며, 강도치사죄는 강도죄와 과실치사죄의 결합범으로서 결과적 가중범이다.

■ 강도강간죄

> **제339조(강도강간)** 강도가 부녀를 강간한 때에는 무기 또는 10년 이상의 징역에 처한다.
>
> **제342조(미수범)** 제329조 내지 제341조의 미수범은 처벌한다. [전문개정 1995.12.29]

- 강도강간죄는 강도죄와 강간죄의 결합범이다. 본죄는 친고죄가 아니다.

■ 해상강도죄

제340조(해상강도) ① 다중의 위력으로 해상에서 선박을 강취하거나 선박 내에 침입하여 타인의 재물을 강취한 자는 무기 또는 7년 이상의 징역에 처한다.
② 제1항의 죄를 범한 자가 사람을 상해하거나 상해에 이르게 한 때에는 무기 또는 10년 이상의 징역에 처한다. 〈개정 1995.12.29〉
③ 제1항의 죄를 범한 자가 사람을 살해 또는 사망에 이르게 하거나 부녀를 강간한 때에는 사형 또는 무기징역에 처한다. 〈개정 1995.12.29〉
제342조(미수범) 제329조 내지 제341조의 미수범은 처벌한다. [전문개정 1995.12.29]

■ 상습강도죄

제341조(상습범) 상습으로 제333조, 제334조, 제336조 또는 전조 제1항의 죄를 범한 자는 무기 또는 10년 이상의 징역에 처한다.
제342조(미수범) 제329조 내지 제341조의 미수범은 처벌한다. [전문개정 1995.12.29]

■ 강도예비 · 음모죄

제343조(예비, 음모) 강도할 목적으로 예비 또는 음모한 자는 7년 이하의 징역에 처한다.

제2절 범죄학적 논의

1. 강도의 의의

강도란 피해자를 공포에 떨게 하거나 폭력과 무력의 사용[3]과 위협으로 타인의 가치 있

3) 무기의 사용은 도구적 기능과 표출적 기능을 가지며, i) 도구적 기능(instrumental function)은 흉기가 강도의 성공적 수행을 가능케 하는 직접적인 도구로 사용되는 것이며, ii) 표출적 기능(expressive function)은 흉기가 피해자를 위협하고 통제함으로써 피해자를 지배해야 할 심리적 필요성을 성취시켜 주는 기능을 말한다.

는 물품을 빼앗는 것으로써, 재산범죄와 폭력범죄의 요소가 동시에 결합된 형태의 강력범죄이다.

2. 강도의 유형4)

콩클린(J. Conklin)은 강도범의 행태를 다음과 같은 기준으로 분류하고 있다.

전문강도 (professional robber)	• 직업 삼아 강도를 저지르는 자
기회강도 (opportunity robber)	• 여러 종류의 재산범죄를 저지르면서 기회가 주어지면 강도행각을 일삼는 유형의 범죄자
중독강도 (addict robber)	• 마약류에 중독된 상태에서 마약류 구입비를 마련하기 위해 강도범행을 저지르는 자
음주강도 (alcoholic robber)	• 술을 마신 상태에서 금품을 탈취하고 싶은 충동을 느껴 강도범행을 저지르는 자. 기회강도의 속성과 중독강도의 속성이 혼합된 형태

4) 조병인, 현대사회와 범죄, 법문사, 2000:61–63.

제08장 강간과 성범죄

제1절 형법적 논의

1. 강간죄와 추행의 의의

1) 의의

강간과 추행의 죄란 개인의 성적 자유를 침해하는 것을 내용으로 하는 범죄이다.

2) 보호법익

보호법익은 개인의 성적 자기결정의 자유이다. 다만 폭행 또는 협박을 수단으로 하는 범죄에서는 신체의 건재성 내지 의사결정의 자유도 부차적인 보호법익이 된다. 보호의 정도는 침해범이다.(다수설)

3) 특별법의 적용

"성폭력 범죄의 처벌에 관한 특례법"에서는 13세 미만의 미성년자에 대한 강간 · 강제추행 · 준강간 · 준강제추행의 죄를 가중처벌하고 있고(동법 제7조), "아동 · 청소년의 성보호에 관한 법률"에서는 아동과 청소년(만 19세 미만의 자)에 대한 강간죄 · 강제추행죄 · 준강간죄 · 준강제추행죄 · 위계위력 간음추행죄를 가중처벌하고 있다.

4) 형법 주요 개정사항

형법

[시행 2013.6.19] [법률 제11574호, 2012.12.18, 일부개정]

◇ **개정이유**

변화된 시대 상황을 반영하여 다양화된 성범죄에 효과적으로 대처하기 위하여 유사강간죄를 신설하고, 성범죄의 객체를 "부녀"에서 "사람"으로 확대하며, 친고죄 및 혼인빙자간음죄를 폐지하려는 것임.

◇ **주요내용**

가. 성폭력 범죄의 객체를 "부녀"에서 "사람"으로 변경함(안 제242조, 제288조제2항, 제297조, 제303조제1항 · 제2항, 제305조, 제339조 및 제340조제3항).

나. 추행 · 간음 목적의 약취 · 유인 · 수수 · 은닉죄 및 강간죄 등 성범죄에 관하여 고소가 있어야 공소를 제기할 수 있도록 한 규정을 삭제함(현행 제296조 및 제306조 삭제).

다. 폭행 또는 협박으로 사람에 대하여 구강, 항문 등 신체의 내부에 성기를 넣거나 성기, 항문에 신체의 일부 또는 도구를 넣는 유사강간행위를 한 자는 2년 이상의 유기징역에 처하도록 하고, 관련 조문을 정비함(안 제297조의2 신설, 제299조부터 제301조까지, 제301조의2, 제305조 및 제305조의2).

라. 실효성이 미약하고, 여성의 성적 주체성을 훼손하는 혼인빙자간음죄를 폐지함(현행 제304조 삭제).

〈법제처 제공〉

2. 강간죄

개정 전	개정 후
제297조(강간) 폭행 또는 협박으로 부녀를 강간한 자는 3년 이상의 유기징역에 처한다.	**제297조(강간)** 폭행 또는 협박으로 사람을 강간한 자는 3년 이상의 유기징역에 처한다. 〈개정 2012.12.18〉

개정 전	개정 후
신설	**제297조의2(유사강간)** 폭행 또는 협박으로 사람에 대하여 구강, 항문 등 신체(성기는 제외한다)의 내부에 성기를 넣거나 성기, 항문에 손가락 등 신체(성기는 제외한다)의 일부 또는 도구를 넣는 행위를 한 사람은 2년 이상의 유기징역에 처한다. [본조신설 2012.12.18] **제300조(미수범)** 제297조, 제297조의2, 제298조 및 제299조의 미수범은 처벌한다. 〈개정 2012.12.18〉

제296조 친고죄 조항 폐지(2012.12.18 형법 개정, 2013.6.19 시행)

1) 강간죄

(1) 의의

강간죄는 '폭행 또는 협박으로 사람을 강간함으로써 성립하는 범죄'이다.

(2) 보호법익 및 보호정도

강간죄의 보호법익은 사람의 성적 자기결정의 자유이다. 성적 자기결정권은 성행위 여부와 파트너 선택에 있어서의 자기결정권을 내포한다. 보호의 정도는 침해범이다.

2) 객관적 구성요건

(1) 행위주체

행위주체에는 제한이 없다. 본죄의 불법의 핵심이 간음 자체에 있기보다는 폭행・협박에 의한 간음행위에 있으므로 여자도 폭행・협박행위를 분담함으로써 남자와 함께 강간죄의 공동 정범이 될 수 있고, 정신병자인 남자를 이용하여 간접정범이 될 수도 있다.

(2) 행위객체

본죄의 행위객체는 사람이다. 기혼・미혼, 성년・미성년을 불문하며 매춘부와 늙은 부녀도 포함된다.

> ***개정내용**(2012.12.18 형 법 개정, 2013.6.19 시행)
>
> 강간죄의 객체가 '부녀'에서 '사람'으로 개정됨

① 법률상 처의 강간죄 객체성 여부
부부관계의 특수성을 고려하여 법률상의 처는 강간죄의 객체가 될 수 없고 폭행죄·협박죄 또는 강요죄가 성립할 수 있을 뿐이라는 견해가 다수설이다. 판례는 혼인이 파탄되어 별거 중인 처에 한하여 제한적으로 긍정하는 입장이다.

(3) 행 위

폭행·협박에 의하여 사람을 강간하는 것이다.

① 폭행 또는 협박: 폭행은 사람에 대한 유형력의 행사를 의미하며, 제3자에 대한 폭행은 사람에 대하여 협박에 해당할 수 있다. 폭행·협박은 상대방의 반항을 불가능하게 하는 경우뿐만 아니라 현저히 곤란하게 하는 경우도 포함된다. 또한 폭행에는 절대적 폭력 예 (마취제·수면제의 사용) 이외에 강제적 폭력도 포함된다.

② 강간: 강간이 성립하기 위하여는 폭행·협박과 간음 사이에 인과관계가 있어야 한다. 따라서 폭행·협박은 간음이 종료되기 이전에 이루어져야 한다. 간음 종료 후의 피해자의 사후동의는 강간죄의 성립에 영향을 주지 않는다. 실행의 착수 전에 부녀의 동의는 구성요건 해당성이 조각되고(양해), 폭행·협박 후에 부녀가 간음에 동의한 경우는 강간미수죄가 성립할 뿐이다(다수설).

③ 착수시기·기수시기: 폭행·협박을 개시하면 실행의 착수가 인정되며, 실제로 피해자의 항거가 불능하게 되거나 현저히 곤란하게 되어야만 실행의 착수가 인정되는 것은 아니다(판례). 남자의 성기가 여자의 성기 안으로 들어가기 시작하는 순간 기수로 된다(삽입설).

3) 주관적 구성요건

폭행·협박에 의하여 사람을 강간한다는 인식과 의사가 있어야 한다. 피해자의 동의가 있다고 오인한 때에는 고의가 조각된다.

4) 죄수 및 타 죄와의 관계

- 동일한 폭행·협박을 이용하여 여러 번 간음한 경우에는 강간죄의 단순일죄가 성립한다. 본죄가 성립한 경우에는 폭행·협박죄는 별도로 성립되지 않는다(흡수관계).
- 강간을 하기 위해 감금을 한 경우에는 강간죄와 감금죄의 상상적 경합이 된다. 반면 감금 중에 강간한 경우에는 양죄의 실체적 경합이 된다.
- 주거에 침입하여 강간한 경우에는 주거침입죄와 강간죄의 경합범이 된다.

5) 친고죄 폐지

▷ **제306조 친고죄** 조항 폐지(2012.12.18 형법 개정, 2013.6.19 시행)

3. 강제추행죄

> **제298조(강제추행)** 폭행 또는 협박으로 사람에 대하여 추행을 한 자는 10년 이하의 징역 또는 1천500만원 이하의 벌금에 처한다. 〈개정 1995.12.29〉

1) 객관적 구성요건

(1) 행위주체

본죄의 행위주체는 제한이 없으므로 여자도 본죄의 단독정범이 된다(신분범도 자수범도 아님).

(2) 행위객체

본죄의 행위객체는 사람이다. 남자도 객체가 된다. 강간죄와 마찬가지로 법률상의 처는 부부관계의 특수성을 고려하여 강요죄의 성립 여부가 문제된다(다수설).

(3) 행 위

폭행·협박으로 추행하는 것이다.

① 폭행・협박의 정도: 다수설은 강간죄와 같이 상대방의 반항을 불가능하게 하거나 현저히 곤란하게 할 정도에 이를 것을 요한다는 입장이나, 판례는 반드시 상대방의 의사를 억압할 정도의 것임을 요하지 않고 상대방의 의사에 반하는 유형력의 행사가 있는 이상 그 힘의 대소강약을 불문한다고 한다.

② 폭행・협박의 시기: 폭행・협박은 반드시 추행행위 이전에 있을 필요가 없다. 추행과 동시에 이루어질 수도 있고, 폭행 자체가 추행에 해당할 수도 있다.

③ 추행: 추행이란 객관적으로 일반인에게 성적 수치심과 혐오의 감정을 일으키게 하는 간음을 제외한 일체의 음란행위를 말하며 주관적인 동기나 목적은 문제되지 아니한다(다수설・판례).

2) 주관적 구성요건

고의, 즉 폭행・협박에 의하여 사람에 대하여 추행한다는 인식과 인용이 있어야 한다. 그러나 목적범, 경향범에 해당하지 않으므로 성욕의 흥분・자극 또는 만족한다는 경향이나 목적을 요하지 않는다.

3) 소추조건

제306조 친고죄 조항 폐지(2012.12.18 형법개정, 2013.6.19 시행)

4. 준강간죄・준강제추행죄

개정 전	개정 후
제299조(준강간, 준강제추행) 사람의 심신상실 또는 항거불능의 상태를 이용하여 간음 또는 추행을 한 자는 전2조의 예에 의한다.	**제299조(준강간, 준강제추행)** 사람의 심신상실 또는 항거불능의 상태를 이용하여 간음 또는 추행을 한 자는 제297조, 제297조의2 및 제298조의 예에 의한다. 〈개정 2012.12.18〉

제306조 친고죄 조항 폐지, 개정내용(2012.12.18 형법 개정, 2013.6.19 시행)

1) 준강간죄 · 준강제추행죄

(1) 의의

본죄는 사람의 심신상실 또는 항거불능의 상태를 이용하여 간음 또는 추행함으로써 성립하는 범죄이다.

(2) 법적 성격

본죄가 자수범인가에 대해서는 견해 대립이 있으나 부정설이 다수설이다. 부정설에 의하면 준강간죄의 간접정범이 성립할 수 있다.

예 만취한 여자를 정신병자로 하여금 간음하게 한 경우

2) 객관적 구성요건

(1) 행위객체

심신상실이나 항거불능의 상태에 있는 사람이다.

① 심신상실: 정신기능의 장애로 인해 성행위에 대한 정상적인 판단능력이 없는 상태를 말한다. 본죄의 심신상실은 생물학적 기초에 제한되지 않으므로 제10조의 심신상실보다 범위가 넓다. 따라서 수면 중이거나(대판 2000.1.14, 99도5187) 일시 의식을 잃고 있는 부녀도 여기에 해당한다. 다만 형법은 심신미약자에 대한 간음 · 추행죄를 별도로 규정하고 있으므로(제302조), 심신미약자는 본죄의 객체에 포함되지 않는다(다수설).

② 항거불능: 심신상실 이외의 원인으로 인하여 육체적(예 포박되어 있는 부녀를 간음한 경우) · 심리적(예 의사가 자기를 신뢰한 여자환자를 치료를 가장하여 간음한 경우)으로 반항이 불가능하거나 현저히 곤란한 경우를 말한다.

③ 심신상실 · 항거불능의 원인: 심신상실 · 항거불능에 이르게 된 원인은 묻지 않는다. 그러나 행위자가 간음 또는 추행을 하기 위하여 마취제 · 수면제 등을 사용하여 이러한 상태를 야기한 때에는 본죄가 아닌 강간죄 또는 강제추행죄가 성립한다.

(2) 행위

심신상실 또는 항거불능을 이용하여 간음 · 추행하는 것이다.

5. 미성년자 의제강간 · 강제추행죄

개정 전	개정 후
제305조(미성년자에 대한 간음, 추행) 13세 미만의 부녀를 간음하거나 13세 미만의 사람에게 추행을 한 자는 제297조, 제298조, 제301조 또는 제301조의2의 예에 의한다. 〈개정 1995.12.29〉	**제305조(미성년자에 대한 간음, 추행)** 13세 미만의 사람에 대하여 간음 또는 추행을 한 자는 제297조, 제297조의2, 제298조, 제301조 또는 제301조의2의 예에 의한다. 〈개정 1995.12.29, 2012.12.18〉

제306조 친고죄 조항 폐지, 개정내용(2012.12.18 형법 개정, 2013.6.19 시행)

1) 의의

13세 미만의 사람을 간음하거나 13세 미만의 사람에게 추행함으로써 성립하는 범죄이다.

2) 객관적 구성요건

(1) 행위객체

미성년자 의제강간죄의 객체는 13세 미만의 사람이고, 미성년자 의제강제추행죄의 객체는 13세 미만의 사람으로서 남녀를 불문한다.

(2) 행위

① 13세 미만자에 대하여 간음 또는 추행하는 것이다. 수단에는 제한이 없으므로 위계나 위력을 행사하거나 피해자의 동의가 있어도 본죄가 성립한다.

② 13세 미만자라도 폭행 · 협박에 의해 간음이나 강제추행한 때에는 강간죄나 강제추행죄가 성립한다.

3) 주관적 구성요건

상대방이 13세 미만이라는 사실과 간음 또는 추행에 대한 인식 · 인용이 있어야 한다.

4) 미수의 처벌 및 소추조건

본죄의 미수범 처벌규정은 없으나, 본죄는 강간죄·강제추행죄의 예에 의하므로 학설·판례는 일치하여 미수범의 처벌을 긍정한다.

6. 강간 등 상해·치상죄

개정 전	개정 후
제301조(강간 등 상해·치상) 제297조 내지 제300조의 죄를 범한 자가 사람을 상해하거나 상해에 이르게 한 때에는 무기 또는 5년 이상의 징역에 처한다. [전문개정 1995.12.29]	**제301조(강간 등 상해·치상)** 제297조, 제297조의2 및 제298조부터 제300조까지의 죄를 범한 자가 사람을 상해하거나 상해에 이르게 한 때에는 무기 또는 5년 이상의 징역에 처한다. 〈개정 2012.12.18〉 [전문개정 1995.12.29]

1) 강간 등 상해·치상죄

(1) 의 의

본죄는 강간죄, 강제추행죄, 준강간·강제추행죄, 미성년자 의제강간·강제추행죄 및 그 미수범을 범한 자가 사람을 상해하거나 상해에 이르게 함으로써 성립하는 범죄이다.

(2) 법적 성격

본죄는 친고죄가 아니다.

2) 객관적 구성요건

(1) 행위주체

강간죄, 강제추행죄, 준강간·강제추행죄, 미성년자 의제강간·강제추행죄의 죄를 범한 자 및 그 미수범이다.

(2) 행위

사람을 상해하거나 상해에 이르게 하는 것이다. 본죄의 상해도 상해죄의 상해와 동일한 개념으로 보는 것이 다수설이지만, 본죄의 법정형이 상해죄에 비하여 중하고 본죄의 상해의 발생여부는 친고죄 여부를 결정하는 기준이 되므로 상해죄의 상해와는 달리 상당한 정도에 달해야 한다는 상대적 상해개념이 주장되고 있다.

(3) 인과관계 및 객관적 귀속(간음 또는 추행의 기회)

상해의 결과는 간음・추행의 기회에 발생한 것이면 족하다. 따라서 본죄의 상해는 강간의 수단으로서 행사된 폭행으로 인해 발생한 것임을 요하지 않고 간음행위 그 자체로부터 발생한 경우나 강간에 수반되는 행위에 의해서 발생한 경우도 포함된다.

(4) 기수시기 및 미수의 처벌

간음이나 추행의 기회에 상해가 발생한 이상 강간죄 또는 강제추행죄가 미수에 그친 경우에도 강간상해죄는 물론 강간치상죄도 기수가 된다(다수설・판례). 강간 등 상해죄는 고의범이므로 강간의 기회에 고의로 상해하려고 하였으나 미수에 그친 경우 형법상 강간상해죄의 미수범처벌규정이 없으므로 강간죄(또는 강간미수죄)와 상해미수죄가 성립할 뿐이다.

3) 주관적 구성요건

- 강간 등 상해죄는 강간 등의 행위와 상해에 대한 고의가 있어야 한다.
- 강간 등 치상죄는 진정결과적 가중범이므로 강간 등의 행위에 대한 고의와 상해에 대한 예견가능성(과실)이 있어야 한다.

4) 죄수 및 타 죄와의 관계

- 강간치상 후 범행발각이 두려워 피해자를 살해한 경우 강간치상죄와 살인죄의 경합범이 된다.
- 강간치상의 범행을 저지른 자가 그 범행으로 인하여 실신상태에 있는 피해자를 구호하지 않고 방치하였다고 하더라도 그 행위는 포괄적으로 단일의 강간치상죄만을 구성한다(대판 1980.6.24. 80도726).

7. 강간 등 살인 · 치사죄

개정 전	개정 후
제301조의2(강간 등 살인 · 치사) 제297조 내지 제300조의 죄를 범한 자가 사람을 살해한 때에는 사형 또는 무기징역에 처한다. 사망에 이르게 한 때에는 무기 또는 10년 이상의 징역에 처한다. [본조신설 1995.12.29]	**제301조의2(강간 등 살인 · 치사)** 제297조, 제297조의2 및 제298조부터 제300조까지의 죄를 범한 자가 사람을 살해한 때에는 사형 또는 무기징역에 처한다. 사망에 이르게 한 때에는 무기 또는 10년 이상의 징역에 처한다. 〈개정 2012.12.18〉 [본조신설 1995.12.29]

1) 강간 등 살인 · 치사죄

(1) 의의

본죄는 강간죄, 강제추행죄, 준강간 · 강제추행죄, 미성년자 의제강간 · 강제추행죄 및 그 미수범을 범한 자가 사람을 살해하거나 사망에 이르게 함으로써 성립하는 범죄이다

(2) 법적 성격

① 강간 등 살인죄는 강간죄 등과 살인죄의 결합범이고, 강간 등 치사죄는 강간죄 등과 과실치사죄의 결합범으로 강간죄에 대한(진정)결과적 가중범이다.

② 본죄는 친고죄가 아니다.

2) 구성요건

- 강간 · 추행 등의 행위와 사망 사이에 인과관계와 객관적 귀속이 있어야 한다.
- 사망의 결과는 간음 · 추행행위 그 자체에서 일어나거나 그 수단인 폭행 · 협박에 의하여 일어나거나 간음 · 추행행위에 수반하여 발생한 경우 모두 해당된다(대판 1999.4.9. 99도519).
- 강간 · 추행 등의 기본행위가 기수로 되었건 미수에 그쳤건 관계없이 사망의 결과가 발생하면 본죄가 성립한다.

8. 미성년자 · 심신미약자 간음 · 추행죄

> **제302조(미성년자 등에 대한 간음)** 미성년자 또는 심신미약자에 대하여 위계 또는 위력으로써 간음 또는 추행을 한 자는 5년 이하의 징역에 처한다.

1) 행위객체

미성년자 또는 심신미약자이다.

(1) 미성년자

제305조(미성년자 의제강간 · 강제추행죄)와의 관계상 19세 미만 13세 이상인 자를 말한다. 혼인한 미성년자도 미성년자로 보아야 한다(다수설).

(2) 심신미약자

정신기능의 장애로 판단능력이 부족한 자를 말하며 연령을 불문한다.

2) 행위

위계 · 위력에 의하여 간음 · 추행하는 것이다.

(1) 위계

간음목적으로 상대방에게 오인, 착각, 부지를 일으키고 상대방의 그러한 심적 상태를 이용하여 간음의 목적을 달성하는 것을 말한다. 기망, 유혹, 상대방의 신뢰를 이용하는 것도 포함된다. **예** 치료나 종교의식을 빙자하여 상대방이 간음당한다는 사실을 알지 못하게 하는 경우

(2) 위력

사람의 의사를 제압할 수 있는 힘을 말하며, 폭행 · 협박은 물론 사회적 · 정치적 권세를 이용하는 것도 포함된다. 다만, 강간죄에서 요구하는 폭행 · 협박을 사용한 경우에는 미성년자나 심신미약자라도 본죄가 아닌 강간죄나 강제추행죄가 성립한다(대판 1965.3.30, 65도45).

9. 피보호 · 감독 부녀간음죄(업무상 위력간음죄)

개정 전	개정 후
제303조(업무상위력 등에 의한 간음) ① 업무, 고용 기타 관계로 인하여 자기의 보호 또는 감독을 받는 부녀에 대하여 위계 또는 위력으로써 간음한 자는 5년 이하의 징역 또는 1천500만원 이하의 벌금에 처한다. 〈개정 1995.12.29〉 ② 법률에 의하여 구금된 부녀를 감호하는 자가 그 부녀를 간음한 때에는 7년 이하의 징역에 처한다.	제303조(업무상위력 등에 의한 간음) ① 업무, 고용 기타 관계로 인하여 자기의 보호 또는 감독을 받는 사람에 대하여 위계 또는 위력으로써 간음한 자는 5년 이하의 징역 또는 1천500만원 이하의 벌금에 처한다. 〈개정 1995.12.29, 2012.12.18〉 ② 법률에 의하여 구금된 사람을 감호하는 자가 그 사람을 간음한 때에는 7년 이하의 징역에 처한다. 〈개정 2012.12.18〉

제306조 친고죄 조항 폐지, 개정내용(2012.12.18 형법 개정, 2013.6.19 시행)

1) 피보호 · 감독 부녀간음죄(업무상 위력간음죄)

(1) 의의

업무, 고용 기타 관계로 인하여 자기의 보호 또는 감독을 받는 부녀에 대하여 위계 또는 위력을 사용하여 간음함으로써 성립하는 범죄이다. 진정신분범이다.

(2) 법적 성격

친고죄 폐지

2) 행위객체

(1) 업 무

본죄의 업무에는 공적 업무와 사적 업무를 불문한다.

(2) 고 용

고용이란 사용자와 피용자와의 관계에 있음을 말한다.

(3) 기타 관계

보호・감독의 원인을 불문하므로 사실상 보호・감독을 받는 부녀도 포함된다.

3) 행 위

(1) 위계・위력

위계나 위력으로 간음하는 것이다. 강간죄에서 요구하는 정도의 폭행・협박을 사용한 경우에는 강간죄가 성립한다.

(2) 추행의 경우

부녀에게 위계나 위력을 사용하여 '추행'한 경우에는 본죄가 아니라 「성폭력범죄의 처벌 등에 관한 특례법」이 적용된다(동법 제10조 제1항).

10. 피구금부녀간음죄

개정 전	개정 후
제303조(업무상위력 등에 의한 간음) ① 업무, 고용 기타 관계로 인하여 자기의 보호 또는 감독을 받는 부녀에 대하여 위계 또는 위력으로써 간음한 자는 5년 이하의 징역 또는 1천500만원 이하의 벌금에 처한다. 〈개정 1995.12.29〉 ② 법률에 의하여 구금된 부녀를 감호하는 자가 그 부녀를 간음한 때에는 7년 이하의 징역에 처한다.	제303조(업무상위력 등에 의한 간음) ① 업무, 고용 기타 관계로 인하여 자기의 보호 또는 감독을 받는 사람에 대하여 위계 또는 위력으로써 간음한 자는 5년 이하의 징역 또는 1천500만원 이하의 벌금에 처한다. 〈개정 1995.12.29, 2012.12.18〉 ② 법률에 의하여 구금된 사람을 감호하는 자가 그 사람을 간음한 때에는 7년 이하의 징역에 처한다. 〈개정 2012.12.18〉

제306조 친고죄 조항 폐지, 개정내용(2012.12.18 형법 개정, 2013.6.19 시행)

1) 피구금부녀간음죄

(1) 의의

본죄는 법률에 의하여 구금된 사람을 감호하는 자(검찰 · 경찰 · 교정직공무원)가 그 사람을 간음함으로써 성립하는 범죄이며 친고죄이다.

(2) 보호법익

보호법익은 피구금자의 성적 자기결정권 외에 감호자의 청렴성에 대한 일반인의 신뢰도 부차적으로 보호한다(통설).

2) 구성요건

(1) 행위주체

본죄의 주체는 법률에 의하여 구금된 사람을 감호하는 자이다(진정신분범).

(2) 행위객체

본죄의 객체는 법률에 의하여 구금된 사람이다. 형집행 중인 자, 노역장에 유치된 자, 구속된 피고인 · 피의자가 모두 포함된다. 그러나 현재 구금 중이 아닌 선고유예 · 집행유예 중에 있는 자, 보호관찰을 받는 자는 본죄의 객체가 아니다.

(3) 행 위

① 간음이다. 특별한 수단을 요하지 않으므로 피구금자의 동의를 얻어 간음한 경우는 물론 위계 · 위력을 사용한 경우에도 본죄에 해당한다(통설).

② 피구금자에 대하여 폭행 · 협박을 사용하여 간음한 경우에는 강간죄가 성립한다.

③ 피구금자에게 위계나 위력을 사용하여 '추행'한 경우에는 본죄가 아니라 「성폭력범죄의 처벌 등에 관한 특례법」이 적용된다(동법 제10조 제2항).

(4) 타 죄와의 관계

13세 미만인 피구금자를 간음한 경우에는 미성년자 의제강간죄가 성립한다.

11. 상습범

개정 전	개정 후
제305조의2(상습범) 상습으로 제297조부터 제300조까지, 제302조, 제303조 또는 제305조의 죄를 범한 자는 그 죄에 정한 형의 2분의 1까지 가중한다.	**제305조의2(상습범)** 상습으로 제297조, 제297조의2, 제298조부터 제300조까지, 제302조, 제303조 또는 제305조의 죄를 범한 자는 그 죄에 정한 형의 2분의 1까지 가중한다. 〈개정 2012.12.18〉 [본조신설 2010.4.15]

- 본죄는 2010.4.15의 형법 개정에서 신설되었다.
- 상습범으로서 가중처벌되는 대상범죄는 강간죄(제297조), 강제추행죄(제298조), 준강간・강제추행죄(제299조), 이 3가지 범죄의 미수범(제300조), 미성년자등간음죄(제302조), 업무상위력등간음죄(제303조), 13세 미만자 의제강간・강제추행죄(제305조)이다.

12. 군형법 관련

군형법

제15장 강간과 추행의 죄 〈개정 2009.11.2〉

제92조(강간) 폭행이나 협박으로 제1조제1항부터 제3항까지에 규정된 사람을 강간한 사람은 5년 이상의 유기징역에 처한다. 〈개정 2013.4.5〉

[전문개정 2009.11.2]

제92조의2(유사강간) 폭행이나 협박으로 제1조제1항부터 제3항까지에 규정된 사람에 대하여 구강, 항문 등 신체(성기는 제외한다)의 내부에 성기를 넣거나 성기, 항문에 손가락 등 신체(성기는 제외한다)의 일부 또는 도구를 넣는 행위를 한 사람은 3년 이상의 유기징역에 처한다.

[본조신설 2013.4.5]

[종전 제92조의2는 제92조의3으로 이동 〈2013.4.5〉]

제92조의3(강제추행) 폭행이나 협박으로 제1조제1항부터 제3항까지에 규정된 사람에 대하여 추행을 한 사람은 1년 이상의 유기징역에 처한다.

[본조신설 2009.11.2]

[제92조의2에서 이동, 종전 제92조의3은 제92조의4로 이동 〈2013.4.5〉]

제92조의4(준강간, 준강제추행) 제1조제1항부터 제3항까지에 규정된 사람의 심신상실 또는 항거불능 상태를 이용하여 간음 또는 추행을 한 사람은 제92조, 제92조의2 및 제92조의3의 예에 따른다. 〈개정 2013.4.5〉

[본조신설 2009.11.2]

[제92조의3에서 이동, 종전 제92조의4는 제92조의5로 이동 〈2013.4.5〉]

제92조의5(미수범) 제92조, 제92조의2부터 제92조의4까지의 미수범은 처벌한다.

〈개정 2013.4.5〉

[본조신설 2009.11.2]

[제92조의4에서 이동, 종전 제92조의5는 제92조의6으로 이동 〈2013.4.5〉]

제92조의6(추행) 제1조제1항부터 제3항까지에 규정된 사람에 대하여 항문성교나 그 밖의 추행을 한 사람은 2년 이하의 징역에 처한다. 〈개정 2013.4.5〉

[본조신설 2009.11.2]

[제92조의5에서 이동, 종전 제92조의6은 제92조의7로 이동 〈2013.4.5〉]

제92조의7(강간 등 상해 · 치상) 제92조 및 제92조의2부터 제92조의5까지의 죄를 범한 사람이 제1조제1항부터 제3항까지에 규정된 사람을 상해하거나 상해에 이르게 한 때에는 무기 또는 7년 이상의 징역에 처한다. 〈개정 2013.4.5〉

[본조신설 2009.11.2]

[제92조의6에서 이동, 종전 제92조의7은 제92조의8로 이동 〈2013.4.5〉]

제92조의8(강간 등 살인 · 치사) 제92조 및 제92조의2부터 제92조의5까지의 죄를 범한 사람이 제1조제1항부터 제3항까지에 규정된 사람을 살해한 때에는 사형 또는 무기징역에 처하고, 사망에 이르게 한 때에는 사형, 무기 또는 10년 이상의 징역에 처한다.

〈개정 2013.4.5〉

[본조신설 2009.11.2]

[제92조의7에서 이동, 종전 제92조의8은 삭제]

제2절 범죄학적 논의

1. 강간범죄의 의의

- 강간은 남성이 완력 또는 힘을 이용한 무력을 동원하여[1] 여성이 원치 않는 강압적인 성행위를 하는 것을 의미한다.[2]
- 강간의 피해자 책임론[3]과 피해자 동정론이 논란의 대상이 되고 있다.

2. 강간의 유형

1) 대상별 강간의 유형

(1) 어린이 강간

- 어린이 강간이란 만 13세 미만의 어린이에게 가해지는 강간이다.
- 어린이 성폭력의 약 80%는 아는 사람에 의해서 발생한다. 아는 사람은 2가지 유형으로 나눌 수 있는데, 첫 번째는 친부나 의부, 삼촌, 이모부, 할아버지 등 혈족 혹은 인척에 의해 일어나는 것이다. 이를 친족 성폭력이라고 한다. 또 다른 유형은 교사나 교직

---

1) Andrew Karmen, Crime Victims : An Introduction to Victimology, Belmont : Thomson Wadsworth, 2006:242.

2) • Dean John Champion, The American Dictionary of Criminal Justice : Key Terms and Major Court Cases, L.A. California : Roxbury Publishing Company, 2005:213.
- 여성이 “NO”라고 말했음에도 불구하고 성관계가 이루어지면 그것은 강간에 해당된다. 강숙자, “한국 여성운동 이념정립을 위한 시론”, 이화여자대학교 박사학위논문, 2004:198.
- 특히 이와 같은 “NO”의 의사표시는 부부 간에도 적용된다. 박기석, “부부강간행위의 강간죄 성립여부”, 형사정책연구, 제15권, 제4호, 한국형사정책연구원, 2004:81-82.
- 남재성은 강간은 성폭력보다는 보다 직접적인 의미인 “완력 또는 신체손상의 위협에 의하거나, 또는 피해자가 동의할 능력이 없을 때 수행된 성기, 항문 또는 입을 통한 강제성교”라고 정의하고 있다. 성폭력은 강간이나 아내 구타와 같이 신체적인 피해나 상처가 명시적이고 명확한 폭력의 형태로부터 성적 괴롭힘과 같은 위협적인 폭력형태를 포괄하는 개념으로 확장될 수 있다. 남재성, “강간 범죄자의 표적선택요인에 관한 연구”, 교정연구, 제35호, 2007:201-228.
- 강간(rape)은 상대방의 동의 없는 성교행위를 말하며, 윤간(multiple rape)은 집단적 성폭행이다.

3) 강간의 피해자 책임론은 피해자를 비난하는 입장으로서 촉발강간이 지적되고 있다. 또한 여성의 피학음란증에 대한 주장은 강간을 통한 고통과 학대라는 마조히즘적 경험을 통해서 쾌락을 얻기 때문에, 강간은 피해자에게 즐거움을 주는 일종의 피해자 없는 범죄(victimless crime)라는 잘못된 통념이다.

원, 유치원 원장, 통학버스 기사, 이웃 사람, 아파트 경비 등 일상생활에서 접촉하기 쉬운 사람들에 의해 일어나는 것이다.

- 많은 가해자들은 자신의 성폭력 사실을 비밀로 지키라며 회유하거나 과장된 협박을 한다.
- 어린이들은 자신이 당한 피해가 성폭력이라는 것을 곧바로 인식하는 데 어려움을 겪는다. 그런 까닭에 어린이 성폭력은 금방 드러나지 않는 경우가 많으므로 어린이가 공포심을 갖는다거나, 혼자 자는 것을 두려워한다거나, 성기 등에 통증을 느낀다거나 하는 일이 생기면 주의깊게 관찰하고 성폭력 피해가 있는 것은 아닌지 의심해 보아야 한다.

(2) 청소년 강간[4)]

- 청소년 강간이란 만 13세 이상 18세 이하의 청소년에게 발생하는 강간을 의미한다.
- 청소년 강간의 경우, 어린이나 성인의 성폭력 피해에 비해 윤간(輪姦)이나 강도강간 등 특수강간의 비율이 높다. 이는 청소년들이 학교 폭력배나 불량배 등의 집단폭행, 강도, 흉기 사용, 침입 등의 주요 표적이 되고 있기 때문이다.
- 다른 연령층과 비교하여 친족 내의 피해, 선배나 동급생에 의한 피해, 교사나 강사 등에 의한 피해의 비율이 높게 나타나고 있다.

---

4) 청소년에 대한 연령 규정은 법규마다 다르나, 청소년기본법에는 9세에서 24세 사이의 사람으로 규정되어 있다. 흔히 '청소년'이라 하면 만 13세에서 만 18세 사이의 사람을 칭하며, 통상 중학교와 고등학교의 시기에 해당된다.

- 19세부터 성년, 장애인 · 노약자를 위한 성년후견제, 미성년자 입양 시 법원 허가를 받아야 하는 등 바뀐 민법이 2013년 7월 1일부터 시행되었다. 만 19세 이상이면 부모 동의 없이 원룸 전세계약, 휴대전화 개통, 신용카드 개설, 보험가입 등을 할 수 있으며, 변리사 · 공인노무사 등 전문자격시험 응시도 할 수 있다. 또 정신지체자 등에게 독자적으로 법률행위를 할 수 없도록 한 금치산 · 한정치산 제도를 폐지하고 성년후견제를 도입하였다. 성년후견제는 사무처리 능력이 떨어지는 장애인 · 노약자 등이 법률행위 조력을 받을 수 있도록 하기 위한 것으로 성년후견 · 한정후견 · 특정후견 · 계약후견 등 4가지로 시행되며, 후견인은 복수 · 법인 선임을 할 수 있으며 변호사 · 법무사 · 세무사 · 사회복지사나 전문법인이 후견에 참여할 수 있다. 미성년자를 입양할 때는 가정법원의 양부모 양육능력과 입양능력 심사를 거쳐 허가를 받아야 한다. 또 이혼 후 단독친권자로 지정된 아버지나 어머니가 사망하면 자동으로 그 상대 배우자가 친권자가 되는 친권 자동 부활제가 폐지되어, 생존한 아버지나 어머니, 친족은 가정법원에 친권자 지정을 청구할 수 있고, 법원은 직권 또는 신청으로 친권자나 미성년후견인을 선임할 수 있다.

- 어린이 강간은 폭력 사용 여부, 동의 여부, 저항 여부와 무관하게 범죄로 취급되어 엄한 처벌을 받지만 청소년 성폭력의 경우 때때로 동의된 성관계로 오인받기도 하고, 피해자에 대한 비난여론이 형성되기도 한다. 이는 현재의 청소년들이 성에 대해 개방적이고 자발적이며, 어느 정도의 판단능력과 방어능력이 있다는 이중적(二重的) 통념이 있기 때문이다.

(3) 남성 강간

- 남성들은 성폭행 피해를 입었을 때, 그로 인한 분노와 고통에도 불구하고 '남성인 자신이 성폭력 피해를 입었다'는 사실에 대한 수치심으로 힘들어한다. 그러나 한편으로는 "내가 여자도 아닌데, 별일 아니다"라는 식으로 자신의 힘든 감정을 외면하려고 하는 경우도 많다.
- 어떤 피해자도 수치스러워하고 부끄러워할 이유는 없다. 또한 자신이 입은 피해에 대해 정당하게 문제를 제기하는 것을 부적절하거나 남자답지 못한 것이라고 생각하지 않아야 할 것이다.
- 같은 남성에게 입은 피해를 인정하고 싶어 하지 않기 때문에 신고율도 매우 낮다. 남성 간 성폭력은 특히 군대에서 많이 일어난다.

(4) 동성 간 강간

- 동성(同性)에게 피해를 입었을 경우, 성폭력이라는 사실 자체를 인지하지 못하는 경우가 많다. 그러나 동성 간에도 상대방의 의사에 반했을 경우에는 강간이다.

(5) 장애인 강간

- 피해자가 장애인인 경우, 피해 당시에 저항할 수 있는 정도가 제한되어 있고 상대적으로 더 취약한 위치에 놓여 있기 때문에 현행법으로도 더 엄중히 처벌하도록 되어 있다.
- 장애인은 흔히 성별과 성욕이 없는 존재로 인식되는 경향이 있기도 한다. 그러나 장애인 역시 성적 자기결정권이 있으며, 이를 존중하기 위해서는 다양한 몸의 차이를 인정해야 할 것이다. 예 도가니 사건

〈도가니법(法)〉

- 2011년 10월 28일 국회를 통과한 아동·장애인 성폭력 범죄에 대한 처벌을 강화하는 내용을 골자로 한 '성폭력 범죄의 처벌 등에 관한 특례법 개정안'의 별칭이다.
- 2011년 9월 개봉된 〈도가니〉라는 영화를 통해 전 국민의 관심이 집중된 후, 이와 관련된 법률안이 긴급하게 처리되어 2011년 11월 17일 시행되었다.
- 이 법은 2011년 9월 개봉한 영화 〈도가니〉를 통해 알려진 장애인학교 교직원의 장애인 성폭행사건을 계기로, 법률 개정안이 국회에서 논의되어 개정된 후 2011년 11월 17일부터 시행됐다. 개정 법률에 따르면 장애인과 13세 미만의 아동을 성폭행했을 경우 7년, 10년으로 형량을 대폭 늘렸으며, 무기징역까지 범위를 넓혔다. 또한 장애인 여성·13세 미만 아동에 대한 성폭행범죄의 공소시효도 폐지됐다. 아울러 장애인 보호·교육 시설의 장(長)이나 직원이 장애인을 성폭행하면 법정형의 2분의 1까지 형이 가중된다.
- 장애인 성범죄와 관련해 솜방망이 처벌의 근거가 돼왔다고 비판받았던, 피해자가 '항거불능'일 경우에만 성폭행으로 인정하는 조항도 삭제했다. 기존 법에는 장애인 대상 성범죄자를 '신체적인 또는 정신적인 장애로 항거불능인 상태에 있음을 이용하여 여자를 간음하거나 사람에 대하여 추행을 한 사람'이라고 돼 있지만, 이를 '신체적인 또는 정신적인 장애가 있는 여자에 대해 강간죄를 범한 사람'으로 고쳤다. 또한 2012년 8월부터는 교장, 교사 등 업무상 지위를 이용해 미성년자를 성추행한 경우 피해자에 대한 처벌 의사와 상관없이 처벌된다.
- 2011년 9월 개봉한 영화 〈도가니〉는 2005년 광주의 한 청각장애학교에서 실제로 발생한 성폭행사건을 토대로 한 공지영 작가의 동명의 소설을 영화화해 사회적으로 큰 반향을 일으켰다. 영화를 본 관객들은 인화학교사건의 재수사와 시설폐쇄를 요구하는 서명운동을 벌였고, 이후 〈도가니〉는 단순히 영화를 넘어서 사회적 약자에 대한 성폭력과 학대를 공론화하는 계기가 됐고, 사건 재수사와 관련 법 개정으로 이어지는 등 엄청난 변화를 몰고 왔다.
- 사건 발생 6년 만에 인화학교 성폭력사건의 전면 재수사에 나선 경찰은 2011년 11월 18일 성폭행과 법인 비리에 연루된 인화학교 전현직 교사, 교직원 등 40명 중 14명을 형사입건하기로 했다는 최종 수사결과를 발표했다. 아울러 광주시는 이날 인화학교와 인화원을 운영하는 복지법인 우석에 대해 법인 허가를 취소하는 조치를 취했다.

〈출처: 시사상식사전, pmg 지식엔진연구소, 박문각, 2013〉

(6) 친족강간

- 친족강간은 가까운 가족이나 친척에게 피해가 있어 배신감과 상실감이 크지만 주변에 알려 도움을 받는 것이 어려워 그 피해가 지속적인 경우가 많다.
- 피해특성상 피해 사실을 알게 된 가까운 가족이나 친척 등이 충격과 혼란으로 인해 사실을 믿으려 하지 않거나 회피하고 거부하는 경우가 많다. 주위 사람들은 분노하거나 두려워하기도 하고, 피해자를 도와주거나 보호하지 못했다는 죄책감에 시달리기도 한다.

(7) 직장 내 강간

직장 내 성폭력의 경우 가해자가 피해자보다 높은 사회적 위치와 많은 권력을 가지고 있어 어려움을 겪는 경우가 많다.

〈부부강간〉

1. 부부강간의 의의

1) 부부강간의 개념

- 부부 간에 발생하는 강제적인 성관계로써 부부강간의 경우 아내가 피해자이며 남편이 가해자인 경우가 대부분이다.
- 부부강간에서 강간이란 낯선 이에게 당하는 성폭력이 아니라 합의하지 않은 상태에서 자행하는 일방적이고 폭력적으로 강요하는 모든 성행위로써 정조(貞操)가 기준이 아니라 사랑하는 사람이든 남편이든 파트너의 성적 자기결정권이 기준이다.

2) 유형

〈배우자에 대한 성적 폭력의 유형〉

유 형		수(명)	비율(%)
구타동반한 강간	도구 또는 흉기로 위협하며 구타를 동반한 강간	2	2.2
	구타를 동반한 강간	16	17.2

<table>
<tr><th colspan="2">유 형</th><th>수(명)</th><th>비율(%)</th></tr>
<tr><td>강압적 강간</td><td>직접 폭력은 없었으나 계속적인 구타, 폭언, 협박이 있어 성관계를 거부할 수 없었던 경우</td><td>20</td><td>21.5</td></tr>
<tr><td rowspan="5">가학적 성학대 및 모욕</td><td>이물질 등의 삽입</td><td>4</td><td>4.3</td></tr>
<tr><td>성기학대(음모제거, 성기부분 구타 및 학대)</td><td>5</td><td>5.4</td></tr>
<tr><td>성적 모욕(정액검사, 속옷검사, 음부촬영 후 타인에게 노출)</td><td>7</td><td>7.5</td></tr>
<tr><td>옷을 벗기고 구타</td><td>9</td><td>9.7</td></tr>
<tr><td>변태적 성관계 요구</td><td>7</td><td>7.5</td></tr>
<tr><td>강제적 성행위 불응 시 폭력 행사</td><td>성관계 거부 후 심한 폭언, 폭력 행사</td><td>20</td><td>21.5</td></tr>
<tr><td>기타</td><td>제3자를 통한 강간 등</td><td>3</td><td>3.2</td></tr>
<tr><td colspan="2">합 계</td><td>93</td><td>100</td></tr>
</table>

※ 2002년 한국가정법률상담소에서 가정폭력 피해여성 100명을 대상으로 상담한 사례 중 배우자에 대한 성적 폭력의 유형

2. 입법례

- 한국과 달리 유럽 등 서구 국가에서는 20~30년 전부터 부부강간을 범죄로 인정·처벌하고 있다.
- 유럽의회는 1986년 혼인관계 여부에 상관없이 모든 강간을 처벌해야 한다고 촉구했고, 이를 계기로 이탈리아와 독일은 1997년 전후로 강간죄 성립 범위를 '혼인 외 성교'로 한정했던 형법을 개정하고 부부강간을 처벌하기 시작했다.

1) 독일

- 1997년, 형법개정을 통해 강간죄의 구성요건 중 '혼인 외 성교'라는 문언을 삭제함으로써 아내 강간죄를 받아들였다.
- 배우자강간 혹은 혼인 내 강간의 인정여부에 대해서 강간죄의 성립을 인정하고 있으며, 성적 자기결정권에 반(反)하는 성폭력범죄에 대한 처벌강화는 최근 독일의 입법경향이다.

2) 미국

- 1857년, 매사추세츠주 법원이 "혼인계약의 조건에는 아내는 남편이 원할 때는 언제나 성교에 응한다는 철회할 수 없는 동의가 포함된다"는 법 이론을 최초로 채택한 후 그대로 적용해 왔다.
- 1984년, 뉴욕 항소법원이 "혼인증명서가 남편이 형사면책권을 갖고서 아내를 강간할 수 있는 자격증으로 파악돼서는 안 된다"며 '아내강간의 면책' 법리를 폐기하고 부부 강간죄를 인정했다.
- 부부 사이의 강간을 인정하지 않는 '결혼 강간 면제'법 조항이 1976년까지 있었으나, 이후 한 주(州)씩 해당 조항을 폐기하기 시작해 1996년에는 17개 주에서 모두 폐지됐다. 현재 미국은 모든 주(州)에서 부부강간을 성폭행 범죄로 다루고 있고, 피해자는 민사소송도 제기할 수 있다.

3) 영국

- 1991년, 최고법원의 전원합의체 판결을 계기로 아내 강간죄를 공식적으로 인정해 오고 있다.
- 1994년 형사정의 및 공공질서법을 제정하며 부부강간을 강간죄에 포함시켰다.
- '불법적인 성교'에서 '불법적'이라는 단어를 삭제하여 배우자강간의 처벌이 가능해졌다.

4) 프랑스

- 부부강간을 강간죄로 처벌한다. 이는 프랑스 형법이 강간을 폭력·강요·위협·충격을 이용해 '타인'에게 가하는 모든 형태의 성적 삽입 행위로 규정하고 있기 때문이다.

5) 네덜란드

- 성범죄에 대하여 매우 폭넓게 처벌하는 입장으로, 혼인 내·외 모두 강간 및 강제추행을 처벌하고 있다.

6) 일본

- 일본법원은 '혼인관계가 실질적으로 파탄되지 않는 한 강간죄가 성립하지 않는다'며 부부강간을 제한적으로 인정하고 있다. 일본 최고재판소는 일관되게 "부부는 성생활의 의무가 있다"고 판결하고 있다.

2) 학자별 분류

(1) 코헨(Albert Cohen)의 분류[5)]

대체적 공격	1) 배우자, 애인 등으로부터 성적 거절을 당했을 때 그 불만을 해소하기 위해 자기를 좌절시킨 특정여성에게 성적 공격을 하지 않고 임의로 선택된 낯선 여성에게 성적 공격을 하게 된다. • 폭력은 성적 영역에서 야만적인 경우가 많다. • 강간은 보통 자동차 안이나 피해자의 가정, 유원지 또는 산 등에서 발생한다. • 강간범은 성적 행위를 하는 순간에 공격을 하지만, 발기와 성적 흥분(erection and orgasm)을 느끼지 못한다. 개인적 · 사회적 활동과 결혼의 적응은 잘 할 수 있다. 2) 심리요법은 불만의 근원을 찾는 데 중점을 두어야 하고, 사회적으로 관용할 수 있는 방법으로 불만을 표현할 수 있는 방법을 가르쳐야 한다.
보상적 공격	1) 여자친구를 찾으려고 노력하기는 부적당한 사람이다. • 강간범의 대부분은 내성적이고 사회에 적응을 못 한다. • 강간범의 행동은 피해자가 항복하여 그에게 순종하도록 요구하는 것이다. 그런 피해자는 여성 중에서 그의 취향에 맞는 여성이 선택되고, 공격은 공원이나 사람의 왕래가 드문 거리 등과 같은 장소에서 발생한다. 그는 피해자에게 접근하여 피해자의 유방이나 생식기를 만진다. 그의 목표는 성적 행위를 하는 것이고 가끔 빨리 사정하기도 한다. • 이런 강간범은 대부분이 가정적 수준이 뒤떨어지고 지능이 낮고 미혼자가 대부분이다. 2) 심리요법은 사회적 · 개인적 적응에 중점을 두어야 한다. • 사회적인 기술을 교육받을 필요가 있고 가정적 · 정서적 안정으로 도움을 주어야 하고, 이런 변화를 위해서는 많은 후원자가 필요하다.
성(性) 공격 동시수행	1) 성을 공격과 관련시키고 있다. • 만약 피해자가 공격을 한다면 그는 더 많은 흥분을 하게 되고 강간은 닥치는 대로 야만적으로 하게 된다. 그러나 그가 갖는 감정은 성적이지 분노적인 것이 아니다. • 전형적으로 이런 강간범은 데이트를 하고 결혼을 하기도 하나 모든 관계가 폭력과 관련되어 있다. 그의 결혼은 불안하고 그의 직장기록은 해고가 포함되며 그는 폭력에 대한 범죄기록을 가질 수 있다. 이럴 때 그는 동물에 대한 잔인성, 무단결석, 가출과 같은 행동을 할 것이다. 2) 치료는 매우 어렵고 완전한 성격재구성에 목표를 두어야 한다.

5) 이상현, 범죄심리학, 박영사, 2004:248-249; D. Lester & G. Lester, Crime of Passion, Chicago : Nelson Hall, 1975:67-69.

충동	1) 순간적인 충동이 일어날 때 변덕적 · 폭발적으로 강간을 하게 된다. • 정신병질적 특성을 가지는 경향이 있고, 모든 종류의 범죄를 포함하는 범죄기록을 가질 것이다. 2) 치료와 대책은 개인의 역동적 이해와 그런 행동을 일으키는 사회적 동인을 알아서 양면의 장애를 제거해 가는 것이 중요하다.

(2) Groth, Burgess, Holstrom의 강간의 분류6)

권력 · 완력강간 (power rape)	남성다움을 표현하거나 여성의 지배 또는 남성다움에 대한 의혹을 해소하기 위한 강간
분노강간(anger rape)	여성에 대한 분노, 경멸, 미움 등을 표출하기 위한 강간
가학적 강간(sadistic rape)	여성의 고통을 즐기려 하는 강간

(3) 그로스 등의 분류7)

지배강간(power robber)	• 패배감이나 굴욕감을 극복하기 위한 강간이며, 성취감 · 소유감 · 정복감 · 승리감 등의 쾌감을 경험하기 위한 강간이다. • 남성으로서의 우월감과 지배욕을 과시(誇示)하는 데 목적이 있기 때문에 처음에는 상대여성이 반항을 하지만 결국은 굴복하고 기쁘게 응할 것으로 기대한다. • 자기의 주체성 · 성능력 · 힘 · 지배력을 증명함으로써 자신 속에 있는 열등감 · 왜소감을 부정하려고 안간힘을 쓰며 자주 같은 범행을 저지른다.
분노강간(anger robber)	• 여성에 대해 분노 · 경멸감 · 증오심 등을 지닌 남성이 그러한 심리상태를 극복하기 위한 강간이다. • 여성에 대한 분노 · 경멸 · 증오 등의 감정을 해소하는 데 목적이 있기 때문에 범행 도중에 상대를 때리고 옷을 찢으며, '쌍년' · '갈보' 등과 같은 저속한 욕을 내뱉고 몸에 상처를 낸다. • 범인의 여성관계가 갈등 · 좌절 · 질투 · 폭력으로 점철되어 있어서 여성을 해치고 여성에게 복수하기 위해 강간을 저지르는 것으므로 경우에 따라서는 살인으로 이어질 수도 있다.

6) A. N. Groth, A. W. Burgess & L. L. Holstom. "Rape : Power, Anger and Sexuality", American Journal of Psychiatry, 1977:1239–1243.

7) • 조병인, 현대사회와 범죄, 법문사, 2000:71–73.
• Groth 등이 분류한 강간의 종류에는 분노강간(anger rape), 권력 · 완력강간(power rape), 가학적 강간(sadistic rape)이 있다. 2000 기출

3. 강간의 원인

1) 강간의 일반적 원인

(1) 성차별적인 사회구조

• 우리 사회는 여성이나 어린이를 남성이나 어른보다 약하고 낮은 존재라 여기고 있다.
• 가정이나 직장, 학교 등 수많은 공간에서 여성-남성, 어린이-어른 간에 지배-복종의 위계관계가 발생한다. 이는 보다 낮은 위치에 놓인 사람을 함부로 대해도 괜찮다는 잘못된 생각을 낳으며, 이로 인해 여성들은 남성들의 성적 폭력에 쉽게 노출된다.
• 성차별적인 사회분위기는 남성의 성폭력을 방관하고 허용할 뿐만 아니라 부추기기까지 하며, 성폭력을 한 가해자에게 면죄부를 주기까지 한다는 것이다.

(2) 왜곡된 성문화

• 한 살이라도 더 어린 여성을 옆에 앉히고 술을 마시려는 남자들과 이를 부추기는 향락·퇴폐문화, 건전한 성관계보다 변태적인 성행위를 더 좋은 것처럼 보여주는 음란물, 여성의 가치를 오직 '성'으로만 다루는 광고와 영화 등 왜곡된 성문화는 여성을 성적 대상, 강간의 대상으로 만든다는 것이다.

(3) 의사소통의 불일치

• 우리 사회에는 여성과 남성의 성(性)에 대한 태도를 서로 다른 잣대로 평가한다. 여성은 성(性)에 무지하고 소극적이어야 하지만, 남성은 성(性)에 적극적이고 과장된 표현을 해도 괜찮다고 생각한다.
• 여성과 남성이 성에 대해 원활한 의사소통을 할 수 없는 문화 속에서, 성폭력이라는 극심한 위기상황에서 여성이 "싫다"거나 "안된다"고 의사표현을 해도 이를 긍정적 대답의 완곡한 표현으로 받아들여 성폭력을 행하는 남성들이 생겨난다는 것이다.

(4) 성교육의 부재

• 온 가족이 함께 텔레비전을 보다가 조금만 야한 장면이 나오면 얼굴을 붉히고 쑥스러워하고, 학교에서는 남녀의 신체구조나 생리적 현상 등 생물학적인 성지식을 전달하는 것을 성교육이라는 이름으로 실시하고 있다.

• 이런 현실 속에서는 성에 대한 가치나 성적 행동에 대해 생각하고 고민해 보는 열린 교육이 이루어질 수 없기에, 제대로 된 성교육 대신 포르노 비디오나 잡지 등에서 보여주는 과장되고 가학적인 성적 표현과 또래집단 사이의 잘못된 성지식을 여과없이 받아들인 많은 청소년들은 죄의식조차 느끼지 못한 채 강간을 저지르게 된다는 것이다.

(5) 강간에 대한 사법계의 인식부족

• 많은 피해자들이 경찰이나 검찰의 조사과정에서 남성의 입장에서 사건을 바라보고 처리하는 형사나 경찰로 인해 자신이 죄인인 것 같은 느낌을 받게 된다.
• 사법계에서는 여전히 성폭력에 대한 잘못된 통념들을 수용하고 있고, 2차 피해로 인해 많은 피해자들이 아예 고소를 하지 못하거나, 고소를 했다가도 취하하는 경우가 많다.
• 사법계의 인식부족은 피해자들이 피해사실을 은폐하거나 법정(法廷)에서의 과정을 포기하게 만들고, 가해자는 아무런 처벌도 받지 않게 되며, 오히려 재범을 저지르는 가해자가 늘어나게 된다는 것이다.

2) 학자별 강간의 원인

Lundberg, Geffner의 강간발생의 요소[8]	i) 성적 학대를 위한 동기강화 요소, ii) 내적 방해를 감소시키는 요소, iii) 외적 방해를 감소시키는 요소 iv) 피해자저항을 감소시키는 등의 4가지 요소가 필수적으로 형성될 때 강간이 발생한다고 설명하고 있다.
Simon[9]	성범죄의 원인으로 가해자의 낮은 자존감, 외로움, 여성에 대한 분노, 우울증, 약물오남용, 성적 환상, 지나친 성적 관심 등과 같은 심리적 요소들이 성범죄의 발생과 밀접한 원인이 있다고 지적한다.

8) William G. Doerner & Steven P. Lab, Victimology, Cincinnati : Anderson Publishing Co., 1998:110.
9) L. M. J. Simom, "Do Criminal Offenders Specialize in Crime Types", Applied and Preventive Psychol., 6, 1997:35-37.

그로스[10)]	강간범들은 성적 쾌감을 즐기기 위해서 강간을 하는 것이 아니라, 여성에 대한 패배감 · 굴욕감 · 증오심 등을 극복하기 위해 강간을 한다고 한다.
전대양[11)]	• 연쇄강간범죄 가해자의 측면의 특징으로 나타나는 공통적인 요소는 어린 시절의 부정적인 발달과정과 성적인 환상과 같은 개인의 심리적 문제, 그리고 낯선 사람들을 강간의 대상으로 삼는 전형적인 강간범의 형태를 가지고 있다고 한다. • 연쇄강간범들은 범행동기가 매우 다양하게 나타나며, 특히 연쇄살인범과 같은 범죄적 특징을 공유한다고 한다.
개인적 · 사회적 원인[12)]	• 개인적 원인으로는 i) 충동에 대한 자제력 부족 ii) 순간적인 충동의 저변에 깔려 있는 복합적인 개인의 감정상태 iii) 강간범죄자의 신경증적(neurotic)혹은 정신병적(psychotic) 인성구조 등이 제시되고 있다. • 사회적 원인으로는 i) 친구집단의 영향 ii) 외설적인 필름의 영향을 들고 있다.

10) 조병인, 현대사회와 범죄(제3판), 법문사, 2000:71-73.
- Groth는 500명의 성폭행자를 대상으로 임상연구를 한 결과 강간은 성기접촉을 포함하는 성폭행의 모습을 띠기는 하지만, 성적 쾌락이나 성적 만족보다는 분노나 적대감, 세력이나 지위의 확인, 통제력, 지배 등의 공격성과 관련된 남성들의 비성적인 욕구를 만족시키려 하는 행위라고 결론내리고 있다. 또한 많은 강간가해자들은 강간 시 성적으로는 오히려 불유쾌감을 경험하며, 공격성과 지배감정의 쾌감을 경험하는데 이는 바로 강간이 갈등과 불안증세에서 비롯되기 때문이라고 하였다(Fortune, 1983).

11) 전대양, "연쇄 강간범의 범죄심리학적 특성", 한국범죄심리연구, 제2권, 제1호(2006년 봄호), 한국범죄심리학회, 2006:45-46.
- 한국형사정책연구원, 강간범죄의 실태에 관한 연구, 서울 : 한국형사정책연구원, 1992.

12) 최인섭 · 전영실, 한국형사정책연구원, 1992:25-26.
- 장다혜는 강간범죄의 원인이 남성위주의 가부장적 사회에서 기인하며, 그러한 사회구조로 인해 강간에 대한 법률적 규정이 남성적 가치와 언어를 반영하고 있어 단순강간과 같은 특정한 강간의 유형에 대한 처벌을 어렵게 만들고 있다고 보고 있다. 장다혜, "단순강간의 형사법상 판단기준에 관한 여성주의적 연구", 이화여자대학교 대학원 박사학위논문, 2004: 146-149.
- 사회적 폭력으로서의 강간은 1) 고대에서부터 오늘까지 사회적으로 허용되는 강간이 존재해 왔다. 이때의 강간은 승리자가 획득한 권력과 우월성을 여자를 통해 과시하는 것으로서, 섹스는 힘을 과시하는 수단이 되는 것이었다. 2) 여성노동자를 통제하기 위한 수단이나 고문의 한 형태로 나타나는 경우도 있다. 이러한 강간은 정치적 또는 사회적 권력행사의 한 형태로서 강간을 제도화하는 데 기여한다. 성폭행이나 강간은 여성들 특히 미혼녀들에게 사회에서 강요하는 '순결'을 지켜야 한다는 이데올로기 속에서 훌륭한 통제정책이 될 수 있다. 예 남성고용주가 10대 여공들에게 강간 등 성폭행을 가하고 강간사실이 알려질 것을 두려워하도록 위협을 가하여 여공들의 이직을 막는다거나, 자백하지 않으면 강간하겠다는 위협의 형태. 3) 사회적 폭력으로서의 강간범들의 특징은 모험, 성취, 소유, 승자 등의 개인주의적 특성이 있는가 하면 복수, 처벌, 강도의 사회적 요소도 있고, 제도적 권력의 과시가 개입되는 것을 볼 수 있다.

3) 강간범죄의 원인에 대한 접근방법

성적 부적절성의 문제	강간범들은 거세(去勢)감정이나 성적 부적절성을 느끼고 있어서 과다하게 공격적인 성행위를 통하여 자신의 감정을 숨기려 한다.
폭력의 하위문화	강간범 자신은 정상이지만 단지 강간을 조장하는 폭력적 하위문화에 의해 기대되는 바가 범죄적 양상을 띤 행동으로 표출된 것이다.
상대적 좌절감의 문제	성이 개방되고 성적 기회가 많은 사회에서 성적 기회를 갖지 못하는 사람은 성의 폐쇄로 인해 기회가 적은 사회에서 성적 기회가 적은 사람보다 더 많은 상대적 좌절감을 느끼기에 개방된 사회에서 강간범죄가 더 많이 발생한다.
차별적 통제 (differential control)	여성에게만 성적 제한이 가해지고, 남성에게는 개방적이기 때문에 강간이 많이 일어날 수밖에 없다.
남녀성비의 불균형	사회의 성비(性比)가 여자에 비해 남자가 월등하게 많은 경우 성적 배출구가 부족하게 되고, 성적 상대를 찾는 데 있어서 사회적 긴장이 고조되므로 강간이 성행한다.
세력이론(power theory)13)	• 상류세력집단은 사실상 강간의 기회는 더 많은 반면, 사회적 통제는 적게 받는다. • 상류세력집단들의 강간은 인지되지 않고 숨겨지며, 처벌받지 않는 경향이 많아서, 상류계층의 강간을 지속적으로 부추기는 경우가 된다.

제3절 전자감시제도(electronic monitoring system)

1. 의의

• 전자감시제도(electronic monitoring system)는 법에 정한 감시대상 범죄자가 특정한 시간에 특정된 장소에 있는지 여부를 확인하기 위하여 범죄자의 손목 또는 발목 등에 전자감응장치(전자발찌)를 부착시켜 전자파를 발신하고 추적하는 원리를 이용하여 위치를 확인하거나 이동경로를 탐지함으로써 원격 감시하는 새로운 제재유형의 하나이다.14)

13) 성매매에 대한 유엔의 입장은 원칙적으로 금지주의이며, 우리나라도 역시 금지주의 입장을 취하고 있다. 청소년 성매매사범의 신상정보는 경찰서에서도 열람할 수 있다. 2008 기출

• 2007년 4월 27일, "특정 성폭력범죄자에 대한 위치추적 전자장치 부착에 대한 법률"이 제정・공포되었으며[15], 2009년 8월 9일, "특정 범죄자에 대한 위치추적 전자장치 부착 등에 관한 법률"로 개정되었다.

2. 성폭력범죄자에 대한 전자감시의 필요성 유무

1) 성폭력범죄의 실태

성폭력범죄는 상습성[16]이 있으므로 같은 범죄자에 의하여 반복될 개연성이 많아 그 재범률이 높다.

2) 성폭력범죄의 특수성

(1) 피해의 심각성

• 성폭력범죄는 다른 어떤 범죄보다도 공동의 피해자가 발생하는 심각한 범죄이다.
• 강간피해자들이 겪는 피해증상으로는 정신적 공황(Crisis),[17] 강간 외상 후 증후군(Rape Trauma Syndrome), 외상 후 스트레스 증후군(PTSD: Post-Traumatic Stress Disorder) 등이 있다.

(2) 다수의 암수범죄 존재

• 성폭력범죄는 암수범죄가 많다.

14) 성폭력범죄자의 재범방지와 성행교정을 통한 재사회화를 위하여 성범죄자의 행적을 추적하여 위치를 확인할 수 있는 전자장치를 부착하는 것을 내용으로 하는 "특정 성폭력범죄자에 대한 위치추적 전자장치 부착에 대한 법률"이 제정・공포됨에 따라 전자감시제도를 도입하게 되었다.
15) • 우리나라의 전자감시제도(전자발찌)는 성폭력범죄를 대상으로 한다. 2010 기출
• 우리나라의 전자감시제도는 교도소 과밀수용문제를 완화하고, 원활한 재사회화와 사회 내 처우제도를 보완하는 것으로 상습 재산범죄자들의 재범방지가 목적이 아니라 성폭력범죄자의 재범방지를 위한 것이다.
2008 기출
16) 13세 이하의 소아에 대한 병적 흥미를 가지는 소아성애증(pedophilia)이라는 정신적 문제를 동반하는 사람의 경우 상습성을 가지기 쉽다고 한다. 김한균・강은영, "성폭력 범죄의 양형분석 및 재범방지를 위한 성폭력 범죄자 사후관리방안," 법무연수원, 2006:65.
17) 조은경, "강간피해의 심리적 반응에 대한 고찰," 피해자학연구, 제3호, 한국피해자학회, 1994:75-76.

• 암수범죄가 많은 이유는 i) 2013.6.14 이전 친고죄인 경우 피해자가 고소를 기피하며, ii) 특히 아동피해자인 경우 표현이 어려운 나머지 형사절차과정까지 이르지 못하게 되는 경우가 많으며, iii) 가해자가 이웃이나 친척 등 알고 있거나 가까운 사이의 사람인 경우에는 더 쉽게 신고하지 못하기 때문이다.

(3) 높은 재범률

2004년의 기준으로, 5년간 성폭력범죄의 재범률은 성인 대상은 37%인 데 반해 아동 대상은 50%에 이른다.

3) 성폭력범죄자에 대한 양형

성폭력범죄자는 중범죄자임에도 불구하고 집행유예를 남발하는 결과가 초래되고 있다.[18)]

3. 현행 전자감시제도의 비교법적 검토 2011 기출

1) "특정 범죄자에 대한 위치추적 전자장치 부착 등에 관한 법률"의 목적

법 제1조(목적) 이 법은 특정 범죄자의 재범 방지와 성행(性行)교정을 통한 재사회화를 위하여 그의 행적을 추적하여 위치를 확인할 수 있는 전자장치를 신체에 부착하게 하는 부가적인 조치를 취함으로써 특정범죄로부터 국민을 보호함을 목적으로 한다. 〈개정 2009.5.8〉

2) 전자장치

법 제2조(정의) 4. "위치추적 전자장치(이하 "전자장치"라 한다)"란 전자파를 발신하고 추적하는 원리를 이용하여 위치를 확인하거나 이동경로를 탐지하는 일련의 기계적 설비로서 대통령령으로 정하는 것을 말한다.

시행령 제2조(위치추적 전자장치의 구성) 「특정 범죄자에 대한 위치추적 전자장치 부착 등에 관한 법률」(이하 "법"이라 한다) 제2조제4호에 따른 위치추적 전자장치(이하 "전자장

18) 집행유예를 선고하는 목적은 단기자유형의 폐단을 피하고(소극적 기능), 더 나아가 그 위반 시 소정의 형을 받아야 한다는 심리강제를 담보로 하여 재범을 방지함과 아울러 범죄자의 자발적 갱생의 실현을 촉진하는 기능(적극적 기능)에 있다. 김재중, "집행유예에 관한 판례 동향과 개선방안", 법학연구, 제19권 제1호, 충북대학교 법학연구소, 2008:297, 참조.

치"라 한다)는 다음 각 호로 구성한다. 〈개정 2009.7.30〉

1. 휴대용 추적장치: 전자장치가 부착된 사람(이하 "피부착자"라 한다)이 휴대하는 것으로서 위성위치확인시스템(Global Positioning System) 및 이동통신망을 통하여 피부착자의 위치를 확인하는 장치
2. 재택(在宅) 감독장치: 휴대용 추적장치를 보조하는 장치로서, 피부착자의 주거지에 설치하여 피부착자의 위치를 확인하는 장치
3. 부착장치: 피부착자의 신체에 부착하여 휴대용 추적장치와 재택 감독장치에 전자파를 송신하는 장치

3) 피부착명령자의 의무

법 제14조(피부착자의 의무) ① 전자장치가 부착된 자(이하 "피부착자"라 한다)는 전자장치의 부착기간 중 전자장치를 신체에서 임의로 분리·손상, 전파 방해 또는 수신자료의 변조, 그 밖의 방법으로 그 효용을 해하여서는 아니된다.

② 피부착자는 특정범죄사건에 대한 형의 집행이 종료되거나 면제·가석방되는 날부터 10일 이내에 주거지를 관할하는 보호관찰소에 출석하여 서면으로 신고하여야 한다. 〈신설 2010.4.15〉

③ 피부착자는 주거를 이전하거나 7일 이상의 국내여행을 하거나 출국할 때에는 미리 보호관찰관의 허가를 받아야 한다. 〈개정 2010.4.15〉

4) 가석방과 전자장치 부착

법 제22조(가석방과 전자장치 부착) ① 제9조에 따른 부착명령 판결을 선고받지 아니한 특정 범죄자로서 형의 집행 중 가석방되어 보호관찰을 받게 되는 자는 준수사항 이행 여부 확인 등을 위하여 가석방기간 동안 전자장치를 부착하여야 한다. 〈개정 2009.5.8〉

② 심사위원회는 제1항에 따라 전자장치를 부착하게 되는 자의 주거지를 관할하는 보호관찰소의 장에게 가석방자의 인적사항 등 전자장치 부착에 필요한 사항을 즉시 통보하여야 한다.

③ 교도소장 등은 가석방 예정자가 석방되기 5일 전까지 그의 주거지를 관할하는 보호관찰소의 장에게 그 사실을 통보하여야 한다.

5) 가종료 등과 전자장치 부착

법 제23조(가종료 등과 전자장치 부착) ①「치료감호법」 제37조에 따른 치료감호심의위원회(이하 "치료감호심의위원회"라 한다)는 제9조에 따른 부착명령 판결을 선고받지 아니한 특정 범죄자로서 치료감호의 집행 중 가종료 또는 치료위탁되는 피치료감호자나 보호감호의 집행 중 가출소되는 피보호감호자(이하 "가종료자 등"이라 한다)에 대하여 「치료감호법」 또는 「사회보호법」(법률 제7656호로 폐지되기 전의 법률을 말한다)에 따른 준수사항 이행 여부 확인 등을 위하여 보호관찰기간의 범위에서 기간을 정하여 전자장치를 부착하게 할 수 있다. 〈개정 2008.6.13, 2009.5.8, 2010.4.15〉

② 치료감호심의위원회는 제1항에 따라 전자장치 부착을 결정한 경우에는 즉시 피부착결정자의 주거지를 관할하는 보호관찰소의 장에게 통보하여야 한다.

③ 치료감호시설의 장·보호감호시설의 장 또는 교도소의 장은 가종료자 등이 가종료 또는 치료위탁되거나 가출소되기 5일 전까지 가종료자 등의 주거지를 관할하는 보호관찰소의 장에게 그 사실을 통보하여야 한다. 〈개정 2010.4.15〉

6) 형의 집행유예와 전자장치 부착

법 제28조(형의 집행유예와 부착명령) ① 법원은 특정범죄를 범한 자에 대하여 형의 집행을 유예하면서 보호관찰을 받을 것을 명할 때에는 보호관찰기간의 범위 내에서 기간을 정하여 준수사항의 이행여부 확인 등을 위하여 전자장치를 부착할 것을 명할 수 있다. 〈개정 2009.5.8〉

② 법원은 제1항에 따른 부착명령기간 중 소재지 인근 의료기관에서의 치료, 지정 상담시설에서의 상담치료 등 대상자의 재범방지를 위하여 필요한 조치들을 과할 수 있다.

③ 법원은 제1항에 따른 전자장치 부착을 명하기 위하여 필요하다고 인정하는 때에는 피고인의 주거지 또는 그 법원의 소재지를 관할하는 보호관찰소의 장에게 범죄의 동기, 피해자와의 관계, 심리상태, 재범의 위험성 등 피고인에 관하여 필요한 사항의 조사를 요청할 수 있다.

제09장 폭력범죄

제1절 형법적 논의

1. 폭행죄(criminal assault)의 의의

1) 폭행의 의의

- 폭행죄는 신체에 대한 침해를 내용으로 하는 범죄이다.
- 보호법익은 사람의 신체의 건재(健在: 안전)이고, 보호의 정도는 형식범[1])으로서의 보호이다.

2) 구성요건

- 폭행죄는 사람의 신체에 대하여 폭행을 가함으로써 성립한다. 신체의 완전성을 침해할 가능성 있는 행위만을 폭행행위라 하고, 구체적인 결과발생의 가능성 여부는 묻지 않는다.

---

1) • 실질범(實質犯)은 법률이 보호하는 법익(法益)을 침해한 결과를 발생시키거나 또는 침해할 위험을 발생시킴으로써 성립하는 범죄를 말한다. 형식범(形式犯)은 단순한 거동(擧動)만으로 성립하는 범죄를 말한다. 실질범을 결과범, 형식범을 거동범이라고도 한다. 예컨대, 형법상 살인죄・상해죄 또는 방화죄는 실질범이며, 공연음란죄는 형식범의 대표적인 예이다.
 • 실질범은 구성요건의 결과가 발생함으로써 성립하는 침해범(예 살인죄 등)과, 구성요건의 결과를 발생시킬 위험성을 발생시킴으로써 성립하는 위험범(예 방화죄 등)의 모두를 포괄한 개념이며, 형법상 대부분의 범죄는 실질범에 속한다. 이에 대하여 형식범은 형법상에서는 많지 않지만, 경범죄처벌법이나 도로교통법 등 각종 행정법규에 많이 있다. 예컨대, 경범죄처벌법상 출입이 금지된 구역이나 시설 또는 장소에 정당한 이유 없이 들어가는 죄(제1조 제49호), 도로교통법상 운전면허증을 휴대하지 아니하거나 제시 요구에 불응하는 죄(77조) 등이다. 형식범은 법익침해의 위험성이 없는데도 행정단속의 필요로 처벌대상이 되는 경우가 많다.

• 행위의 객체는 자연인(自然人)인 타인(他人)의 신체이다.
• 폭행죄의 폭행은 협의의 폭행개념으로, 사람의 신체에 대한 직접적인 유형력의 행사를 의미한다.

2. 폭행죄의 유형

■ 폭행죄
■ 존속폭행죄

제260조(폭행, 존속폭행) ① 사람의 신체에 대하여 폭행을 가한 자는 2년 이하의 징역, 500만원 이하의 벌금, 구류 또는 과료에 처한다. 〈개정 1995.12.29〉
② 자기 또는 배우자의 직계존속에 대하여 제1항의 죄를 범한 때에는 5년 이하의 징역 또는 700만원 이하의 벌금에 처한다. 〈개정 1995.12.29〉

■ 특수폭행죄

제261조(특수폭행) 단체 또는 다중의 위력을 보이거나 위험한 물건을 휴대하여 제260조제1항 또는 제2항의 죄를 범한 때에는 5년 이하의 징역 또는 1천만원 이하의 벌금에 처한다. 〈개정 1995.12.29〉

■ 폭행치사상죄

제262조(폭행치사상) 전2조의 죄를 범하여 사람을 사상에 이르게 한 때에는 제257조 내지 제259조의 예에 의한다.

■ 상습폭행죄

제264조(상습범) 상습으로 제257조, 제258조, 제260조 또는 제261조의 죄를 범한 때에는 그 죄에 정한 형의 2분의 1까지 가중한다.

형법 제257조(상해, 존속상해) ① 사람의 신체를 상해한 자는 7년 이하의 징역, 10년 이하의 자격정지 또는 1천만원 이하의 벌금에 처한다. 〈개정 1995.12.29〉
② 자기 또는 배우자의 직계존속에 대하여 제1항의 죄를 범한 때에는 10년 이하의 징역 또는 1천500만원 이하의 벌금에 처한다. 〈개정 1995.12.29〉
③ 전 2항의 미수범은 처벌한다.

형법 제258조(중상해, 존속중상해) ① 사람의 신체를 상해하여 생명에 대한 위험을 발생하게 한 자는 1년 이상 10년 이하의 징역에 처한다.

② 신체의 상해로 인하여 불구 또는 불치나 난치의 질병에 이르게 한 자도 전항의 형과 같다.

③ 자기 또는 배우자의 직계존속에 대하여 전2항의 죄를 범한 때에는 2년 이상의 유기징역에 처한다.

형법 제259조(상해치사) ① 사람의 신체를 상해하여 사망에 이르게 한 자는 3년 이상의 유기징역에 처한다. 〈개정 1995.12.29〉

② 자기 또는 배우자의 직계존속에 대하여 전항의 죄를 범한 때에는 무기 또는 5년 이상의 징역에 처한다.

제2절 범죄학적 논의

1. 폭력범죄의 일반적 특징 2009, 2010, 2012 기출

- 가정폭력의 피해자는 여성에 한정되지 않고, 남편, 자녀, 노인 등도 피해자가 될 수 있다.
- 폭력범죄와 약물남용과는 상관관계가 많다.2)
- 일반적으로 대도시의 폭력범죄율은 농촌지역의 폭력범죄율보다 높다.
- 남성이 여성보다 폭력범죄를 더 많이 저지른다.
- 일반적으로 20대는 60대보다 폭력범죄를 더 많이 저지른다.
- 문제행동을 일찍 시작한 아이는 폭력범죄를 지속적으로 저지를 가능성이 높다.

2. 데이트 폭력(domestic violence)

1) 개념

- 남녀가 교제에서부터 약혼이나 동거에 이르기까지, 교제하는 기간 동안 합의 없이 상대방에게 해를 끼칠 의도를 가지고 행하게 되는 신체적 · 심리적 · 성적인 유머 행동을 말한다.

---

2) 조직폭력범죄의 특징으로는 폭력과 매수, 위계성, 조직집단 간의 배타성 등을 지적할 수 있다. 2008 기출

- '서로의 인생을 풍요롭게 해주어야 할 밀접한 인간관계에서 한 사람이 다른 한 사람을 폭력으로 통제(control)하는 것. 즉, 데이트 과정에서 일어나는 육체적, 언어적, 정신적 폭력을 의미한다.

2) 특성

- 데이트 폭력은 사랑이라는 이름 아래 숨어 있는 엄연한 범죄이며, 데이트 폭력은 사랑이 아니라 집착이며, 폭력을 행사하는 쪽의 열등감과 정신적 미숙이 원인이라고 밝혀진 바 있다.
- 대부분 성폭력만을 데이트 폭력으로 생각하지만, 데이트 중 발생하는 여러 가지 종류의 작은 구타, 손찌검, 혹은 모욕감이나 수치심을 주는 언어폭력도 데이트 폭력에 해당된다.
- 데이트 폭력의 가장 큰 문제는 두려움을 느껴 연인과 헤어지지 못하는 피해자들이 해결 방법을 찾지 못하는 데 있다.

3) 데이트 폭력의 유형

심리적 폭력	• 상대방의 자아개념을 손상시켜 피해를 주는 행위 • 주로 언어적인 폭력과 상대방의 물건을 부수거나, 때리려고 위협함으로써 심리적인 위해를 가하는 비언어적인 폭력의 형태 예 고함치기, 날카로운 소리 지르기, 상대방에게 모욕적인 말과 행동, 외모 비난하기, 위협하기 등
신체적 폭력	상대방에게 고통이나 상해(傷害)를 야기하려는 의도를 가지고 신체적 힘이나 도구를 사용 예 떠밀기, 움켜잡기, 팔을 잡고 흔들거나 머리카락 잡아당기기, 뺨 때리기, 물건 던지기, 발로 심하게 차기, 목 조르기 등
성적(性的) 폭력	상대방의 의사에 반(反)해서, 상대방에게 원하지 않는 성적 행위를 강요하여 신체적 · 심리적 피해를 주는 행위 예 신체적 일부 쳐다보기, 외설적 그림이나 글을 보게 하기, 외모나 옷차림을 성적으로 평가하기, 음담패설하기, 신체적 일부의 밀착접촉, 껴안기 및 키스하기, 성교 강요하기 등

3. 가정폭력

1) 가정폭력의 개념

- 가정폭력이란 가정구성원 사이의 신체적, 정신적 또는 재산상 피해를 수반하는 행위로써「가정폭력범죄의 처벌 등에 관한 특례법」 제2조 제1호의 행위를 말한다.3)

가정폭력범죄의 처벌 등에 관한 특례법

[시행 2012.8.5] [법률 제11002호, 2011.8.4, 타법개정]

제1장 총칙 〈개정 2011.4.12〉

제1조(목적) 이 법은 가정폭력범죄의 형사처벌 절차에 관한 특례를 정하고 가정폭력범죄를 범한 사람에 대하여 환경의 조정과 성행(性行)의 교정을 위한 보호처분을 함으로써 가정폭력범죄로 파괴된 가정의 평화와 안정을 회복하고 건강한 가정을 가꾸며 피해자와 가족구성원의 인권을 보호함을 목적으로 한다.

[전문개정 2011.4.12]

제2조(정의) 이 법에서 사용하는 용어의 뜻은 다음과 같다. 〈개정 2011.7.25, 2011.8.4, 2012.1.17〉

1. "가정폭력"이란 가정구성원 사이의 신체적, 정신적 또는 재산상 피해를 수반하는 행위를 말한다.
2. "가정구성원"이란 다음 각 목의 어느 하나에 해당하는 사람을 말한다.
   가. 배우자(사실상 혼인관계에 있는 사람을 포함한다. 이하 같다) 또는 배우자였던 사람
   나. 자기 또는 배우자와 직계존비속관계(사실상의 양친자관계를 포함한다. 이하 같다)에 있거나 있었던 사람
   다. 계부모와 자녀의 관계 또는 적모(嫡母)와 서자(庶子)의 관계에 있거나 있었던 사람
   라. 동거하는 친족
3. "가정폭력범죄"란 가정폭력으로서 다음 각 목의 어느 하나에 해당하는 죄를 말한다.

3) 일본의 경우 가정폭력(Domestic Violence : DV)이란 배우자나 내연관계 그리고 부모·아이·형제·친척 등의 가족으로부터 받는 가정 내 폭력을 말한다. 'Domestic'은 원래 '가정의 것'이라는 의미이지만, 최근 일본 내 가정폭력(DV)의 개념은 동거 유무를 불문하고, 헤어진 부부나 연인 등 근친자 사이에 일어나는 폭력 전반을 가리키는 경우가 많다.

가. 「형법」 제2편제25장 상해와 폭행의 죄 중 제257조(상해, 존속상해), 제258조(중상해, 존속중상해), 제260조(폭행, 존속폭행)제1항·제2항, 제261조(특수폭행) 및 제264조(상습범)의 죄

나. 「형법」 제2편제28장 유기와 학대의 죄 중 제271조(유기, 존속유기)제1항·제2항, 제272조(영아유기), 제273조(학대, 존속학대) 및 제274조(아동혹사)의 죄

다. 「형법」 제2편제29장 체포와 감금의 죄 중 제276조(체포, 감금, 존속체포, 존속감금), 제277조(중체포, 중감금, 존속중체포, 존속중감금), 제278조(특수체포, 특수감금), 제279조(상습범) 및 제280조(미수범)의 죄

라. 「형법」 제2편제30장 협박의 죄 중 제283조(협박, 존속협박)제1항·제2항, 제284조(특수협박), 제285조(상습범)(제283조의 죄에만 해당한다) 및 제286조(미수범)의 죄

마. 「형법」 제2편제32장 강간과 추행의 죄 중 제297조(강간), 제298조(강제추행), 제299조(준강간, 준강제추행), 제300조(미수범), 제301조(강간 등 상해·치상), 제301조의2(강간등 살인·치사), 제302조(미성년자 등에 대한 간음), 제305조(미성년자에 대한 간음, 추행), 제305조의2(상습범)(제297조부터 제300조까지의 죄에 한한다)의 죄

바. 「형법」 제2편제33장 명예에 관한 죄 중 제307조(명예훼손), 제308조(사자의 명예훼손), 제309조(출판물등에 의한 명예훼손) 및 제311조(모욕)의 죄

사. 「형법」 제2편제36장 주거침입의 죄 중 제321조(주거·신체 수색)의 죄

아. 「형법」 제2편제37장 권리행사를 방해하는 죄 중 제324조(강요) 및 제324조의5(미수범)(제324조의 죄에만 해당한다)의 죄

자. 「형법」 제2편제39장 사기와 공갈의 죄 중 제350조(공갈) 및 제352조(미수범)(제350조의 죄에만 해당한다)의 죄

차. 「형법」 제2편제42장 손괴의 죄 중 제366조(재물손괴 등)의 죄

카. 가목부터 차목까지의 죄로서 다른 법률에 따라 가중처벌되는 죄

4. "가정폭력행위자"란 가정폭력범죄를 범한 사람 및 가정구성원인 공범을 말한다.

5. "피해자"란 가정폭력범죄로 인하여 직접적으로 피해를 입은 사람을 말한다.

6. "가정보호사건"이란 가정폭력범죄로 인하여 이 법에 따른 보호처분의 대상이 되는 사건을 말한다.

7. "보호처분"이란 법원이 가정보호사건에 대하여 심리를 거쳐 가정폭력행위자에게 하는 제40조에 따른 처분을 말한다.

7의2. "피해자보호명령사건"이란 가정폭력범죄로 인하여 제55조의2에 따른 피해자보호명령의 대상이 되는 사건을 말한다.

8. "아동"이란 「아동복지법」 제3조제1호에 따른 아동을 말한다.

[전문개정 2011.4.12]

「가정폭력방지 및 피해자보호 등에 관한 법률」

[시행 2011.2.5] [법률 제10038호, 2010.2.4, 일부개정]

제1조(목적) 이 법은 가정폭력을 예방하고 가정폭력의 피해자를 보호·지원함을 목적으로 한다.

[전문개정 2006.4.28]

제2조(정의) 이 법에서 사용하는 용어의 뜻은 다음과 같다.

1. "가정폭력"이란 「가정폭력범죄의 처벌 등에 관한 특례법」 제2조제1호의 행위를 말한다.
2. "가정폭력행위자"란 「가정폭력범죄의 처벌 등에 관한 특례법」 제2조제4호의 자를 말한다.
3. "피해자"란 가정폭력으로 인하여 직접적으로 피해를 입은 자를 말한다.
4. "아동"이란 18세 미만인 자를 말한다.

[전문개정 2007.10.17]

2) 가정폭력의 특징

- 가족구성원이라는 고정된 대상에게 지속적이고 반복적으로 행사된다.
- 경제적 수준을 살펴보면 하층계급에만 국한된 문제가 아니며, 가정이라고 하는 사적인 공간에서 발생하는 폭력이다.
- 유년시절 가정폭력 피해자는 성인이 되어 가정폭력 가해자가 될 가능성이 높다. 2008 기출

3) 가정폭력의 원인

(1) 생물학적 요인

- 공격적인 성향의 증가와 충동조절 능력에 문제가 초래되는 경우 폭력행위가 증가하며, 주로 유전적인 폭력성, 간질발작, 뇌졸중, 교통사고로 인한 두부 손상, 알코올 중독, 약물중독 및 금단상태 등의 생물학적 요인이 있다.

(2) 심리적 요인

성격장애	반사회적 인격장애, 충동조절 장애, 가학적이고 의존적이고 미숙한 성격, 분노처리가 행동화되는 성격 등
어린 시절의 폭력 경험	자신이 소아시절에 가정폭력을 목격하면서 성장한 경우가 많다.
피해자의 요인	어린시절 가정폭력을 경험했거나 건강상태가 나쁠수록, 경제력과 사회능력이 낮을수록 노예화되는 경향이 있다.
기타	의처증과 의부증, 우울증, 정신장애 등

(3) 사회적 요인

가부장적 사회제도	왜곡된 가부장적인 가족구조가 가족 간 갈등과 폭력을 심화시키는 요인으로 작용
사회적 스트레스	스트레스를 많이 느끼는 가장(家長)일수록 돌발적인 분노표출방법이자 단기 해결수단
결손가정	결손가정의 아동은 가정폭력을 경험
사회경제적 상태	주로 사회경제적 수준이 낮을수록 폭력이 많지만, 실제로는 상류・하류 사회계층을 막론하고 가정폭력이 발생
왜곡된 사회적 통념[4)	내 아내와 내 자식을 내 마음대로 할 수 있다는 소유의식, 사회전반에 만연한 폭력 문화, 남의 집안 문제에 끼어들면 안 된다는 잘못된 사회적 인식

4) 가정폭력 유형

(1) 부부폭력

① 매 맞는 아내(아내구타)

• 부부 사이의 합의하에 일어나는 가학적 - 피(彼)가학적 관계가 아니라 쌍방의 합의 없이 남편이 아내에게 신체적・정신적・성적・경제적인 힘을 남용하는 행위이다.

---

4) 여자와 북어는 때려야 부드러워진다?, 맞을 짓을 했으니까 맞았겠지?, 귀한 자식일수록 매로 가르쳐야 한다?, 부부싸움은 칼로 물 베기다? 등의 잘못된 사회적 통념이 아직 만연하고 있다.

- 유형으로는 신체적 학대, 언어적 · 정서적 학대, 성적 학대, 경제적 학대, 방임 · 유기 등이 있다.
- 가족해체의 직접적인 원인이 되며 다른 가족구성원들에게도 장기적이고 심각한 영향을 미치는 특성이 있다.
- "더 자주, 더 심하게" 즉, 반복성과 심각성의 증가가 특징적이며, 피해정도는 멍듦부터 골절상, 각종 상처, 유산, 심지어 사망에까지 이른다.
- 구타유형으로는 목조르기, 주먹이나 발로 온몸 구타, 골프채 · 몽둥이로 구타, 칼 등 흉기위협(찌르기), 옷을 벗기고 때림(감금 포함) 등

② 매 맞는 남편

- 경제적 능력이 위축된 남성들의 증가와 가장(家長)으로서 점점 설 자리를 잃어가는 메마른 가정으로 인해 매 맞는 남편이 늘고 있는 형편이다.
- 특히 피해자 남성은 문제가 노출될 경우 주위로부터 조롱거리가 될 것을 두려워하며 반격행동에 대한 사법처리에의 염려, 경제적 어려움 때문에 상황을 벗어나기가 좀처럼 여의치 않다고 느낀다.
- 주로 나이든 남성이 훨씬 젊은 여성과 결혼했을 때 남편학대가 발생하는 것으로 보고되고 있다.
- 피해유형으로는 할퀴고 꼬집고, 따귀 또는 던진 집기에 맞는 수준이 대부분이다. 그러나 마구잡이 폭행, 무차별 폭언도 행해진다.

(2) 아동/청소년 학대

- 한국의 부모는 훈육을 목적으로 하는 체벌 등으로 자녀를 구타한 경험이 있으며 이는 세계에서 가장 높은 비율이다.
- 남편과 아내는 자신의 부모로부터 구타당한 것으로 보고되고 있으며, 자녀를 구타하는 부모들은 부부폭력이 많아 부부폭력과 아동구타는 매우 상관성이 높다고 보고되고 있다.
- 피해유형으로는 뇌손상으로 인한 정신지체나 정서불안, 신체적 손상으로는 폭력으로 인한 타박상, 장기(臟器) 등의 파열, 두개골 골절 등 각종 골절상으로 인하여 심하게는 사망하는 경우도 있다.

(3) 노인폭력(직계존속 학대)

- 노인들은 사회와 가정에서 지위와 권위를 상실하고 경제력이 떨어지면서 여러 종류의 폭력을 당하게 되지만 수치심 때문에 주위 사람들에게 잘 알리지 않는다.
- 피해유형으로는 주로 정서적 학대(무시, 멸시 등)가 많으며, 유기, 태만뿐만 아니라 물리적인 신체구타도 보인다.

5) 가정폭력의 피해와 영향

(1) 피해자에게 미치는 정신적 · 심리적 후유증

우울증	반복적 구타로 인한 자존심의 손상이 심하며, 스스로의 모멸감과 자괴심에 의해 우울증에 빠지는 경우가 많다.
자살	우울증과도 상당한 관련이 있다.
불안장애	가정폭력을 연상시키는 모든 것에 불안증세를 보인다. 충격 후 스트레스성 장애가 생기기도 한다.
화병	가정폭력으로 인한 울화증으로 마음 대신 몸이 우는 장애증상이다.
복수심으로 인한 또 다른 폭력	지속적인 구타를 당하던 아내가 술 취해 잠든 남편을 살해하는 결과를 낳기도 한다.
자녀에 대한 영향	부부간에 폭력을 행사하게 되면 자녀도 상처를 받아 자아존중감이 낮아지고 불행감, 무력감, 거부감, 죄의식, 분노를 느끼게 된다. 따라서 두통, 야뇨증, 불면증, 말더듬 같은 신체이상을 보이기도 하고 각종 비행행동이나 학습장애를 보이거나 자살에도 이른다.

(2) 가정생활 및 사회에 미치는 영향

① 폭력가정의 대물림

폭력가정의 대부분이 어렸을 때 아버지가 어머니를 때리거나 아동학대 등을 경험했다는 점에서 세대를 거쳐 가정폭력이 이어질 수 있다. 아들은 폭력남편이 될 가능성이 높고 딸은 남성 혐오증, 남성 기피증을 보일 수 있다.

② 사회에 미치는 영향

가정폭력이 반복될 경우 마침내 가정파괴로 이어져 청소년의 학원폭력, 각종 비행 등으로 인한 사회문제로 이어질 수 있다.

4. 학교폭력

1) 학교폭력의 의의 2012 기출

학교폭력예방 및 대책에 관한 법률
[시행 2014.1.31] [법률 제11948호, 2013.7.30, 일부개정]

제1조(목적) 이 법은 학교폭력의 예방과 대책에 필요한 사항을 규정함으로써 피해학생의 보호, 가해학생의 선도·교육 및 피해학생과 가해학생 간의 분쟁조정을 통하여 학생의 인권을 보호하고 학생을 건전한 사회구성원으로 육성함을 목적으로 한다.

제2조(정의) 이 법에서 사용하는 용어의 정의는 다음 각 호와 같다. 〈개정 2009.5.8, 2012.1.26, 2012.3.21〉

1. "학교폭력"이란 학교 내외에서 학생을 대상으로 발생한 상해, 폭행, 감금, 협박, 약취·유인, 명예훼손·모욕, 공갈, 강요·강제적인 심부름 및 성폭력, 따돌림, 사이버 따돌림, 정보통신망을 이용한 음란·폭력 정보 등에 의하여 신체·정신 또는 재산상의 피해를 수반하는 행위를 말한다.

1의2. "따돌림"이란 학교 내외에서 2명 이상의 학생들이 특정인이나 특정집단의 학생들을 대상으로 지속적이거나 반복적으로 신체적 또는 심리적 공격을 가하여 상대방이 고통을 느끼도록 하는 일체의 행위를 말한다.

1의3. "사이버 따돌림"이란 인터넷, 휴대전화 등 정보통신기기를 이용하여 학생들이 특정 학생들을 대상으로 지속적, 반복적으로 심리적 공격을 가하거나, 특정 학생과 관련된 개인정보 또는 허위사실을 유포하여 상대방이 고통을 느끼도록 하는 일체의 행위를 말한다.

2. "학교"란 「초·중등교육법」 제2조에 따른 초등학교·중학교·고등학교·특수학교 및 각종학교와 같은 법 제61조에 따라 운영하는 학교를 말한다.
3. "가해학생"이란 가해자 중에서 학교폭력을 행사하거나 그 행위에 가담한 학생을 말한다.
4. "피해학생"이란 학교폭력으로 인하여 피해를 입은 학생을 말한다.
5. "장애학생"이란 신체적·정신적·지적 장애 등으로 「장애인 등에 대한 특수교육법」 제15조에서 규정하는 특수교육을 필요로 하는 학생을 말한다.

2) 학교폭력의 유형

폭력의 양태에 따라 물리적 폭력과 정신적 폭력으로 대별할 수 있고, 여기에 언어적 폭력, 금품갈취, 괴롭힘의 일종으로 집단따돌림 등의 유형이 있다.

제 10 장 절도범죄

제1절 형법적 논의

1. 절도죄(竊盜罪)의 의의

1) 절도죄의 의의

- 절도죄는 타인이 점유하는 타인의 재물을 절취함으로써 성립하는 범죄이다. 타인이라 함은 자기 이외의 자연인, 법인, 법인격 없는 단체를 포함한다.
- 재산죄 중에서 재물만을 객체로 하는 순수한 재물죄이다. 보호법익은 소유권이다.[1]
- 가중적 구성요건으로는 야간 주거침입절도죄, 특수절도죄 및 상습절도죄가 있다.

2) 요건

- 절도죄의 객체는 타인의 소유 및 점유의 재물이다.
- 타인의 소유란 타인의 단독소유 또는 행위자와 타인의 공동소유에 속하는 재물을 말한다.[2]
- 타인의 점유는 재물이 타인의 단독점유, 행위자와 타인의 공동점유인 경우에 점유의 타인성이 인정된다. 재물은 관리할 수 있는 유체물과 동력을 말한다.

---

1) 소유권의 내용인 사용·수익·처분이 방해되는 것도 소유권의 침해이므로 침해범이라는 견해가 타당하다(다수설).
2) 재물의 타인성이란 재물이 범인 이외에 다른 사람의 소유에 속하는 것을 의미한다. 따라서 타인의 단독소유, 행위자와 타인의 공동소유인 경우에도 타인성이 인정된다.

- 주관적 요건으로 타인이 점유하는 타인의 재물을 절취한다는 데 대한 인식과 의사인 고의와 불법영득의사가 있어야 한다.

3) 행위

- 타인의 매물을 절취하는 것을 말한다. 절취란 타인이 점유하고 있는 타인의 재물을 점유자의 의사에 반하여 그 점유를 배제하고 자기 또는 제3자의 점유로 옮기는 것을 말하며, 타인의 점유배제와 새로운 점유취득을 그 내용으로 한다.
- 본죄의 실행의 착수시기는 타인의 점유를 배제하는 행위를 개시한 때이다. 기수시기는 재물을 자기의 지배하에 두면 족하므로 재물을 취득할 때 기수가 된다는 취득설이 타당하다(다수설 · 판례).

2. 절도죄의 유형

■ 절도죄

제329조(절도) 타인의 재물을 절취한 자는 6년 이하의 징역 또는 1천만원 이하의 벌금에 처한다. 〈개정 1995.12.29〉

■ 야간주거침입 절도죄

제330조(야간주거침입절도) 야간에 사람의 주거, 간수하는 저택, 건조물이나 선박 또는 점유하는 방실에 침입하여 타인의 재물을 절취한 자는 10년 이하의 징역에 처한다.

- 야간이라는 시간적 제약을 받는 주거침입죄와 절도죄의 경합범이다.

■ 특수절도죄

제331조(특수절도) ① 야간에 문호 또는 장벽 기타 건조물의 일부를 손괴하고 전조의 장소에 침입하여 타인의 재물을 절취한 자는 1년 이상 10년 이하의 징역에 처한다. ② 흉기를 휴대하거나 2인 이상이 합동하여 타인의 재물을 절취한 자도 전항의 형과 같다.

• 제1항은 야간주거침입절도가 침입방법으로 건조물의 일부를 손괴하는 그 수단의 강폭성 때문에 가중처벌하고, 제2항은 흉기휴대라는 위험성, 2인 이상이 합동하는 집단성 때문에 형을 가중한 것이다.

■ 자동차 등 불법사용죄[3)]

제331조의2(자동차등 불법사용) 권리자의 동의 없이 타인의 자동차, 선박, 항공기 또는 원동기장치자전차를 일시 사용한 자는 3년 이하의 징역, 500만원 이하의 벌금, 구류 또는 과료에 처한다. [본조신설 1995.12.29]

■ 상습절도죄

제332조(상습범) 상습으로 제329조 내지 제331조의2의 죄를 범한 자는 그 죄에 정한 형의 2분의 1까지 가중한다. 〈개정 1995.12.29〉

• 상습으로 절도죄 · 야간주거침입절도죄 및 특수절도죄를 범한 경우에 성립하는 범죄이다. 행위자의 상습성으로 책임이 가중되는 가중적 구성요건이다.

제2절 범죄학적 논의

1. 스카르의 절도유형[4)]

전문적 침입절도	• 직업적으로 남의 집이나 사무실 등에 침입하여 금품을 훔치는 유형
아마추어 침입절도	• 침입에 필요한 전문기술이나 수법에 익숙하지 않은 사람이 다른 사람의 금품에 욕심이 생겨 침입절도를 행하는 유형

3) 원칙적으로 불법영득의사가 없는 사용절도는 처벌할 수 없다. 그러나 타인의 자동차 등을 불법사용하는 행위가 증가하는 현상과 자동차 등 불법사용으로 인한 피해 및 처벌하지 않는 경우의 피해자의 법감정을 고려하여 개정형법이 신설한 규정이다.

4) 1973년에 워싱턴 D.C 지역의 침입절도를 연구하면서 범행에 대한 집착의 정도, 주수입원(主收入原), 범행의 숙련도 및 조직화의 정도, 범행동기 등을 기준으로 절도유형을 '전문적 침입절도'와 '아마추어 침입절도'로 구분하였다. 조병인, 현대사회와 범죄, 법문사, 2000:76-78.

2. 월쉬의 절도유형

도전적 침입절도 (challenge burglaries)	• 재물 자체가 욕심이 나서가 아니라 그 소유자에게 재산피해를 주기 위해 침입절도를 저지르는 경우
만용적 침입절도 (dare burglaries)	• 아동이나 청소년들이 또래에게 자신의 용맹을 과시하기 위해 무모하게 침입절도를 저지르는 경우
탈취적 침입절도 (dispossesive burglaries)	• 침입절도의 전형적 형태로서 오로지 현금이나 귀중품을 훔칠 목적으로 침입절도를 저지르는 경우

제11장 사기범죄

제1절 형법적 논의

1. 사기의 죄

1) 의의

• 사기죄는 사람을 기망(欺罔)하여 재물을 편취(騙取)하거나 재산상의 이익을 취득하거나 제3자로 하여금 취득하게 함으로써 성립하는 범죄이다. 재물(재물죄)과 재산상의 이익(이득죄)이 모두 객체이다.

• 상대방의 하자(瑕疵)있는 의사에 의하여 재물을 취득한다는 점에서 공갈죄와 같이 편취죄이나, 사기죄는 행위수단으로 기망[1]을, 공갈죄는 폭행・협박을 수단으로 하는 점에서 차이가 난다.

2) 보호법익

전체로서의 재산권이라는 견해(다수설), 재산권 외에 거래의 진실성도 보호법익에 해당한다는 견해의 대립이 있다. 보호의 정도는 침해범이다.

1) 사기죄의 요건으로서의 기망(欺罔)은 널리 재산상의 거래관계에 있어서 서로 지켜야 할 신의와 성실의 의무를 저버리는 모든 적극적 및 소극적 행위로서 사람으로 하여금 착오(錯誤)를 일으키게 하는 것을 말하며, 사기죄의 본질은 기망에 의한 재물이나 재산상 이익의 취득에 있고, 상대방에게 현실적으로 재산상 손해가 발생함을 그 요건으로 하지 아니한다(대판 1997.9.9. 97도1561)

2. 유형

1) 사기죄

> **제347조(사기)** ① 사람을 기망하여 재물의 교부를 받거나 재산상의 이익을 취득한 자는 10년 이하의 징역 또는 2천만원 이하의 벌금에 처한다. 〈개정 1995.12.29〉
> ② 전항의 방법으로 제삼자로 하여금 재물의 교부를 받게 하거나 재산상의 이익을 취득하게 한 때에도 전항의 형과 같다.
> **제352조(미수범)** 제347조 내지 제348조의2, 제350조와 제351조의 미수범은 처벌한다.
> [전문개정 1995.12.29]
> **제353조(자격정지의 병과)** 본장의 죄에는 10년 이하의 자격정지를 병과할 수 있다.
> **제354조(친족간의 범행, 동력)** 제328조와 제346조의 규정은 본장의 죄에 준용한다.

본죄는 사람을 기망하여 재물의 교부를 받거나 재산상의 이익을 취득한다든지 제3자로 하여금 교부 또는 취득하게 함으로써 성립하는 범죄이다. 재물과 재산상 이익을 모두 객체로 한다.

2) 컴퓨터 등 사용사기죄

> **제347조의2(컴퓨터등 사용사기)** 컴퓨터 등 정보처리장치에 허위의 정보 또는 부정한 명령을 입력하거나 권한 없이 정보를 입력·변경하여 정보처리를 하게 함으로써 재산상의 이익을 취득하거나 제3자로 하여금 취득하게 한 자는 10년 이하의 징역 또는 2천만원 이하의 벌금에 처한다.
> [전문개정 2001.12.29]
> **제352조(미수범)** 제347조 내지 제348조의2, 제350조와 제351조의 미수범은 처벌한다.
> [전문개정 1995.12.29]
> **제353조(자격정지의 병과)** 본장의 죄에는 10년 이하의 자격정지를 병과할 수 있다.
> **제354조(친족간의 범행, 동력)** 제328조와 제346조의 규정은 본장의 죄에 준용한다.

- 본죄는 컴퓨터 등 정보처리장치에 허위의 정보 또는 부정한 명령을 입력하거나 권한 없이 정보를 입력·변경하여 정보처리를 하게 함으로써, 재산상의 이익을 취득하거나 제3자로 하여금 취득하게 함으로써 성립하는 범죄이다.

• 보호법익은 사기죄와 같이 재산권이고 보호 정도는 침해범이다.

3) 준사기죄

제348조(준사기) ① 미성년자의 지려천박 또는 사람의 심신장애를 이용하여 재물의 교부를 받거나 재산상의 이익을 취득한 자는 10년 이하의 징역 또는 2천만원 이하의 벌금에 처한다. 〈개정 1995.12.29〉
② 전항의 방법으로 제삼자로 하여금 재물의 교부를 받게 하거나 재산상의 이익을 취득하게 한 때에도 전항의 형과 같다.
제352조(미수범) 제347조 내지 제348조의2, 제350조와 제351조의 미수범은 처벌한다.
[전문개정 1995.12.29]

• 미성년자의 지려천박(智慮淺薄: 지적 능력부족) 또는 사람의 심신장애를 이용하여 재물을 취득하거나 제3자로 하여금 재물을 교부받게 하거나 재산상의 이익을 취득하게 함으로써 성립하는 범죄이다.
• 기망(欺罔)을 수단으로 하지 않지만 존재하는 의사(意思)의 하자(瑕疵)를 이용한다는 점에서 기망수단에 의한 의사의 하자를 이용하는 사기죄와 유사하므로 사기죄에 준하여 처벌된다.
• 보호법익은 재산권이고 보호의 정도는 침해범이다.

4) 편의시설부정이용죄

제348조의2(편의시설부정이용) 부정한 방법으로 대가를 지급하지 아니하고 자동판매기, 공중전화 기타 유료자동설비를 이용하여 재물 또는 재산상의 이익을 취득한 자는 3년 이하의 징역, 500만원 이하의 벌금, 구류 또는 과료에 처한다.
[본조신설 1995.12.29]
제352조(미수범) 제347조 내지 제348조의2, 제350조와 제351조의 미수범은 처벌한다.
[전문개정 1995.12.29]
제353조(자격정지의 병과) 본장의 죄에는 10년 이하의 자격정지를 병과할 수 있다.
제354조(친족간의 범행, 동력) 제328조와 제346조의 규정은 본장의 죄에 준용한다.

(1) 유료자동설비

대가지불을 조건으로 기계 또는 전자장치의 작동에 의하여 일정한 물건 또는 편익을 제공하는 일체의 자동설비를 말한다. 예 자동판매기, 공중전화

(2) 부정이용

- 대가를 지급하지 않고 자동설비를 부정한 방법으로 조종하여 그 용법에 따라 작동시키는 것을 말한다. 예 가짜 동전을 투입하여 자판기 커피를 뽑는 것
- 절취한 타인의 일반공중전화카드로 통화한 경우는 대가가 지불된 것이므로 본죄에 해당하지 않으며, 자동설비를 손괴하고 그 속의 내용물을 가져가는 것은 절도죄와 손괴죄의 경합범이 된다.

5) 부당이득죄

제349조(부당이득) ① 사람의 궁박한 상태를 이용하여 현저하게 부당한 이익을 취득한 자는 3년 이하의 징역 또는 1천만원 이하의 벌금에 처한다. 〈개정 1995.12.29〉

② 전항의 방법으로 제삼자로 하여금 부당한 이익을 취득하게 한 때에도 전항의 형과 같다.

제353조(자격정지의 병과) 본장의 죄에는 10년 이하의 자격정지를 병과할 수 있다.

제354조(친족간의 범행, 동력) 제328조와 제346조의 규정은 본장의 죄에 준용한다.

사람의 궁박(窮迫)한 상태를 이용하여 현저하게 부당한 이익을 취득한 경우 또는 제3자로 하여금 부당한 이익을 취득하게 한 경우에 성립하는 범죄이다.

6) 상습사기죄

제351조(상습범) 상습으로 제347조 내지 전조의 죄를 범한 자는 그 죄에 정한 형의 2분의 1까지 가중한다.

제352조(미수범) 제347조 내지 제348조의2, 제350조와 제351조의 미수범은 처벌한다.
[전문개정 1995.12.29]

제353조(자격정지의 병과) 본장의 죄에는 10년 이하의 자격정지를 병과할 수 있다.

제354조(친족간의 범행, 동력) 제328조와 제346조의 규정은 본장의 죄에 준용한다.

상습성으로 인하여 책임이 가중되는 가중적 구성요건으로서 부진정 신분범이다. 상습범은 포괄일죄(包括一罪)에 해당한다.

제2절 범죄학적 논의

1. 사기범죄의 의의[2)]

- 사기의 수단과 방법은 다종다양하기에 여러 가지 수법이 있고, 상습성을 보이는 경우가 많으며, 사기범에 따라 그 수단과 방법은 고정화되는 경향이 있어 수사학에서 수법범죄로 다루고 있다.[3)]
- 사기는 비폭력적 범죄(nonviolent crime)이고, 피해자의 자발적인 협력이 있어야 가능하며, 범죄가 규명될 때까지는 어느 정도의 시간이 필요하다는 점에서 상대방에게 물리력을 행사하거나 주거에 침입하는 등의 침해행위를 벌이는 강도나 절도 등의 폭력적인 범죄와는 다른 특성을 가진다.
- 사기의 대표적 수단인 타인에 대한 기망은 반드시 그 대상의 무지나 어리석음 등이 원인이 되는 것은 아니며, 오히려 개인의 신뢰감을 역이용한 것이라는 데 사기의 폐해가 있다.
- 사기범의 경우 범인 스스로뿐만 아니라 주위 사람들까지도 그를 범인으로 생각하지 않는 등 법적 제재의 효과가 의문시되고 있다.
- 사기는 발생영역이 광범위하고 이에 따른 재산적 피해가 비교적 심각한 범죄유형이다.
- 사기에서 비롯된 재정적 손실은 절도나 강도와 같은 통상의 재산범죄에 의한 재정적 손실보다 훨씬 더 크다.

---

2) 이순래 외, 현대사회와 범죄, 청목출판사, 2012:311-323.

3) 범죄수법이란 범인이 일정한 수단·방법으로써 반복하여 범행하는 습벽을 말한다. 따라서 강도·절도·사기와 같은 수법범죄의 경우 범행시간과 장소 그리고 범죄행위에 표현된 수단·방법·습벽 등을 토대로 범죄수법을 유형화하여 범인을 특정하는 수사를 하게 되며, 이를 수법수사라 한다.

2. 사기범죄자의 특징

1) 사기범죄의 성공요인

- 사기범죄자들은 연령, 소득, 지역, 학력, 지식 등에 상관없이 사기대상을 확대하고 있어 누구나 피해를 입을 수 있다.
- 사기범죄자들은 전문적인 마케팅자료, 세밀히 연구되고 다듬어진 대본, 친밀한 톤의 목소리와 매력적으로 포장된 제안, 까다로운 질문에 대한 설득력 있는 대답, 상대방의 반감을 전문적으로 다루는 방법에 관해 정교한 기술을 보유하고 있다.

2) 사기범죄의 특징

- 사기범죄자는 범행의 반복으로 인한 지능화 경향이 나타나며, 피해자를 찾아서 이동하는 특성 때문에 범죄의 광역화 경향이 나타난다.
- 상습성과 고정화에 따라 높은 재범률을 보이기 때문에, 사기사건을 수사할 때는 사기범죄자가 이미 같은 수법의 사기사건으로 수사기관에서 여러 차례 조사받은 전력이 있는 경우가 많다.
- 범죄경력조회상에 나타난 처분미상 전과는 물론 경찰서에서 조사받은 사실에 대하여 사건송치서 사본상의 의견서를 통하여 범죄사실과 수법을 확인하여야 한다.
- 최근에는 인터넷의 급속한 확산으로 인하여 컴퓨터 및 인터넷상의 사기가 급증하는 추세를 보이고 있다.

〈표 2-1〉 사기 등 지능범죄와 일반 강력범죄의 비교

구분	사기 등 지능범죄	일반 강력범죄
계획성	합법을 가장하여 계획적·조직적으로 은밀히 이루어진다.	대부분 우발적인 범행이다.
사회·경제정세와의 관련성	밀접한 관련이 있다.	관련이 적다.
범인의 신분	범인의 지능이 높고 사회적 신분이 높다.	서민층이 대부분이다.
범행의 외적 성격	범행 피해가 잠재적이다.	피해가 뚜렷하다.

피해규모	피해자・피해지역・피해액이 크다.	피해자가 특정 개인인 경우가 많다.
증거인멸	계획적으로 증거인멸이 이루어지므로 채증(증거의 채집)이 어렵다.	대부분 범죄현장에 물적 증거가 남아 있다.
적용 법령	범위가 넓다.	범위가 좁다.
수사착수시기	신중한 검토 후 착수한다.	신속히 착수한다.

출처: 이순래 외, 현대사회와 범죄, 청목출판사, 2012:315.

제 12 장 조직범죄

제1절 조직범죄의 의의

1. 조직범죄의 개념[1)]

1) 범죄실무가들의 정의

(1) 미국연방조직범죄규제법(Organized Crime Control Act of 1970)은 조직범죄는 복잡한 조직구조를 이용하여 불법적인 활동에 연루되는 것을 피하는 두목과 자체규범을 준수하는 조직원으로 구성되어, 질서정연하고 체계적인 공모에 의하여 활동하는 범죄조직의 형태로 보고 있다.[2)] 또한 영속성 · 조직성 · 규범의 존재 · 뇌물수수를 기본요건으로 한다고 규정하고 있다.

- 조직범죄는 필요에 따라 전적으로 또는 부분적으로 불법적이며 은폐된 수단과 적법한 수단을 사용하여 금전적 · 상업적인 이윤을 얻고 뇌물수수를 통하여 자체의 활동을 보호하는 것을 목적으로 하는 조직이다.

(2) 1978년 펜실베이니아 범죄위원회(Pennsylvania Crime Commission)는 조직범죄를 "도박 · 매춘 · 고리대금 · 노동착취 · 범죄적 모의 · 기타 불법적 활동 등의 불법상품과 서비스를 불법거래하는 불법적인 활동으로써, 사기와 강압적인 수단을 사용하고 부적절하게 정부에 영향력을 행사하여 경제적 이익을 극대화시키는 것을 목적으로 하고 있다"고 정의하고 있다.

(3) 1983년 조직범죄에 대한 대통령위원회(The President's Commission on Organized

---

1) 전대양 · 송병호, 조직범죄론, 형설출판사, 2004:19-27.
2) U. S. Organized Crime Control Act of 1970.

Crime : PCOC)는 범죄조직은 불법적인 이익과 권력을 추구하기 위하여 협박, 기타 필요하다면 복잡한 재정적인 조작을 통하여 형법에 위반하는 것을 주로 하는 사람들의 집단을 모두 포함한다고 하였다.

2) 범죄학자들의 정의

- 서덜랜드(Edwin H. Sutherland)는 저서 『화이트칼라 범죄(White Collar Crime)』에서 화이트칼라 범죄가 곧 조직범죄화되고 있다고 하였다.[3] 또한 조직범죄를 기업이 소비자 · 경쟁자 · 주주 · 투자자 · 발명가 · 고용인이나 국가에 대해서 행하는 모든 범죄라고 정의하고 있다.
- 블록(Alan Block)과 챔블리스(William Chambliss)는 조직범죄를 폭력 · 공갈 · 강요 · 약탈 · 마약밀매 · 사기도박 · 고리대금 · 매춘 등 비윤리적 행위를 관리하고 조종하는 위법한 행위로 보았다.[4]
- 스미스(Dwight Smith)는 저서 『마피아의 신비(The Mafia Mystique)』에서, 조직범죄의 경제적 의미를 중시하여 "이윤을 추구하는 불법한 기업이 잠재적인 불법한 수요를 충족시키기 위하여 그 활동범위를 공개된 합법시장으로 확장시키며 행하는 범죄"라고 하였다.
- 이아니(Francis Ianni)는 조직범죄 또는 적어도 이탈리아계 미국인의 조직범죄는 현대의 관료주의와는 무관한 가치와 행동체계로 구성된 전통적 사회체계로서 그들 조직을 혈연조직망론으로 설명하고 있다.
- 일반적인 조직범죄의 정의를 보면 "조직범죄는 상당한 대중적 수요가 있는 불법활동으로부터 이득을 얻기 위해 합리적으로 움직이는 지속적인 범죄활동으로, 조직의 존속은 무력 · 위협의 사용, 공무원의 부패 등을 통해 유지되는 특성을 갖는다"는 것이다.[5]

---

3) Edwin H. Sutherland, White Collar Crime, N.Y. : Dryden Press, 1969:9.

4) 블록은 조직범죄는 기업적 신디케이트와 힘의 신디케이트라는 2가지의 특수한 형태를 가진다고 하였다. "기업적 신디케이트"는 도박 · 매춘 · 마약 등의 불법상품과 서비스를 제공하는 조직범죄이고, "힘의 신디케이트"는 폭력 등의 힘을 사용하는 덜 구조화되고 유연한 조직을 말한다. 챔블리스는 조직범죄를 통제시스템 없이 정치적 · 경제적 · 사회적 급변에 적응하기 위한 조직으로 보았다. 전문사기 · 오토바이강도 등은 조직범죄에서 제외하였다. Alan Block & William Chambliss, Organized Crime, Elsevier Science, 1982:12.

- 하겐(Frank E. Hagan)은 1983년, 조직범죄의 개념정의에 동원된 특성들을 지적하면서[6] 조직범죄는 i) 조직적 위계질서의 지속, ii) 범죄를 통한 이익추구, iii) 이를 위한 무력의 사용이나 위협, iv) 면책을 위한 매수, v) 용역에 대한 공공수요 등의 특성을 갖는다고 하고 있다.[7]
- 탈이데올로기성(non-ideology)과 불법적 이득(illegal economic profit), 폭력(violence), 조직성(membership) 등이 중요한 요소이다. 즉, 조직범죄는 경제적 이득의 추구가 제1의 속성이므로 정치적 성격을 배제하며, 경제적 이득은 불법적 방법으로 획득하고, 비폭력적 수단으로 목적을 달성할 수 없을 때에는 언제라도 폭력을 사용하며, 이를 위해 조직을 형성하고 조직 내 위계질서를 유지하여 조직의 영속성을 보장한다는 것이다.[8]

구 분	조직범죄의 내용
비이념적	• 테러조직들과는 달리 정치적 목적이 없다.
계급조직	• 자체질서의 유지 목적
지속적	• 조직원 결원 시 즉시 대치
제한적이며 배타적인 조직원	• 민족 · 혈연 · 인종 · 동료 등의 동질성 유지
불법적인 폭력과 뇌물의 사용	• 폭력은 규율을 추종케 하는 수단이자 의도전달수단, 뇌물은 기업운영 및 비밀유지수단
업무의 분화	• 조직목표의 달성을 위한 분업화된 특수업무 수행
독점적	• '독점'을 통해 자유거래를 제한하여 이익을 극대화
비밀엄수를 포함한 규율에의 복종	• 합법적인 사업의 성공을 위한 조직원 규합 목적

5) Jay Albanese, Organized Crime in America, Cininnati : Anderson, 1989:5.
6) • 계층구조의 지속(organized hierarchy continuing), 범죄를 통한 이윤추구(rational profit crime), 폭력 및 협박의 행사(use of force or threat), 면책을 위한 부정 · 부패(corruption to maintain immunity), 서비스에 대한 수요 존재(public demand for services), 특정시장을 통한 독점(monopoly over particular market), 제한된 구성원(restrected membership), 비이념적(non–ideological), 전문화(specialization), 비밀주의(code of secrecy), 광범위한 기획(extensive plan)
• 최인섭, "조직범죄의 특성과 실태", 제12회 형사정책세미나자료, 한국형사정책연구원, 1994:15.
7) Frank E. Hagan, "The Organized Crime Continuum : A Further Specification of a New Conceptual", Criminal Justice Review, 8, 1983:52.
8) Dennis J. Kenny & James O. Finckenauer, Organized Crime in America, Belmont, CA : Wadsworth Publishing Company, 1995:3–6.

3) 우리나라의 정의

(1) 현행 형법에 의하면 조직범죄는 범죄단체 내지 범죄조직에 의해서 저질러지는 범죄, 즉 범죄를 범할 목적으로 구성된 다수인이 통솔체계를 갖춘 조직으로 수행하는 범죄라고 정의할 수 있다.9)

- 현행법규에서 조직범죄를 규정하고 있는 것으로는 형법 제114조 제1항, 폭력행위 등 처벌에 관한 법률 제4조, 특정 범죄 가중처벌 등에 관한 법률 제5조 등이 있는데, 이 중 가장 기본이 되는 것은 일반법인 형법 제144조 제1항이다.

제114조(범죄단체의 조직) ① 범죄를 목적으로 하는 단체를 조직하거나 이에 가입한 자는 그 목적한 죄에 정한 형으로 처단한다. 단, 형을 감경할 수 있다.
② 병역 또는 납세의 의무를 거부할 목적으로 단체를 조직하거나 이에 가입한 자는 10년 이하의 징역이나 금고 또는 1천500만원 이하의 벌금에 처한다. 〈개정 1995.12.29〉
③ 전2항의 죄를 범하여 유기의 징역이나 금고 또는 벌금에 처한 자에 대하여는 10년 이하의 자격정지를 병과할 수 있다.

제4조(단체 등의 구성·활동 〈개정 1993.12.10〉**)** ① 이 법에 규정된 범죄를 목적으로 한 단체 또는 집단을 구성하거나 그러한 단체 또는 집단에 가입하거나 그 구성원으로 활동한 자는 다음의 구별에 의하여 처벌한다. 〈개정 1990.12.31, 1993.12.10, 2006.3.24〉
1. 수괴는 사형, 무기 또는 10년 이상의 징역에 처한다.
2. 간부는 무기 또는 7년 이상의 징역에 처한다.
3. 그 외의 자는 2년 이상의 유기징역에 처한다.

② 제1항의 단체 또는 집단을 구성하거나 그러한 단체 또는 집단에 가입한 자가 단체 또는 집단의 위력을 과시하거나 단체 또는 집단의 존속·유지를 위하여 다음 각호의 1의 행위를 한 때에는 그 죄에 대한 형의 장기 및 단기의 2분의 1까지 가중한다. 〈신설 1993.12.10, 2006.3.24〉
1. 「형법」 제8장 공무방해에 관한 죄중 제136조(공무집행방해)·제141조(공용서류 등의 무효·공용물의 파괴)의 죄, 동법 제24장 살인의 죄중 제250조제1항(살인)·제252조(촉탁, 승낙에 의한 살인등)·제253조(위계 등에 의한 촉탁살인 등)·제255조(예비, 음모)의 죄, 동법 제34장 신용, 업무와 경매에 관한 죄중 제314조(업무방해)·제315조(경매, 입찰의 방해)의 죄, 동법 제38장 절도와 강도의 죄 중 제333조(강도)·제334조(특수강도)·제335조(준강도)·제336조(약취강도)·제337조(강도상해, 치상)·제339조(강도강간)·제340조제1항

9) 박재오, "조직폭력의 문제점과 근절방안", 강력검사연구논문집(Ⅳ), 대검찰청, 1994:23.

(해상강도) 및 제2항(해상강도상해, 치상) · 제341조(상습범) · 제343조(예비, 음모)의 죄를 범한 자
2. 이 법 제2조 또는 제3조의 죄를 범한 자
③ 타인에게 제1항의 단체 또는 집단에 가입할 것을 강요하거나 권유한 자는 2년 이상의 유기징역에 처한다. 〈신설 1993.12.10〉
④ 제1항의 단체 또는 집단을 구성하거나 그러한 단체 또는 집단에 가입하여 단체 또는 집단의 존속 · 유지를 위하여 금품을 모집한 자는 3년 이상의 유기징역에 처한다. 〈신설 1993.12.10〉

(2) 대법원 판례에 의하면 범죄단체를 "특정다수인이 특정한 범죄를 범할 공동목적하에서 이루어진 계속적인 결합체로서 그 단체를 주도하는 최소한의 통솔체계를 갖춘 것"이라고 정의하고 있다.[10)]

(3) 이상현은 조직범죄는 "범죄를 범할 목적으로 한 사람 이상의 범죄자가 서로 연합하여 저지른 범죄로, 그 목적은 정치적이거나 경제적인 이익을 위한 것이며, 정치적으로는 현존질서의 파괴에, 경제적으로는 합법적인 사업과 비합법적인 사업을 모두 이용하는 범죄"로 보고 있다.[11)]

2. 조직범죄의 특징[12)]

1) 조직

(1) 일정한 조직

- 조직범죄는 조직 · 기능 · 권위 등에서 회사조직과 유사하다.
- 조직범죄는 관료조직을 유지하기 위해 특별한 논공행상과 승진체계[13)]를 갖는다.
- 조직범죄는 목표를 달성하기 위해 구성원 사이에 계층적 질서를 확립하고 그 사이에서 전문화와 분업화가 이루어진다.

10) 대법원 1976.4.13 선고 76도 340 판결, 1977.1.27 선고 77도 3469 판결.
11) 이상현, 범죄심리학, 박영사, 2004:258.
12) 전대양 · 송병호, 조직범죄론, 형설출판사, 2004:49-63.
13) 교도소나 소년원에 수감되는 전과가 그 조직에서 승진의 기회가 되는 경우이다.

- 위반자에 대한 엄격한 제재수단을 보유하는 등 직업적 부문화(occupational subculture)가 발달되어 있다.[14]

(2) 관료제적 조직

조직범죄는 특정한 목적을 달성하기 위해 의식적으로 구성되는 합리성과 지속적인 운영체계 및 공적 조직을 가진다.

(3) 의사(擬似) 혈연적 조직

조직 내의 맹목적 충성과 상호보호를 위해서 혈연공동체로 발전했다.

2) 활동

(1) 경제적 이익의 추구

- 조직범죄활동은 한마디로 합법적 · 비합법적 활동을 모두 포함한다.
- 조직범죄는 경제적 이익의 추구를 최고의 목적으로 한다.[15]
- 합법적 사업보다는 불법적 사업을 추구하게 되기에 주로 지하불법경제를 이용하게 된다.

(2) 광범위한 비호세력의 존재

조직범죄는 그들의 활동을 보호해 주는 비호세력을 갖고 있다. 비호세력은 조직범죄를 이용하여 자신들의 이익을 얻고 그 대가로 범죄조직을 합법적인 조직인 것처럼 가장해 주거나 법집행으로부터 보호해 주는 주변집단이다.

(3) 수단의 다양성

조직범죄는 활동영역이 넓고 그 수단도 매우 다양하다. 조직범죄의 고전적인 불법활동은 고리대금업 · 도박장운영 · 마약거래 · 이득갈취 · 공직자매수 · 매춘 등이었으나, 최근에는 유흥업소경영 · 주류도매상경영 · 연예인공급사업독점 · 사채업관여 · 부동산업계진출 · 건설업계침투 · 기업상대갈취 · 노사분규개입 · 종교분쟁개입 · 선거운동개입

14) John A. Mack, "The Organized and Professional Labels Criticized", International Journal of Crime and Penology, 1, 1973:295.
15) Donald Cressey, Theft of the Nations, Harper Torchbooks, 1977:72–108.

등이 새로이 부각되고 있다.[16)]

(4) 범죄모의의 은밀성

조직범죄는 대부분이 사전에 계획적으로 이루어진다.[17)] 즉, 범행모의가 사전에 은밀히 이루어지고 관료제적 내부조직체계를 통하여 범행지시가 내려간다.

3) 수단

조직범죄집단은 그 조직의 유지 및 활동을 위하여 폭력·공갈·협박 등을 주로 사용한다. 폭력의 사용은 집단내부의 기강확립이나 외부에의 세력권 확대 등을 위하여 수시로 사용된다.

(1) 일반인 상대 폭력

조직폭력배가 자신들의 목적달성을 위하여 일반적으로 자행하는 폭력을 말한다.

(2) 조직 사이의 폭력

조직적인 집단투쟁행위로 조직구성원의 행동방식이나 기여도가 조직 내에서 구성원의 지위를 결정하며, 더 나아가 폭력조직의 존속 및 확장여부를 결정짓는 중요한 요소로 작용하게 된다.

(3) 조직 내의 폭력

조직폭력배들은 조직 내의 질서를 유지하기 위해서도 폭력을 사용한다.

4) 해악성

- 사회전반에 걸쳐 불안감이 고조되어 국민들의 일상생활이 위축된다.
- 공권력의 위신이 실추되어 사회질서를 유지하기가 곤란해진다.
- 범죄조직을 비호하는 공직자가 생겨나고 공직자사회 전체가 부조리의 온상이 된다.
- 자유경쟁질서의 붕괴로 국가경제질서가 중대한 위기를 맞게 된다.

16) 고건호, "폭력조직의 활동영역과 대책", 강력검사연구논문집(Ⅳ), 대검찰청, 1994:56-62.
17) 김주현, "조직범죄수사에 필요한 제도개선방향에 관한 소고", 강력검사연구논문집(Ⅳ), 대검찰청, 1994:100.

- 불법자금이 정치부문으로 유입되어 정치인이 조직범죄의 하수인이 된다.
- 불법자금의 언론으로의 유입으로 여론형성이 오도될 수 있다.
- 청소년들이 폭력세계를 동경하는 등 타락의 길로 인도하게 된다.[18)]

〈조직범죄의 특징〉

구분	내용
Abadinsky 2012 기출	• 정치적 목적이나 이해관계가 개입되지 않으며, 일부 정치적 참여는 자신들의 보호나 면책을 위한 수단에 지나지 않는 비이념적인 특징을 가지고 있다. • 매우 위계적 · 계층적이다. • 조직구성원이 매우 제한적이며 배타적이다. • 조직활동이나 구성원의 참여가 거의 영구적일 정도로 영속적이다. • 목표달성을 쉽고 빠르게 하기 위하여 불법적 폭력과 뇌물을 활용한다. • 전문성에 따라 또는 조직 내 위치에 따라 임무와 역할이 철저하게 분업화되고 전문화되어 있다. • 이익을 증대시키기 위하여 폭력을 사용하거나 관료를 매수하는 등의 방법으로 특정지역이나 사업분야를 독점한다. • 합법적 조직과 마찬가지로 조직의 규칙과 규정에 의해 통제된다.
Haskell과 Yablonsky	• 대기업이나 군대와 유사한 계층구조를 가지고 있다. • 통상 무력을 사용하거나 무력으로 위협한다. • 기업운영, 인사관리, 정치인과 경찰과의 관계, 이익배분 등에 관한 철저한 계획을 한다. • 비교적 형사처벌로부터 면책되는 경우가 많다. • 관련된 집단의 지도자들끼리 상호 맞물려 있다.

18) • 사회적 측면에서는 조직범죄가 마약류 · 향정신성 의약품 등을 유통시켜 사회의 건강을 해치고 개인과 가정 나아가서 사회 전체의 안전유지를 위한 상품과 서비스의 구입비용을 증대시킨다. 그리고 질서 및 풍속을 저해하거나 서민생활을 침해한다.
• 경제적 측면에서는 조직범죄의 암거래로 인한 불법수익의 획득과 세금포탈 등으로 시장경제질서를 위협하고 국가재정을 해한다. 아울러 경제계에 침투해서 폭력을 행사하여 업무를 방해하거나 폭력을 수단으로 이익을 노린다.
• 정치적 측면에서는 조직범죄집단이 정부기관에의 영향력 행사, 공직매수, 선거운동에의 개입 등을 통해 정치와 정부에 대한 불신을 가져오는 등 사회 전체에 대하여 적지 않은 영향을 미친다. 그리고 정치활동에 폭력을 행사하거나 정치적 조직폭력과 테러행위를 자행한다.

3. 조직범죄의 활동범위

1) 일반적 활동범위[19)]

조직범죄의 활동범위로는 불법서비스의 제공・불법상품의 제공・음모・합법적 사업으로의 확장・강탈・매수 등을 들 수 있다.[20)]

① 불법서비스의 제공(provision of illicit services): 불법적인 서비스란 법률 등으로 금지되어 합법적인 기업들이 제공하지 않거나 않으려는 도박장의 운영이나 보호세의 징수・고리 대금업・매춘 등을 제공하는 것이다.

② 불법상품의 제공(provision of illicit goods): 합법적인 사회에서 통용될 수 없는 것으로 악과 관련된(vice-related) 상품을 제공하는 것이다.[21)]

③ 범죄행위자들의 공모(conspiracy): 마약거래・장물처리・고리대금・도박 등의 행위 시에 불법적인 합의 즉, 공모가 필수적으로 수반된다.

④ 자금원을 숨기거나 합법적인 사업에 의한 수입임을 가장: 합법적 사업은 조직범죄의 불법적인 수입원을 감출 수 있고, 시민들의 의심이나 형사사법기관의 수사를 피할 수 있게 한다.

⑤ 조직범죄가 합법적인 사업으로 확장하는 과정은 주로 강탈(extortion): 강탈이란 절도의 형식 즉, 남의 물건을 가져가는 것과 그 가져가는 방식이 폭력이나 물리적 강제력을 사용한다는 데 있다.

⑥ 비호세력에 대한 매수(corruption): 법집행기관의 공무원・시장・은행원・변호사・회계사・정치인 등과 같은 공적 혹은 사적인 인물들을 매수한다.

2) 우리나라 조직범죄의 활동유형

우리나라의 경우에는 ⅰ) 유흥업소의 주도권을 쟁탈하기 위한 폭력조직의 물리력 행사 등을 행하는 조직폭력사범(organized violence), ⅱ) 무기・마약・장기 등을 거래하는 불법

19) 일반적 활동영역으로는 매춘, 카지노, 마약 등이 있다. 2009 기출
20) Michael D. Lyman & Gary W. Potter, op. cit., pp. 9-10.
21) 특히 암시장에서 가장 많이 불법거래되는 것이 마리화나(marijuana)・코카인(cocaine)・헤로인(heroin) 같은 마약이다. 매춘업을 위해 부녀를 인신매매하고, 그 부산물로 제작된 포르노그래피를 암시장에 유통시키며, 매년 등록되지 않은 권총 등 불법무기를 제공하며, 합법적인 시장에 유통시킬 수 없는 장물들의 유통도 조직범죄의 몫이라고 한다.

거래사범(illicit trafficking), iii) 마약이나 주류 등의 불법제조행위를 행하는 불법제조사범(illegal manufacture), iv) 불법 오락실 · 투기장 개장 등을 행하는 도박(gambling), v) 윤락조직의 대규모 · 조직원 운영에 관련된 매춘(prostitution), vi) 관련 공직자에게 범죄의 묵인 · 정보제공의 대가로 제공하는 금품거래와 관련된 증뢰(bribery of government officials), vii) 이념단체(ideological organization)나 범죄단체가 특정목적을 위하여 사회의 혼란을 기도하는 물리력 행사 행위와 관련된 테러(terror) 등으로 분류하고 있다.

4. 조직범죄의 통제전략과 국제협력[22]

1) 조직범죄 규제법규의 완비

(1) 조직범죄의 입법적 대응방안

부정수익의 몰수제도와 자금세탁의 규제문제, 조직폭력의 각종 자금취득 활동의 근절방안, 공직부패의 방지대책, 피해자(증인)보호의 강화방안, 도청과 정보협력자의 활동, 새로운 수사기법의 도입 등을 반영한 종합적인 대조직폭력범죄 규제법령의 제정이 필요하다.[23]

(2) 자금세탁 규제법규의 제정

금융정보 등을 수사기관이 적절히 활용할 수 있는 방안, 금융기관의 임직원이 일정한 거래를 당국에 보고한 사실이나 자료의 열람 · 등사 · 제출 사실 등을 거래 당사자에게 누설하는 것을 금지하는 제도, 고객 및 수익자의 신원확인, 관계서류의 보존, 의심스러운 거래 등의 통보에 관한 제도 등이 마련되어야 한다.

(3) 증인 · 피해자 보호제도의 강화

피해자나 참고인 등의 조직폭력 범죄자와의 대질이나 그 면전에서의 증언이 지양되어야 하고, 조직폭력 범죄자의 보복으로부터 보호하는 제도의 제정이 필요하다.

---

22) • 전대양 · 송병호, 조직범죄론, 형설출판사, 2004:376-396.
• 조직범죄에 대한 양형 및 처우상의 대책으로는 과학적 수사기법 개발과 엄정한 형벌의 적용, 불법자금원의 차단, 피해자와 신고자의 보호 등이 있다. 2005 기출

23) 고건호, 전게논문, pp. 62-63.

(4) 부정수익몰수제도의 도입

조직폭력범죄의 경제적 기반이 되는 범죄수익을 박탈하는 것이 가장 효과적인 방법이다.

2) 규제활동의 강화

(1) 조직범죄 서식환경의 정비

- 조직폭력범죄가 서식하기 쉬운 주변 환경에 대한 집중적인 정비를 실시하여 조직폭력범죄가 기생하지 못하도록 하여야 할 것이다.
- 관계기관과 단속대상 업주 간에 유착의 의혹이 없도록 엄정한 단속과 함께 업주 스스로 조직폭력의 취업요구나 금품요구를 거부하는 풍토를 조성하여야 할 것이다.
- 비호세력에 대한 수사를 철저히 하여 강력한 처벌이 뒤따라야 할 것이며, 조직폭력범죄에 대한 배제활동은 시민 한 사람 한 사람이 보다 현실적으로 조직폭력범죄에 대한 위기감・해악감을 갖게 하는 한편 조직폭력범죄의 공포이미지를 저하시키는 것도 중요하다.

(2) 단속활동의 개선

- 지속적인 정보수집과 계속적인 정보관리, 전국적인 수사체제와 수사기관 간의 정보교환, 지속적 감시 등 전문적・지속적인 대처가 요구된다. 따라서 조직범죄의 수사를 지휘하고 정보를 수집・전파하는 전담부서의 보강이 필요하다.
- 경찰, 검찰 등 수사기관에서는 조직폭력 전담수사요원을 양성하여 전문적으로 조직폭력범죄를 수사하도록 하여야 한다. 조직폭력범죄의 단속에 있어서 군소조직보다는 대형조직에 중점을 두고 지속적・반복적으로 단속활동을 전개해 나가야 한다.

(3) 수사기법의 개선

- 미국의 증인면책제도의 도입을 검토할 필요가 있다.[24)]
- 조직범죄에 대한 효과적인 대책을 위해서 수사기관들은 주거에 대한 감청 내지 도청이 필요하다.
- 사생활 침해를 최대한 억제하면서도 불가피한 경우 예외적으로 도청 등의 수사기법

24) 문영호・정진수, 전게논문, p. 89.

이 활용될 수 있도록 법적 장치가 마련되어야 한다.

(4) 조직범죄자료의 전산화

조직폭력범죄의 체계적인 정보관리를 위하여 모든 자료가 전산화되어야 한다.

3) 형벌과 교정활동의 강화

(1) 형벌주의

조직폭력의 세력을 약화시키기 위해서는 사회방위차원에서 사회에서 장기간 격리시킬 필요가 있다.

(2) 사회복귀를 위한 교정활동

- 출소 후 조직을 이탈하고 정상적인 직업을 가질 수 있도록 하는 것이다.
- 출소 후 직업을 가지고 정상인으로서 생활할 수 있도록 직업훈련에 중점을 두어야 한다. 또한 유관기관과 민간단체에서도 이들에 대한 직업을 위해 제반수단을 강구하여야 할 것이다.[25]

4) 국제공조체제 강화

- 조직범죄의 국제화현상에 효율적으로 대처하기 위해서는 국가 간의 긴밀한 협력이 필수적이다.
- 국제조약과 출입국관리, 국제수사공조절차, 국내외의 법제 및 외국인의 취급 등에 관한 광범위한 지식을 갖춘 전문수사관의 육성이 시급하다.
- 국제적 차원의 수사공조뿐만 아니라 국내 수사기관 상호 간의 공조와 유관기관 간의 협조가 종횡으로 원활하게 이루어질 수 있도록 제도적 장치도 필수적이라 하겠다.

25) 문영호 · 정진수, "조직폭력의 실태와 대책", 한국형사정책연구보고서, 한국형사정책연구원, 1993:136.

제13장 증오 및 스토킹 범죄

제1절 증오범죄

1. 증오범죄(hate crimes)의 의의 2012 기출

- 편견에 기인하여 사람이나 사물에 대하여 불법행위를 하는 것 또는 인종, 종교, 장애, 성적 편향 등에 의해 동기화되는 범죄를 말한다.1)
- 미국, 1990년 증오범죄통제법은 살인, 치사, 강간, 폭력, 위협, 방화, 재물의 파괴나 손괴 등의 범죄를 포함하는 인종·종교·성적 성향·민족에 기초한 편견의 증거가 분명한 범죄라고 규정하고 있다. 예 로마에서의 기독교인에 대한 박해, 유대인에 대한 나치의 최후의 해결, 보스니아에서의 인종청소, 르완다에서의 대량학살, 미국에서의 흑인에 대한 백인우월주의자들의 공격, 독일에서의 우익폭력이나 외국인을 증오하는 폭력, LA에서의 한국인에 대한 폭동

2. 특징

- 비합리성 : 합리적 사고로는 범죄의 이유나 목적을 파악하기 어렵다.
- 잔인성 : 원한과 같은 감정에 기인한 범죄이기에 불필요하게 과도한 폭력이나 극단적인 잔인성이 표출되는 경향이 있다.2)

---

1) • 김진혁, 한국형 증오범죄에 관한 연구, 2010:31-57.
 • 증오범죄는 특정집단에 대한 편견에 의하여 동기화된 범죄이다. 2009 기출

2) 증오범죄의 보편적 특징은 주로 낯선 사람, 절반 이상이 20세 미만자에 의해 저질러지며, 신체적 폭력을 동반하는 경우가 많기 때문에 상당히 잔인하며 통상적인 범죄의 공격에 비해 매우 심각한 부상을 초래하게 된다. 이윤호, 범죄학, 박영사, 2007:159.

- 대량성 : 피해대상 전체 또는 불특정다수 전체를 공격대상으로 삼기 때문에 피해자가 대량으로 발생할 수 있다. 예 폭탄테러
- 무차별성 : 피해대상이 특정집단이나 특정인으로 확정되지 않는 경향이 있다.
- 지속성 : KKK단의 경우처럼 세대를 이어서 범죄가 되물림되는 경우가 있다.
- 모방성 : 유사한 범죄가 일시에 확산되는 경향을 볼 수 있다. 예 알 카에다와 같은 아랍권의 테러가 감행되었을 때 불특정 중동인들이 동시다발적인 위협에 노출되는 경우
- 보복범죄의 유발 : 피해집단이나 피해자가 다시 범죄자로 전환되는 경우이다.

3. 유형

1) 신념형 : 개인이나 집단의 편향된 신념에 의하여 특정대상에 물리적 · 정신적 · 재산적 피해를 가하는 유형 예 Ku Klux Klan의 KKK단은 120년의 역사, 스킨헤드족
2) 복수형: 여성에게 박대받았다고 생각하여 여성만을 대상으로 범행을 저지르는 강간범 · 살인범, 경제적 상류층을 대상으로 한 강도 · 살인
3) 무연관형: 적절한 대상 없는 증오 또는 이유 없는 증오 예 일본의 은둔형 증오범죄[3)]

4. 증오집단에 대한 법률적 대치

1) 특정의 위협적 행동을 금지함 예 미국, 종교적 장소에서의 의도적 방해나 기물파손 등 금지, 십자가를 불태우거나 위협할 의도로 타인의 재물에 표식이나 상징 등 부착금지
2) 편견에 의하여 동기지어진 일반적 행동의 금기 예 뉴욕, 증오범죄법 – 편견에 의하여 동기지어진 차별이나 희롱 등 금지
3) 편견에 의하여 동기지어진 범죄행동에 대한 처벌 예 최고의 형으로 처벌

3) '아카하바라 살인사건'(2008.6.8)은 단지 사람을 죽이고 싶었다며 7명을 숨지게 하고 10명에게 부상을 입혔다. 도쿄 지요다구(區) 아키하바라 전차교차로에서 2톤 트럭이 돌진하여 보행자를 덮쳤다. 차에서 내린 범인은 등산용 칼로 길가는 행인을 무차별하게 공격하였다. 연합뉴스, 2008.12.12.

제2절 스토킹범죄

1. 스토킹(미행: stalking)의 의의

1) 스토킹의 의의

- 스토킹은 일정기간 동안 의도적·반복적으로 행하여 정상적인 판단능력이 있는 일반인이라면 누구나 공포나 불안을 느낄 만한 일련의 행동으로 특정인이나 그 가족들에게 정신적·육체적 피해를 입히는 일방적이고 병적인 행동을 말한다.
- 1990년, 미국, 미행금지법을 제정함 예 미국, 여배우인 Rebecca Schaffer는 그녀를 추종하던 남성팬에 의해 살해됨
- 결별폭행(separation assault)은 여성을 떠나게 할 의사가 없는 남성이 여성의 뒤를 추적하고 위협하여 괴롭히거나 폭행하는 것을 말한다.

2) 스토킹의 법률적 논점과 특성

(1) 미행과 미행자의 특성

미행자의 행위가 시간이 갈수록 그리고 횟수가 늘어날수록 점점 더 위협적이고 심각하며 폭력적으로 되어간다.

(2) 스토킹의 법률적 요소

- 행위의 연속성 : 일련의 미행행위가 연속적으로 이루어져서 종횡적으로 보아 일정한 행동유형을 보여주는 것을 전제로 한다.
- 위협의 요건 : 미행자가 피해자에게 합리적인 사람이라면 누구나 두려움을 느끼게 되는 정도나 방법으로 행동하거나 위협을 가할 것을 필요로 한다. 예 검은 장미 배달, 손으로 권총 겨냥, 집 앞에 동물시체 배달
- 미행자의 의도 : 피해자에게 공포를 야기하려는 범죄적 의사 즉, 범의(犯意)가 있어야 한다.

2. 특징

1) 스토킹의 특징

- 대부분 안면이 있거나 과거의 친밀한 관계에 있는 자들에 의해서 스토킹이 일어난다.
- 사소한 범행에서 심각한 범행으로 진행한다. 즉, 상대방의 단순한 사생활을 침해하는 정도에서 그치는 것이 아니라 심하면 폭행이나 강간 그리고 살인에 이르는 위험한 범죄행위에까지 이르게 된다.
- 스토킹의 중단은 대체로 피해자가 멀리 떠나버리거나 경찰의 관여가 있을 때 또는 다른 애정대상을 만났을 때 나타나는 경우가 대부분이다.
- 편집증적으로 집착하는 경향이 있으며, 경계성 인격장애 성향을 보이며, 스토킹 기간이 장기간에 걸쳐 이루어진다. 2008 기출

2) 스토커의 특성

- 스토커의 인구통계학적 특성을 보면, 이들의 대다수는 남자들이라는 점이다. 스토커는 대인관계의 미숙이나 결혼 등에 실패한 사람이 대부분이다.
- 스토커의 대다수가 직업이 없거나 직업이 불안정하며 또 스토킹을 하는 시점에 불안정한 직업경력을 가지고 있다.
- 스토커의 교육수준은 평균 이상이다. 스토커가 일반인보다 지능이 높기 때문에 지능적이고 교활하여 스토킹 관련 범죄수사에서 유죄의 입증을 하기가 상당히 어렵다.
- 스토커 중 일부는 심한 정신병으로 편집증, 지나친 소유욕 그리고 매우 불안정한 성격을 가지고 있어 범죄의 우려가 대단히 높다.

제14장 피해자 없는 범죄

제1절 의의

1. 피해자 없는 범죄(victimless crimes)의 의의 2011 기출

- 가해자와 피해자의 관계에서 볼 때, 동일범죄의 가해자가 동시에 피해자가 되어 전통적 가해자와 피해자의 상대적 관계가 형성되지 않는다거나(개인적 차원의 범행) 또는 범죄의 피해자가 특정인이 아닌 불특정 다수인이어서 가해자와의 관계가 분명치 않은 경우(기업차원의 범죄)의 범죄를 말한다.
- 가해자가 동시에 피해자가 되는 범죄인 마약사용 등이 있으며, 피해자가 동의·기여한 범죄인 마약매매, 매춘, 동의낙태, 도박 등이 있다.
- 피해자 없는 범죄는 특별히 개인적으로 피해를 입은 자가 없고 서로 동의하에 저질러진 경우 대개 신고되지 않거나 인지되지 않아 암수범죄가 되기 쉽다.

2. 유형

1) 개인범죄와 기업범죄

- 피해자와 가해자가 동일인인 개인범죄 예 매춘
- 피해자가 불특정 다수인인 기업범죄(corporate crime)[1)]

---

1) • 피해자 없는 범죄는 피해자와 가해자의 관계가 불분명한 것으로써, 특히 피해자가 불특정다수인 기업범죄도 피해자 없는 범죄에 해당된다. 2004 기출
• 피해자 없는 범죄의 유형에는 약물, 매춘, 낙태, 기업범죄 등이 있다. 2007 기출
• 피해자 없는 범죄에는 성매매, 도박, 약물남용 등이 있다. 2009 기출

2) 피해자를 기준으로

- 소비자 : 독과점과 같은 공정거래위반 관련 범죄(antitrust violations), 허위광고(false advertising), 위험물질의 생산과 판매 등
- 일반시민대중 : 환경범죄, 안전위해범죄 등

제2절 성매매

1. 관련 법령

성매매알선 등 행위의 처벌에 관한 법률
[시행 2013.4.5] [법률 제11731호, 2013.4.5, 타법개정]

제2조(정의) ① 이 법에서 사용하는 용어의 뜻은 다음과 같다. 〈개정 2011.9.15〉

1. "성매매"란 불특정인을 상대로 금품이나 그 밖의 재산상의 이익을 수수(收受)하거나 수수하기로 약속하고 다음 각 목의 어느 하나에 해당하는 행위를 하거나 그 상대방이 되는 것을 말한다.
   가. 성교행위
   나. 구강, 항문 등 신체의 일부 또는 도구를 이용한 유사 성교행위
2. "성매매알선 등 행위"란 다음 각 목의 어느 하나에 해당하는 행위를 하는 것을 말한다.
   가. 성매매를 알선, 권유, 유인 또는 강요하는 행위
   나. 성매매의 장소를 제공하는 행위
   다. 성매매에 제공되는 사실을 알면서 자금, 토지 또는 건물을 제공하는 행위
3. "성매매 목적의 인신매매"란 다음 각 목의 어느 하나에 해당하는 행위를 하는 것을 말한다.
   가. 성을 파는 행위 또는 「형법」 제245조에 따른 음란행위를 하게 하거나, 성교행위 등 음란한 내용을 표현하는 사진・영상물 등의 촬영 대상으로 삼을 목적으로 위계(僞計), 위력(威力), 그 밖에 이에 준하는 방법으로 대상자를 지배・관리하면서 제3자에게 인계하는 행위
   나. 가목과 같은 목적으로 「청소년 보호법」 제2조제1호에 따른 청소년(이하 "청소년"이라 한다), 사물을 변별하거나 의사를 결정할 능력이 없거나 미약한 사람 또는 대통령령으로 정하는 중대한 장애가 있는 사람이나 그를 보호・감독하는 사람에게 선불금 등 금품이나 그 밖의 재산상의 이익을 제공하거나 제공하기로 약속하고 대상자

를 지배·관리하면서 제3자에게 인계하는 행위

다. 가목 및 나목의 행위가 행하여지는 것을 알면서 가목과 같은 목적이나 전매를 위하여 대상자를 인계받는 행위

라. 가목부터 다목까지의 행위를 위하여 대상자를 모집·이동·은닉하는 행위

4. "성매매피해자"란 다음 각 목의 어느 하나에 해당하는 사람을 말한다.

가. 위계, 위력, 그 밖에 이에 준하는 방법으로 성매매를 강요당한 사람

나. 업무관계, 고용관계, 그 밖의 관계로 인하여 보호 또는 감독하는 사람에 의하여 「마약류관리에 관한 법률」 제2조에 따른 마약·향정신성의약품 또는 대마(이하 "마약등"이라 한다)에 중독되어 성매매를 한 사람

다. 청소년, 사물을 변별하거나 의사를 결정할 능력이 없거나 미약한 사람 또는 대통령령으로 정하는 중대한 장애가 있는 사람으로서 성매매를 하도록 알선·유인된 사람

라. 성매매 목적의 인신매매를 당한 사람

② 다음 각 호의 어느 하나에 해당하는 경우에는 대상자를 제1항제3호가목에 따른 지배·관리하에 둔 것으로 본다.

1. 선불금 제공 등의 방법으로 대상자의 동의를 받은 경우라도 그 의사에 반하여 이탈을 제지한 경우

2. 다른 사람을 고용·감독하는 사람, 출입국·직업을 알선하는 사람 또는 그를 보조하는 사람이 성을 파는 행위를 하게 할 목적으로 여권이나 여권을 갈음하는 증명서를 채무이행 확보 등의 명목으로 받은 경우

[전문개정 2011.5.23]

제18조(벌칙) ① 다음 각 호의 어느 하나에 해당하는 사람은 10년 이하의 징역 또는 1억원 이하의 벌금에 처한다.

1. 폭행이나 협박으로 성을 파는 행위를 하게 한 사람

2. 위계 또는 이에 준하는 방법으로 성을 파는 사람을 곤경에 빠뜨려 성을 파는 행위를 하게 한 사람

3. 친족관계, 고용관계, 그 밖의 관계로 인하여 다른 사람을 보호·감독하는 것을 이용하여 성을 파는 행위를 하게 한 사람

4. 위계 또는 위력으로 성교행위 등 음란한 내용을 표현하는 영상물 등을 촬영한 사람

② 다음 각 호의 어느 하나에 해당하는 사람은 1년 이상의 유기징역에 처한다.

1. 제1항의 죄(미수범을 포함한다)를 범하고 그 대가의 전부 또는 일부를 받거나 이를 요구·약속한 사람

2. 위계 또는 위력으로 청소년, 사물을 변별하거나 의사를 결정할 능력이 없거나 미약한

사람 또는 대통령령으로 정하는 중대한 장애가 있는 사람으로 하여금 성을 파는 행위를 하게 한 사람

3. 「폭력행위 등 처벌에 관한 법률」 제4조에 규정된 단체나 집단의 구성원으로서 제1항의 죄를 범한 사람

③ 다음 각 호의 어느 하나에 해당하는 사람은 3년 이상의 유기징역에 처한다.

1. 다른 사람을 감금하거나 단체 또는 다중(多衆)의 위력을 보이는 방법으로 성매매를 강요한 사람
2. 성을 파는 행위를 하였거나 할 사람을 고용·관리하는 것을 이용하여 위계 또는 위력으로 낙태하게 하거나 불임시술을 받게 한 사람
3. 삭제 〈2013.4.5〉
4. 「폭력행위 등 처벌에 관한 법률」 제4조에 규정된 단체나 집단의 구성원으로서 제2항제1호 또는 제2호의 죄를 범한 사람

④ 다음 각 호의 어느 하나에 해당하는 사람은 5년 이상의 유기징역에 처한다.

1. 업무관계, 고용관계, 그 밖의 관계로 인하여 보호 또는 감독을 받는 사람에게 마약 등을 사용하여 성을 파는 행위를 하게 한 사람
2. 「폭력행위 등 처벌에 관한 법률」 제4조에 규정된 단체나 집단의 구성원으로서 제3항제1호부터 제3호까지의 죄를 범한 사람

[전문개정 2011.5.23]

제19조(벌칙) ① 다음 각 호의 어느 하나에 해당하는 사람은 3년 이하의 징역 또는 3천만원 이하의 벌금에 처한다.

1. 성매매알선 등 행위를 한 사람
2. 성을 파는 행위를 할 사람을 모집한 사람
3. 성을 파는 행위를 하도록 직업을 소개·알선한 사람

② 다음 각 호의 어느 하나에 해당하는 사람은 7년 이하의 징역 또는 7천만원 이하의 벌금에 처한다.

1. 영업으로 성매매알선 등 행위를 한 사람
2. 성을 파는 행위를 할 사람을 모집하고 그 대가를 지급받은 사람
3. 성을 파는 행위를 하도록 직업을 소개·알선하고 그 대가를 지급받은 사람

[전문개정 2011.5.23]

제20조(벌칙) ① 다음 각 호의 어느 하나에 해당하는 사람은 3년 이하의 징역 또는 3천만원 이하의 벌금에 처한다.

1. 성을 파는 행위 또는 「형법」 제245조에 따른 음란행위 등을 하도록 직업을 소개·알선

할 목적으로 광고(각종 간행물, 유인물, 전화, 인터넷, 그 밖의 매체를 통한 행위를 포함한다. 이하 같다)를 한 사람

2. 성매매 또는 성매매알선 등 행위가 행하여지는 업소에 대한 광고를 한 사람

3. 성을 사는 행위를 권유하거나 유인하는 광고를 한 사람

② 영업으로 제1항에 따른 광고물을 제작·공급하거나 광고를 게재한 사람은 2년 이하의 징역 또는 1천만원 이하의 벌금에 처한다.

③ 영업으로 제1항에 따른 광고물이나 광고가 게재된 출판물을 배포한 사람은 1년 이하의 징역 또는 500만원 이하의 벌금에 처한다.

[전문개정 2011.5.23]

제21조(벌칙) ① 성매매를 한 사람은 1년 이하의 징역이나 300만원 이하의 벌금·구류 또는 과료(科料)에 처한다.

② 제7조제3항을 위반한 사람은 500만원 이하의 벌금에 처한다.

[전문개정 2011.5.23]

제22조(범죄단체의 가중처벌) 제18조 또는 제19조에 규정된 범죄를 목적으로 단체 또는 집단을 구성하거나 그러한 단체 또는 집단에 가입한 사람은 「폭력행위 등 처벌에 관한 법률」 제4조의 예에 따라 처벌한다.

[전문개정 2011.5.23]

제23조(미수범) 제18조부터 제20조까지에 규정된 죄의 미수범은 처벌한다.

[전문개정 2011.5.23]

아동·청소년의 성보호에 관한 법률

[시행 2013.6.19] [법률 제11574호, 2012.12.18, 타법개정]

제2조(정의) 이 법에서 사용하는 용어의 뜻은 다음과 같다. 〈개정 2012.12.18〉

1. "아동·청소년"이란 19세 미만의 자를 말한다. 다만, 19세에 도달하는 연도의 1월 1일을 맞이한 자는 제외한다.
2. "아동·청소년대상 성범죄"란 다음 각 목의 어느 하나에 해당하는 죄를 말한다.
   가. 제7조부터 제15조까지의 죄
   나. 아동·청소년에 대한 「성폭력범죄의 처벌 등에 관한 특례법」 제3조부터 제15조까지의 죄
   다. 아동·청소년에 대한 「형법」 제297조, 제297조의2 및 제298조부터 제301조까지, 제301조의2, 제302조, 제303조, 제305조 및 제339조의 죄
   라. 아동·청소년에 대한 「아동복지법」 제17조제2호 및 제4호의 죄

3. “아동·청소년대상 성폭력범죄”란 아동·청소년대상 성범죄에서 제11조부터 제15조까지의 죄를 제외한 죄를 말한다.
4. “아동·청소년의 성을 사는 행위”란 아동·청소년, 아동·청소년의 성(性)을 사는 행위를 알선한 자 또는 아동·청소년을 실질적으로 보호·감독하는 자 등에게 금품이나 그 밖의 재산상 이익, 직무·편의제공 등 대가를 제공하거나 약속하고 다음 각 목의 어느 하나에 해당하는 행위를 아동·청소년을 대상으로 하거나 아동·청소년으로 하여금 하게 하는 것을 말한다.
   가. 성교 행위
   나. 구강·항문 등 신체의 일부나 도구를 이용한 유사 성교 행위
   다. 신체의 전부 또는 일부를 접촉·노출하는 행위로서 일반인의 성적 수치심이나 혐오감을 일으키는 행위
   라. 자위 행위
5. “아동·청소년이용음란물”이란 아동·청소년 또는 아동·청소년으로 명백하게 인식될 수 있는 사람이나 표현물이 등장하여 제4호의 어느 하나에 해당하는 행위를 하거나 그 밖의 성적 행위를 하는 내용을 표현하는 것으로서 필름·비디오물·게임물 또는 컴퓨터나 그 밖의 통신매체를 통한 화상·영상 등의 형태로 된 것을 말한다.
6. “피해아동·청소년”이란 제2호 나목부터 라목까지, 제7조부터 제14조(제13조제1항의 죄는 제외한다)까지의 죄의 피해자가 된 아동·청소년을 말한다.
7. “대상아동·청소년”이란 제13조제1항의 죄의 상대방이 된 아동·청소년을 말한다.
8. “온라인서비스제공자”란 다른 사람들이 정보통신망(「정보통신망 이용촉진 및 정보보호 등에 관한 법률」 제2조제1항제1호의 정보통신망을 말한다. 이하 같다)을 통하여 온라인 자료를 이용할 수 있도록 서비스를 제공하는 자로서 대통령령으로 정하는 자를 말한다.
9. “등록정보”란 법무부장관이 「성폭력범죄의 처벌 등에 관한 특례법」 제42조제1항의 등록대상자에 대하여 같은 법 제44조제1항에 따라 등록한 정보를 말한다.

제13조(아동·청소년의 성을 사는 행위 등) ① 아동·청소년의 성을 사는 행위를 한 자는 1년 이상 10년 이하의 징역 또는 2천만원 이상 5천만원 이하의 벌금에 처한다.
② 아동·청소년의 성을 사기 위하여 아동·청소년을 유인하거나 성을 팔도록 권유한 자는 1년 이하의 징역 또는 1천만원 이하의 벌금에 처한다.

2. 성매매의 유형

<table>
<tr><th colspan="2">구분</th><th colspan="2">정의</th><th>유형</th><th>비고</th></tr>
<tr><td colspan="2" rowspan="2">전통형 성매매</td><td colspan="2" rowspan="2">특정지역을 거점으로 매매춘만을 목적으로 하는 업소에서 이루어짐</td><td>대규모 매춘 집결지</td><td>서울 용산, 청량리588, 천호동, 영등포, 미아리텍사스, 경기도 용주골 등에서 이루어지는 성매매</td></tr>
<tr><td>미군 기지촌</td><td>경기도 용주골</td></tr>
<tr><td colspan="2" rowspan="4">산업형 성매매</td><td rowspan="4">본래의 업소(업종)의 목적과 달리 성매매 행위가 이루어지거나 성매매 행위를 알선함</td><td rowspan="3">서비스를 매개로 업소 내에서 혹은 밖으로 나가서 성매매 행위를 함</td><td>식품접객업소</td><td>대중음식점(카페), 단란주점, 유흥주점(룸싸롱, 외국인 관광클럽)을 통해 이루어지는 성매매</td></tr>
<tr><td>위생접객업소</td><td>호텔이나 여관 등의 숙박업소, 사우나, 증기탕 등의 목욕장 업소, 이발소 등에서 이루어지는 성매매</td></tr>
<tr><td>안마시술소</td><td>안마소에서 안마사 혹은 보조원 등을 통해 이루어지는 성매매</td></tr>
<tr><td>연결(알선)을 통해서 성매매 행위를 함</td><td>이벤트사 성매매</td><td>주부, 직업여성, 미혼여성, 대학생 등을 대상으로 직업상담소, 결혼상담소, 이벤트사 등에서 알선하는 성매매</td></tr>
<tr><td rowspan="6">기타</td><td rowspan="3">매개체/장소가 있는 경우</td><td colspan="2" rowspan="3">일정 매개장소나 매개체가 있어서 매매춘이 이루어짐</td><td>외국인 성매매</td><td>국내에서 취업 중인 외국인들이 업소의 알선으로 하는 성매매</td></tr>
<tr><td>전화방, 폰팅</td><td>전화방 등을 통해 연결되며, 서로 조건이 맞으면 하는 성매매</td></tr>
<tr><td>연예계 성매매</td><td>특정인의 소개로 여자 연예인, 고급 콜걸들이 사회고위층을 상대로 하는 성매매</td></tr>
<tr><td rowspan="3">직접 연결하는 경우</td><td colspan="2" rowspan="3">중간에서 매춘을 연결해주는 사람이 있지 않고 매춘 여성이 직접 매춘 상대자와 연결함(PC 성매매, 길거리 성매매의 경우 10대 청소년들이 행하는 경우가 많음)</td><td>박카스 아줌마, 들병이</td><td>등산객, 운전수, 탑골공원의 노인 등을 대상으로 직접 호객하는 성매매</td></tr>
<tr><td>고속 성매매
거리 성매매</td><td>고속도로나 거리에서 이루어지는 성매매</td></tr>
<tr><td>PC 성매매</td><td>PC를 매개로 하는 성매매</td></tr>
</table>

자료: 변화순 · 황정임(1998), "산업형 매매춘에 관한 연구", 한국여성개발원.

3. 성매매방지를 위한 대책들

전통적으로 성매매를 억제하기 위한 정책은 성판매자에 초점을 두어왔으나, 최근 금지주의(미국, 스웨덴), 비범죄주의(영국), 합법적 규제주의(캐나다) 국가들이 성구매 행위에 제재를 가하는 정책들을 시도하고 있다.

1) "성구매자 재범방지 교육(John School)"

미국, 영국, 캐나다에서 실시되고 있는 "성구매자 재범방지 교육(John School)"은 재범률 감소의 효과를 거두었고, 시행지역을 점차 확대하고 있었다. 교육대상은 주로 "초범자"를 대상으로 하며, 교육시간은 8시간 정도이고 약 25~40명을 대상으로 해당 시의 경찰청에서 한 달에 한번 진행하며, 참가자들에게 집행요금을 내게 한다. 집행요금은 처벌에 준하는 재정적 부담의 효과를 거두는 한편, 집행요금을 성판매 여성을 위한 프로그램 비용에 재투입함으로써 사회적 비용을 절감하는 이중의 효과를 거두고 있다.

〈우리나라의 존스쿨(John School) 교육〉

- 존스쿨(John School) 교육이란 성매매에 대해 규제주의 입장을 취하고 있는 미국의 샌프란시스코에서 비롯된 성구매자 재범방지교육 시스템이다. 미국의 성매매 피해여성 지원단체인 세이지(SAGE)가 1995년부터 초범 성구매자 남성의 의식개혁을 목적으로 실시하고 있는 성매매 재발 예방교육프로그램이다.
- 우리나라는 존스쿨(John School)을 2005년 8월부터 도입하여 서울 보호관찰소 등 전국 보호관찰소에서 확대 실시하고 있다.
- 교육대상은 보호관찰소가 실시하는 성구매자 교육을 이수하는 조건으로 기소유예처분된 자로 주로 성구매 초범자가 대상이다.
- 교육시간은 1일 8시간으로 교육내용은 성매매 행위의 범죄성에 대한 법률적 설명, 성매매의 범죄성과 해악성, 폭력성과 반인권적 측면 고찰, 성매매와 신체・정신 건강과의 연관성, 집단토론, 자기통제계획수립, 소시오 드라마를 통한 성(性)에 대한 이해 등과 교육효과를 측정하기 위해 교육 실시 전과 후의 의식변화에 대한 설문 등으로 구성되어 있다.
- 존스쿨 교육은 남성중심의 왜곡된 성인식을 교정하고 성매매의 범죄성과 반인권성을 인식하게 함으로써 재발을 효과적으로 방지하고자 한다.
- 초범 성구매자들에게 교육이수 조건부 기소유예라는 기회를 주어 형사절차에서 조기에 벗어나 사회에 정상적으로 복귀하도록 하는 효과를 위한 것이다.

2) 신상공개 및 고객창피주기 캠페인

미국 미네소타 등 몇몇 지역에서는 경찰국 홈페이지, 라디오와 신문, 성범죄자 케이블 TV(John TV) 등을 통해 성구매자 신상공개를 실시하고 있었다. 캐나다 밴쿠버에서는 특별수사대가 주축이 되어 성매매 지역에서 발견되는 차량의 사진과 경고성 편지를 발송하는 "고객창피주기" 캠페인이 실시되고 있었다.

3) 성구매자 단속: 미수, 흥정행위 처벌 및 함정수사

미국, 캐나다, 영국, 스웨덴은 성매매 흥정 및 미수행위를 처벌대상에 포함시키고, 미국, 캐나다에서는 단속을 위해 "함정수사"가 이용되고 있었다.

4) 성구매자 상담 서비스 실시

스웨덴 괴테보르그에서는 성구매 남성에 대한 상담과 조정 활동을 실시하고 있었다. 상담 내용에는 남성 구매자의 가족 상담을 포함하고 있었는데, 성매매 문제를 통해 가족 문제를 지원한다.

〈매춘〉

1. 매춘(賣春)의 의의

- 직업으로써 또는 일로써 돈을 받고 성(性)을 교환하는 여성의 행위 즉, 재물이나 금전을 목적으로 하는 성적 교환을 말한다.[2)]
- 태프트(Donald R. Taft)는 저서 『범죄학(Criminology)』에서 매매춘은 "성교행위를 가져야 하며 그 대가로 보수가 있어야 하고, 성교는 불특정인과의 성교여야 한다"고 정의하고 있다.[3)]
- 현행, 우리나라 형법은 제242조, 제288조에서 이에 관해 규정하고 있다.

2) 매매춘은 일반적으로 윤락·매춘·매음·매매춘·매매음 등의 용어로 불리고 있다. 법적인 용어로 '윤락(淪落)'이란 "스스로 타락하여 몸을 버린다"는 의미로 쓰이고 있다. 구 윤락행위 등 방지법에서의 '윤락행위'는 "불특정인을 상대로 금품 기타 재산상의 이익을 받거나 받을 것을 약속하고 성행위를 하는 것"으로 정의하였다.

3) 전대양·송병호, 조직범죄론, 형설출판사, 2004:240-272.

제242조(음행매개) 영리의 목적으로 미성년 또는 음행의 상습없는 부녀를 매개하여 간음하게 한 자는 3년 이하의 징역 또는 1천500만원 이하의 벌금에 처한다. 〈개정 1995.12.29〉

제288조(영리등을 위한 약취, 유인, 매매 등) ① 추행, 간음 또는 영리의 목적으로 사람을 약취 또는 유인한 자는 1년 이상의 유기징역에 처한다.

② 추업에 사용할 목적으로 부녀를 매매한 자도 전항의 형과 같다.

③ 상습으로 전2항의 죄를 범한 자는 2년 이상의 유기징역에 처한다.

2. 매춘의 요인[4]

1) 소인적 요인(predisposing factors)

결손가정, 부모의 난잡함, 매춘을 관용하거나 허용하는 근친사회의 분위기, 정신장애를 유발할 수 있는 노이로제(부모의 학대와 태만, 가정파괴) 등

2) 유인적 요인(attracting factors)

많은 소득, 쉬운 생활, 흥미로운 생활, 성적 만족과 쾌락의 기대(직업으로서 매춘이 갖는 독립성, 경제성, 모험, 성적 만족) 등

3) 촉진적 요인(precipitating factors)

경제적 압박, 바람직한 결혼기회의 부재, 포주로부터의 유혹, 불행한 사랑행각, 좋은 기회 등

3. 매매춘의 분류

전업정도 \ 조직참가정도		상 완전조직	중 불완전조직	하 비조직적 자영업수준
상	• 전업매매춘	• 매음굴 창녀	• 콜걸	• 거리의 창녀, 고속도로 매매춘
중	• 겸업매매춘	• 스트리퍼	• 호스티스, 웨이트리스, 바걸, 댄서	• 안마시술소, 이발관, 증기탕, 다방과 찻집 종업원
하	• 부업매매춘	• 연예인의 부업매매춘	• 각종 이벤트사를 통한 매매춘, 직장인, 여대생 등 부업이나 단지 매춘참가자	• 담요부대, 기타 유흥 접객업소 종업원, 전화방, 폰팅, PC 매매춘

자료: 한국여성개발원(http://pro-web.suwon-c.ac.kr/~honglan/table/m.html).
출처: 전대양·송병호, 조직범죄론, 형설출판사, 2004:245, 재인용.

4) Benjamin과 Masters가 지적한 매춘부가 되는 요인이다.

4. 매매춘의 대책

각국의 성매매정책들은 성매매행위 자체의 처벌여부에 따라 금지주의 · 비범죄주의 · 합법적 규제주의로 분류할 수 있다.[5)]

1) 금지주의(penalization)

- 성매매 자체를 불법한 행위로 간주하며, 성판매자에 대한 처벌을 근간으로 하고 있다.
- 우리나라는 성을 사는 자와 성을 사는 행위의 상대방이 된 자 및 이를 알선한 모두를 처벌함으로써 성매매에 대한 전면적 금지주의를 채택하고 있다.

2) 비범죄주의(abolition)

- 법적으로 성매매행위 자체를 규제하거나 금지하지 않는다.
- 국가에 따라 학교 · 병원 등의 특정지역, 특정시간, 특정유형은 불법으로 간주하기도 하고 세금을 징수하는 등 다양한 정책을 펴고 있으나, 대체로 호객행위 · 광고 등은 불법으로 규제한다.

3) 합법적 규제주의(regulation)

일정한 형태의 성매매를 법적으로 인정하며, 이에 대한 세금을 징수하며 등록증, 의료감시체계를 의무화하거나 특정지역, 특정시간에는 성거래를 통제하는 정책을 취하고 있다. 거리의 성매매의 경우 판매자나 구매자 모두 처벌되는 경우가 많다.

〈표 2-2〉 성매매에 대한 각국의 정책 분류

분류	주요 특징	세부사항	해당 국가	기타
금지주의	• 모든 종류의 성매매행위를 금지하며, 처벌규정을 두고 있음	• 성구매행위만 금지	• 스웨덴	• 필리핀 : 국회법안 상정
		• 성판매행위만 금지	• 일본, 대만, 필리핀	
		• 구매 및 판매행위 금지	• 한국, 중국, 태국, 알바니아, 미국 뉴욕, 샌프란시스코, 워싱턴 등	
비범죄주의	• 성매매행위 자체를 처벌하는 규정은 없음(규제하지도 합법적으로 인정하지도 않음)	• 주로 호객행위, 광고 등을 불법으로 간주	• 프랑스, 영국, 노르웨이, 덴마크, 브라질, 스페인, 폴란드, 핀란드, 이탈리아, 아일랜드, 호주 퀸즐랜드 주 등	• 영국 잉글랜드, 웨일스 : 거리 성매매 구입 행위 금지 • 노르웨이 : 성구매 행위 처벌법 제정

5) 여성부, "성매매방지를 위한 국외사례연구", 정책자료 2001-18, 2001:2.

<table>
<tr><td rowspan="2">합법적 규제주의</td><td rowspan="2">• 일정한 형태의 성매매를 법적으로 인정하고 이에 대한 세금징수, 의료감시체계를 가지며, 활동지역을 규제함</td><td>• 합법적인 직업으로 인정, 영업허가제</td><td>• 네덜란드</td><td rowspan="2">• 캐나다 : 거리 성매매행위(판매・구입・흥정행위) 처벌</td></tr>
<tr><td>• 등록증, 허가증, 건강검진, 세금징수, 특정지역에만 허용</td><td>• 독일, 스위스, 헝가리, 호주 빅토리아 주, 멕시코, 캐나다, 오스트리아, 터키, 미국 네바다 주 등</td></tr>
</table>

자료: 여성부, “성매매방지를 위한 국외대안사례연구”, 정책자료 2001-18, 2001.
출처: 전대양・송병호, 조직범죄론, 형설출판사, 2004:25, 재인용.

제3절 약물범죄[6)]

1. 약물의 종류와 약리효과

천연약물	자연에서 재배해서 얻어지는 것 또는 이것을 원료로 해서 제조되는 약물
합성약물	자연원료를 사용하지 않고 화학적 합성과정을 통해서 얻어지는 약물
대용약물	남용의 목적으로 만들어지지는 않지만 다양한 방법으로 남용되는 약물 예 본드, 신나

1) 천연약물

아편계통, 코카계통, 대마계통의 크게 3가지로 나눌 수 있다.

(1) 아편계통 2012 기출

앵속, 약담배, 아편꽃 등으로 불리는 양귀비(Opium poppy)에서 추출한 것

6) 이순래 외, 현대사회와 범죄, 청목출판사, 2012:324-340.

아편(Opium)	• 양귀비의 익지 않은 열매에 상처를 내어 받은 유즙을 섭씨 60도 이하의 온도로 건조한 것 • 주로 인도, 터키, 유고, 파키스탄에서 재배 • 중추신경을 마비시켜 진정제, 진통제로 쓰이지만 남용할 경우 강한 의존효과를 가진다. • 아편은 생아편, 의료용인 아편말, 흡연용 아편으로 분류됨[7] • 양질의 아편에는 모르핀(Morphine)이 9~14% 정도 함유되어 있다. • 19세기 초에 처음 분리되어 주로 강한 진통제로 쓰이고 있다. 보통 정맥주사의 방법으로 남용되는데, 남용하면 아편보다 더 강한 중독성과 금단현상을 가져온다.
헤로인(Heroin)	• 아편계통의 약물로서 모르핀으로부터 만들어지는 디아세틸모르핀이라고 한다.[8] • 형태는 향기가 없는 결정화된 무색 분말로 제조방법에 따라 다양한 색상을 띠며, 주로 코로 흡입하거나 주사 또는 흡연의 방법으로 남용된다. • 마취제, 진통제, 진해제로 사용. 중독되면 강한 의존성과 금단현상을 가지며, 약효는 모르핀에 비해 수 배나 강해서 산모가 남용하면 태아도 중독된다고 한다.
그 외 아편계통의 약물	• 코데인(Codeine), 테바인(Thebaine), 옥시코돈(Oxycodone), 하이드로모르핀(Hydromorphine) 등 • 헤로인에 비해 모두 약효가 약해서 인기가 낮다.

(2) 코카계통

코카인(Cocaine)	• 코카나무잎에서 채취 • 코카잎 성분의 70~80%가 코카인이라고 하며, 주로 페루, 볼리비아, 콜롬비아, 인도네시아, 스리랑카, 대만 등의 해발 700~1,700미터 정도 되는 비가 많이 내리는 곳에서 재배된다. • 코로 흡입하거나, 흡연, 정맥주사를 통해 남용되며, 먹는 경우도 있다. • 1862년부터 주로 국부마취제로 사용했으며, 특유의 환각작용이 있고, 벌레가 몸 위를 기어다니는 느낌이 나며, 공격적 행동을 유발한다. • 남용하면 영양장애와 함께 우울증, 불안감, 수면장애, 만성피로, 정신장애를 일으킨다.

7) 아편말은 생아편을 가루로 하여 모르핀의 함유량을 10%로 조절한 것으로 갈색의 가루형태를 띤다. 흡연용 아편은 생아편을 물에 녹여 찌꺼기를 제거하고 증발, 농축시켜 액상으로 만든 것이다.

8) 헤로인(Heroin)의 어원은 "강하다"를 의미하는 독일어 heroisch에서 유래되었다고 하며, 1874년에 최초로 제조되었다.

크랙(Crack)	• 코카인을 농축한 것으로 1985년 이후에 출현한 것으로 농축코카인으로 불린다. • 일반적으로 대롱을 통해 연기를 흡입하는 방식으로 남용하며, 약효가 신속, 강렬하고 코카인에 비해 싸다. • 복용하면 큰 황홀감; 코카인에 비해 남용과 중독, 폭력의 위험성이 크다.

(3) 대마계통

대마초[9]	• 온대기후지역 대부분에 서식하며 우리나라에서도 가끔 야생에서 발견된다. • 삼베의 원료가 되기 때문에 농가에서 허가받아 재배한다. • 외국에서는 마리화나(Marihuana) 또는 카나비스(Canabis)라는 이름으로 통용되는데, 주로 가공되지 않은 대마초를 카나비스라 한다. • 민간에서는 진통제, 경련 진정제로 쓰였으며, 주로 흡연을 통해서 남용된다. • 약리효과는 흥분과 억제 2가지 작용을 모두 가지며, 많이 복용하면 환각증상이나 정신이상도 나타난다.
해시시(Hashish)	• 대마초로부터 채취된 대마수지를 건조, 압착한 것 • 파키스탄, 아프가니스탄, 레바논 등 중동 지역과 동남아, 인도, 멕시코, 아프리카, 북미에서 생산
해시시 오일 (Hashish Oil)	• 해시시를 증류공정 등을 반복하여 고도로 농축한 것 • 한두 방울이 대마초 담배 한 개비의 효과에 해당

2) 합성약물

메스암페타민 (속칭 히로뽕)	• 1919년에 처음으로 합성되었으며, 정맥주사 또는 술이나 음료수에 타서 복용하거나 분말을 코로 흡입하거나 열을 가하여 가스를 흡입하거나, 심지어는 상처를 내어 바르는 방법에 의해 남용된다. • 실제로는 대부분 정맥주사를 이용하며, 약리효과는 큰 황홀감을 느끼게 하며, 식욕을 억제하는 효과가 있어 다이어트의 목적으로 이용되기도 한다. • 신체적 의존성은 없으나 정신적 의존성이 있는 것으로 알려져 있다

9) 대마초는 보통 약물남용자들이 처음으로 접하는 약물이라고 할 수 있으며, 보통 다른 약물로 거쳐가는 통로가 된다. 이 때문에 대마초를 더 강한 약물중독의 세계로 들어가는 진입약물(gateway drug)이라고 한다.

	(쾌감의 유혹에 빠짐). • 반복 사용하면, 보통 3개월 정도에서 만성중독상태를 초래하여 환각, 망상을 수반하는 정신장애에 빠진다고 한다.
엑스터시(속칭 도리도리)	• 엑스터시는 '야바'와 함께 미국, 유럽, 한국 등에서 테크노 음악과 함께 최근에 급속히 퍼진 약물이다. • 복용하고 머리를 좌우로 흔들면 큰 황홀감을 가져다준다고 하며, 실제로 테크노 댄스클럽에서 열리는 레이브파티에 이 약물이 거의 필수적으로 이용된다. • 엑스터시는 가격이 상대적으로 싸서, 청소년들이 많이 남용하고 있다.
LSD	• 매우 소량으로 환각작용을 경험할 수 있으며, 흰색 가루나 정제 또는 맑은 액체의 형태로 무색, 무미, 무취의 특성을 띤다. • 약리효과는 히로뽕에 비해 강하며, 심지어는 자신의 모습을 제3자의 입장에서 관찰할 수 있다는 환각을 느끼거나 음악에서 색채감이나 맛을 느낄 수 있다는 착각을 일으킨다고 한다.
바르비튜레이트	• 불안감; 긴장, 불면증의 치료에 사용되었던 억제제로서, 많은 양을 복용하면 잠이 오며, 안정효과를 얻기 전에 흥분감을 경험하는 경우도 있다고 한다. • 최면이나 마취, 심지어 안락사에 이용되며, 미국에서 발생하는 자살의 약 6%가 이 약물의 남용에 의한 것이라고 한다.
GHB(감마 하이드록시 부티레이트, 속칭 물뽕)	• 특히 외국의 대학생들이 데이트 강간용으로 많이 사용한다. • 음료수나 알코올에 몇 방울을 타서 마시면 10~15분 내에 약효가 나타나서 3~4시간을 지속하는데, 기분이 좋아지고 취한 듯하면서 몸이 처지는 느낌을 주며 테이프가 끊기는 경험을 하는 경우가 많다고 한다. • 24시간 내에 인체를 빠져나가기 때문에 사후 추적이 어렵다는 점도 이 약물을 선호하는 원인이다.

3) 대용약물

- 남용을 목적으로 만들어진 것이 아닌 각각의 고유한 용도가 있는 화학물질들이다.
- 본드나 신나, 부탄가스 등으로 의사합법약물(quasi-legal drug)이라고도 한다.
- 한국에서 주로 많이 사용하는 유해약물로는 본드, 신나, 가스, 수면제, 각성제 등이 있으며, 이들은 크게 유기용제류, 각성제나 수면제 등의 알약류, 술이나 담배류로 나눌 수 있다.

(1) 유기용제류(흡입제)

- 본드나 가스에 함유된 것으로 유기용제는 휘발성이어서 증발하는데, 이 증발가스(유기용제 가스)를 흡입하면 정신기능이 왜곡된다.
- 본드, 가스 외에 가솔린, 신나, 아교, 에어로졸, 스프레이, 래커(lacquer) 희석제, 매니큐어 제거제, 라이터액, 드라이클리닝액, 타자수정액 등을 들 수 있다.
- 주로 냄새를 코로 흡입함으로써 남용되는데, 시각과 청각장애, 현기증 등의 증세가 나타나며 심하면 환각증상이 나타난다.
- 내성이 있어서 지속적으로 흡입한 경우 처음과 같은 효과를 느끼기 위해서는 훨씬 많은 양을 흡입해야 하며, 심각한 정도는 아니지만, 신체적 의존성 및 정신적 의존성이 있으며, 심하면 영구적인 뇌의 손상을 가져올 수 있다.

(2) 알약형태

- 향정신성 의약품에는 각성제(흥분제: 타이밍, 나이트 에스나인, 레그린 등), 진정제(안정제: 아티반, 바리움, 세코날, 바르비탈류, 벤조디아제핀류, 루미날 등), 진통제(폰날, 세다핀, 누바인(염산날부핀), 카리소프로돌(S정) 등), 진해제(덱스트로메토르판(러미나, 루비킹, 덱시판), 지놀타, 지페프롤 등), 그리고 항히스타민제(이빌, 프라콩, 페니라민 등) 등 매우 다양한 약물로 구성된다.

〈표 2-3〉 남용되는 약물의 종류 · 관련법규 및 독성

구분	종류	약리학적 분류	투여 방법	신체적 증상 및 행동	독성
억제제 (진정제, 수면제)	Barbiturates Phenobarbital Amytal Seconal Nembutal Tuinal	중추신경 억제제	경구 주사	동공축소, 취한 행동, 말더듬, 사고산만, 억제, 졸리움, 멍청함, 과량사용 시 무의식, 혼수, 호흡마비로 사망	정신적 의존, 신체적 의존, 오판과 조정력 상실에 의한 위험, 금단증상, 신장장애, 뇌손상, 간장장애, 과량 사용 시 사망(술과 함께 복용 시 상승작용)
신경 안정제	Valium Librium Ativan Quaalude	중추신경 억제제	경구	중추신경 억제제와 유사한 평온, 즐거움과 안정감, 발한, 감정억제, 정신적 침체, 배뇨장애, 노여움, 긴장, 불안, 정	억제제와 유사(그러나 보다 강함), 정신적 · 신체적 의존, 술, 마약, 수면제와 겸용 시 상승효과, 시각장애, 현기증, 졸리움, 금단

				신적 흥분, 언어장애	증상(흥분, 오심, 감정 억제, 경련 등)
흡입제 (본드·가스)	Toluene Hexane Acetone Gasoline Thinner	중추신경 억제제	흡입	술과 유사함. 동공축소, 혼수, 언어장애, 현기증, 도취감, 시각과 청각왜곡, 환각작용, 콧물, 눈물, 침, 근조절장애, 취한 행동, 성냄, 흥분, 졸리움, 무의식	정신적 의존, 판단장애로 오는 위험, 공격적 행위, 반사회적 행동, 간장장애, 심장장애, 골수장애, 영구적 뇌손상 가능, 식욕감퇴, 체중저하, 사망.

출처 : 이순래 외, 현대사회와 범죄, 청목출판사, 2012:311-323; 이훈규·이경재, 1996:31-32에서 재작성.

2. 약물의 국제이동과 남용실태[10)]

1) 해외의 3대 약물 생산지역과 국제이동 2011 기출

1) 황금의 삼각지역 (Golden Triangle)	• 태국, 미얀마, 라오스의 접경지대에 위치하고 있으며, 과거 전 세계의 아편과 헤로인의 60~70%를 생산했던 지역이다.
2) 황금의 초승달지역 (Golden Crescent)	• 이란, 파키스탄, 아프가니스탄의 접경지역에 위치하고 있으며, 1980년대 후반부터 아편생산지대로 떠올랐다. 과거 유럽의 75%, 미국의 25% 정도를 점유했었다.
3) 코카인 삼각지역 (Cocain Triangle)	• 콜롬비아, 페루, 볼리비아의 접경지역에 위치하고 있으며, 전 세계 코카인의 거의 전부라고 할 수 있는 약 98%를 생산한다. • 코카인 삼각지역 주변 국가들의 사용량 외에는 대부분 미국이나 유럽으로 수출하고 있다. • 생산지역 주변인 남미 외에, 주로 북미와 유럽, 그리고 아프리카로 수출되고 있으며, 소량으로 아시아나 오세아니아 지역으로도 수출되고 있다.

10) 이순래 외, 현대사회와 범죄, 청목출판사, 2012:334-340.

2) 기타 약물

대마초	• 잎담배의 형태로 유통되는 것은 전 세계에 광범위하게 걸쳐서 나타나며, 소비도 코카인과는 달리 전 세계에 걸쳐서 매우 광범위하게 분포하고 있다. • 유럽의 경우 잎담배의 형태로 유통되는 대마는 줄어들고 있지만, 대신 대마수지(canabis resin)의 형태로 유통되는 경우가 급속히 증가하고 있다. • 대마류는 다른 천연약물에 비해서 비교적 생산지와 소비지가 고르게 분포해 있는 것이 특징이다. • 우리나라의 경우 대마류 약물의 남용률이 세계적으로 볼 때 주변의 중국이나 일본보다 더 높은 1그룹이 속해 있다(UNODC, 2009:112).
합성약물	• 천연약물과는 달리 적절한 기후와 사회적 여건을 갖춘 재배지를 따로 필요로 하지 않기 때문에, 생산지와 소비지가 그렇게 멀리 떨어져 있지 않은 것이 특징이다. • 우리나라의 경우 주로 홍콩, 중국 그리고 캐나다를 통하여 많은 합성약물이 들어오고 있다.

〈표 2-4〉 약물범죄의 2가지 하위유형

투약범죄	• 보통 가해자이면서 피해자가 되는 경우 • 범죄가 상습적, 반복적으로 행해지며, 보통 폭력범죄, 재산범죄, 풍속범죄를 동반하는 것
약물제조범죄나 약물유통범죄	• 전문가에 의해 행해지는 전형적인 조직범죄 • 국제성을 띠는 광역범죄이며 한번 가담하면 헤어나기 어렵고, 보통 공무원의 부패가 함께 개입되어 있는 경우가 대부분

〈주요 약물의 유형〉[11)]

마리화나(Marijuana)	• 대마초의 꽃, 씨앗, 줄기, 잎을 말리고 부순 초록, 회색 또는 갈색의 혼합물 • 기억과 학습장애, 왜곡된 인식, 사고와 문제해결의 어려움, 조정력의 상실, 심장박동의 증대, 불안 등

11) 이윤호, 현대사회와 범죄, 박영사, 2011:405-413.

메스암페타민 (Methamphetamine)	• 주사로 투입, 코로 흡입, 담배처럼 흡연, 입으로 먹을 수도 있는 매우 중독성이 강한 중앙신경계통 자극제 • 짧지만 매우 강한 황홀감(rush), 활동성의 증대, 식욕의 감소, 6~8시간 지속되는 행복감, 발작, 주의력 결손장애 • 비만의 치료를 위한 의료용으로 제한
헤로인(Heroin)	• 양귀비의 씨앗으로부터 추출된 모르핀(morphine)에서 제조 • 주사 투입, 담배처럼 흡입, 코로 흡입 • 복용의 가장 중요한 결과는 중독
크랙(Crack)	• 연기로 마시는 매우 중독성이 강한 형태의 코카인 • 코카인은 강력한 중앙신경계통 자극제이며, 강력한 중독성 약물
LSD[12]	• 호밀이나 기타작물을 성장, 발육시키는 균류인 맥각(ergot)에서 발견되는 리세르그 산(lysergic acid)에서 제조 • 알약이나 캡슐, 액체형태로도 거래 • 향기가 없고 색깔도 없으며 약간 쓴맛을 내며 보통 입으로 삼켜서 복용하는 약물
클럽 약물[13] **- 엑스터시** (Ecstasy)	• 흥분과 환각적 효과를 유발
흡입제(inhalants)	• 휘발성 용매와 상업적 접착제, 라이터 연료, 세제, 페인트 용품 등에서 일반적으로 발견되는 물질로 제조
근육증강제(anabolic steroids) **- 스테로이드** (Steroids)	• 입으로 삼킬 수도 있고, 근육주사로 주입할 수도 있으며, 젤이나 크림의 형태도 있음

제4절 마약범죄

1. 마약류

1) 마약류의 의의

• 세계보건기구(WHO)는 마약을 ⅰ) 약물사용에 대한 욕구가 강제적일 정도로 강하고

12) 보통 '산(acid)'으로 알려진 LSD는 원래 순환기와 호흡기 자극제로 개발되었다.
13) 나이트클럽이나 카페 또는 레이브 파티(rave party) 등에서 젊은이들에게 널리 퍼지고 있는 일부 약물을 총칭하여 '클럽 약물(club drug)'이라고 한다.

(의존성), ii) 사용약물의 양이 증가하는 경향이 있으며(내성), iii) 사용을 중지하면 온몸에 견디기 힘든 증상이 나타나며(금단증상), iv) 개인에만 한정되는 것이 아니라 사회에도 해를 끼치는 약물[14])로 규정하고 있다.

- 우리나라는 마약 · 향정신성의약품 · 대마 및 원료물질의 취급 · 관리를 적절히 함으로써 그 오용 또는 남용으로 인한 보건상의 위해를 방지하여 국민보건 향상에 이바지함을 목적으로 기존의 "마약법"(1957년 제정), "향정신성 의약품관리법"(1979년 제정) 및 "대마관리법"(1976년 제정)을 통합하여 "마약류관리에 관한 법률"(법률 제6146호)을 제정하여 2000년 7월 1일부터 시행하고 있다.
- 마약류관리에 관한 법률에서 "마약류"라 함은 마약 · 향정신성의약품 및 대마를 말한다.
- 우리나라에서는 마약에 관한 단일협약(Single Convention on Narcotic Drugs; 1916), 향정신성물질에 관한 협약(Convention on Psychotropic Substance; 1971), 마약 및 향정신성물질의 불법거래방지에 관한 협약(United Nations Convention against Illicit Traffic in Narcotic Drugs and Psychotropic Substances; 1988)에 가입하고 있다.

「마약류 관리에 관한 법률」

[시행 2012.6.8] [법률 제10786호, 2011.6.7, 일부개정]

제1장 총칙 〈개정 2011.6.7〉

제1조(목적) 이 법은 마약 · 향정신성의약품 · 대마 및 원료물질의 취급 · 관리를 적정히 함으로써 그 오용 또는 남용으로 인한 보건상의 위해를 방지하여 국민보건 향상에 이바지함을 목적으로 한다. 〈개정 2002.12.26〉

제2조(정의) 이 법에서 사용하는 용어의 정의는 다음과 같다.
〈개정 2002.12.26, 2004.1.20, 2008.2.29, 2010.1.18〉

1. "마약류"라 함은 마약 · 향정신성의약품 및 대마를 말한다.
2. "마약"이라 함은 다음 각목의 1에 해당하는 것을 말한다.
   가. 양귀비 · 아편 또는 코카엽
   나. 양귀비 · 아편 또는 코카엽에서 추출되는 모든 알칼로이드로서 대통령령이 정하는 것
   다. 가목 및 나목에 열거된 것과 동일하게 남용되거나 해독작용을 일으킬 우려가 있는 화학적 합성품으로서 대통령령이 정하는 것

14) 최정호, 마약범죄수사론, 경찰대학, 2008:4.

라. 가목 내지 다목에 열거된 것을 함유하는 혼합물질 또는 혼합제제. 다만, 다른 약물이나 물질과 혼합되어 가목 내지 다목에 열거된 것으로 다시 제조 또는 제제할 수 없고, 그것에 의하여 신체적 또는 정신적 의존성을 일으키지 아니하는 것으로서 보건복지부령이 정하는 것(이하 "한외마약"이라 한다)을 제외한다.

4. "향정신성의약품"이라 함은 인간의 중추신경계에 작용하는 것으로서 이를 오용 또는 남용할 경우 인체에 현저한 위해가 있다고 인정되는 다음 각목의 1에 해당하는 것으로서 대통령령이 정하는 것을 말한다.

5. "대마"라 함은 대마초(칸나비스사티바엘)와 그 수지 및 대마초 또는 그 수지를 원료로 하여 제조된 일체의 제품을 말한다. 다만, 대마초의 종자·뿌리 및 성숙한 대마초의 줄기와 그 제품을 제외한다.

7. "원료물질"이라 함은 마약류가 아닌 물질 중 마약 또는 향정신성의약품의 제조에 사용되는 물질로서 대통령령이 정하는 것을 말한다.

〈표 2-5〉 주요 마약류 체계

<table>
<tr><td rowspan="12">마약류</td><td rowspan="3">• 향정신성 의약품</td><td colspan="2">• 각성제 : 메스암페타민(필로폰), MDMA(엑스터시) 등</td></tr>
<tr><td colspan="2">• 환각제 : L.S.D.(Lysergic acid diethylamide) 등</td></tr>
<tr><td colspan="2">• 억제제(안정제) : 바르비탈염제류 등</td></tr>
<tr><td rowspan="7">• 마약</td><td colspan="2">• 천연마약 : 양귀비(앵속 → 아편 → 모르핀 등)</td></tr>
<tr><td colspan="2">• 코카엽 : 코카인(Cocaine), 크랙(Crack)</td></tr>
<tr><td colspan="2">• 한외마약 : 코데솔, 코데날, 코데잘, 유코데 등</td></tr>
<tr><td rowspan="3">• 합성마약</td><td>• 페치딘(Pethidine)계</td></tr>
<tr><td>• 메사돈(Methadone)계</td></tr>
<tr><td>• 모르피난(Morphinane)계 등</td></tr>
<tr><td colspan="2">• 반합성마약 : 헤로인, 히드로폰, 옥시포돈 등</td></tr>
<tr><td rowspan="2">• 대마</td><td colspan="2">• 대마초(마리화나)</td></tr>
<tr><td colspan="2">• 대마수지(해시시, 해시시오일)</td></tr>
</table>

출처: 최정호, 마약범죄수사론, 경찰대학, 2008:4.

***합성마약[15)]**

합성마약은 모르핀 등 천연마약의 진통효과를 가지면서 의존성 내지 습관성이 적은 의약품을 개발하는 과정에서 만들어졌다.

메사돈계·페치딘계·모프리난계·아미노부텐계·벤조몰판계 등이 있지만, 대표적인 것으로 메사돈계와 페치딘계가 있다.[16)]

〈표 2-6〉 마약의 사용효과

분류		종류	약리작용(흥분/억제)	의약용도	사용방법	남용효과	작용시간
향정신성 의약품		메스암페타민	흥분	식욕억제	경구 주사 코흡입	환시, 환청, 환촉, 피해망상, 사망	12~34
		LSD	환각	없음	경구 주사	환각, 환청, 환시	8~12
		바르비탈유	억제	진정·수면	경구 주사	취한 행동, 뇌손상, 호흡기장애, 감각상실	1~6
마약	천연 마약	아편	억제	진정·진통	경구 주사	도취감, 신체조정력 상실, 사망	3~6
		모르핀	억제	진정·진통	경구 주사		
		헤로인	억제	진정·진통	경구 주사		
		코카인	흥분	국소마취	주사 코흡입	흥분, 정신혼동, 사망	2
	합성 마약	염산페치딘	억제	진정·진통	경구 주사	아편과 동일	3~6
		메사돈	억제	진정·진통	주사	〃	12~24
대마		대마	환각	없음	경구 흡연	도취감, 약한 환각	2~4

출처: 최정호, 마약범죄수사론, 경찰대학, 2008:23.

15) 전대양·송병호, 조직범죄론, 형설출판사, 2004:205-206.

16) • 메사돈계(methadone): 메사돈(methadone)은 2차 세계대전 중 모르핀이 부족하여 독일의 과학자가 합성하여 개발했다. 메사돈의 약효는 모르핀보다 긴 24시간 지속되면서도 헤로인이나 모르핀의 효과가 있어 다른 마약중독자의 치료과정에 사용되고 있다. 하지만 메사돈도 속도가 느리긴 하지만 내성 내지 의존성을 유발하며 금단증상도 나타난다.

• 페치딘계(pethidine): 페치딘(pethidine)은 1939년, 이젤레브(O. Eiseleb)가 합성하였고, 사우만(O. Schaumann)이 모르핀과 유사한 진통효과가 있음을 발견하여 '돌란틴(Dolantine)'이란 이름으로 시판되었다. 페치딘은 중추신경에 작용하여 진통효과를 가져오며 진정작용도 있다. 남용자는 졸리고 멍해지며 호흡이 느려지는 증상을 나타낸다. 다량사용의 경우 경련도 유발할 수 있고 내성과 의존성도 동반한다.

대검찰청, 마약류범죄백서, 대검찰청, 2001:14.

2) 마약류의 남용[17]

(1) 마약류의 특성[18]

중독성(한 번 사용하면 계속 사용하고 싶은 충동), 환촉(얼굴 등에 벌레가 기어가는 듯한 느낌), 내성(사용횟수에 비례 양을 늘리지 않으면 효과가 없음), 금단증상(사용을 중지하면 온몸에 참기 힘든 이상증세를 느낌), 반사회성(개인뿐 아니라 사회 더 나아가 온 인류에 해를 끼침) 등이 있다.

(2) 마약류 남용의 이유

걱정을 줄이고, 긍정적 느낌을 갖기 위해서, 두려움·충동심을 억제하기 위해서, 책임회피·반항심·호기심을 위해서, 잘못된 행동·지루함을 탈피하기 위해서, 자신감·관심·애정을 얻기 위해서 남용이 이루어지고 있다.

2. 약물남용[19]

1) 의의

- 약물의 불법성 규정은 특정 약물에 대한 사회의 인식과 그 인식을 바탕으로 한 법률적 지위에 의해 결정된다. 즉, 불법약물의 규정과 개념은 시대와 장소에 따라 달라지는 상대적 개념이다. 예 담배와 마리화나
- 약물남용의 영향을 이해하기 위해서는 약물의 종류, 사용자, 상황 등을 함께 고려해야 한다.

---

17) 최정호, 마약범죄수사론, 경찰대학, 2008:31.

18) 마약범죄는 피해자 없는 범죄의 전형을 이루며, 경마약의 복용은 중마약의 복용으로 이어지기 쉬우며, 우리나라는 엄벌주의를 취하고 있으며, 형법의 예방효과는 일반적으로 작다고 평가된다. 2004 기출

19) 약물중독으로 인한 금단현상이 충동적 범죄의 원인이 될 수 있으며, 약물중독과 비교적 관련이 적은 범죄는 사기이다. 또한 약물중독에 따른 범죄의 대책으로 형벌보다는 치료와 교정이 선행되어야 하며, 마약류 범죄는 본질적으로 국제성을 가진 범죄이며, 조직범죄와 깊은 관련이 있다. 2005 기출

2) 약물남용의 진행과정

(1) 일반적인 약물남용 진행과정

호기심 → 약물 첫 사용→ 쾌감→ 동료집단의 소속감→ 집단명예 → 가족과 멀어짐 → 성격장애적 행동 → 습관성 → 약물의존 및 내성 형성 → 신체적 쇠퇴 → 심한 사회질병적 인격붕괴

(2) 청소년의 약물남용 심화과정

담배 → 술 → 본드 → 가스 → 약품 → 대마초 → 필로폰

3. 마약범죄

1) 마약류사범의 시대적 흐름[20)]

50~60년대 아편과 메사돈 남용, 60~70년대 필로폰을 밀제조하여 일본으로 밀수출, 70년대 월남전에서 대마초 유입 흡연, 80년대 필로폰 투약자 부산 등 전국 확산, 90년대 범죄와의 전쟁으로 필로폰 제조책 중국으로 진출, 2000년 신종마약 엑스터시 등이 외국인 · 해외 유학생들을 중심으로 국내확산, 2003년 4월 중국 마약류단속강화로 필리핀으로부터 유입 등의 흐름을 지적할 수 있다.

2) 마약범죄의 특성

희생자가 없는 범죄(피해자가 국가), 국경이 없는 범죄, 전문조직 범죄, 점조직으로 된 범죄(상선과 하선이 분리), 암수범죄(비노출 범죄), 함정수사가 일부 허용된 범죄(대법원 판례) 등의 특성을 가진다.

20) 최정호, 마약범죄수사론, 경찰대학, 2008:43.

〈표 2-7〉 시대별 마약류 및 법규의 변천

시대	남용 약물	관련 법규
조선말	• 아편 · 모르핀	–
일제시대	• 아편 · 모르핀 · 헤로인	• 조선아편취체령(1919) • 아편단속법(1930)
해방 이후	• 아편 · 헤로인	• 마약단속규정(1946) • 마약취체령(1946)
1950년대	• 아편	• 형법(1953) • 마약법(1957)
1960년대	• 아편 · 메사돈	• 마약법 • 특정범죄가중처벌임시법(1961) • 독물 및 극물에 관한 법률 • 특가법(1966)
1970년대	• 대마초 · 필로폰 · LSD	• 마약법 • 독물 및 극물에 관한 법률 • 습관성의 약품관리법(1970) • 대마관리법(1976) • 향정신성의약품관리법(1979)
1980년대	• 대마초 · 필로폰	
1990년대	• 필로폰 · MDMA	• 마약법 • 향정신성의약품관리법 • 대마관리법
2000~현재	• 필로폰 · MDMA · 야바	• 마약류관리에 관한 법(2000)

출처: 최정호, 마약범죄수사론, 경찰대학, 2008:44.

제5절 화이트칼라 범죄

1. 화이트칼라(white-collar) 범죄의 의의 2011 기출

• 1939년 Sutherland[21]는 하류계층보다 사회적 지위가 높으며 비교적 존경받는 사람이

21) • 화이트칼라 범죄란 Sutherland가 부유한 사람과 권력 있는 사람들의 범죄활동을 기술하기 위해 처음 사용한 용어이다.
• 비행친구의 영향력에 관심을 가졌던 학자로서, 절도나 강도와 같은 전통적 범죄보다 훨씬 심각한 영향을 주는 화이트칼라의 범죄는 쉽게 용납되고 있음을 주장한 학자는 서덜랜드(Sutherland)

자신의 직업과정에서 수행되는 직업적 범죄라고 정의하였다.[22]

- 모든 사회계층 사람들이 자신의 직업적 과정에서 범행하는 직업지향적 법률위반으로써, 자신의 직무상의 권한과 영향력을 악용하여 저지르는 불법행위이다. 일반적 범죄자에 비하여 자신을 범죄자로 생각하지 않는 경향이 있다. 2009 기출
- 화이트칼라 범죄의 피해는 천천히 오래 지속되며, 그 원인이나 가해자를 직접적으로 추적하기 쉽지 않기 때문에 그 피해가 확산되고 심화될 수 있는 지연된 폭력이다.

[그림 2-1] Sutherland's concept of white-collar crime

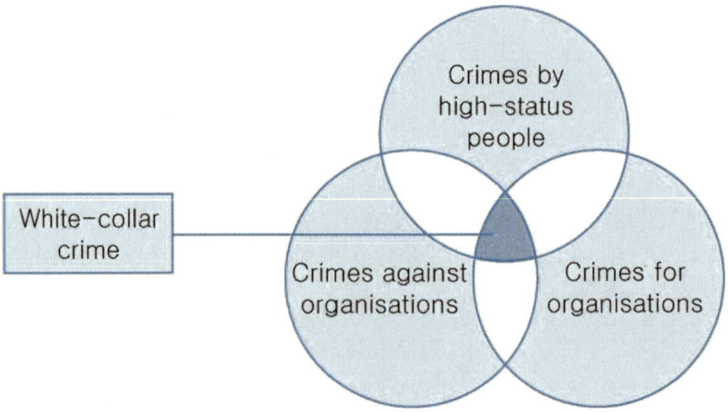

출처: Tim Newburn, Criminology, Willan Publishing, 2007:375.

2. 화이트칼라 범죄의 특성 2008 기출

범행의 합리성(rational execution)과 그 결과 초래되는 높은 이익, 피해자의 무의식적 협조, 사회적 무관심, 범죄자의 비범죄적 자기인상(자신을 범죄자로 보지 않고 존경의 대상으로 봄)[23]

이다. 2007 기출

22) Conklin은 기업범죄(business crime), 일부 학자는 상사범죄(corporate crime)라고 한다.

23) • 화이트칼라 범죄는 피해자가 명확하지 않은 경우가 많으며, 피해범위가 광범위한 경우가 많으며, 피해자는 피해사실을 잘 모르는 경우가 많으며, 범죄사실의 입증이 매우 어렵다. 2005 기출

3. 화이트칼라 범죄의 원인에 대한 이론

1) 심리적 소질론

- 화이트칼라 범죄는 기본적으로 정직한 기업세계의 극히 일부인 '썩은 사과(rotten apples)'를 대표하는 희귀한 현상으로 보고, 화이트칼라 범죄자는 비범죄자와 다른 심리학적 기질을 가지고 있다고 본다.
- 화이트칼라 범죄자는 기회만 주어진다면 남을 속이려는 타고난 소질을 가지고 있으며, 법을 위반할 의향이나 유혹에 대한 저항이 낮은 인성을 갖는다.

2) Sutherland의 차별적 접촉이론

- 화이트칼라 범죄자는 화이트칼라 범죄행위를 부정적으로 규정하는 정직한 기업인들보다 이를 긍정적으로 규정하는 다른 화이트칼라 범죄자들과 더 많은 접촉을 가졌기 때문에 그 범죄행위를 학습하게 된다.

- 화이트칼라 범죄는 직무상의 전문지식이나 조직체계를 이용하기 때문에 범죄로 인식하기 어려우며, 해당 범죄에 대하여 직접적으로 책임 있는 사람을 가려내기 어려우며, 분명히 드러난 피해자가 드물며 피해의 규모가 크다. 또한 쉽게 발각되기 어려우며 관대한 처벌을 받는 경향이 있다. 2008 기출
- 1) 범죄의 전문성과 복잡성: 화이트칼라 범죄는 직업상의 전문지식이나 조직체계를 이용하므로 일반인들은 그러한 행위를 범죄로 인식하기 어려우며, 범죄자가 범죄에 이용하는 지식은 대개 전문성이 강한 것으로 과학적이거나 공학적이거나, 회계상에 관한 것이거나 법률적인 것이다.
  2) 범죄의 전문성과 은폐성: 화이트칼라 범죄는 고도의 전문성과 은폐성을 갖는다. 발생형태 또한 범죄인과 피해자 간의 긴밀한 연결관계에 의하여 이루어지고, 해당 범죄에 대하여 직접적으로 책임 있는 자를 가려내기 어려우며, 실정법상의 허점을 이용하는 경우가 있어 외부적으로 범죄라고 하기 어려운 경우도 있다.
  3) 피해파악의 곤란성: 화이트칼라 범죄는 불특정 다수인을 대상으로 하거나 은폐되어 행해지기 때문에 피해자조차도 자신의 피해를 인식하지 못하거나 피해사실을 부인하는 경우가 발생한다. 즉, 분명하게 드러나는 피해자는 드물며 피해의 규모는 크지만, 피해자는 정부나 기업과 같은 추상적인 실체이거나, 단지 사소한 피해를 입은 다수의 사람이 된다.
  4) 처벌의 곤란성: 화이트칼라 범죄는 쉽게 발각하기 어려우며, 처벌하기도 곤란하여 비록 기소된다고 하더라도 관대한 처벌을 받는 경향이 있다. 화이트칼라 범죄자 중에서 소수에게만 실형이 선고되며, 대부분의 사람들은 집행유예를 선고받거나 아주 적은 액수의 벌금만 선고받는다.
  5) 범죄자의 비범죄적 자기인상: 화이트칼라 범죄자는 자신을 범죄자로 보지 않고 존경의 대상으로 보아 자신들의 비범죄적 인상을 유지할 수 있게 된다.

- 화이트칼라 범죄는 부정직한 기업인과의 차별적 접촉을 통한 학습과 부정적인 기업 관행을 통제하고자 하는 사회적 노력의 부족에서 기인한다.

3) 중화이론

화이트칼라 범죄자들은 자신의 범죄를 정당화 내지 합리화한다.

제6절 Hightech범죄

1. Hightech범죄의 의의

Hightech범죄란 컴퓨터 및 과학기술과 동시에 관련이 있거나 혹은 어느 한쪽과 관련이 있는 범법행위[24] 또는 컴퓨터를 불법행위의 도구 또는 범법행위의 목적물로 이용한 범죄행위[25]를 말한다.

2. Hightech범죄의 특징[26]

- 시간과 공간을 초월하여 동시에 다수의 이용자와 접속할 수 있기 때문에 간단한 한번의 속임수로도 많은 사람들에게 반복적으로 계속하여 많은 피해를 입힐 수 있다.
- 이용자의 신분이 노출되지 않고, 목격자가 있기 어려워 범죄현장의 발견과 범인의 현장검거 또는 신고에 의한 체포 등을 기대하기 어렵다.
- 범행현장을 알기도 어렵고 설사 현장을 알 수 있더라도 통치권(統治權)의 문제로 아무런 도움이 되지 않는 경우가 많다.
- '피해자가 없는 범죄'와 같이 피해자가 피해사실을 알지 못하거나 뒤늦게 알게 된다.
- 범행의 흔적이 잘 남지 않고, 이용자의 신분이 노출되지 않고, 범행 장소가 불특정하기 때문에, 증거의 확보가 어렵고, 확보된 증거도 활용하기가 쉽지 않다.

---

24) 미국, 하이테크범죄수사협회(High Technology Crime Investigation Association)의 정의이다.
25) 미국, 하이테크범죄조합(High Tech Crime Consortium)의 정의이다.
26) 강동범, "사이버범죄와 형사법적 대책", 한국형사정책연구원, 형사정책연구, 제11권 제2호(통권 제42호), 2000:69-72.

- 행위자들이 자신의 얼굴을 드러내지 않는 비대면성(非對面性)으로 인하여 범죄가 보다 과격하고 대담해질 수 있고, 범행을 위하여 고도의 전문적 지식과 기술을 요하며, 시공(時空)을 초월하는 특성으로 인하여 범죄피해가 빨리 확산될 수 있어서 피해규모가 엄청날 수 있다.

3. Hightech범죄의 동기[27)]

- 범죄자 개인의 잘못된 우월감과 성취감 예 해커의 해킹
- 개인의 감정적 문제 예 cyber stalking, 해킹, 바이러스 유포
- 경제적 이욕(利慾) 예 예금인출, 전자상거래의 사기, 산업스파이 행위
- 다른 범행의 수단 예 마약밀거래 등의 불법자금 세탁

4. Hightech범죄의 규제

1) 규제의 어려움[28)]

- 현실세계가 아닌 가상공간에서 행하여지므로 법률적 규제가 미흡하고, 추적이 곤란하며 암호체계를 이용하고 있다.
- 범행현장에서 즉시 해결이 곤란하며, 사후적발도 어렵다.
- 여러 가지 수법이 결합되어 행하여지며, 고도의 전문적 지식과 기술이 사용되며, 조직 내부의 소행인 경우 조직의 명예와 신용을 고려한 은폐가 있다.

2) 구체적 전략

방화벽(firewall) 설치, 공개 키 암호화 체계(public key encryption system) 도입 등이 있다.

27) 조병인, "하이테크 범죄의 실태와 대책", 1999년도 한국공안행정학회 국제범죄 학술세미나 자료집, pp. 40-44, 참조.
28) 한국정보보호센터, "정보보호 통계자료", 정보보호뉴스 제14호, 1999년 8월, pp. 31-32, 참조.

제7절 사이버범죄

1. 사이버범죄의 의의[29)]

- 사이버범죄(cybercrime)란 일반적으로 인터넷과 같은 정보통신망으로 연결된 컴퓨터 시스템이나 이들을 매개로 형성되는 사이버공간(cyberspace)을 중심으로 발생하는 범죄행위를 총칭하는 표현으로 사용된다.[30)]
- 은행에서 초기의 전산망이 구축되기 시작한 지 얼마 되지 않은 1958년, 미국 미니애폴리스(Minneapolis) 은행에서 살라미 기법(salami slicing)[31)]에 의한 최초의 컴퓨터 남용(computer abuse) 사례가 보고되었다.

2. 사이버범죄의 분류

1) Carter의 분류[32)]

(1) 목표물로서의 컴퓨터(Computer as the Target)

지적재산권의 절취, 시장정보의 절취(고객리스트, 가격 데이터, 판촉계획), 컴퓨터화된 파일에서 얻어진 정보에 기초한 갈취(의료정보, 개인의 이력, 성적 선호도)

---

29) • 사이버범죄라는 개념의 구조화는 1930년대 Sutherland가 제시한 화이트칼라 범죄(white-collar crime)로부터 시작되었다. Sutherland는 노동자로 대변되는 블루칼라와 다른 은행가, 변호사, 회계사 등 지식과 신뢰받는 사회적 지위 · 권력을 지닌 자들이 그것을 남용하여 이루어지는 범죄인 화이트칼라 범죄의 개념을 일반화시켰다.
• 1940~50년대에 학자들은 화이트칼라에 의해 자주 이루어지는 금전이나 다른 자산에 대한 절취나 횡령, 사기, 위조 등의 범죄에 대해 재정범죄(financial crime)라는 새로운 개념구조를 도입하였다. 양근원 · 장윤식, 사이버범죄수사론, 경찰대학, 2008:1.

30) Cybercrime이라는 용어는 1995년 Sussman과 Heuston 등에 의해 사용되고, 1997년 미국정부에서 공식적으로 인용한 이후에 전 세계적으로 널리 사용되었다. 국내에서도 1999년 경찰청의 '컴퓨터범죄수사대'를 '사이버범죄수사대'로 확대개편하여 정부에서 공식적인 용어로 사용하였다. 양근원 · 장윤식, 사이버범죄수사론, 경찰대학, 2008:1-3. 양근원, 사이버범죄의 특징과 수사방향, 수사연구, 수사연구사, 2000년 6월, p. 16.

31) 쉽게 발각되지 않게 소수점 이하에 이를 정도의 아주 작은 단위의 낙전을 지정한 계좌로 모이도록 컴퓨터를 조작하여 횡령하는 수법이다.

32) 기능적인 유형의 분류방식이다. D. L. Carter, "Computer Crime Categories", FBI Law Enforcement Bulletin, 64, no. 7, 1995; 양근원 · 장윤식, 사이버범죄수사론, 경찰대학, 2008:4-6.

(2) 범죄 수단으로서의 컴퓨터(Computer as Instrumentality of the Crime)

현금입출금기(Automated Teller Machine; ATM)카드와 계정에 대한 사기적인 이용과 이자금의 절취, 전환, 또는 계좌이체, 신용카드 사기, 컴퓨터 거래에서의 사기(증권거래, 매매, 환어음), 전기통신 사기 등

(3) 컴퓨터가 다른 범죄에서 부수적인 경우(Computer Is Incidental to Other Crimes)

돈세탁과 불법금융거래, 조직범죄 기록과 장부 및 장부작성 등 불법행위를 지원하는 전자게시판 포함

(4) 컴퓨터의 보급과 관련된 범죄(Crimes Associated with the Prevalence of Computers)

소프트웨어 해적행위와 위작, 컴퓨터 프로그램의 저작권 침해와 장치위조, 컴퓨터 장치와 프로그램의 암거래, 기술적인 설비의 절취 등

- phone phreaking : 컴퓨터를 이용하여 전화교환 시스템에 침입하여 장거리전화를 거는 것을 말한다.
- 피싱(fishing) : 은행 · 쇼핑몰 · 온라인게임 등 유명기관을 사칭하여 가짜 홈페이지 주소가 들어 있는 이메일을 보내고, 위장된 홈페이지에 개인정보를 입력하도록 유도한 뒤 수집한 정보를 악용하는 신종금융사기를 말한다.[33] 2009 기출

  보이스 피싱(voice fishing): 전화를 이용하여 타인의 금융정보를 빼내는 사기수법이다.
- 파밍(Pharming): 합법적으로 소유하고 있던 사용자의 도메인을 탈취하거나 도메인 네임시스템(DNS) 이름을 속여 사용자들이 진짜 사이트로 오인하도록 유도, 개인정보를 훔치는 새로운 수법이다.

33) 김용준, 범죄피해자학, 백산출판사, 2009:194-195.

2) 인터폴(Interpol, 국제형사경찰기구)의 분류[34)]

〈표 2-8〉 인터폴의 컴퓨터범죄 분류

대분류	소분류
• 인가받지 않은 접속(Unauthorized Access)과 가로채기(Interception)	• 해킹(Hacking), 가로채기(Interception), 시간절도(Time Theft)
• 컴퓨터데이터의 변경 (Alteration of Computer Data)	• 논리폭탄(Logic Bomb), 트로이전 호스(Trojan Horse), 바이러스(Virus), 웜(Worm)
• 컴퓨터관련 사기 (Computer-Related Fraud)	• 현금지급기이용(Cash Dispensers), 컴퓨터위조(Computer Forgery), 도박기(Gaming Machines), 투입/산출/프로그램조작(Input/Output/Program Manipulations), 지불수단(Means of Payment), 전화공짜사용(Telephone Phreaking)
• 인가받지 않은 복제 (Unauthorized Reproduction)	• 컴퓨터게임(Computer Games), 기타 소프트웨어(Other Software), 반도체배치설계도(Semiconductor Topography)
• 컴퓨터 파괴 (Computer Sabotage)	• 하드웨어(Hardware), 소프트웨어(Software)
• 기타 컴퓨터관련 범죄 (Other Computer-Related Crime)	• 전자게시판(Bulletin Board Systems), 무역비밀절도(Theft of Trade Secrets), 금제품취급(Indictable Material)

출처: 양근원 · 장윤식, 사이버범죄수사론, 경찰대학, 2008:6.

3) 경찰의 분류[35)]

(1) 사이버테러형 범죄

• 정보보호 내지 정보보안(information security)의 3가지 목표인 정보의 기밀성(Confidentiality), 무결성(Integrity), 가용성(Availability)을 침해하는 범죄이다.

• 정보보안의 목표를 위협하는 요소는 통신도청이나 비밀침해 등 가로채기(interception),

---

34) 인터폴 내 유럽 컴퓨터범죄 운영그룹(Interpol European Computer Crime Working Group)의 분류이다.

35) 양근원 · 장윤식, 사이버범죄수사론, 경찰대학, 2008:7-8.

파일손괴나 운영방해와 같은 방해(interruption), 정보의 위변조(modification and fabrication)를 들 수 있다.[36)]

- 방법은 해킹, 컴퓨터바이러스, 서비스거부 공격(DoS, Denial of Service), 인터넷웜(internet worm) 등

(2) 일반 사이버범죄

통신을 이용한 사기, 음란물 등 불법물의 인터넷상 유통행위, 도박·음란·범죄방조 등 불법적인 사이트 운영, 사이버 명예훼손 및 사이버 스토킹 등 사이버 성폭력, 개인정보침해, 협박이나 공갈 등

3. 사이버범죄의 일반적 특징[37)] 2011, 2012 기출

1) 디지털 자료로 인한 특징

컴퓨터에서 정보는 디지털 정보이며 매우 빠른 속도로 처리될 수 있기 때문에 쉽게 작성·변경·삭제될 수 있으며 전기공급, 자기 등 물리적인 변화에도 비교적 민감하다.

2) 자동성

컴퓨터를 통한 자료처리의 컴퓨터 프로그램이나 하드웨어 장치에 정해진 내용에 따라 자동적으로 진행된다.[38)] 따라서 목표한 동작이 일어나는 시간은 임의로 정할 수 있고, 실제로 동작이 일어나는 시간에 이미 실행자는 그 동작을 통제할 필요가 없으므로 시간과

---

36) Charles P. Pfleeger, Security in Computing, U.S: Prentice Hall PTR, 1997:3.
양근원·장윤식, 사이버범죄수사론, 경찰대학, 2008:7.

37) • 양근원·장윤식, 사이버범죄수사론, 경찰대학, 2008:19-20.
- 사이버범죄의 특징으로는 범죄자의 익명성, 범행의 비대면성, 범죄피해의 광범위성 등이 있다. 2007 기출.
- 컴퓨터범죄의 특징으로는 입증의 곤란성, 높은 암수범죄율, 피해의 광범위성, 비대면적 범죄성 등이 있다. 2004 기출
- 1. 피해자가 피해사실을 알지 못하거나 뒤늦게 알게 되는 경우가 많다. 2. 간단한 조작으로 많은 사람들에게 광범위한 피해를 입힐 수 있다. 3. 범죄피해가 빠르게 확산될 수 있다. 4. 범죄현장의 발견과 범인의 현장검거가 전통적 범죄에 비해 상대적으로 어렵다. 2010 기출

38) 경찰수사보안연수원, 컴퓨터범죄수사, 2000년 2월, p. 296.

공간적인 혼란이 발생하며, 행위는 연속하거나 반복되어 발생할 수 있다.

3) 개방성 및 광역성[39]

인터넷은 인터넷에 접속할 수 있는 모든 불특정 다수에 개방된 것이므로, 전 세계의 원격지에서 쉽게 접근할 수 있다.[40] 또한 네트워크를 통해 일대일 또는 일대 다수의 동시 또는 비동시적인 접속이 가능하기 때문에 행위의 결과는 불특정한 다수에 영향을 미칠 수도 있다. 따라서 때에 따라 행위자의 의도와는 무관하게 피해가 엄청난 규모로 확대될 수도 있다.

4) 익명성

개방성과 광역성 및 인터넷에 고유한 주소체계와 컴퓨터의 특징으로 인하여, 사용자는 신분을 노출시키지 않고 인터넷을 이용하는 것이 가능하다.

5) 간접성

인터넷에서의 활동은 컴퓨터시스템의 통신을 수단으로 하므로 상대방과의 직접적인 대면을 필요로 하지 않는다. 또한 통신은 또 다른 매개체에의 연쇄적인 통신을 가능하게 한다.

4. 사이버범죄의 형법 적용

1) 사이버 폭력행위

- 사이버상의 각종 폭력행위는 물리적인 폭력을 동반하지는 않지만 심리적으로 상당한 압박을 가하는 것이 사실이며 건전한 사이버 생활을 방해하며, 상대방의 의사를 무

39) 정보통신부, 정보화역기능 방지 종합대책(안), p. 14.

40) 사이버범죄의 국제적인 문제로는 인터넷은 국경이 없으나 현실법은 그렇지 못하다. 서비스의 제공자, 서비스 제공 컴퓨터, 사용자가 서로 법체계가 다른 나라에 있어 적용되는 법률이 다른 경우, 범인이 여러 서버를 경유하여 범행을 하여 역추적을 하던 중에 외국 수사기관과의 공조를 하고자 하나 형사공조의 한계에 따른 문제, 집행의 범위를 벗어난 외국에 대한 자국기관의 행정적인 조치의 불가능 등 많은 문제로 인하여 조치의 실효성을 담보하기 곤란할 뿐 아니라 자칫 국제적인 분쟁을 야기할 수도 있다. 양근원·장윤식, 사이버범죄수사론, 경찰대학, 2008:22.

시하고 일방적으로 지속적으로 행해질 수 있다는 문제가 있다.

- 특히 오프라인 공간에서의 단순 스토킹 행위에 대해서는 형사처벌을 할 수 없는 반면 사이버스토킹에 대해서는 처벌규정이 마련되어 있다.
- 사이버상의 성폭력 즉, 자기 또는 다른 사람의 성적 욕망을 유발하거나 만족시킬 목적으로 전화·우편·컴퓨터, 기타 통신매체를 통하여 성적 수치심이나 혐오감을 일으키는 말이나 음향, 글이나 도화, 영상 또는 물건을 상대방에게 도달하게 한 자는 성폭력처벌 및 피해자보호 등에 관한 법률 제14조(통신매체를 이용한 음란행위)에 의해 2년 이하의 징역 또는 500만원 이하의 벌금에 처해진다.

> **제12조(통신매체를 이용한 음란행위)** 자기 또는 다른 사람의 성적 욕망을 유발하거나 만족시킬 목적으로 전화, 우편, 컴퓨터, 그 밖의 통신매체를 통하여 성적 수치심이나 혐오감을 일으키는 말, 음향, 글, 그림, 영상 또는 물건을 상대방에게 도달하게 한 사람은 2년 이하의 징역 또는 500만원 이하의 벌금에 처한다.

- 카메라, 기타 이와 유사한 기능을 갖춘 기계장치를 이용하여 성적 욕망 또는 수치심을 유발할 수 있는 타인의 신체를 그 의사에 반하여 촬영한 자는 성폭력처벌법 제13조(카메라 등을 이용한 촬영)에 의하여 5년 이하의 징역 또는 1천만원 이하의 벌금에 처해진다.

> **제13조(카메라 등을 이용한 촬영)** ① 카메라나 그 밖에 이와 유사한 기능을 갖춘 기계장치를 이용하여 성적 욕망 또는 수치심을 유발할 수 있는 다른 사람의 신체를 그 의사에 반하여 촬영하거나 그 촬영물을 반포·판매·임대 또는 공공연하게 전시·상영한 자는 5년 이하의 징역 또는 1천만원 이하의 벌금에 처한다.
>
> ② 영리를 목적으로 제1항의 촬영물을 「정보통신망 이용촉진 및 정보보호 등에 관한 법률」 제2조제1항제1호의 정보통신망(이하 "정보통신망"이라 한다)을 이용하여 유포한 자는 7년 이하의 징역 또는 3천만원 이하의 벌금에 처한다.

- 사이버스토킹은 「정보통신망 이용촉진 및 정보보호 등에 관한 법률」 제44조의7(불법정보의 유통금지 등)에 규정하고 있다.

「정보통신망 이용촉진 및 정보보호 등에 관한 법률」

[시행 2011.9.30] [법률 제10465호, 2011.3.29, 타법개정]

제44조의7(불법정보의 유통금지 등) ① 누구든지 정보통신망을 통하여 다음 각 호의 어느 하나에 해당하는 정보를 유통하여서는 아니된다.

1. 음란한 부호·문언·음향·화상 또는 영상을 배포·판매·임대하거나 공공연하게 전시하는 내용의 정보
2. 사람을 비방할 목적으로 공공연하게 사실이나 거짓의 사실을 드러내어 타인의 명예를 훼손하는 내용의 정보
3. 공포심이나 불안감을 유발하는 부호·문언·음향·화상 또는 영상을 반복적으로 상대방에게 도달하도록 하는 내용의 정보
4. 정당한 사유 없이 정보통신시스템, 데이터 또는 프로그램 등을 훼손·멸실·변경·위조하거나 그 운용을 방해하는 내용의 정보
5. 「청소년보호법」에 따른 청소년유해매체물로서 상대방의 연령 확인, 표시의무 등 법령에 따른 의무를 이행하지 아니하고 영리를 목적으로 제공하는 내용의 정보
6. 법령에 따라 금지되는 사행행위에 해당하는 내용의 정보
7. 법령에 따라 분류된 비밀 등 국가기밀을 누설하는 내용의 정보
8. 「국가보안법」에서 금지하는 행위를 수행하는 내용의 정보
9. 그 밖에 범죄를 목적으로 하거나 교사(敎唆) 또는 방조하는 내용의 정보

② 방송통신위원회는 제1항제1호부터 제6호까지의 정보에 대하여는 심의위원회의 심의를 거쳐 정보통신서비스 제공자 또는 게시판 관리·운영자로 하여금 그 취급을 거부·정지 또는 제한하도록 명할 수 있다. 다만, 제1항제2호 및 제3호에 따른 정보의 경우에는 해당 정보로 인하여 피해를 받은 자가 구체적으로 밝힌 의사에 반하여 그 취급의 거부·정지 또는 제한을 명할 수 없다.

③ 방송통신위원회는 제1항제7호부터 제9호까지의 정보가 다음 각 호의 모두에 해당하는 경우에는 정보통신서비스 제공자 또는 게시판 관리·운영자에게 해당 정보의 취급을 거부·정지 또는 제한하도록 명하여야 한다.

1. 관계 중앙행정기관의 장의 요청이 있었을 것
2. 제1호의 요청을 받은 날부터 7일 이내에 심의위원회의 심의를 거친 후 「방송통신위원회의 설치 및 운영에 관한 법률」 제21조제4호에 따른 시정 요구를 하였을 것
3. 정보통신서비스 제공자나 게시판 관리·운영자가 시정 요구에 따르지 아니하였을 것

④ 방송통신위원회는 제2항 및 제3항에 따른 명령의 대상이 되는 정보통신서비스 제공자, 게시판 관리·운영자 또는 해당 이용자에게 미리 의견 제출의 기회를 주어야 한다. 다만, 다음 각 호의 어느 하나에 해당하는 경우에는 의견 제출의 기회를 주지 아니할 수 있다.

1. 공공의 안전 또는 복리를 위하여 긴급히 처분을 할 필요가 있는 경우
2. 의견청취가 뚜렷이 곤란하거나 명백히 불필요한 경우로서 대통령령으로 정하는 경우
3. 의견 제출의 기회를 포기한다는 뜻을 명백히 표시한 경우 [전문개정 2008.6.13]

2) 사이버 원조교제

사이버상에서 원조교제를 하는 경우에는 현실공간에서의 원조교제와 동일한 규정에 의하여 처벌받는다. 즉, 청소년의 성을 사는 행위를 한 자는 아동·청소년의 성보호에 관한 법률 제10조에 의하여 5년 이하의 징역 또는 3천만원 이하의 벌금에 처해진다.

「아동·청소년의 성보호에 관한 법률」
[시행 2012.1.1] [법률 제10582호, 2011.4.12, 타법개정]

제10조(아동·청소년의 성을 사는 행위 등) ① 아동·청소년의 성을 사는 행위를 한 자는 5년 이하의 징역 또는 3천만원 이하의 벌금에 처한다. 〈개정 2010.4.15〉

② 아동·청소년의 성을 사기 위하여 아동·청소년을 유인하거나 성을 팔도록 권유한 자는 1년 이하의 징역 또는 1천만원 이하의 벌금에 처한다.

3) 사이버 도박 등

사이버상에서 재물을 걸고 도박행위를 하는 자에 대해서는 형법 제246조(도박, 상습도박)가 적용된다. 또한 영리의 목적으로 사이버도박장을 개장한 자는 형법 제247조 (도박개장)가 적용된다.

형법 제246조(도박, 상습도박) ① 재물로써 도박한 자는 500만원 이하의 벌금 또는 과료에 처한다. 단, 일시오락정도에 불과한 때에는 예외로 한다. 〈개정 1995.12.29〉
② 상습으로 제1항의 죄를 범한 자는 3년 이하의 징역 또는 2천만원 이하의 벌금에 처한다. 〈개정 1995.12.29〉
형법 제247조(도박개장) 영리의 목적으로 도박을 개장한 자는 3년 이하의 징역 또는 2천만원 이하의 벌금에 처한다. 〈개정 1995.12.29〉

제8절 환경범죄

1. 환경범죄(environmental crimes)의 의의

1) 환경범죄의 개념

- 사람의 건강에 위해를 주거나 환경을 저해하는 환경오염행위[41] 또는 이와 관련된 행위로서 법에 의하여 처벌되는 행위를 말한다.
- 1991년 대구 페놀사건을 계기로 1991년 5월 31일 법률 제4390호로 환경범죄의 단속에 관한 특별조치법이 제정되었다.
- 수질환경보전법, 대기환경보전법, 토양환경보전법 등 환경행정법상의 벌칙규정으로 존재하는 환경행정형법과는 달리, 제정의 목적이 환경범죄와 이에 대한 처벌을 정하기 위한 것이고 내용도 모두 환경범죄와 처벌로 이루어진 형사특별법이라는 것이다.

41) 환경정책기본법 제3조는 '환경오염'이라 함은 사업활동 기타 사람의 활동에 따라 발생되는 대기오염, 수질오염, 토양오염, 해양오염, 방사능오염, 소음・진동, 악취, 일조방해 등으로서 사람의 건강이나 환경에 피해를 주는 상태를 말한다.

「환경정책기본법」
[시행 2011.10.26] [법률 제10911호, 2011.7.25, 타법개정]

제3조(정의) 이 법에서 사용하는 용어의 정의는 다음과 같다. 〈개정 1999.12.31, 2002.12.30, 2005.5.31〉

1. "환경"이라 함은 자연환경과 생활환경을 말한다.
2. "자연환경"이라 함은 지하·지표(해양을 포함한다) 및 지상의 모든 생물과 이들을 둘러싸고 있는 비생물적인 것을 포함한 자연의 상태(생태계 및 자연경관을 포함한다)를 말한다.
3. "생활환경"이라 함은 대기, 물, 폐기물, 소음·진동, 악취, 일조 등 사람의 일상생활과 관계되는 환경을 말한다.
4. "환경오염"이라 함은 사업활동 기타 사람의 활동에 따라 발생되는 대기오염, 수질오염, 토양오염, 해양오염, 방사능오염, 소음·진동, 악취, 일조방해 등으로서 사람의 건강이나 환경에 피해를 주는 상태를 말한다.

4의2. "환경훼손"이라 함은 야생동·식물의 남획 및 그 서식지의 파괴, 생태계질서의 교란, 자연경관의 훼손, 표토(表土)의 유실 등으로 인하여 자연환경의 본래적 기능에 중대한 손상을 주는 상태를 말한다.

5. "환경보전"이라 함은 환경오염 및 환경훼손으로부터 환경을 보호하고 오염되거나 훼손된 환경을 개선함과 동시에 쾌적한 환경의 상태를 유지·조성하기 위한 행위를 말한다.
6. "환경용량"이라 함은 일정한 지역 안에서 환경의 질을 유지하고 환경오염 또는 환경훼손에 대하여 환경이 스스로 수용·정화 및 복원할 수 있는 한계를 말한다.
7. "사전환경성검토"라 함은 환경에 영향을 미치는 행정계획의 수립 또는 개발사업(행정계획의 수립이 요구되지 아니하는 개발사업을 말한다. 이하 같다)의 허가·인가·승인·면허·결정·지정 등(이하 "허가등"이라 한다)을 함에 있어서 해당 행정계획 또는 개발사업에 대한 대안의 설정·분석 등 평가를 통하여 미리 환경측면의 적정성 및 입지의 타당성 등을 검토하는 것을 말한다.

2) 환경범죄의 특성[42] 2012 기출

(1) 침해의 간접성 즉, 인위적 활동에 의해 발생되며 침해가 간접적이다. 환경오염 자체는 유해물질을 배출·폐기함으로써 직접적으로 나타나지만 공중의 생명·신체에

42) 법무연수원, 1987:26-27.

대한 위험은 유해물질의 배출・폐기를 통하여 대기, 토양 등이 오염됨으로써 간접적으로 나타난다. 이 때문에 형사법적 처리가 어렵다.

(2) 침해의 완만성 즉, 대부분의 유해물질이 서서히 축적되어 환경을 오염시키고 상당기간이 지난 후에 위험을 초래하게 되는 경우가 많다.

(3) 피해의 불특정성 즉, 환경범죄의 주체를 확정하기 어렵다. 환경침해 및 그로 인한 사람의 생명・건강에 대한 위험을 야기시킨 유해물질을 배출・폐기하는 기업이 집단으로 몰려 있는 경우는 어느 회사가 행위의 주체인지 확정하기가 곤란하다. 또한 침해행위의 상관성으로 인해 고의・과실이 불분명하여 경계선상에 있는 경우가 많이 발생한다는 특징이 있다.

(4) 피해의 광역성 즉, 환경재의 특수성으로 말미암아 한번의 오염이 확산・전파된다.[43]

(5) 기타, 기업범죄로서의 환경범죄, 범죄피해의 국제화, 환경오염자로부터의 정부, 나무심기, 돌고래 보호 등 자연보호운동에 헌금하는 등의 환경친화적 가식(假飾)행위, 환경당국과 산업체는 회전문(回轉門)의 관계로 인한 규제의 덫(regulatory capture) 등이 지적되고 있다.

2. 환경범죄의 이론적 배경

1) 범죄활동과 범행의 방법은 사회적으로 용인되는 행위로써 학습되는 것이라는 차별적 접촉이론(differential association theory)이 있다.

2) 환경범죄가 발생하는 제도적 구조와 미시적 문화 전반에 초점을 맞추고 있는 신아노미이론(neo-Mertonian Anomie theory)이 있다.

---

43) 환경범죄의 특성으로는 침해의 간접성, 침해의 계속성, 피해의 광역성과 불특정성 등이 있다.
2005 기출
- 환경범죄의 특수성으로 환경범죄의 주체는 생산을 담당하는 사업자가 대다수를 차지하기에 경제적 지위가 상위에 있는 계층이라고 할 수 있으며, 범죄발생의 인과관계나 고의・과실을 확정하기 곤란하며, 피해자가 불특정다수이며, 피해범위를 확정하기 곤란하며, 가해자가 자신이 범죄를 저질렀다는 죄의식이 상대적으로 적다는 것이다.

3. 환경범죄의 규제전략

1) 억제전략(deterrence strategy)

위반사항을 적발하여 위반자들 처벌하는 전략이다. 예 아이보리코스트 : 20년 실형(實刑)이나 1백만 달러가 넘는 벌금부과 / 나이지리아 : 화학폐기물 불법폐기에는 사형 / 케냐 : 코끼리 밀렵자 현장사살

2) 준수전략(compliance strategy)

대결보다는 협조, 강제보다는 회유와 조정을 찾는 전략이다.

제3편

범죄원인론

〈범죄원인에 대한 설명의 수준〉[1]

개인적 수준에서의 범죄설명	생물학적 이론과 심리학적 이론	
사회학적 수준에서의 설명	미시적 수준(microlevel)	사회적 과정을 중시
	거시적 수준(macrolevel)	사회적 구조를 중시

1. **개인적 수준에서의 설명**

- 생물학적 이론과 심리생물학적 이론(psychobiological theory), 심리통계적 접근(psychometric approach), 임상심리적 이론 그리고 사회학적인 관점으로서 역할이론과 차별적 접촉이론 및 기타 학습이론을 들 수 있다.
- 개인의 범행가담을 설명하기 위해서 어떠한 개인적 특성과 경험에 초점을 맞추고 있다.

2. **사회학적 수준에서의 설명** 2011, 2012 기출

- 사회학적 이론은 사회구조를 강조하는 입장과 사회과정을 강조하는 입장으로 구분할 수 있다.

1) 사회구조를 강조하는 입장: 거시적 수준(macrolevel)	• 사회적 상호작용의 반복적인 안정된 유형으로서 규범위반을 설명하는 이론이다. • 범죄의 유형과 정도의 다양성을 설명하기 위해 하위문화를 포함한 문화 및 사회제도의 속성을 중시한다. 예 다양한 형태의 기능주의(functionalism), 갈등이론(conflict theory), 마르크스주의 이론과 아노미이론, 차별적 사회조직화(differential social organization), 하위문화이론(subcultural theories) 등 • 왜 상이한 사회제도·문화·하위문화 등이 상이한 유형과 정도의 범죄를 유발하는가 또는 왜 범죄가 특정한 방법으로 유형화되는가를 설명하고자 한다.
2) 사회과정을 강조하는 입장: 미시적 수준(microlevel)	• 시간에 따른 사회적 상호작용의 계속적인 변화와 발전의 견지에서 규범 위반을 설명하는 이론이다. • 집단과 개인의 상호작용의 결과와 유형에 초점을 맞춘다. • 어떠한 상호작용의 발전과 구조가 범죄를 유발하는가를 공식화하고자 노력한다. 예 다양한 형태의 사회학습적 이론들

1) 이윤호, 범죄학, 박영사, 2007:199-202.

제 15 장 생물학적 범죄원인론

제1절 생물학적 범죄원인론의 전개

1. 롬브로조(Lombroso, Cesare)

1) 의의

- 롬브로조(Lombroso)는 최초의 실증주의 범죄학자로서, 선천적으로 타고난 범죄적 유전자에 의해 범죄를 하게 되는 '생래적 범죄인(born criminal)'이 있다고 하였다.[1)]
- '생래적 범죄인'은 원래 생물학적으로 원시적인 형질을 가지고 태어났기 때문에 범죄를 저지를 수밖에 없다고 보았다. 2009, 2011 기출
- '생래적 범죄인'은 교화교정이 거의 불가능하기 때문에 영구격리 또는 사형을 행하지 않으면 안 된다고 주장하였으며, 근대과학적 형사정책의 아버지라고 할 수 있다.[2)]

---

1) • 타고난 범죄자가 대부분이라 믿었고 범죄자들은 격세유전에 의해 출현한다고 주장한 학자는 '롬브로조'이다. 2007 기출
- 이탈리아 각지의 감옥을 찾아다니며 사형수 383명과 일반수형자 3,839명의 두개골 및 기타 신체상의 특징을 분석하고, 그들의 정신 · 성격상의 특징과 비교하여 통계적으로 정리해서 "범죄인론"을 발표하였다. 범죄자들은 진화 전(前) 원인류의 제반 특징을 갖고 있는 특이 변종인간이라는 것이며, 이들은 생래적으로 범죄자로 태어나기 때문에 특수한 범죄억제적 환경에서가 아니면 범죄자로 나타나게 마련이라는 것이다.
- 범죄자의 생물학적 요인으로는 염색체, 중추신경, 호르몬 등이 있다. 2007 기출
- 범죄생물학적 관점의 연구로는 가계연구, 쌍생아 연구, 호르몬 연구 등이 있으며, 인성연구는 범죄심리학적 관점의 연구이다. 2008 기출

2) 인간본성에 대한 기본 가정은 고전주의는 자유의지에 기반하며, 실증주의는 결정론에 기반한다. 2005 기출

2) 생래적 범죄인의 특징

형태학적으로 두개골의 이상, 신체적 · 생리적 이상, 정신적 이상, 사회적 특징 등의 퇴행적 특성을 갖는 자를 생래적 범죄인이라고 하였다.

〈표 3-1〉 생래적 범죄인의 특징

두개골의 이상	• 구부러진 코, 쑥 들어간 턱, 늘어진 귀, 튀어나온 이마, 높은 광대뼈, 큰 눈썹, 듬성듬성한 턱수염, 부정한 치열, 빨간 머리카락
신체적 특징	• 이마의 돌출, 후두부의 특수성, 깎아낸 듯한 이마 · 턱 관절의 강한 발달, 돌출된 광대뼈, 치열의 부정 · 턱수염의 결여, 모발의 이상 • 비틀린 코, 납작코, 매부리코, 구강의 돌출, 늘어진 귀 · 눈의 결함이나 특이성, 극단적으로 긴 팔 · 두개골의 불균형, 손가락 · 발가락 수의 과부족, 왼손잡이, 매우 긴 팔, 기형손가락, 빈약한 체모, 손바닥의 외선, 나이에 비해 많은 주름살, 소두증, 대두증, 사팔뜨기, 비대칭적인 안면
정신적 특징	• 도덕감정의 결여, 오만과 허영심, 위태감, 사행심 · 충동성(폭발성), 복수심, 잔혹성 · 낮은 지능, 성적 충동의 조숙, 무모함, 지나친 게으름, 충동성, 자기중심적
사회적 특징	• 문신 새기기, 잔인한 놀이 즐기기, 주색이나 도박에의 취향 • 무생물의 인격화(미신), 신조 은어 만들기, 특수하거나 상징적인 그림 그리기, 몸에 문신, 과도한 몸동작, 유창한 화술, 과도한 도박 · 음주, 무생물의 인격화

3) 범죄인 분류

(1) 생래적 범죄인	• 초범이라도 무기구금이나 도태처분 • 잔혹한 행위를 반복하는 자는 극형
(2) 정신병적 범죄인	• 정신적 결함에 의한 범행
(3) 기회범죄인	• 사이비범죄인–자신의 명예나 생존을 위한 범행 • 준범죄인–경미한 생래적 · 퇴행적 특징
(4) 격정적 · 우발적 범죄인	• 분노 · 사랑 · 명예 등 순간적 흥분에 의해 범행한 자로 단기자유형보다는 벌금형
(5) 관습범죄인	• 환경의 영향에 의해 범행
(6) 잠재적 범죄인	• 알코올, 분노감 등에 의한 범행

출처: 공정식, 2011:55, 참조.

2. 페리(Enrico Ferri) 2012 기출

- 범죄포화의 법칙(Law of Criminal Saturation)에서 "범죄는 물리적 · 지리적 · 인류학적 · 사회적 요인의 종합적 산물이며, 일정 사회환경에 일정한 인적 · 물적 상태가 수반하게 되면 범죄의 수는 일정하다"고 주장하였다.[3)]
- 페리는 인간의 자유의지는 하나의 순수한 환상에 불과하다고 하면서 고전주의 범죄학을 비판하였다.
- 인간의 모든 행위는 개인적 · 사회적 · 자연적 요소의 복합적 관계에 의해 결정된다고 보았으며, 범죄의 원인은 인류학적 · 물리적 · 사회적 요인이 영향을 주며 그중에서 사회적 요인을 중시하였다.[4)] 이에 따라 "범죄포화의 법칙(Law of Criminal Saturation)"과 "범죄 과포화의 법칙"을 주장하였다.
- 대용형법(Penal Substitute)을 주장하여 결정론적 시각에서의 범죄행위에 대한 도덕적 책임을 부정하고 사회적 책임론을 주장하였으며, 범죄대책으로 형벌보다 사회정책이 필요하다고 주장하였다.[5)]
- 형사처분은 보안처분으로 일원화하고 도덕적 색채를 배제한 사회방위처분론을 주장하였다.

범죄포화의 법칙 (Law of Criminal Saturation)	• 범죄원인이 되는 요소들이 일정한 양으로 존재하는 사회에는 이에 상응하는 일정한 양의 범죄가 반드시 발생한다.
범죄과포화의 법칙[6)]	• 사회 · 물리적인 예외조건의 발생으로 반사적 · 부수적인 범죄가 증가한다.

3) 케틀레(A. Quetelet)는 "사회는 범죄의 씨앗을 품고 있으면서 범죄를 준비한다. 사회가 준비한 범죄를 범죄자는 이를 실행할 따름이다"라고 하였으며, 뒤르켐(E. Durkheim)은 "범죄는 사회를 움직이는 윤활유의 역할을 하고 있다"고 주장하였다.

4) 개인적 요인에는 연령, 성별, 교육 정도, 사회적 계급, 기질적 · 정신적 구조 등을, 사회적 요인에는 인구, 여론, 관습, 종교, 정치 · 재정, 생산과 분배, 치안행정, 교육, 보건, 입법(페리가 가장 중요하다고 본 범죄원인) 등을, 자연적 요인에는 기후, 토질, 계절, 밤낮의 장단, 평균기온 등을 제시하였다.

5) 대용형법이란 형벌 대신 실업에 기인한 곤궁범죄의 경우에는 이민의 자유를, 정치범죄는 사상의 자유를, 사기나 문서위조범죄는 과세절감 등을 시행하는 것을 말한다. 사회정책으로는 일반인에 대하여 범죄의 근본적인 대책을 위해서 자유거래, 독점철폐, 값싼 노동자숙소의 건립, 공공저축은행, 거리조명의 개선, 산아제한, 혼인 및 이혼의 자유, 무기제작의 국가적 규제, 기아보호소의 설립 등을 주장하였다.

• 범죄인의 분류에 있어서는 롬브로조의 잠재적 범죄인을 없애고 5가지로 분류하였다.

〈표 3-2〉 페리가 분류한 범죄자의 유형과 대책

범죄자 유형	대 책
(1) 선천성 범죄자	• 무기한 격리
(2) 정신장애 범죄자	• 정신병원 수용
(3) 격정 범죄자	• 손해배상명령, 이주명령
(4) 기회 범죄자	• 농장형무소 훈련, 손해배상명령, 이주명령
(5) 습관성 범죄자	• (개선 가능한 경우) 농장형무소 훈련, 손해배상명령, 이주명령
	• (개선 불가능한 경우) 무기유형

출처: 이만종, 범죄학개론, 학현사, 2005:52.

3. 가로팔로(Raffaele Garofalo)

1) 의의

• 가로팔로(Garofalo: 1852~1934)는 1885년 저서 『범죄학(Criminologia)』에서 국가마다 상이한 형법질서에의 의존성으로부터 범죄학을 분리시켜, 시대와 국가를 초월한 독자적인 범죄개념을 주장하였다.

• 범죄인을 자연범과 법정범, 과실범으로 구분하고[7], 범죄의 본질은 자연범에게 있다고 하였다.

• 자연범(Natural crime)은 연민과 성실이라는 2가지 도덕적 정서에 반하는 행위를 하는 자로서, 인간의 기본적인 사랑의 감정이 소질적으로 퇴화되거나 결여된 자로 보았다.

• 범죄는 체형적 특질이 지능의 저하, 이타적 감정의 결여를 유발하여 심리적 결여에 의해 범죄가 발생한다고 보았다.

• 롬브로조의 범죄인관을 긍정하고, 롬브로조와 유사한 범죄대책을 제시하였다.

6) 기본적·전형적인 범죄란 살인·강도·절도·간통이고, 그 반사적·부수적 범죄란 살인·강도 등에 따르는 공무집행방해, 불법무기소지 등과 절도에 따르는 장물범죄들, 그리고 간통에 따르는 명예훼손·위증 등의 범죄를 말한다.

7) 법정범은 일정기간 구금이 필요하며, 과실범은 처분하지 말 것을 주장하였다.

2) 범죄인의 분류

〈표 3-3〉 가로팔로의 범죄자 유형과 대책

범죄자 유형	대 책	
① 살인범	• 연민과 성실의 정이 모두 결여된 자	• 사회적응가능성이 없는 경우에는 사형
② 폭력범	• 연민의 정이 결여	• 원칙적으로 무기 유배형이 적용되지만, 청소년의 경우에는 농장집단에 수용
③ 절도범	• 성실의 정이 결여	
④ 성범죄인	• 도덕적 감수성의 결여	• 부정기 유배형
⑤ 기타	• 연민과 성실의 정의 결여 정도가 낮은 경우	• 손해배상명령(범죄위험성이 적음)

출처: 이만종, 범죄학개론, 학현사, 2005:54, 참조, 일부 수정.

제2절 범죄와 체형

1. 크레치머(Kretschmer)의 체형의 범인성 이론

- 1925년 독일에서 260명의 정신병자를 조사한 결과 정신병자들에게 특징적인 신체타입이 있다는 것을 발견하였다.
- 체형을 세장형(asthenic: 쇠약형), 운동형(athletic: 강건형, 투사형), 비만형(pyknic), 그리고 혼합형으로 나누었다.

〈표 3-4〉 체형의 분류

체격	기질	정신병질	정신병
세장형	분열성	분열병질	정신분열증
비만형	순환성	순환병질	조울증
투사형	점착성	간질병질	간질

주) 1. 세장형과 투사형(운동형)은 정신분열증과 연관, 비만형은 조울증과 연관 있다고 주장되고 있다.
2. 폭력범에는 투사형의 체형을 가진 사람이 많고, 절도범이나 사기범 중에는 세장형이 많으며, 비만형의 체형을 가진 사람은 범죄를 적게 범하는 경향이 있는데 범죄를 범하는 경우에는 대체로 사기범이 많고 그 다음으로 폭력범죄가 많다.

2. 모어와 건드래크

- 1929년 미국 일리노이에 있는 주(州) 형무소에 재소하고 있는 254명의 백인남자를 연구했다.
- 비만형은 사기, 폭력, 성범죄와 연관되어 있고, 세장형과 투사형(운동형)은 주거침입 절도, 강도와 절도와 연관되어 있다는 것을 발견하였다.

3. 후튼(E. Hooton)의 체형의 범인성 이론

- 고링의 조사방법을 비판하면서, 미국 18개주에서 17,000명의 범죄자와 비범죄자를 뽑아서 신체타입과 범죄와의 관계를 조사했다.
- 범죄자들은 일반인에 비해 거의 모든 신체조건이 열등하다는 것을 발견했다.

4. 셀던(Sheldon)의 체형의 범인성 이론

1) 의의

1949년 15세부터 21세까지 200명의 소년들을 대상으로 체격, 지성, 비행과의 관계를 조사한 결과를 바탕으로, 비행지수(index of delinquency)를 작성하여 1~10까지의 단계 중 7을 초과하는 소년들에 대해서는 보호시설수감이 필요하다고 주장하고, 비행청소년들은 범죄성을 가진 부모로부터 태어나는 것이므로 비행을 만드는 요소는 유전(inherited)이라고 결론지었다.

2) 체형의 분류

소년들의 체격을 몸의 각 부분을 1부터 7까지 점수를 매겨, 내배엽 우월형(비만형), 중배엽 우월형(투사형), 외배엽 우월형(세장형) 등 3가지로 분류하였다.[8)]

---

8) • 체형은 태아가 형성될 때 기본적인 3개의 세포 즉, 내배엽, 중배엽, 외배엽이 어떻게 구성되는가에 따라 구별할 수 있다. 내배엽은 소화기관, 중배엽은 근육, 뼈, 외배엽은 피부, 신경체계가 발달하므로 이들의 구성형태에 따라 신체유형을 알 수 있다. 셀던(Sheldon)은 체형에 따른 기질을 밝혔으며, 사람들은 3가지 신체적 특징을 어느 정도는 각각 가지고 있다고 본다.
• 범죄자의 신체유형을 내배엽, 중배엽, 외배엽으로 나누고, 근육질의 운동형 신체를 가진 사람이 공격적인 성향으로 인해 범죄를 많이 저지르게 된다고 주장한 생물학적 범죄학자는 '셀던'이다. 2007 기출

(1) 내배엽형

비만형으로 소화기관이 발달, 살이 찐 편이고, 전신이 둥글고 부드러운 편이다.

(2) 중배엽형

근육형으로 운동근육이 발달되어 있고, 몸이 건장하며, 몸집이 크다.

(3) 외배엽형

세장형으로 피부와 신경체계가 발달되어 있으며, 예민하고 내향적인 기질을 갖고 있다.

〈표 3-5〉 셸던(Sheldon)의 신체유형과 기질유형

구분	신체유형	기질유형	크레치머의 체격형
내배엽형	• 상대적으로 소화기관이 크게 발달 • 살이 찐 편이다. • 전신부위가 부드럽고 둥근 편이다. • 팔과 다리가 가늘고 짧다. • 골격이 작다. • 피부가 부드럽다.	• 내장 긴장형 • 몸가짐이 대체로 이완되어 있다. • 편안한 성격이다. • 부드러우며 사치품 등을 좋아한다. • 온순하지만 기본적으로 외향적 성격이다.	비만형
중배엽형	• 근육, 골격, 운동조작이 탁월하다. • 몸통이나 가슴이 크다. • 손목이나 손이 크다. • 야윈 경우는 각이 진 체형이다. • 야위지 않은 경우는 우람한 체형이다.	• 신체 긴장형 • 활동적이며 역동적인 성격이다. • 단호한 걸음걸이, 언어구사, 제스처, 행동이 공격적이다.	투사형
외배엽형	• 피부, 신경계 기관 등이 탁월하다. • 여위고 가냘픈 체형이다. • 얼굴이 작고 코가 높다. • 몸무게는 작지만 피부면적은 넓다.	• 두뇌 긴장형 • 내향적인 성격이다. • 신체기능에 대한 불평이 많다. • 소음이나 외부자극에 민감하다. • 비사교적인 성격이다.	세장형

5. 글뤽(S. Glueck)부부

- 소년범죄의 원인연구에서 Sheldon의 연구를 적용한 결과, 비행소년은 보통소년과 차이점이 있다고 하였다.
- 비행소년은 정상소년보다 체격적으로 투사형이 약 2배 정도 더 많고, 심리적으로는 직접적·구체적 표현을 하는 경향이 있으며, 기질적으로는 침착성이 부족하고, 문제에 대해서는 무계획적이며, 일반적으로 태도는 적대적·의혹적이라고 하였다.

제3절 범죄와 유전 2012 기출

1. 유전적 결함에 대한 연구[9)] 2008, 2010 기출

1) 의의

유전에 의한 내인성 정신병, 정신병질, 지적 장애, 음주벽, 범죄상습성, 폭력성을 부모로부터 자손이 물려받아 범죄의 원인이 되는 경우를 말한다.[10)]

2) 슈툼플(F. Stumpfl)의 내인성 정신병

내인성 정신병의 경우 유전적 결함이 부모에게 나타난 정도를 보면 일반적인 범죄자들보다 상습적인 범죄자들에서 높게 나타나, 내인성 정신병의 유전적 영향을 발견할 수 있었다.[11)]

3) 글뤽부부(Sheldon Glueck & Eleaner Glueck)의 연구

비행소년이 정신박약이나 정서장애를 가진 경우에는 부모 중에 유전적 결함이 있는 경

9) 유전과 범죄의 관계에 관한 연구에는 쌍생아 연구, 범죄가계연구, 입양아 연구 등이 있다. 2007 기출

10) 정신병 등의 유전부인(遺傳負因)이 범죄자의 혈연 가운데 많이 발견될 때 이를 범인성 유전부인이라 한다. 결함이 부모에게 있는 경우를 직접부인(直接負因), 조부모에게 있는 경우를 간접부인(間接負因), 부모의 형제에게 있는 경우를 방계부인(傍系負因)이라 한다.

11) 누범, 조발범, 중한 풍속범 등의 경우에 유전이 나타나는 확률이 높다고 주장했다.

우가 많다는 것을 발견하였다. 특히, 아버지보다 어머니의 유전적 영향이 더 크다고 주장하였다.

4) 리들(Riedl)

- 범죄자집단을 범죄성 출현시기에 따라 범죄혈통군, 조발범군(早發犯群), 지발범군(遲發犯群)으로 분류하여 연구했다.[12)]
- 유전적 결함은 범죄혈통군, 조발범군, 지발범군 순으로 나타났고 특히, 어머니보다 아버지의 유전적 영향이 더 크다고 주장하였다.

2. 범죄인 가계 연구

1) 의의

범죄인 가계란 특정범죄자 등이 많이 출생한 가계로 이를 조사·연구함으로써 그 가계 내에서 범죄성의 유전여부를 분석·평가하는 것이다.

2) 학자별 연구

(1) 고다드(Henry Goddard)의 칼리카크(Kallikaks)가(家) 연구

- 미국 남북전쟁 중 민병대원이었던 '칼리카크'라는 병사(兵士)와 정신박약 소녀 사이에서 태어난 '마틴'의 자손 480명 중 지적 장애자, 성적(性的) 비정상인, 알코올 중독자, 간질환자, 조사자(早死者), 범죄인, 매춘업자가 대부분이었고 정상인은 4명에 불과하였다.
- '칼리카크'라는 병사가 후에 독실한 청교도 여자와 결혼하여 얻은 자손 496명 중 대부분은 의사, 변호사, 교육자 등 사회적으로 명망있는 자들이었으며 정신이상자 1명, 종교적 광신자 1명, 조사자(早死者) 1명, 음주습벽자 2명에 불과하였다. 이는 정신병질 등이 유전한다는 증거라고 주장했다.

12) 범죄혈통군이란 혈연에서 범죄자가 5명 이상인 집단을 말하며, 조발범군이란 18세 이전에 범죄를 범한 집단을, 지발범군이란 30세 이후에 범죄를 범한 집단을 말한다.

(2) 덕데일(Richard Dugdale)의 주크(Jukes)가(家) 연구

한 교도소에 일가족 6명이 동시에 수용된 주크가(家)를 발견하여, 그 가계의 7대에 걸쳐 709명을 조사한바, 알코올중독자, 매춘부, 범죄자 등이 절반 이상이라는 것을 발견하였다.

3. 쌍생아 연구

1) 의의

일란성 쌍생아와 이란성 쌍생아가 각기 범죄를 저지르는 일치율을 비교하여 유전이 범죄소질에 미치는 영향을 알 수 있다는 가정 아래, 일란성 쌍생아가 이란성 쌍생아보다 그 일치율이 높은 경우 범죄에 있어 유전소질의 중요성을 인정할 수 있다는 연구이다.

2) 학자별 연구

(1) 갈튼(F. Galton)

범죄일치율에 대한 사고를 기초로 쌍생아 연구의 단서를 마련한 최초의 학자이다.

(2) 랑게(J. Lange)[13)]

1929년 저서 『운명으로서의 범죄』를 통해 쌍생아연구를 범죄생물학에 도입하였으며, 연구결과 일란성 쌍생아의 범죄일치율은 64.4%, 이란성 쌍생아는 28.9%라 하며 범죄성에 대한 유전적 소질이 매우 크다고 주장하였다.

(3) 크리스티얀센(Christiansen)

1974년, 쌍생아 기록을 검토하고, 쌍생아계수를 사용하여 사회학적 방법에 따라 일정한 변수에 따른 범죄의 유전성을 조사하였는데, 그 결과 쌍생아의 범죄일치율은 범죄의 종류, 출생지역, 사회계층 및 범죄에 대한 집단저항의 강도에 따라 차이가 난다고 주장하였다.

---

13) 쌍생아 연구방법을 범죄생물학에 도입하여 범죄성의 형성은 유전소질에 의하여 결정적으로 좌우된다고 주장한 학자는 '랑게(Lange)'이다. 2005 기출

(4) 슈툼플(Stumpfl)

누범자연구에서 일란성 쌍생아의 일치율이 이란성 쌍생아보다 높다고 주장하였으며, 쌍생아의 범죄율 일치조사에 있어, 일치의 개념을 5단계로 나누어 연구의 치밀성을 높였다.

1단계	2단계	3단계	4단계	5단계
양 쌍생아가 처벌된 경우	범죄의 비중이 일치하는 경우	범죄의 실행방법이 일치하는 경우	사회적 행상이 일치하는 경우	성격구조가 일치하는 경우

4. 양자 연구

1) 의의

범죄자 중 양자(養子, 입양자, adoption)를 조사하여 그 생부모와 양부모의 범죄성을 대비하였을 때, 생부모가 범죄성을 소유한 경우 양자의 범죄발생정도가 양부모보다 현저히 우세하면 유전적 범죄성향을 인정할 수 있다는 방법이다.

2) 학자별 연구

(1) 슐싱어(F. Schulsinger)의 연구

양자연구를 통해 범죄의 유전성을 밝히고자 한 최초의 학자로, 정신적 결함이 혈연관계를 통하여 전수하는지 여부를 연구하였다.

(2) 허칭스와 메드닉(Hutchings & Mednick)의 연구

- 범죄성향의 유전성을 밝히기 위해 양자연구를 통해, 생부모의 범죄적 성향이 후손인 양자들에게까지 미치고 있다고 하였다. 2008 기출
- 생부모가 전과자인 경우 양자가 범죄자가 될 경우가 더 높고, 양부모와 생부모의 범죄성은 상관관계가 있어 양쪽 모두 범죄자일 경우 양자의 범죄확률이 높다.

5. 성염색체 연구

1) 의의

성염색체 연구는 범죄발생에 있어서 유전적 특성인 성염색체 이상(異常)인 XYY, XXY,

XXXY 등이 있다.

2) Kleinfelter증후군에 관한 연구

- 클라인펠터(Kleinfelter)증후군은 여성적 특징을 나타내는 X염색체의 수가 증가하는 경우로 특히 XXY형이 문제된다.14)
- 신체적으로는 저능아, 고환의 퇴화, 무정자증, 여성형 유방, 장신 등의 특징이 있고, 인격적으로는 지능이 낮고 반사회적 경향이 있고, 자신감이 결여되어 있다. 범죄경향으로는 동성애, 성범죄, 절도죄의 경향이 있다고 주장되었다.

3) XYY형 성염색체 이상

- XYY형(초남성: supermale)은 남성적 특징을 나타내는 Y염색체가 증가한 경우로서 범죄와 관련하여 특히 문제되는 유형이다.
- 1961년, 샌드버그(Sandberg)는 XYY염색체를 가진 사람들이 XY형보다 범죄성향을 띠기가 더욱 쉽다고 주장하였다.
- 특징으로는 장신, 성적인 조숙, 정신적 불안과 저지능, 난폭한 성격, 조발성 범죄자가 많고 일반인에 비해 범죄율이 60배 이상 높은 것으로 주장되었다.
- 범죄경향으로는 초범 연령이 13~14세로 일반인의 18세에 비하여 상당히 빠르며 공격성을 띠고 있고 성범죄나 살인, 방화 등의 강력범죄를 범하기 쉽다고 주장하였다.15)

제4절 현대의 생물학적 범죄원인론

1. 영양장애와 범죄

1) 비타민 · 미네랄 결핍

- 비타민과 미네랄 등이 결핍되면 뇌기능에 이상이 생기고 그 결과 정서불안을 야기함

14) 인간의 염색체는 상염색체 44개와 성염색체 2개로 구성되어 있다.
15) 폭력적 범죄와 관련이 높다고 주장되는 염색체는 XYY이다. 2009 기출

으로써 이상행동을 낳는다는 영양분결핍이론이다.

- 비타민 B와 C가 부족하거나 이에 대한 신체적 의존성이 지나치게 높을 경우 두뇌작용에 이상을 일으키며 이것이 결과적으로 범죄나 비행과 같은 반사회적 행위를 유발하게 된다는 의학적 보고가 있다.
- 1990년대 연구로 나트륨, 칼륨, 칼슘, 아미노산, 모노아민, 펩티드 등이 부족할 경우에는 우울증, 광증, 인지작용상의 장애, 기억상실, 비정상적 성욕 등과 같은 문제를 야기한다는 결과가 있다.

2) 저혈당증

- 저혈당은 뇌의 작용을 저하시키거나 과도하게 작용하도록 함으로써 비정상적인 행동, 우울증, 과도한 폭력성, 심한 두통, 머릿속의 혼란 등을 유발한다는 것이다.
- 심각한 저혈당 증세를 나타내고 있는 재소자들이 더 폭력적이고 과격하며 비정상적인 사고를 하고 있는 것으로 나타났으며, 충동적인 범죄행위를 저지를 수 있는 가능성이 크다는 것이다.

2. 생화학적 이상과 범죄성

성범죄자의 생화학적 특성에 대한 연구는 크게 1) 호르몬 연구와 2) 신경전달물질 연구로 대별된다.[16]

1) 호르몬 연구

- 일반적으로 생리학적 신호에는 1) 자기분비(autocrine)호르몬, 2) 이상(異狀)분비(paracrine)호르몬 3) 내분비(endocrine)호르몬의 3가지가 있다.[17]
- 여러 분비선에서 분비되는 호르몬의 양과 질에 따라 범죄와 연관이 있다고 보는 것이 생리학적 범죄학자들의 주장이다.

---

16) 이순래 외, 현대사회와 범죄, 청목출판사, 2012:271-273.

17) 우리가 일상적으로 말하는 호르몬이란 주로 내분비호르몬을 가리키는데, 이는 내분비조직(endocrine tissue)에 의해 소량으로 합성된 물질로서 혈관이나 임파선을 통해 신체의 각 부위로 이동한다. 호르몬은 주로 송과선(샘), 뇌하수체선(샘), 갑성선(샘), 부갑상선(샘), 부신피질, 흉선(샘) 및 성선(샘) 등 7가지의 내분비선(샘)에 의해 체내에서 체내로 분비되는데, 분비선의 유형 및 양에 따라 체중, 체격, 지능, 성격, 기질, 감정 등 신체 각 부위의 기능이 변화한다.

• 성범죄와 관계가 있는 분비선은 갑상선, 성선 및 뇌하수체선이다. 대체로 갑상선호르몬(티록신)과 성선 호르몬의 분비가 많을수록 그리고 뇌하수체 호르몬의 분비가 적을수록 성폭행의 개연성이 증가한다.

2) 신경전달물질 2011 기출

신경전달물질은 사람의 기분을 결정하고 충동을 조절하며 졸음이나 배고픔을 느끼게 해준다. 가장 잘 알려진 신경전달물질로는 도파민(Dopamine), 세로토닌(Serotonin), 노르에피네프린(Norepinephrine) 등이 있다.

구분	내용
도파민[18]	• 도파민이 너무 많이 분비되면 오히려 공격성과 폭력성을 띠게 된다. • 도파민의 수치가 반드시 공격성과 연관되는 것은 아니지만 대체로 도파민의 수치가 낮을수록 공격성이 낮아진다고 할 수 있다.
세로토닌[19]	• 세로토닌이 다량으로 분비되면 공격적이거나 폭력적인 성향이 줄어들게 된다. • 세로토닌은 범죄성뿐만 아니라 자살이나 우울증, 주의결핍과 같은 문제들을 호전시키는 역할을 한다.
노르에피네프린 (노르아드레날린 (Noradrenaline))	노르에피네프린은 도파민과 같이 흥분제적 신경전달물질로써 싸우느냐 피하느냐와 같은 중요한 결정을 내릴 필요가 있을 때 다량으로 분비되면 공격적인 성향을 띠게 한다.

1) 테스토스테론

- 테스토스테론(testosterone)은 공격성을 야기하는 남성호르몬으로 반사회적 공격적 행동과 관련이 있다는 것이다.
- 미국에서는 남성 성범죄자들의 처우방법으로 테스토스테론의 수준을 떨어뜨리는 약물을 사용하거나, 여성호르몬인 에스트로겐(estrogen)을 주입하여 성능력을 저하시키는 방법 등이 이용되기도 한다.

18) 도파민은 흥분제적 신경전달물질로서 처벌과 보상체계에 연결되어 사람의 기분을 결정한다. 어떤 행위로부터 보상을 많이 받을 상황에 처하면 좋은 기분을 갖게 되는 반면, 처벌을 받을 상황에 놓이면 우울해진다. 즉, 정신기능을 향상시키고 행위를 결정하는 역할을 한다.

19) 세로토닌은 대뇌피질에 골고루 분포되어 선하고 좋은 기분을 유도하는 것으로 알려져 있으며, 개인의 기분상태를 결정하는 데 중요한 역할을 한다. 도파민이나 노르에피네프린이 흥분제의 효과가 있다면 세로토닌은 억제제의 효과가 있다.

2) 생리전기 증후군(PMS: Premenstrual Syndrome)

- '생리전기 증후군(PMS: Premenstrual Syndrome, 생리도벽)'이 심각하면 정신적으로는 우울증, 신경과민, 충동·공격적 성향, 주의집중 결여, 기억력 장애, 자살충동, 피로감, 분노 등이 나타나며, 육체적으로는 불면증과 과식증, 하복부·유방·관절의 통증, 몸이 붓는 증상, 구토·오심·발한 등이 나타난다고 한다.[20]

3. 신경계통의 이상과 범죄성

1) 중앙신경계 뇌손상

- 중앙신경계통의 비정상적인 활동이 범행과 관련이 있다는 것으로 뇌파(EEG: Electro Encephalo Graph)를 분석한다.
- 비정상적인 EEG수치를 보이는 사람들은 자신의 행동에 대한 통제능력과 억제능력이 상대적으로 현저하게 떨어지며, 타인에 대해 적대적인 경향이 짙으며 자신에게 방해가 되거나 경쟁적인 입장을 가지는 사람에 대해 대단히 공격적인 성향을 보인다는 것이다.

2) 자율신경계

자율신경계 기능의 장애로 인하여 처벌이 예견되는 상황에서 불안반응이 즉각적으로 발현되지 않거나 혹은 그 반대로 상황이 종료되었는데도 불안반응이 신속히 제거되지 못하여 범죄의 원인이 된다는 것이다.

3) 간질

- 간질로 인한 뇌기능장애의 경우, 폭력적이고 통제불능의 상태에 빠질 확률이 높고, 실제로도 교도소 수용자에게서는 일반인보다 간질보유 비율이 높게 나타나고 있다는 것이다.
- 뇌종양이 우울증, 신경과민, 격분, 살해기도 등에 빠질 확률을 높일 수도 있다는 것이다.

20) 전대양, 현대사회와 범죄, 형설출판사, 2002:75.

제16장 심리학적 범죄원인론

제1절 정신분석이론

1. 범죄심리학의 의의

- 범죄심리학(Criminal Psychology)이란 지능·인성·학습 등 인간의 정신적 특징에서 범죄원인을 찾는 실증주의 범죄학이다.
- 심리학분야인 지각·인지, 학습, 기억, 사고, 지능, 정동(情動) 등의 기초적 영역과 인접학문인 인류학, 생물학, 생리학, 사회학, 정신의학, 통계학 등의 광범위한 지식으로 범죄자나 비행자의 행동을 사회문화적·개체적·집단적으로 규명하려는 학문이다.[1)]

2. 정신분석과 범죄

1) 프로이드(S. Freud)의 정신분석의 의의

- 프로이드(S. Freud)는 범죄행동은 무의식 속에 잠재하는 갈등의 결과로 보고 있다.
- 신프로이드 이론에 의하면 범죄자는 자아(ego)가 약하고 본능(id)은 지나치게 높은 사람이라고 할 수 있다. 즉, 범죄는 본능적인 충동을 갖는 id와 행위에 대한 사회적 기대 및 금지를 나타내는 superego 사이의 갈등에서 ego가 이를 적절하고 균형있게 조절하지 못한 결과이다.[2)]

---

1) • 이상현, 범죄심리학, 박영사, 2004:11.
  • 범죄심리학자로는 아이젱크(Eysenck), 슈나이더(Schneider), 프로이드(Freud), 고프, 타르드, 톨만, 반두라, 피아제, 콜버그, 페스팅거, 스키너 등이 있다. 2010 기출
2) • 정신분석이론은 원본능과 초자아 간의 갈등 혹은 초자아의 미발달에서 범죄가 비롯된다고 보았다. 2004 기출

• 프로이드는 형벌은 위하력이 없으며, 범죄인에 대해서는 인간의 무의식적인 동기를 의식화시키는 의학적 치료와 사회적 보호처분이 필요하다고 하였다.

〈표 3-6〉 인성 구분

구 분	내 용
본능 (id, 원초적 자아)	• 선천적으로 가지고 태어나는 것 • 비합리적 · 본능적 · 반사회적인 무의식 상태로 쾌락을 추구 • 사회생활에 잘 적응하기 위해서는 통제되고 다듬어져야 함
자아 (ego)	• 의식적 · 합리적인 부분 • 본능과 초자아의 균형을 잡아줌
초자아 (superego)	• 범죄와 관련해서 가장 중요한 부분. 미숙할 때에는 범죄를 초래 • 도덕적 · 양심적인 부분 • 자아비판력, 양심, 내적 규제 • 남근기(3~6세)에 발달

2) 프로이드의 성격발달의 5단계

• 프로이드는 성격의 발달은 5단계로 이루어진다고 주장하였다. 즉, 1단계는 입을 통해 쾌락을 얻는 '구강기', 2단계는 배설을 통해 쾌락을 추구하는 '항문기', 3단계는 아버지 또는 어머니와 나를 동일시하게 되어 '오이디푸스 콤플렉스'와 '엘렉트라 콤플렉스'[3)] 가 형성되는 '남근기', 4단계는 성에 대한 관심이 억제되고, 또래들과 사회성을 기르는 '잠복기', 5단계는 사춘기와 질풍노도의 시기인 '생식기' 단계로 나누었다.

• 성격은 6세 이전 즉, '남근기' 이전에 형성된다고 보았으며, 이 시기에 성격이 정상적으로 형성되지 않으면 범죄를 저지를 확률이 높다고 주장하였다.

• 프로이드의 정신분석학적 입장에서 범죄에 대한 개념과 관련되는 것으로는 리비도, 무의식(id), 자아(ego), 초자아(superego), 오이디푸스 콤플렉스 등이 있다. 1997, 1999, 2008 기출

3) • 오이디푸스 콤플렉스는 이성의 부모에게 강한 성애적인 감정을 보이며 동성(同性)의 부모에게는 질투나 적의를 나타내는 콤플렉스를 말한다. 이는 남성이 지니고 있는 어머니에 대한 성적 감정(근친상간 소망)과 아버지에 대한 적대감정(살인 소망)을 가리킨다.

• 엘렉트라 콤플렉스는 여성이 페니스가 없는 자신을 남성보다 열등한 존재로 여겨 그러한 상태로 자신을 낳아준 어머니에 대한 실망과 아버지의 자식을 임신한다고 하는 환상을 말한다. 이만종, 범죄학개론, 학현사, 2005:65.

〈표 3-7〉 성격발달의 5단계

순 서	구 분	나 이
1단계	구강기	0~1세
2단계	항문기	1~3세
3단계	남근기	3~6세
4단계	잠복기	6~12세
5단계	생식기	12세 이후

3. 성격과 범죄

1) 의의

범죄행위란 충동성, 폭력성, 자극 추구성, 반발성, 적대감 등과 같은 개인의 성향이 표현된 것뿐이라고 한다.

2) 성격연구

(1) 글뤽부부의 '로르샤흐(Rorschach) 검사' 연구

비행소년 500명과 일반소년 500명을 성격의 심층심리상의 특징을 보여주는 로샤 테스트에 의해 비교한 후, 전체적으로 비행소년들은 외향적이고, 활발하며, 충동적이고, 자제력이 약하였을 뿐만 아니라 적대적이고, 화를 잘 냈으며, 도전적이었고, 의심이 많았고, 파괴적이었다. 또한 정상소년에 비해 실패나 패배를 별로 두려워하지 않았다.

(2) 왈도(Waldo)와 디니츠(Dinitz)의 MMPI 연구

- 1950년에서 1965년 사이에 다면적 인성검사(The Minnesota Multiphasic Personality Inventory: MMPI)를 이용하여 범죄자의 성격프로파일을 조사한 94편의 연구들을 재분석하였다.
- 그 결과 94편의 연구 중 80%에서 범죄자와 정상인 사이에 통계적으로 주목할 만한 성격 프로파일 차이가 있다는 것을 알 수 있었다.[4)]

4) 10가지 성격측면에서 가장 현저한 차이가 있었던 곳은 제4척도 즉, 정신병리적 일탈부분이었으며 이에 따라 왈도와 디니츠는 범죄자들은 일반인에 비해 정신병리적 일탈경향이 강한 성격으로 특징지을 수 있다고 보았으며, 이는 가석방 판결 시 사용되기도 하였다.

3) 정신병리적 성격과 범죄

- 정신병리적(사회병리적 · 반사회적) 성격은 성격의 이상 정도가 정상성을 크게 벗어나 거의 병적으로 볼 수 있는 경우이다.
- 성격상의 근본적인 장애로 인해 조그마한 자극에 대하여도 격렬한 감정의 폭발을 일으키는 자극과 반응의 부조화를 경험한다든지, 생물학적 욕망 등 감정생활을 적절히 조절할 수 있는 능력이 결핍되어, 행위관련 요소 간에 기능적인 협동관계가 이루어지지 않아 반사회적 행위에 그만큼 쉽게 빠져든다는 것이다.

4. 사이코패스

1) 의의

- 1920년대 독일의 슈나이더(K. Schneider)가 처음 소개한 개념으로 보통 반사회적 인격장애증을 앓고 있는 사람을 가리킨다.
- 발정 · 광신 · 자기현실 의지결여 · 폭발적 성격 · 무기력 등의 특징을 지닌다.
- 평소에는 내부에 잠재되어 있다가 범행을 통하여서만 밖으로 드러나기 때문에 주변 사람들이 알아차리지 못하는 것이 보통이다.

2) 특징

- 타인의 고통을 느끼는 공감능력이 결여되어 있다.[5)]
- 죄책감이 결여되어 있고 자기 합리화를 한다.
- 교활하고 상습적으로 거짓말을 한다.

5) 이는 끔찍한 장면을 보았을 때, 정상인과 사이코패스 살인범과의 뇌 비교를 통해 알 수 있다. 미국 브르크하멜국립연구소의 연구결과에 따르면, 감정을 지배하는 전두엽 기능이 일반인의 15%밖에 되지 않아 다른 사람의 고통에 무감각하고 양심의 가책을 느끼지 않는다. 고통에 무감각하므로 자신이 저지른 죄의 대가로 받게 될 처벌을 두려워하지 않음으로써 재범률도 높고 연쇄범죄를 저지를 가능성도 일반범죄자들보다 높다. 또 공격적 성향을 억제하는 분비물인 세로토닌이 부족하여 사소한 일에도 강한 공격적 성향을 드러낸다고 한다. 사이코패스는 이 같은 유전적 · 생물학적 요인에 사회적 · 환경적 요인이 결합되어 나타나는 전인격적 병리현상으로 본다.

3) 사이코패스(psychopath)의 원인

(1) 유전적 · 생물학적(선천적) 요인

선천적 요인으로는 뇌파의 이상, 비정상적인 균형을 보이는 뇌반구의 기능, 호르몬 분비 이상, 자율신경계가 있다.[6]

(2) 후천적 요인인 환경

- 사이코패스의 유전적 요인이 매우 높더라도 성장환경이 건전할 경우 사이코패스 발현가능성은 낮아진다.
- 반대로 유전적 요인은 다소 낮더라도 나쁜 환경에서 성장할 경우 내부적으로 스스로 사이코패스 성향을 학습하게 되어 사이코패스 발현가능성이 매우 높아진다.
- 후천적 요인으로는 유년기 학대경험, 범죄경험, 경쟁사회 등을 들 수 있다.

〈표 3-8〉 연쇄살인심리의 7단계

단계	명칭	내용
1단계	심리적 준비단계 (Aure Phase)	• 살인대상을 찾고 포획하는 작업에 들어가는 단계
↓		
2단계	낚시질단계 (Trolling Phase)	• 연쇄살인범은 낚시꾼과 유사하다. 희생자를 낚아 올리기 위해 낚싯대를 드리울 위치를 정하는데 살인자들마다 선호지역이 있다고 한다. 어둠침침한 지하주차장이나 인적이 드문 밤거리, 외진 골목길, 야산 샛길을 좋아하는데 이런 장소를 배회하면서 기회를 노린다.
↓		
3단계	구애단계 (Wooing Phase)	• 피해자를 유혹하여 덫으로 끌어들이는 단계다. 대개 신임을 얻어 경계심을 허문 다음 유인한다. 유괴범들도 비슷하다. 도와달라고 하면서 유인한다. 이들에게 발견되는 아주 놀라운 점은 이들이 결코 혐오스럽게 생겼거나 무서운 얼굴이 아니라는 점이다. 그들은 폭력을 함부로 쓰지 않고 마각을 드러내기 전까지는 순진한 모습으로 유혹한다. 고양이와 매가 사냥하기 전 발톱을 감추는 것과 비슷하다.

6) 사이코패스의 뇌반구 기능은 얼굴에 나타나는 감정의 표현을 정확히 읽는 좌뇌와 감정을 경험하는 우뇌가 결함을 보이는 것이다. 호르몬 분비 이상은 몸속의 효소를 조절하는 유전자가 전두엽의 기능을 줄어들게 하여 공격성을 증가시키는 원인이 된다. 자율신경계는 둔감한 교감신경계와 민감한 부교감신경계로 구성되어 있는데, 사이코패스는 스트레스 상황에서 매우 담담하고, 말초신경계가 둔감하여 무감정적이다. 그리고 공감이나 후회, 자책이 결여되어 있으며, 쉽게 거짓말할 수 있는 능력을 가지고 있다.

4단계	포획단계 (Capture)	• 포획은 전광석화처럼 빠르게 이루어진다. 갑자기 차문을 잠가 버리거나 피해자의 얼굴에 주먹을 날려 순간적으로 무력화시킨다.
5단계	살인 (Murder)	• 생명을 빼앗는 단계다.
6단계	회상기 (Totem Phase)	• 신체 일부를 기념품화한다. 사진으로 남기는 범인들도 있다.
7단계	침체기 (Depression Phase)	• 다시 우울함으로 돌아가는 단계다. 그러다 다시 1단계로 돌아간다.

제2절 정신적 결함이론

1. 고다드(Goddard)의 범죄자의 정신박약설

- 수형자들의 지능을 측정한 결과, 수행자의 대부분이 저지능이라는 점을 밝혀 정신박약과 범죄 사이에 관계가 있음을 강조하였다.
- 지능과 범죄의 관계에 대해서 논란의 여지가 있으나 둘 사이에 관계가 있는 것은 어느 정도 사실이다. 그러나 낮은 지능과 범죄를 연결짓는 것은 단순하지 않다.
- 지능 자체가 선천적 요인과 환경적 요인 모두와 관련을 가진 측면이 있을 뿐만 아니라 지능과 비행의 관계 역시 이들 두 가지 측면이 상호 작용한 결과라고 보아야 한다.

2. 고프(Gough)의 반사회적 인성과 범죄

1) 의의

- '반사회적 인성'은 일반적으로 '정신병리', '사회병리'와 동의어로 사용된다.
- 지능의 부족, 뇌의 구조적인 질환, 신경증적 정신병을 앓고 있지는 않지만 사회적 적응능력이 부족한 퍼스낼러티를 지칭한다.
- 일반적으로 사회의 중요한 가치나 규범을 내면화하는 데 실패한 결점이 있는 퍼스낼러티를 말한다.

2) 반사회적 인성의 특성

- 미래에 대한 목표보다는 현실의 목표를 과대평가한다.
- 충동적 행동을 취하며, 자극의 강도와 자극에 대한 행동적 반응이 일치하지 않는다.
- 타인과 깊고 영속성 있는 애정관계를 형성할 수 없기에, 깊숙한 대인관계를 유지할 수 없다.
- 자기가 정한 목표에 도달할 때까지의 사고와 계획성이 결여되어 있다.
- 사회적 부적응에 대한 불안과 고민이 결여되어 있고, 자기 잘못을 타인에게 돌리며 실패에 대한 책임을 지지 않는다.
- 하찮은 일에도 변명하며, 전혀 신뢰할 수 없으며 책임도 지지 않으며, 감정이 결핍되어 있다.

3) 반사회적 인성의 원인

부모의 애정결핍, 아버지가 정신병자이거나 알코올중독자일 가능성, 기타 불우한 아동기의 경험(가정폭력의 경험) 등이 지적되고 있다.

3. 슈나이더(Schneider)의 정신병질(psychopathy)과 범죄 1999 기출

1) 발양성 정신병질자

- 자신의 능력과 운명에 대해 과도하게 낙관적이며, 경솔하고 불안정적인 면을 갖는 성격이다.
- 다혈질적이고 활동적이어서 어디서나 떠들고 야단법석을 벌이며 실현가능성이 없는 약속도 깊은 고려 없이 남발함으로써 상습사기범이 되기 쉽다.
- 무전취식자로 돌아다니기도 하며 닥치는 대로 훔치기도 한다.
- 순간적인 충동에 따라서 움직이고 쉽게 범죄유혹에 빠지기도 한다.

2) 우울성 정신병질자

- 염세적·비관적인 인생관에 빠져 항상 우울하게 지내고 자책적이다.
- 항상 최악의 상황을 생각하고 과거를 후회하고 미래를 걱정한다.
- 강박관념에 빠져 자살할 가능성이 높다.
- 적극적으로 범죄에 가담하지 않는 편이지만 강박증상으로 드물기는 하지만 살인이나 성범죄를 저지르기도 한다.

3) 의지박약성 정신병질자

- 외형적 의지, 내면적 의지 양자 모두에서 박약성을 지녀 주위 상황과 주변 사람들의 태도에 따라 우왕좌왕한다. 대개 지능이 낮은 편이다.
- 좋은 환경 아래에서는 온순하고 모범적으로 생활하나, 나쁜 환경 아래에서는 범죄의 유혹에 직면하게 되면 쉽게 빠지고 그 후에는 헤어나지 못한다.
- 상습누범자 중에 많고[7], 창녀, 알코올중독자, 마약중독자 중에 많다.

4) 무정성(정성박약성) 정신병질자

- 인간이 보편적으로 갖고 있는 타인에 대한 동정심이나 연민의 감정, 수치심, 명예심, 공동의식, 양심의 가책 등이 결핍되어 함부로 행동한다.
- 자신의 목적달성을 위해서는 냉혹·잔인하게 행동하고 그에 대한 죄책감을 느끼지 못하고, 복수심도 강하고 완고하며 교활하다.
- 사이코패스, 도덕적 백치 또는 도덕적 박약자(moral imbecile) 등으로 불리며, 흉악범죄인 살인, 강도, 강간과 관련이 깊고, 가로팔로의 자연범과 유사하며, 범죄학에서 가장 주목을 받는 정신병질자이다.
- 롬브로조의 생래적 범죄자, XYY형 범죄자 등이 여기에 해당한다.

5) 폭발성 정신병질자(병적 흥분자)

- 사소한 자극에 대해 병적으로 과도하게 격렬한 반응을 일으키고, 전후를 고려함이 없이 닥치는 대로 던지고 때리고 폭언하기를 주저하지 않는다.
- 타인에 대한 공격뿐 아니라 자해행위를 하기도 한다. 이런 경향은 알코올 음용 이후에 더욱 잘 나타난다.
- 뇌파검사를 하면 간질성 기질이 나타나기도 한다. 평소에는 조용하고 친절하며 분별력 있게 지내기도 한다. 이들은 충동범죄인 살상, 폭행, 모욕, 손괴 등의 범죄행위를 많이 저지른다.

6) 기분이변성 정신병질자

- 기분의 동요가 심하여 예측할 수 없는 것이 특징이다.
- 갑자기 어떤 감동이 발하여 이상한 행동과 기분을 내다가 곧 주저앉는 등 변화가 심하다.
- 폭력성과 마찬가지로 간질성 기질이 나타나기도 한다. 방랑과 폭음, 낭비를 일삼는 경우가 많고, 초범, 방화범과 상해범 중에 이런 성향이 많다.

7) 자기현시욕성(허영성) 정신병질자

- 자기를 사물의 중심으로 생각하는 등 자기를 실제 이상으로 높이 인식하는 성격이다.

---

7) 의지박약형은 누범자에게 가장 많이 나타나는 정신병질의 유형이다. 1999 기출

- 다른 사람의 주목과 평판의 대상이 되고자 공상적인 거짓말을 일삼기 때문에 고급사기범이 되기 쉽다.
- 욕구가 좌절되면 신체적 질환으로 도피하여 히스테리성 반응을 보이기도 한다.

8) 자신결핍성(자기불확실성) 정신병질자

- 자신의 우월성을 나타내고자 하는 마음은 많으나 능력부족을 늘 의식하여 주변 사정에 민감하고 어떤 강박현상에 쫓기는 듯한 복잡한 심경의 소유자이다.
- 주변 사정에 민감하여 도덕성을 지키기 때문에 범죄와는 거리가 멀다.

9) 열광성(광신성) 정신병질자

- 어떤 가치나 신념에 열중하여 외부에 적극적으로 선전하고 주장을 펼치는 등 소신에 따라 행동하는 강한 성격의 소유자이다.
- 정의감에 따라 소송을 즐기기도 하고 비현실적 주장을 펼치기도 한다(종교적 광신자나 정치적 확신범).

10) 무력성 정신병질자

- 심신의 부조화 상태를 호소하며, 관심을 자기에게 돌리기를 바라고 동정을 바라는 성격이다.
- 인격성의 상실에 빠져 번민하기도 하고 신경질적이다.
- 범죄성과 적극적인 관련성을 가진 것은 발양성, 의지박약성, 폭력성, 기분이변성, 자기현시욕성, 열광성, 무정성의 7가지이며, 우울성, 자신결핍성, 무력성은 소극적인 관계를 가진다고 보았다.

〈표 3-9〉 슈나이더의 10가지 정신병질의 종류

내용/유형	성격적 특징	관련되는 범죄유형
발양성 (hyperthymisch)	• 자기의 운명과 능력에 낙천적, 경솔, 부정적 비판 · 감정제어능력 결여(폭발성 · 무정성 · 광신성 등과 관련)	• 상습죄, 누범 중에 많음 • 모욕죄 · 사기죄와 관련 • 무정성과 관련되면 알코올중독 위험
우울성 (depressive)	• 염세적 · 회의적 인간관, 자책성 · 발기제지성 · 불평	• 범죄와 관련 적음. 자살유혹이 강함. 강박관념에 의한 살상 · 성범죄 가능
의지박약성 (willenslos)	• 모든 영향에 대한 저항상실지능이 낮음 ※ 항상 범죄적 경향으로만 기우는 무절조성과 구별	• 좋은 환경하에서는 범죄와 관련 적음. 누죄의 60%. 각종 중독자 계획을 요하지 않는 소규모 절도, 사기

무정성 (Gemutlos)	• 동정심·수치심(혐오) 등 인간의 고등감정 결여, 광신성의 사후변질결과로도 나타남(발양성, 무지박약성, 기분역변성 등과 관련)	• 목적달성을 위한 흉악범(강도·살인·강간 등), 범죄단체조직·누범
폭발성 (explosive)	• 자극에 대한 지나친 반응, 병적 흥분, 음주 시 무정성·의지박약성과 결합되면 매우 위험. 타 유형에 비하여 자기치료가 가능(자기결핍성 이외의 모든 유형과 관련)	• 살상·모욕·손괴·폭행 등 충동적 범죄의 대부분과 관련. 충동적 자살도 가능
기분이변성 (stimmungslabil)	• 기분동요의 심각으로 예측 곤란 폭발성과 유사하나 정도가 낮음. 정신병질자의 50%, 의지박약·정신박약과 결합 시 위험	• 방화·도벽·음주광·과식, 격정범으로 상해·모욕·군기위반 가능
자기현시욕성·과장성 (geltungsvedurftig)	• 자신에의 주목·관심유도, egocentric 자기 기망적 히스테리성 반응 (박약성, 광신성 등과 관련)	• 기망적 성격에 따른 고등사기(Hochstapler), 구금수형자 중 거짓병 앓는 자가 많음
자신결핍성 (selbstunsicher)	• 능력부족인식으로 우월성 억제 강박관념, 주변에 대한 인식으로 도덕성 강함	• 범죄와 관련 적음. 감수성이 예민한 경우 강박관념으로 인한 범죄(살상, 성범죄 등 가능)
광신성·열광성 (fanatisch)	• 개인적·이념성 사상에 열중 타인에 대한 불신으로 범죄가능	• 호소광(Querluant), 투쟁적 광신자의 경우, 정치범이 많음
무력성 (asthenisch)	• 심신의 부조화상태·타인 관심요구, 신경증의 증상	• 범죄와 관련 적음

출처: 이만종, 범죄학개론, 학현사, 2005:63.

4. 정신병질과 범죄[8)]

1) 정신병질

- 정신병질은 반사회적 성격장애(antisocial personality disorder)로 다양한 성격장애와 품행장애를 보인다. 즉, 규칙위반, 남을 속임, 충동성, 공격적인 행동, 무분별, 책임의식 결여 등의 성격측면의 장애와 이에 따른 행동장애를 보인다.
- 성격장애란 개인의 고유한 성격특질이 그가 속한 사회문화적 기대로부터 심하게 벗어나 있고, 이 특질이 경직되어 있어서 부적응적으로 아무 상황에서나 반복적으로 나타나며, 이 때문에 사회적으로나 직업적으로 심각한 기능장애를 야기하거나 주관적인 고통을 유발하는 경우를 말한다.[9)]
- 성격장애는 작은 자극에도 격렬한 감정의 폭발을 보이기도 하고, 여러 가지 욕망을 적절히 통제할 수 있는 능력이 결여되어 범죄나 반사회적 행동에 그만큼 쉽게 노출되는 셈이다.

2) 정신분열증

- 정신분열증(schizophrenia)은 현실에서 이해할 수 없는 소리를 듣거나 어떤 보이지 않는 힘에 의하여 자기가 조종당한다는 생각을 사실로 믿는 정신병(psychosis)[10)]의 일종이다.
- 사고장애의 망상에는 i) 다른 사람들에 의해 자신의 생각과 행동이 지배받고 있다는 조종망상, ii) 다른 사람이 나를 괴롭히거나 내가 피해를 입고 있다는 피해망상, iii) 자기가 세상 구원자이거나 주요한 임무를 띠고 있다고 생각하는 과대망상, iv) 자기의 생각을 다른 사람들이 다 알고 있다고 생각하는 사고전파, v) 외계인이 자기에게 생각을 넣고 있다는 사고투입 등이 있다.

---

8) • 정신병으로 인한 범죄자 중에서 가장 많이 발견되는 증상은 정신분열증이다. 2004 기출
 • 전대양, 현대사회와 범죄, 형설출판사, 2002:81-88.

9) 전대양, 현대사회와 범죄, 형설출판사, 2002:93.

10) 정신병이란 지각 · 사고 · 의식의 변화를 포함하는 장애로서 현실에 대해 이해할 수 없는 엉뚱한 추론을 하며, 자신을 비현실적으로 추론할 뿐만 아니라 이를 실제의 것으로 믿는 것을 말한다.

3) 편집증

편집증(paranoia)은 전반적으로 근거 없는 의심을 많이 하고 사람을 믿지 않으며 극도로 다른 사람을 경계하고 정서는 메말라 있는 것이 주요 특징이다.

4) 불안신경증

- 신경증(neurosis)은 노이로제로 흔히 알려져 있으며, 최근에는 불안장애로 부르고 있다. 불안신경증(anxiety neurosis)은 여러 가지 공황장애나 일반화된 불안장애를 갖고 있는 불안장애의 일종이다.
- 공황장애(panic disorder)는 예기치 못한 갑작스러운 두려움이 몰려오고 그 두려움이 너무 극심해서 견디기 힘든 상황에까지 이르는 경험을 말하는 것이다.
- 일반화된 불안장애(generalized anxiety disorder)는 ⅰ) 실제로는 위협이 되지 않는 대상이나 상황에 대해서 심한 공포와 두려움을 보이는 것이고, ⅱ) 이런 공포자극을 비합리적인 줄 알면서도 회피하고자 하는 것이다.
- 불안을 이기지 못해 또는 불안에서 벗어나고자 범죄를 범하고 이 때문에 체포되어 처벌받음으로써 해방감을 만끽하고자 한다. 이를 '죄책감 콤플렉스에 의한 범죄'라고도 한다.

5) 강박신경증

- 강박신경증(obsessive compulsive disorder)이란 강박적 사고나 강박행동을 말한다. 강박관념(obsession)이란 본인도 불합리하고 얼토당토않은 줄 알지만 통제할 수 없는 어떤 생각이나 심상이 반복적이고 지속적으로 떠오르는 것을 말한다.
- 강박행동(compulsion)이란 어떤 의식적 행동(손씻기, 정돈하기, 확인하기 등)이나 정신적 활동(기도하기, 숫자세기 등)을 몇 번이고 되풀이하여 반복하려는 억제할 수 없는 충동에 따른 행동으로서, 보통 강박관념에 대한 반응으로서 나타난다.
- 방화광(pyromania), 절도광(kleptomania), 음주광(dipsomania) 등에 강박신경증 환자가 많다고 하며, 특히 방화광들은 성적인 장애에 기인하여 방화행동을 반복한다고 한다.

제3절 인성이론

1. 의의

- 범죄자는 일반인과 다른 비정상적이고 부적합한 범죄적 성향을 가지고 있다고 보고, 범죄행동은 이와 같은 개인적 성향 즉, 충동성, 폭력성, 자극추구성, 반발성, 적대감 등이 표출된 것으로 본다.
- 정신분석학적 설명은 인간에게 겉으로 잘 드러나지 않는 무의식 같은 것이 표출된 행동을 중시하는 반면, 인성을 통한 설명은 각종 심리검사에 의해 드러난 특성을 중심으로 인간의 행동을 설명하고 예측하는 점에서 차이가 있다.
- 인성이론은 정신병리적 성격 논의에 비해 보다 넓은 관점에서 성격특성을 분류하는 데 관심이 있으며, 여러 가지 심리검사나 측정방법을 통해 성격적 차이를 규명하는 데 주력한다.

2. 아이젱크(Eysenck)의 성격이론(인성이론) 2009 기출

1) 의의

- 성격을 환경에 대한 개인의 독특한 적응에 영향을 미치는 인격, 기질, 지성, 신체요소들이 안정되고 영속적으로 조직화된 것이라고 정의하였다.
- 매우 반사회적 성향을 가진 사람의 경우에 정신이상, 외향성, 신경증의 정도가 모두 높을 것이라고 보았다. 범죄자는 내성적 성격보다 외향적 성격이 높다고 했다. 2004 기출

2) 성격의 3차원(P – E – N 모델) 2009 기출

(1) 정신병적 성향(정신이상: P)

- 정신병을 향한 성향과 반사회적인 이상성격을 포함한다.
- 공격적, 차가움, 자기중심적, 비정함, 비사회적, 비관습적인 것 등으로 특징지어진다.

- 정신병리와 연관이 있을 수도 있지만 개인차는 정상분포를 따르므로 어느 정도는 정신병과 무관하다.

(2) 외향성(E) : 사회성과 충동성에서의 차이와 관련

- 외향성은 사교적이고, 파티를 좋아하고, 친구가 많고 흥미진진한 것을 추구하며 순간의 기분에 따라 행동한다.
- 내향성은 조용하고, 내성적이고, 말수가 적고, 반성적이며, 충동적 결정을 불신하고, 잘 정돈된 삶을 선호한다.
- 내향인은 외향인에 비해 고통에 더 민감하고, 보다 쉽게 피로하고, 흥분이 수행을 저하시키고, 학교공부를 더 잘하고, 혼자 일하는 직업을 선호하고, 암기에 덜 반응하고, 성적으로 덜 활동적이다.
- 내향인은 사건들에 의해 보다 쉽게 각성되고 사회적 금지사항들을 보다 쉽게 학습한다. 그 결과 내향인은 더 억제되어 있다. 학습에서 내향인은 처벌에 의해서 보다 영향을 받고, 외향인은 보상에 의해서 보다 영향을 받는다는 증거도 있다.

(3) 신경증 성향(신경성: N)

- 정서적 안정성-불안정성 측정치로 높은 신경증적 성향은 더 큰 불안정성이 특징이다.
- 정서적으로 불안정하고 변덕스러우며, 걱정, 우울, 불안, 낮은 자존감, 긴장, 수줍음 등의 특징이 있고 신체적 통증의 호소가 빈번하다.

제4절 학습 및 도덕성 발달

1. 의의

- 학습이론은 정신분석학적 접근, 퍼스낼리티 이론 등과 달리 인간을 이해하는 데 있어서 무의식이나 인격 내부의 역동관계 등의 내적 과정을 가정할 필요를 인정하지 않는다.
- 학습이론에서는 관찰가능한 행동 수준에서의 자극과 반응과의 관계를 중시한다.

• 학습(learning)은 경험을 매개로 하여 행동에 비교적 영속적인 변화를 일으키는 과정이며, 학습이론에서는 기억할 수 없는 경험은 제외되며, 기억할 수 있는 경험이 인간의 행동에 영향을 미친다고 본다.
• 학습이론가들은 강화・모방을 범죄의 주요 요인으로 보았다. 2004 기출

2. 타르드(Gabriel Tarde)의 모방이론

1) 의의

범죄를 정상적으로 학습된 행위로 보며, 인간행위의 본질은 사람들이 사회생활을 하는 중에 다른 사람의 행위를 모방하는 것이라고 보았다. 범죄행위도 이런 모방(imitation)의 한 예이다.

2) 모방의 법칙 2000 기출

〈표 3-10〉 모방의 3가지 법칙[11)]

거리의 법칙	• 모방은 사람과 사람 사이의 거리에 반비례하여 강하게 또는 약하게 행하여지고, 거리가 가까울수록 강하게 모방작용이 행하여지는 것이다. 이 경우의 거리는 기하학적 의미만이 아니라 심리학적 의미의 거리도 포함된다.
위에서 아래로의 법칙	• 사회적 우월자를 중심으로, 상위자로부터 하위자로, 봉건시대에는 귀족에서 민중으로, 근대에는 대도시에서 촌락지방으로, 수도에서 지방으로 등의 모방현상이 진행되며, 또 성년에서 소년으로 진행된다.
삽입의 법칙(무한진행의 법칙)	• 모방의 발전과 변화과정에 관한 것으로 처음의 단순한 모방이 유행으로, 그리고 그 유행이 관습으로 발전・삽입되어 간다고 주장하였다.

11) 타르드는 "범죄자를 제외한 모든 사람에게 그 책임이 있다."고 할 정도로 극단적인 환경결정론자였으며, 범죄행위 모방의 3법칙은 거리의 법칙, 방향의 법칙, 삽입의 법칙으로 구성되며, 방향의 법칙은 사회적 지위가 열등한 사람들은 우월한 사람들을 모방한다는 것이다. 2005 기출

3. 콜버그(Kohlberg)의 도덕발달이론

1) 의의

- 도덕성은 개인이 자신의 욕망에 집착하지 않고 타인의 입장을 이해하며, 사회 속에서 적응해 가는 행동경향을 말한다.
- 행위의 옳고 그름에 대한 이해와 그에 상응하는 행동은 3가지 수준의 6단계라는 과정(사회화과정)을 통해서 발달한다고 주장하였다.
- 사람들의 인지능력을 강조했으며, 도덕발달의 6단계 중 1, 2단계에 있는 사람이 범죄가능성이 높다고 했다. 2004 기출

2) 도덕발달단계

(1) 1수준 : **전인습적 도덕성**(pre-morality)

- 1단계 : 처벌받지 않을 행동(처벌과 복종단계)
- 2단계 : 일반적으로 이익이 되는 행동(쾌락주의)

(2) 2수준 : **인습적 도덕성**(conventional conformity)

- 3단계 : 타인의 인정을 받고 비난받지 않을 행동(대인관계 조화)
- 4단계 : 법과 질서에 의해 엄격히 규정된 행동

(3) 3수준 : **후인습적 도덕성**(autonomous principles)

- 5단계 : 법은 대중의 복리를 위한 사회계약이라는 입장에 근거하여 판단
- 6단계 : 보편적인 윤리원칙에 입각해서 판단

제17장 사회학적 범죄원인론

제1절 사회구조이론

[그림 3-1] The three branches of social structure theory

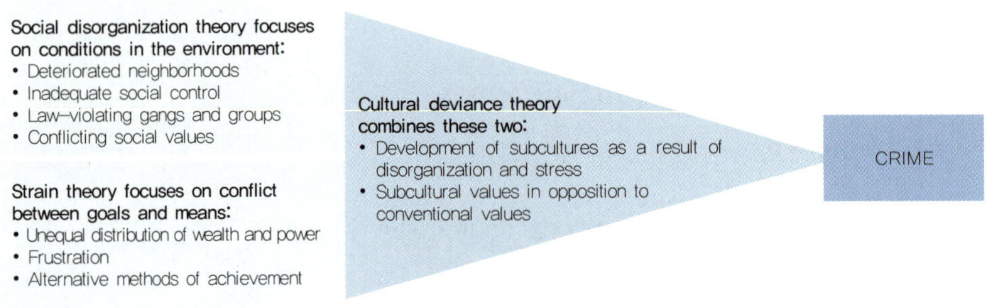

출처: L. J. Siegel & J. J. Senna, Essentials of Criminal Justice, Thomson Wadsworth, 2007:59.

1. 사회해체이론(social disorganization theory)[1)]

• 사회해체란 "공식적 사회통제 또는 비공식적 사회통제가 붕괴되어 가는 과정"을 말하며, 사회조직의 분화(differential social organization)라고도 한다.

• 범죄는 사회해체가 진행되어 나가는 과정에서 반사회적 행위가 일반화함에 따라 나

1) 범죄발생의 원인과 증가를 설명함에 있어, 범죄자의 특성이 아니라 지역사회처럼 사회환경의 특성을 단위로 하여 다루는 거시이론의 대표적인 것은 '사회해체이론'이다. 2005 기출

타나는 것으로 파악한다.

1) 시카고(Chicago)학파

- 1920년대부터 미국 시카고대학을 중심으로 생태학적으로 범죄를 설명한 시카고학파는 범죄를 사회환경 특히, 지역사회(community)에 관련되어 있다고 주장하였다.
- 시카고의 급격한 도시발전, 이민, 가난 등에 의하여 가족, 학교, 교회 등 전통적인 기관들이 제 기능을 하지 못해 가족과 이웃사회의 결합이 약화되는 현상을 가리켜 '사회해체'라 하고, 이는 슬럼(slum)지역 범죄의 주요 원인이라고 밝혔다.
- 시카고 슬럼지역의 거주민이 달라짐에도 계속 높은 범죄율을 보이는 것은, 그 지역의 특수한 환경이 범죄를 발생시키는 요소이며 그러한 환경은 계속 전달되는 것이라고 주장하였다.

2) 버제스(Burgess)의 동심원이론

- 시카고를 5개의 지역(중심상업지역, 전이지역, 노동자 거주지역, 중류계층지역, 외부통근지역)으로 나누어 범죄발생률을 조사해 본 결과, 범죄율이 가장 높은 지역은 제2지역(전이지역)이고, 범죄율이 가장 낮은 지역은 제5지역(외부통근지역)이었다.
- 도심지역과 전이지역의 범죄발생률이 지속적으로 높고, 도심에서 멀어질수록 점차 낮아진다는 것을 발견하였다.[2)]
- 전이지역에서는 급격한 도시발전, 이민, 가난 등에 의하여 전통적 기관들이 깨지거나 제 기능을 하지 못해 긴장상태에 놓여 있어 가족과 이웃의 결합이 약화되는 사회해체 현상이 범죄의 원인이 된다고 주장하였다.
- 범죄는 개인심리의 소산이기보다 열악한 주택사정, 심한 인구이동, 열악한 학교환경 등과 같은 사회적 요인이 주민들 간에 계속 전달된 결과로 보았다.

2. 긴장이론

긴장이론은 아노미이론, 제도적 아노미이론, 일반긴장이론으로 나누어볼 수 있다.

2) A도시의 지역별 범죄분포를 살펴보면, 도심의 범죄율이 높고 외곽의 범죄율은 낮은 것으로 나타난다. 이것은 '사회해체이론'에 의하여 가장 적절히 설명될 수 있다. 2007 기출

1) 아노미이론

(1) 의의

아노미(anomie)는 원래 무규범상태 또는 무규율상태의 의미로 사용되었으나 그 후 신념체계의 갈등 또는 붕괴상태, 도덕적 부적응 등 여러 가지 의미로 사용되고 있다.[3)]

(2) 뒤르켐의 아노미이론

- 아노미는 끝없는 자기욕망을 사회규범이나 도덕으로써 제대로 규제하지 못하는 사회적 상태에서 욕망의 분출 또는 좌절에 의한 긴장의 해소이다.
- 자살, 범죄를 일탈의 한 형태로 파악하며, 사회응집력(cohesion)의 정도에 따라 자살률이 달라지며 사회응집력의 2차원인 '통합'과 '규범'의 정도의 차이가 자살의 원인이 된다.

〈표 3-11〉 자살의 유형

유형	내용
이기주의적 자살	• 통합의 정도가 너무 낮을 때 발생하는 자살
이타주의적 자살	• 통합의 정도가 너무 높을 때 발생하는 자살
아노미적 자살	• 규범이 너무 약해져서 발생하는 자살
숙명론적 자살	• 규범이 강해서 발생할 수 있는 자살

3) • 아노미이론(긴장이론)과 관련된 학자로는 뒤르켐(Durkheim), 머튼(Merton), 애그뉴(Agnew) 등이 있다. 2010 기출
- 아노미란 용어를 처음 사용한 뒤르켐(Durkheim)은 인간의 욕구란 상대적인 것이며, 아노미란 인간의 끝없는 자기 욕망을 사회의 규범이나 도덕으로써 제대로 규제하지 못하는 사회적 상태를 지칭한다고 하였다.
- 머튼(Merton)은 사람들이 추구하는 목표는 생래적인 것이 아니라 그 사회의 문화적 성격에 의해서 영향을 받으며, 이에 도달할 수 있는 수단 역시 문화적으로 일정한 것으로만 제한되어 있다고 보았다. 아노미는 문화적 목표와 사회적 수단 간의 불일치에서 발생한다고 하였다.
- 아노미란 사회와 관계되는 인간의 속성이 아니라 사회구조적 속성에 관계되는 것이다. 아노미상황은 현재의 사회구조가 구성원 개인의 욕구와 욕망에 대한 통제력을 유지할 수 없을 때 일어나며, 집단이나 사회의 무규범성 상태나 조건이다. 뒤르켐은 머튼의 아노미이론에 영향을 주었다. 2004 기출
- 아노미란 무규범상태를 말하며, 급격한 사회변동으로 일탈행위가 증가하며, 뒤르켐의 이론은 머튼의 이론에 영향을 주었다. 2009 기출

(3) 머튼의 아노미이론 2009 기출

① 의의

- 아노미는 문화적 목표와 제도화된 수단 간의 괴리로 인하여 발생하며[4], 범죄는 개인적인 허물이나 결핍에서 오는 증상이 아닌 사회문화적 요인들 즉, 강조되는 문화적 목표에 비해 제한된 성취기회로 인하여 발생한다.
- 머튼 (R. K Merton)은 저서『사회구조와 아노미(Social Structure and Anomie)』에서, 일탈행동은 문화적으로 규정된 목표와 그 목표를 달성하기 위하여 사회적으로 구조(문화적 목표)된 제도적 수단(제도화의 과정)이 서로 조화 있게 작용하지 못할 때 발생하는 것이라고 주장하였다.[5]

② 아노미적 상황에 대처하는 방식에 따른 5가지 적응유형

문화적 목표와 제도적 수단의 '수용'과 '거부'의 결합에 의하여 문화에 순응하려는 사회 속의 개개인의 적응유형을 ⅰ) 동조, ⅱ) 혁신, ⅲ) 의례주의, ⅳ) 도피주의, ⅴ) 반항의 5가지 유형으로 분류하고, 혁신과 도피주의가 범죄와 가장 관계 깊은 유형이라고 하였다.[6]

〈표 3-12〉 머튼의 적응유형 2012 기출

적응유형	목표에 대한 태도	수단에 대한 태도	특 징
동조형 (confirmity)[7]	+	+	• 문화적 목적 즉, 물질적 부의 축적을 달성하기를 원하고 그 목적을 합법적인 수단을 통해서 달성할 수 있는 집단 사회의 성공목표에 대해 용인하고 이에 도달하기 위한 제도적 수단을 받아들임

4) 문화적인 목표와 제도화된 수단 간의 괴리로 인해 사회의 아노미가 발생한다고 주장한 학자는 '머튼'이다. 2007 기출

5) Anomie는 원래 무정부상태, 무규제상태의 의미로 사용되었으나, 그 후 신념체계의 갈등, 붕괴상태, 도덕적 유발, 부도덕 등 여러 의미로 사용되었으며, 특히 목표상실감, 불만, 자기 소외 등 개인적 차원의 무규범상태임. Anomie와 구별하려는 견해도 있다.

6) Merton Robert K., Social Theory and Social Structure, New York : The Free Press, 1957.

7) 문화적 목표와 성공에 필요한 제도화된 수단을 동시에 가지고 있는 사람들은 기존의 사회질서에 순응한다. 문화적 목표를 수용하지만 합법적인 수단을 구비하지 못한 사람들은 절도, 사기 같은 재산범죄를 저지르는 경우가 많다. 문화적 목표와 제도화된 수단을 거부하는 사람들은 알코올중독, 마약중독, 매춘, 도박 등의 퇴행성향을 나타낸다. 2005 기출

개혁형(혁신형, innovation)8)	+	−	• 문화적 목표는 추구하지만 이를 성취할 합법적 틀 내의 수단이 없기 때문에 불법적 수단을 동원해서라도 목표를 달성하려는 유혹을 가장 많이 받을 수 있다. 문화적 목표는 수용하지만 이를 성취하기 위한 합법적 수단은 없는 경우(범죄형)
의례형(의식형, ritualism)	−	+	• 문화적 목표는 부인하면서, 제도적 수단은 용인하는 중하층 관료 등의 적응형태로써, 물질적 성공이라는 문화적 목표가 자기에게는 실현 가능성이 희박하다고 보고 주어진 틀 내에서 규범을 따르며 살아가는 유형 가능한 목표만 세워서 좌절을 줄임(소시민형)
도피형(퇴행형, retreatism)9)	−	−	• 문화적으로 승인된 목표와 사회적으로 받아들여질 수 있는 수단을 모두 거부하는 적응유형으로써, 문화적 목표도 가지고 있지 않고 자연히 그러한 목표를 달성하기 위한 시도조차 포기한 유형 2008 기출 • 기존사회에서 후퇴하여 딴 세상에 산다(폐인형).
반역형(혁명형, 번복형, 반항형, rebellion)	±	±	• 문화적 목표와 제도적 수단 모두를 부정하고 새로운 목표와 수단을 제시함으로써 사회의 반혁을 시도하는 유형 • 기존사회의 목표, 수단을 모두 거부하며 새로운 목표, 수단을 제시하여 사회변혁을 꾀한다(혁명형).

〈표 3-13〉 머튼의 사회 무질서상황과 사람들의 적응형태

적응형태	문화적 목표	제도화된 수단	행위유형	행동양식
동조(순응)	+	+	• 대부분의 정상인	• 무위(無爲)
혁신(개혁)	+	−	• 전통적 재산범죄자	• 규범위반
의례(의식주의)	−	+	• 하층관료 · 샐러리맨	• 목표약화
은둔(도피, 퇴행)	−	−	• 약물중독자 · 부랑자	• 현실도피
반항(전복, 혁명)	±	±	• 반역자 · 혁명가	• 현실타파

주) 기호의 의미 : +는 수용, −는 대체를 의미한다. 범죄학상 문제되는 유형은 혁신 · 은둔 · 반항형이고, 아노미 유형은 동조형을 제외한 나머지 유형들이다. 가장 흔한 적응양태는 동조형이다.
출처: 이만종, 범죄학개론, 학현사, 2005:79.

8) •○○시의 빈곤지역에 사는 초등학생인 A군의 장래희망은 도둑 또는 강도이다. 선생님과 친구에게 "은행강도가 되어서 돈을 벌겠다"고 공공연히 말한다. 이러한 사례에서 A군의 경우는 Merton이 제시한 적응유형 중 '혁신형'에 해당된다. 2004 기출
•불황이 계속되자 절도와 강도 등의 행위가 빈번하고 있다. 머튼(R. Merton)의 사회긴장이론(Social Strain Theory)에 의하면 이와 같은 불법행위는 긴장상태에 대한 '혁신형(innovation)'의 적응유형으로 분류할 수 있다. 2005 기출

9) 머튼의 아노미이론에서 문화적으로 승인된 목표와 사회적으로 받아들여질 수 있는 수단을 모두 거부하는 적응유형은 '도피형'이다. 2008 기출

③ 적응유형과 범죄관련성

범죄를 줄이기 위해서는 우선 경제적 성공이라는 목표의 성취를 위한 합법적 수단의 기회가 적은 하급계급에게 보다 많은 경제적 기회를 제공하는 것이 중요하다. 예 한국, IMF 이후 범죄현상의 증가는 급작스런 경제적 변동에 의한 아노미적 상황이 범죄의 증가에 영향을 준 것으로 해석할 수 있다.

2) 제도적 아노미이론 2011 기출

- 뒤르켐과 머튼의 아노미이론을 계승하여, 현재 미국사회의 범죄현상을 거시적 차원에서 설명하는 이론이다.
- 메스너와 로젠펠드의 저서 『범죄와 미국의 꿈』에서, 문화와 사회구조는 높은 범죄율을 생산하는 데 함께 작동한다고 하였다.
- 자본주의 문화와 구조가 범죄를 조성하고 유지시키는 환경을 조성하게 만든다. 즉, 물질지상주의의 가치체계와 비경제적 사회제도에 대한 경제제도의 우월적 지배는 범죄나 여러 가지 종류의 일탈을 유발할 요인을 더 많이 양산하게끔 하는 것이다.

3) 일반긴장이론

- 긴장이론은 긴장과 좌절을 유발하는 사회환경적 요소가 범죄의 원인이자 동기로 작용한다고 주장한다.
- 1990년대, 애그뉴(Agnew, 1992)는 대입 낙방, 가족의 사망, 이별, 부모의 학대, 친구의 괴롭힘 등의 일상생활에서의 여러 사건과 긴장이 범죄의 원인이 될 수 있다고 주장하였다.
- 목적달성의 실패, 긍정적 자극의 소멸, 부정적 자극의 생성 등 긴장이 부정적 감정을 낳고 이는 다시 비행을 일으키는 원인이 된다는 것이다. 2010 기출
- 긴장요인들로 인해 부정적인 감정(화, 우울)을 경험하기 때문에 범죄를 저지른다고 보았으며 즉, 화와 같은 부정적 감정이 최종적인 범죄의 원인이 되며, 어떻게 보면 부정적 감정을 해소하기 위해 범죄를 하는 것이라고 설명하고 있다.

3. 문화적 일탈이론

1) 밀러(Miller)의 하층계급문화이론(working-class culture theory)

(1) 의의

- 하층계급문화이론은 하급계층의 사람들이 사회 전체의 규범보다는 자신이 속한 집단의 규범에 따라 행동하다 보면 자연스럽게 범죄를 저지를 수밖에 없다는 이론이다.[10]
- 우범지역에 거주하는 하층계급사람들에게는 고유한 문화규범이 있고, 이에 따라 행동함으로써 중류계층의 법규범을 위반하게 되어 범죄가 발생하게 된다는 것이다. 따라서 범죄행위를 특정 하위문화의 자연적 결과로 인식하고 있다.
- 범죄와 비행의 원인을 하층계급문화에의 동조로 보고, 중류계층의 가치와 행동규범에 대한 악의적인 원한이나 울분의 표시가 아니라 하층계급 고유의 집중된 관심의 추구에서 형성된 것으로 파악한다.

(2) 하위계층의 6가지 중심가치(focal concern)[11]

〈표 3-14〉 하류계층의 독특한 문화규범-관심의 초점

말썽거리 (trouble)	• 준법의식 때문이 아니라 말썽을 일으키지 않으려고 범법행위를 삼가는 데 관심이 높다. 또한 법집행기관과의 말썽이 영웅적이거나 정상적이며 성공적인 것으로 간주되는 경향이 있어 이러한 일에도 관심을 갖는다. 또한 주위 사람들의 이목을 끌고 높은 평가를 받기 위하여 사고를 치고, 사고의 결과를 얼마나 잘 회피하느냐에 의해 서로의 위세를 평가하는 경향이 있다.
억셈(강인함) (toughness)	• 남성다움과 육체적 힘의 과시, 여성가장 가구에 대한 반작용으로 볼 수 있다.
영민함(교활) (smartness)	• 다른 사람을 잘 속이는 반면, 자신은 남에게 속아서는 안 된다는 것을 의미하는데, 영리하게 언어를 구사함으로써 정신능력을 최대로 과시하고 완력을 최소로 사용해서 그들 사회에서 인정받고자 하는 경향이다.

---

10) 하류계층의 사람들이 사회 전체의 규범보다는 자신이 속한 집단의 규범을 따라 행동하다 보면 자연스럽게 범죄를 저지를 수밖에 없다고 주장하는 이론은 '하위문화이론'이다. 2008 기출

11) "말썽부리기, 강인, 영악함, 자극추구, 운명주의, 자율성 추구"와 가장 관계 깊은 이론은 '하위문화이론'이다. 2007 기출

	영리함에 대한 관심은 폭력에의 의존을 원치 않으므로 억셈과는 상충되는 관심사이다. 사기도박에 관한 관심사가 여기의 예이다.
흥분함 (excitement)	• 스릴, 모험 및 권태감을 모면하는 데 관한 관심사다. 권태감의 해소가 비행의 주원인이 되고 있다.
운명주의 (fatalism)	• 빈곤한 자들은 때때로 그들의 생활은 그들이 통제할 수 없는 외적 요소에 의하여 지배되고 있다고 믿음으로써, 그들의 현실을 정당화한다. 따라서 범행으로 처벌되는 것도 팔자소관으로 생각하기 때문에 대수롭지 않게 받아들이는 경향이 있다.
자율 (autonomy)	• 자기 자신이 마음대로 자신의 일을 처리하고 싶은 희망을 의미하나, 이는 하류계층의 성원이 자신들의 사회계층제도상의 위치 때문에 항상 타인으로부터 명령과 간섭을 받고 있는 현실에 대한 잠재의식적인 반발로 인해 생성된다.

출처: 이만종, 범죄학개론, 학현사, 2005:81.

2) 코헨(Cohen)의 비행하위문화이론

(1) 의의

- 비행하위문화(delinquent subculture)란 비행집단에 공통된 특정한 가치관이나 신념·지식 등을 포함하는 사고나 이에 따른 행동양식을 말한다.
- 코헨은 저서 『일탈소년들(Delinquent Boys)』에서, 중산층출신의 청소년들보다 하층계급의 청소년들이 비행할 가능성이 높으며, 이는 이들이 느끼는 중산층 지위성취좌절에서 오는 긴장에서 찾았다.[12)]
- 중산층문화에 적응하지 못한 하층계급출신 청소년들이 중산층문화와 정반대의 문화 즉, 반항문화를 구성하여 지배문화를 거부하고 자신들의 적응문제를 집단적으로 해결하려고 비행하위문화를 형성하게 된다는 것이다.[13)]

---

12) "A는 빈민가의 하류계층에서 주위의 비행행위를 보면서 자랐다. A는 학교에 입학한 후 교사의 가르침이 자신의 성장배경과 달라 이에 적응하지 못하였다. A는 자신의 하류계층 친구들과 도둑질과 폭행 등의 행위를 통해 자신들만의 세계를 구축하여 꺾인 자존심과 좌절된 욕구를 충족시키고자 하였다." 이의 사례를 잘 설명할 수 있는 이론과 주창자는 '비행하위문화론의 코헨(Cohen)'이다. 2005 기출

13) • 반동형성(반항형성 : reaction formation) : 코헨은 하류계층의 청소년들이 사회의 일반문화와 정반대되는 방향으로 하위문화의 가치나 규범을 설정하는 과정 즉, 중산층문화에서 권장하는 기준들과는 반대적 성격을 띠게 되는 것을 말한다.

(2) 비행하위문화의 특징

① **비공리성**(non-utilitarian)

범죄행위로부터 얻는 물질적 이익보다 타인에게 피해를 입히고 동료로부터 얻는 명예와 지위 때문에 범죄행위를 한다.

② **악의성**(maliciousness)

다른 사람에게 고통을 주고 금기를 파괴하는 행위를 강조함으로써 중산층문화로부터 소외된 자신들의 실추된 지위를 회복하려고 시도한다.

③ **부정성**(negativism)

사회의 지배적 가치체계에 대해서는 무조건 거부반응을 보임으로써 중산층문화에서 가치를 전도시켜 그들 나름대로의 가치체계를 구축하는 것이다.

④ **단기적 쾌락주의**(short-run hedonism)

장기적인 계획과 목표하에서 사는 것이 아니라 당장에 쾌감을 느끼기에 급급한 심리이다.

⑤ **집단자율성의 강조**(emphasis of group autonomy)

외부에 대한 극도의 적개심과 내부에 대한 응집력의 형성이다.

3) 클라워드(R. Cloward)와 올린(L. E. Ohlin)의 차별적 기회이론

(1) 의의

- 차별적 기회이론(분화적 기회구조이론)은 Durkheim과 Merton의 아노미이론과 Sutherland의 차별적 접촉이론을 하나로 통합한 특성을 지니고 있다.[14)]

- 하층소년들이 중산층 문화의 적응실패로 반동적으로 문화를 이루어 악의적이고 부정적으로 범죄를 하게 된다는 이론은 '코헨의 하위문화이론'이다. 2004 기출
- 청소년비행이 집단적으로 발생한다는 데 주목해서, 지위좌절을 겪은 하층청소년들이 집단적으로 중산층문화에 대한 반항으로 하위문화를 형성한다고 보고, 이를 범죄원인으로 지목한 이론이 '코헨의 비행하위문화이론'이다. 2007 기출

14) 차별적 기회이론은 성공을 추구하는 문화적 목표를 수용하나 구조적으로 합법적인 수단이 없는 사람이 비행을 저지르게 된다고 봄으로써 머튼의 입장을 수용하지만, 그러한 사람들이 불법적 기회가

• 사회구조에 있어서 목표달성을 위한 기회구조는 합법적 수단과 기회가 차별적인 것처럼, 불법적 수단과 기회도 차별적으로 주어지기에, 하층계급의 청소년들은 성공을 위한 합법적 수단과 기회가 제한되므로 불법적 수단과 기회를 이용하는 비행을 저지르게 된다는 것이다. 즉, '합법'과 '비합법'이라는 2개의 기회구조의 관계에서 일탈행위를 한다는 것이다.

(2) 비행하위문화의 3가지 유형 2010, 2012 기출

① **범죄하위문화(criminal subculture)**

범죄조직이 조직화 · 체계화되어 있고, 대대로 범죄기술이 전수되어 재산범죄를 수행해 나가면서 생계를 해결하는 등 불법적 범죄기회구조가 확고한 하위문화를 말한다.[15)]

② **갈등하위문화(conflict subculture)**

주로 거리의 폭력배들한테 발견되는 것으로, 주로 싸움을 잘할 뿐 체계적으로 전수되는 범죄기술은 없다. 불법적 범죄기회는 없으나 폭력을 수용하는 하위문화이다.

③ **도피하위문화(retreatist subculture)**

어떠한 사람들은 성공의 목표를 달성하지 못한 긴장상태에서 불법적 범죄기술을 학습할 기회도 없고, 그렇다고 폭력을 수용하지도 못하여 재산범죄자도 폭력배도 되지 못하는 이중실패자가 되며, 약물과 알코올중독에 빠지게 된다.

4) 쇼와 매케이의 문화전달이론(cultural transmission theory)

• 문화전달이론(cultural transmission theory)은 1930년대 시카고대학의 C. R. Shaw와 H. McKay에 의해 주장되었으며[16)], 비행을 유발하는 사회적 요인으로 말미암아 비행지

어떠한가에 따라 서로 상이한 문화에 접하게 되고, 그에 따라 비행유형도 다르다는 점을 강조한다.

15) 불법적인 기회구조가 발달되어 있는 노동계급지역에서 나타나는 문화이며, 주로 돈벌이와 관련된 절도범죄와 관계있는 문화는 '범죄하위문화'이다. 2005 기출

16) • 쇼(Shaw)와 매케이(McKay)는 공식통계를 이용하여 비행을 측정하고 비행소년이 살고 있는 지역을 중심으로 분석하였다. 인구의 이동이 심하고 문화적 갈등이 상존하여 사회의 비공식적 통제력이 약화된 과도기적인 지역의 도심에 가까울수록 비행이 다발한다는 사실을 발견하였다. 도시성장을 분석함으로써 범죄와 비행의 분포상태는 물론 그와 같은 도시범죄의 분포이유를 규명하고자 하였다. 2004 기출

역에 고유한 하위문화가 형성되고, 하위문화는 그 지역의 구성원이 교체되더라도 계속 다음 세대에 전달되기 때문에 비행이 계속적으로 발생하게 된다고 주장하였다.

- 1942년 저서『소년비행과 도시지역』에서 청소년의 비행원인은 그 지역 특유의 사회문화적 환경에 따른 비행적 문화의 전달 및 학습의 결과라고 보았다. 또한 비행자들의 거주지역에 대한 '범죄지도'를 작성하여 도시생태가 범죄발생에 영향을 미친다는 사실을 지적하였다.
- 오랜 시간에 걸쳐 인종적 구성이 계속 변화되어 왔음에도 불구하고 이민초기에 가장 범죄율이 높았던 지역이 계속해서 높은 범죄율을 유지하였다. 그 이유는
  - i) 인종적 이질성이 높은 까닭으로 문화적 갈등이 생기게 되고 자연히 지역적 통합이 낮아질 수밖에 없다.
  - ii) 이민자들의 잦은 이동으로 비공식적 사회연결망이 생성되기가 어렵고 불안정해짐으로써 사회적 연결망을 통한 사회통합의 정도를 감소시키는 요소로 작용하게 된다. 이는 결국 비공식적 사회통제를 약화시키고, 그 결과로 일탈문화가 생성되기 쉬운 조건을 제공하게 됨으로써 다른 지역에 비해 비행이나 범죄가 더 많이 발생하게 된다.[17)]
- 사회해체가 일어난 지역은 다른 지역에 비해 지역주민들 간의 유대와 비공식적 사회통제가 낮기 때문에 범죄발생률이 높다. 비록 빈곤과 실업률이 높은 지역이라도 집합효율[18)]이 높은 지역은 범죄율이 낮다는 것을 발견하였다. 2011 기출

예 미국 시카고지역의 프로젝트 : 지역 내의 여러 사회적 지원단체들인 학교, 교회, 노조, 클럽의 활동을 잘 묶어주어 활성화시키는 데 목적이 있고 오락프로그램, 여름캠프, 보다 나은 법집행, 지역학교와 공중위생시설의 개선 등을 통해 범죄가 발생할 수 있는 환경을 미리 통제하고자 하였다.

• 쇼(Shaw)와 매케이(McKay)는 지역사회의 해체적 특성에서 범죄원인을 찾는 거시이론가이다. 2009 기출

17) 사회해체지역에서 범죄율이 높은 이유는 높은 인구이동률 때문이다. 2010 기출

18) '집합효율'은 일종의 이웃의 비공식적 통제를 일컫는 용어이다. 샘슨과 그의 동료들은 집합효율은 이웃들 사이의 상호신뢰를 나타내는 것으로서 공동선을 위해 기꺼이 개입하려는 의지를 지칭하는 것이며 주로 이웃공동체의 노력을 의미한다고 보았다. 특정지역에서의 범죄율에 가장 중요한 영향력을 미치는 것은 빈곤, 실업, 편부모의 비율, 특정 소수인종의 비율 등이 아니라 바로 이 집합효율의 정도라는 것이다.

예 보스턴 도심의 프로젝트 : 주로 도심의 갱들에게 활동가를 파견하고 그들과의 원만한 관계 형성을 통해 범죄를 통제하고자 하였다.

제2절 사회학습이론

1. 서덜랜드(E. Sutherland)의 차별적 접촉이론(differential association theory)[19]

1) 의의 2011, 2012 기출

- 서덜랜드(E. Sutherland)[20]는 범죄행동은 타인과 상호접촉을 통해 학습되며, 접촉의 차이는 빈도 · 지속시간 · 시기 등의 차이이다.
- 학습은 접촉에 의한 학습이지만 접촉 자체만으로 범죄가 발생하는 것이 아니라 그 접촉내용에 따라 결정되며, 주로 친밀한 집단 내에서 이루어진다는 것이다.
- 비행친구와의 접촉을 범죄나 비행의 중요한 원인으로 보았다.[21]

19) • 사회심리학적 이론에는 사회학습이론(차별적 접촉이론, 차별강화이론, 중화이론), 사회통제이론(허쉬의 통제이론), 사회반응이론(낙인이론)으로 나누어볼 수 있다.
   • 차별적 접촉이론은 분화적 접촉이론, 차등적 교제이론, 교제차등이론, 접촉차이론, 차등적 접촉이론 등으로 불린다.

20) 서덜랜드(E. Sutherland)는 "친구 따라 강남 간다"는 속담과 관련된 차별적 접촉이론을 주장한 이론가이다. 2008, 2009 기출

21) • 범죄행위는 학습의 결과이며, 상호작용과정에서 의사소통을 통해 학습되며, 학습내용은 범죄기술, 동기, 충동, 합리화, 태도 등이다. 2005 기출
   • 범죄행위는 학습되며, 범죄행위의 동기와 태도도 학습되며, 학습은 친밀한 집단에서 이루어지며, 의사소통을 통해 학습된다. 2007 기출
   • 차별적 접촉이론에서 주장하는 범죄의 원인과 가장 관련되는 주장은 "주변의 비행친구들과 어울리다 보니 나도 모르게 나쁜 물이 들었다."이다. 2004 기출
   • 법과 규범에 순응하는 가치를 가진 학생이 나쁜 친구들의 영향을 받아 비행을 저지르게 된다는 이론이 차별적 접촉이론이다. 2010 기출
   • Sutherland & Cressey, Criminology, Philadelphia, 1970:78.

2) 비행적 사회화과정의 9가지 가설[22)]

1) 범죄(비행)행위는 학습의 결과이다.
2) 범죄(비행)행위는 다른 사람들과 상호작용(교체·접촉)을 수행하는 과정에서 커뮤니케이션을 통해 학습된다.
3) 범죄행위 학습의 주요 부분은 가까운 사집단(가족·친지·동료 등) 내에서 이루어진다.
4) 범죄(비행)행위가 학습의 결과라고 할 때, 학습의 내용은 ① 범행의 기술 ② 동기·욕구·합리화 및 태도의 구체적 관리법을 포함한다.
5) 동기와 욕구의 구체적 관리법은 법규범에 대한 호의적 또는 거부적 정의(definition)들로부터 학습된다.
6) 특정의 개인이 범죄자가 되는 것은 법(또는 사회윤리)의 위반을 호의적으로 해석하는 '정의'들과의 접촉이 법의 위반을 거부적으로 해석하는 '정의'들과의 접촉을 능가하기 때문이다.
7) 이질적 접촉(교제)은 접촉의 빈도(frequency), 기간(duration), 우선위(priority), 강도(intensity)에 있어 각양각색이다.
8) 범죄적 행동양식 및 반범죄적 행동양식과의 접촉을 통해서 이루어지는 범죄(비행)행위의 학습과정은 일상생활 속에서 이루어지는 여타 행위의 학습과정과 동일한 메커니즘을 이룬다.
9) 범죄행위가 일반적 욕구와 가치관의 표현이기는 하지만 일반적 욕구와 가치관만으로는 범죄를 제대로 설명할 수 없다. 그 이유는 준법행위라는 것도 따지고 보면 동일한 욕구와 가치관의 표현이기 때문이다.

- 범죄행위 자체는 유전되지 아니하며 학습의 과정을 통하여 습득함으로써 터득된다. 학습은 1차적 친근집단 구성원과의 접촉을 통하여 강하게 이루어지며, 학습의 내용에는 범행의 기술과 동기, 욕구, 합리화 및 태도의 구체적 관리법이 포함된다.
- 특정 개인이 범죄자가 되는 것은 법의 위반을 호의적으로 해석하는 정의들과의 접촉이 법의 위반을 거부적으로 해석하는 정의들과의 접촉을 빈도·기간·우선순위·강도 면에서 능가할 때이다.[23)]

22) 전대양, 현대사회와 범죄, 형설출판사, 2002:102-103.
23) 서덜랜드는 미국의 상류층에서 화이트칼라(white-collar) 범죄가 끊이지 않는 것은 미국 중상류사회(하나의 하위문화권)에서 화이트칼라 범죄가 긍정적으로 받아들여지고 있고 화이트칼라 범죄양식이 다른 사람에 의하여 학습되기 때문이라는 가설을 세우고 실증적 자료를 제시함으로써 자신의 가설이 타당함을 주장하였다. 전대양, 현대사회와 범죄, 형설출판사, 2002:103.

2. 글레이저(D. Glaser)의 차별적 동일시이론[24)]

- 글레이저(D. Glaser)는 사람들이 동일화되어 가는 과정에서 범죄행동을 수행한다고 하면서, 친밀한 집단뿐만 아니라 사회적으로 먼 준거집단 또한 학습과정에서 중요한 역할을 한다는 것이다. 즉, 동일화과정에서 자기의 태도를 합리화하고 용납함으로써 범죄행위를 한다는 것이다.
- 서덜랜드의 '접촉'의 개념 대신에 '동일화(identification)'의 개념을 사용함으로써 범죄의 발생, 범죄행동과 비범죄행동의 구분을 설명하고자 하였다.

3. 버제스(Burgess)와 에이커스(Akers)의 차별적 강화이론

- 범죄행위는 차별적 접촉의 결과인 모방에 의해 발생하며, 범죄행위의 지속여부는 차별적 강화에 의해 결정된다.
- 사람들은 보상이 있으면 그것을 반복하고 처벌이 있을 것으로 예상되면 그 일을 회피하며, 강화학습 이외에도 주위 사람들의 행동을 관찰・학습하고 모방하게 되어 범죄를 저지를 수 있음을 강조하였다. 즉, 주위 사람들 이외에 TV나 영화로부터 학습・모방할 수 있음도 제시했다.[25)]

4. 사이크스(Sykes)와 맛차(Matza)의 중화기술이론

1) 의의

- 중화기술이론(neutralization theory)이란 범죄자는 자기의 범죄나 비행행위에 대해 자기자신 또는 타인들로부터의 비난을 의식적으로 합리화 내지 정당화시킴으로써 그

---

24) '차별적 동일시이론'은 차별적 접촉이론을 수정・보완한 것으로써 '차등적 자아이론', '차이일체론' 등으로 불린다. 글레이저(D. Glaser)는 매스미디어의 중요성을 강조하고 있다.

25) • 최근 이종격투기의 폭력적인 장면들을 아이들이 모방하여 문제가 되고 있다. 이는 "에이커스의 사회학습이론"에 의해 가장 적절히 설명될 수 있다. 2007 기출
- 에이커스가 사회학습이론에서 주장한 4가지 중요한 개념은 정의(定義), 모방, 차별적 접촉, 차별적 강화이다. 2008 기출
- 차별적 접촉 이외에 차별적 강화, 정의, 태도학습, 모방을 범죄의 학습과정으로 중요하게 다루었다. 2008 기출

비난을 벗어난 안도감에서 범죄 등 비행행위를 저지르게 된다는 이론이다.

- 대부분의 비행자와 범죄자들이 관습적인 가치와 태도를 견지하지만 그들은 이들 가치를 중화(neutralization: 합리화 · 정당화)시키는 기술을 배워서 비합법적인 행위와 관습적 행위 사이를 왔다 갔다 하는 '표류(drift)'를 한다고 주장한다.
- 실제로 비행소년이라 할지라도 대부분의 경우에는 다른 사람과 마찬가지로 일상적이고 준법적인 생활을 하고 특별한 경우에 한하여 범죄를 저지르게 되고, 체포된 후에는 대부분 후회하고 수치심을 느낀다고 지적하였다.

2) 표류이론(drift theory)

- 대부분의 비행소년들은 타고난 본질적 요소에 의하여 강제되거나 비행적 가치를 수용하여 비행을 저지르는 것이 아니라, 단지 사회통제가 느슨한 상태에서 합법과 위법의 사이를 표류하는 '표류자'라는 것이다.
- '표류'란 사회통제가 약화되었을 때 소년들이 합법적인 규범이나 가치에 전념하지 못하고 그렇다고 위법적인 행위양식에도 몰입하지 않는 합법과 위법의 중간단계에 있는 상태를 말한다.

〈표 3-15〉 중화기술의 유형[26] 2011 기출

책임의 부정	• 의도적인 것이 아니었거나 자기의 잘못이 아니라 실수, 주위환경, 친구 등에게 책임을 전가하는 경우 • 자신도 자기를 통제할 수 없는 외부세력의 피해자라고 여기는 경우[27]

26) • 사이크스(G. M. Sykes) 등의 중화이론에서 양심의 가책을 피하는 형태로는 책임의 부정, 손상의 부정, 피해자의 부정 등이 있다. 2004 기출
• A는 뇌물을 받고 부정한 행위를 일삼는 고위공직자 B의 집에 침입하여 귀중품을 훔쳤다. A는 B같이 나쁜 사람의 물건은 훔쳐도 된다고 자기를 정당화하였다. 이는 중화기술 중 '피해자의 부정'에 속한다. 2005 기출
• "어울릴 줄 모르고 튀어서 왕따 당한 아이는 맞아도 싸다"라고 하는 것은 중화의 기술 중 '피해자의 부정'에 속한다. 2007 기출

27) • 비행소년이 부모의 무원칙적인 가정교육이라든가 자녀에 대한 무관심 등으로 자신의 행위를 정당화하는 경우
• 기업가가 자신의 종업원이 자의적 법해석 또는 잘못된 법 이해로 위법을 하게 되었다고 주장하는 경우
• 만약 가게에서 구할 수 있었다면 직장에서 훔치지 않았을 것이라고 정당화하는 경우

가해의 부정	• 자신의 행위가 위법한 것일지는 몰라도 실제로 자신의 행위로 인하여 손상을 입은 사람은 아무도 없다고 주장하며 합리화하는 경우[28)]
피해자의 부정	• 자신의 행위가 피해를 유발한 것은 인정하지만, 그 피해는 마땅히 받아야 하는 응징이라고 변명하는 경우 • 피해를 본 사람이 노출되지 않은 경우에 피해자의 권리를 무시하는 경우[29)]
비난하는 자에 대한 비난	• 법관, 경찰, 선생님, 기성세대, 부모 등과 같이 자기를 비난하는 사람들은 더 부패한 자들로서 자기를 심판할 자격이 없다고 비난하면서 자신의 비행에 대한 죄책감과 수치심을 중화시키는 것[30)]
상위가치에 대한 호소	• 자신의 비행을 인정하면서도 친구들과의 의리나 조직을 위해 어쩔 수 없었다고 하여 형법의 요구보다는 자신이 속한 집단의 연대성이 더 중요하다고 생각하여, 본인의 비행을 합리화하는 경우[31)]

• 그들이 나를 이렇게 만들었다고 하는 경우
• 나는 선택의 여지가 없었다고 하는 경우
• 그것은 내가 아니었더라도 다른 누군가가 했을 것이라는 경우
• 공정식, 살아있는 범죄학, 교육과학사, 2011:104-105.

28) • 소유자가 불확실한 재물을 훔친 경우 훔친 것을 빌린 것이라고 하는 경우
• 자동차절도 또는 가격담합 등의 범죄를 정당화하는 경우, 그들이 보험에 가입했다는 경우
• 그들은 많은 돈을 가지고 있다는 경우
• 그렇게 큰 가게에서 CD 한 장 정도가 무슨 대수냐는 경우
• 자동차를 훔치고는 잠시 빌렸다고 하는 경우
• 방화를 하면 보험회사가 피해를 모두 보상해 줄 것이라는 경우 등

29) • 성적으로 난잡한 여성이나 매춘부는 보호받을 가치가 없는 정조라고 강간범이 자신의 행위를 정당화하는 경우
• 그는 피해당할 만했다는 경우
• 그녀가 말대꾸를 했다는 경우
• 그는 나쁜 사람이라는 경우
• 자기의 절취행위는 부정직한 점포에 대한 보복이라는 경우

30) • 전문 장물아비가 자신의 최고의 고객 중 일부는 판사와 경찰관이라고 지적한 경우
• 은행강도가 자신에 대한 처벌이 뇌물을 받은 정치인이나 은행돈을 횡령한 은행가보다 엄하게 처벌되는 것에 항변하는 경우
• 모두가 도둑놈인데 왜 나만 갖고 그러느냐는 경우
• 내가 그에게 안 했다면 그가 나에게 했을 것이라는 경우

31) • 은행 여직원이 사랑하는 애인을 위하여 원치 않은 돈을 횡령한 경우
• 조직폭력집단의 조직원이 의리 때문에 자신과 상관없는 일에 참여함으로써 범죄행위를 한 경우
• 그는 잘 모르는 사람이잖아! 비겁자는 저리 가라! 나는 내 동료를 보호해야 한다 등의 경우
• 공정식, 살아있는 범죄학, 교육과학사, 2011:105.

제3절 통제이론

1. 의의 2012 기출

- 통제이론에는 내적 통제인 Reckless의 봉쇄이론(견제이론) 등, 외적 통제인 Hirschi의 사회유대이론 등, 법률적 통제인 Gibbs의 억제이론 등으로 나눌 수 있다.
- 일반적으로 범죄의 원인을 설명하는 많은 이론들은 "범죄자가 왜 범죄를 범하게 되는가" 또는 "어떤 사회적 상황이 범죄의 발생을 가져오는가"를 탐구하는 데 비하여, 통제이론은 오히려 "왜 어떤 사람은 사회적 규범을 준수하게 되는가"를 연구하여야 한다고 주장하였다.
- 범죄동기는 인간본성의 일부로서 개인의 범죄동기는 일정하다고 본다. 따라서 연구자들이 연구할 문제는 "왜 사람들이 일탈을 하게 되는가" 하는 것이 아니라 "왜 사람들이 규범적 가치에 동조하게 되는가" 하는 것이다.

2. 레클리스(Reckless) 등의 자아관념이론

- 레클리스(W. C. Reckless), 디니츠(S. Dinitz), 머레이(E. Murray) 등은 선량한 소년들을 비행으로부터 멀어지게 하는 비행절연체(delinquency insularity)를 자아관념(self concept)으로 보았다.[32)]
- 소년들이 범죄나 비행을 유발하는 환경에 노출되어 있음에도 불구하고 비행을 저지르지 않는 이유는 자기가족관계 등을 고려하여 사회적으로 바람직하다고 인정되는 방향으로 '자아관념'을 형성시켜 유지하기 때문이라는 것이다. 즉, 자아관념이 비행적 영향이나 환경적 유인에 대한 방패막이가 된다.
- 범죄다발지역에 살면서 범죄적 집단과 접촉하더라도 범죄에 가담하지 않는 소년에

---

32) 자기관념이론은 강력한 내면적 통제와 이를 보강하는 외부적 통제가 사회적·법적 행위규범의 위반에 대한 절연체를 구성한다는 레클리스(Reckless)의 봉쇄이론(containment theory)으로 발전하였다. W. C. Reckless. "A New Theory of Delinquncy and Crime", Federal Probation, Vol. 25, 1961:42-46.
Walter C. Reckless, Simon Dinitz, and Ellen, E. Murry, Self Concept as Insulator Against Delinquency ASR, Vol. 21, 1956:744-756.

대한 의문에서 착안한 이론으로써, 동일한 범죄접촉하에서도 실제로 비행에 가담여부를 결정하는 개인적인 반응의 차이는 자아관념의 차이 때문이라고 주장하였다.33)

- 가족관계와 같은 절연체가 선량한 소년들로 하여금 비행을 멀리하게 하며, 이를 바탕으로 형성된 자기관념이 그들을 범죄로부터 멀어지게 한다.

3. 레클리스(Reckless)의 봉쇄(억제)이론 2010 기출

1) 의의

- 고전주의학파에 기반하여, 인간은 누구나 쾌락을 추구하고 고통을 피하려 한다고 가정하고 있다. 즉, 인간은 누구나 쾌락을 추구하지만, 처벌을 두려워하기 때문에 처벌만이 범죄를 막을 수 있다고 주장하였다.
- 범죄의 원인을 처벌의 여부와 강약에 주목하고, 처벌이 있거나 강화되면 범죄를 하지 않을 것이고, 반대로 처벌과 통제가 느슨하다면 범죄의 발생가능성은 높을 것이라고 주장한다.
- 사람들은 만일 범죄유발요인이 범죄억제요인보다 강하면 그 사람은 범죄를 저지르게 되고, 범죄억제요인이 강하면 비록 범죄유발요인이 있더라도 범죄와 비행을 자제한다는 것이다. 또한 외적 봉쇄요인이 약하더라도 내적 봉쇄요인이 강하면 범죄나 비행은 통제될 수 있다.
- 사람들은 일반적으로 범죄성을 유인(pulls), 압력(pressures) · 배출(pushes)하는 사회상황에 처해 있으며, 범죄적 성향이 내재해 있지만 범죄 · 비행에 대한 내 · 외적 통제 때문에 내재된 범죄적 성향을 일탈적 행동으로 전환하지 않는다는 것이다.
- 일반억제효과에 주목하여 처벌의 신속성, 확실성, 엄격성의 효과에 주목하여, 처벌이 엄격하고 신속하며 확실할수록 범죄의 억제효과는 커진다고 주장하였다.34)

---

33) 범죄사회학이론 중 동일한 범죄환경 속에서도 어떤 사람은 범죄에 감염되고 어떤 사람은 감염되지 않는 상이한 반응의 문제를 가장 잘 설명할 수 있는 이론은 '자기관념이론'이다. 2004 기출

34) • '신속성'은 범죄발생 즉시 처벌이 얼마나 신속하게 이루어지는가를, '확실성'은 범죄가 발생하면 반드시 처벌이 이루어지는가를, '엄격성'은 처벌이 엄하게 이루어지는가를 말한다.
• 윌리암스와 호킨스(1986년)는 공식기관에 의한 처벌은 단순히 처벌 그 자체의 확실성이나 위험 또는 고통 때문에 범죄의 감소 및 억제를 가져오는 것이 아니며, 처벌의 억제효과는 사회유대와 관련하여 나타난다고 주장한다. 즉, 처벌은 위협적인데 그것은 범죄를 하게 될 경우 처벌을

2) 범죄유발요인

유인요인	• 정상적인 생활로부터 이탈하도록 유인하는 요소 예 나쁜 친구들, 비행이나 범죄하위문화, 범죄조직, 불건전한 대중매체 등
압력요인	• 사람들을 불만족한 상태에 들게 하는 조건 예 빈곤·실업 등 열악한 생활조건, 가족갈등, 열등한 신분적 지위, 성공기회의 박탈 등
배출요인	• 범죄나 비행을 저지르도록 하는 각 개인의 생물학적 또는 심리적 요소 예 불안감, 내적 긴장감, 증오심, 공격성, 즉흥성, 반역성 등

3) 범죄봉쇄요인

레클리스는 내적 봉쇄요인과 외적 봉쇄요인 중에서 어느 한 가지라도 제대로 작용하면 범죄나 비행을 예방할 수 있다고 보았다.

내적 봉쇄요인	• 규범이나 도덕을 내면화함으로써 각자가 내부적으로 형성한 범죄차단력에 관한 요인들 예 자기통제, 선량한 자기관념, 강한 자아의식, 충분히 발달된 초자아, 강한 인내력, 전환에 대항하는 저항력, 강한 책임감, 목적의 설정, 대체적 만족을 발견하는 능력, 긴장을 완화시키는 합리성 등의 자아의 구성요소
외적 봉쇄요인	• 가족이나 주위 사람들과 같이 외부적으로 범죄를 차단하는 요인들 예 행위자에의 일관된 도덕관의 제시, 행위자의 규범, 목표·기대에의 제도적 강화, 합리적·사회적 기대의 존재, 효과적인 관리와 규율, 적절한 활동여지의 제공과 달리 선택할 수 있는 방법과 안전편의 제공, 승인, 동화, 귀속의 기회 등

받으면 사회유대에 있어 많은 손실을 가져오기 때문에 행위자에게 위협적이라고 본 것이다. 따라서 처벌의 억제효과는 어느 정도 사회유대가 형성되어 있는 사람에게만 나타날 것이라는 점에서 이전의 억제이론은 수정될 필요가 있다는 것이다.

- ○○지법 A판사는 인터넷 채팅을 통해 알게 된 10대 소녀와 원조교제를 한 혐의로 기소된 B모(25)씨에게 벌금 1,000만원을 선고하였다. A판사는 "이번 경우는 피의자에게 직접적인 효과가 느껴지지 않는 집행유예보다 벌금형을 선고하는 편이 다른 사람들의 범행을 방지하는 데 효과가 클 것으로 판단했다"고 밝혔다. A판사의 선고가 근거하고 있는 이론은 '억제이론'이다. 2004 기출
- 새로 취임한 법무부장관은 범죄율을 낮추기 위해 더욱 강한 처벌이 필요하다고 한다. 장관은 '억제이론'을 가장 지지할 것이다. 2007 기출

4. 허쉬(T. Hirschi)의 사회적 통제이론(social bonding theory)[35)]

1) 의의 2012 기출

- 사회적 통제이론은 인간은 선천적으로 이기적이고 반사회적이며, 범죄행위는 인간의 본성에서 비롯되므로 고통스런 과정을 거쳐야만 한다고 본다.
- 대부분의 사람에게 어느 정도의 일탈적・범죄적 성향이 있음에도 불구하고 "왜 많은 사람들이 규범이나 법에 동조하는가?"를 설명하는 것으로 범죄를 억제하는 환경적 요인이 무엇인가에 초점을 둔 이론이다.[36)]
- 모든 개인을 잠재적 범죄자로 보고 누구든지 내버려두면 범죄를 저지를 것인데, 이를 통제하는 것이 사회유대이다. 따라서 범죄는 개인이 사회에 대한 유대가 약해졌거나 끊어졌을 때 발생한다고 보았다.
- 허쉬(T. Hirschi)는 1969년 저서 『비행의 원인』에서 개인의 범죄성향을 통제하는 것은 개인과 사회 간의 유대라고 보았고, 특히 가족 간의 유대를 강조하였으며, 범죄자는 타인의 희망과 기대에 상관하지 않는 경향이 있으며, 범죄행위는 법에 역행하고 처벌의 위험이 수반되며, 범죄행위에는 시간이 필요하다고 보았다.
- 범죄원인을 어릴 때 형성된 자기통제력[37)]이라는 내적 성향요소[38)]로 보았다.[39)] 즉, 범죄나 사회유대의 약화, 비행친구와의 접촉은 모두 낮은 자기통제력이라는 공통된

35) '사회적 통제이론(social bonding theory)'을 '사회연대이론', '사회유대이론', '사회결속이론'이라고도 한다.

36) • "왜 사람들은 범죄를 범하지 않는가"라는 의문을 기본전제로 하여, 사람들이 범죄를 저지르는 이유를 사회결속 내지 통제가 약화되었거나 단절되었기 때문이라고 보는 이론은 "사회유대이론(Social Bonding Theory)"이다. 2005 기출
• "왜 사람들은 범죄를 하지 않는가?"라는 문제제기와 가장 관계가 깊은 이론은 '허쉬의 사회통제이론'이다. 2007 기출
• 허쉬의 사회유대이론은 범죄행동의 시작을 사회유대 약화에 연결하여 설명했다. 모든 사람을 잠재적 범죄자로 가정했다. 많은 사람들이 왜 범죄를 저지르지 않는가에 대해 관심을 가졌다. 2008 기출

37) 자기통제력은 순간만족과 충동을 조절할 수 있는지, 스릴과 모험을 추구하기보다는 분별력과 조심성이 있는지, 근시안적이기보다는 앞으로의 일을 생각하는지, 쉽게 흥분하는 성격인지 등을 말하는 것이다.

38) 내적 성향은 어릴 때 형성되며 이는 부모의 양육방법에 의해 결정된다고 보았다. 어릴 때 형성된 자기통제력은 청소년기를 지나 성인이 되어서도 변하지 않는 안정적이고도 지속적인 성향이 된다고 했다.

39) 갓프레드슨과 허쉬가 범죄일반이론에서 주장한 범죄원인은 '자기통제력'이다. 2008 기출

원인에서 비롯되는 결과라고 보았다.[40] 2011 기출

2) 사회유대의 요소[41] 2009, 2012 기출

사회에 애착이 높고, 관여를 하며, 참여를 하고, 사회의 도덕적 신념을 받아들이는 사람들은 범죄를 저지르지 않고 그렇지 못한 사람들이 범죄를 저지른다고 주장한다.

〈표 3-16〉 사회유대의 요소

구분	내용
애착 (유대: attachment)	• 타인에 대한 심리적·정서적 친근 정도 즉, 다른 사람에 대한 감정과 민감성인 상호애정관계 • 가족, 친구, 자신이 존경하고 모방하기를 원하는 대상들에 대한 존경·애정 등의 감정을 통해 영향을 받음[42]
전념 (개입·수용: commitment)	• 전통적인 활동 또는 합법적인 경력, 일종의 생활양식[43]
참여 (참여: involvement)	• 개입에 투자된 시간이나 에너지 즉, 전통적 활동에 합리적으로 투자한 시간[44]
신념 (확신: belief)	• 행위에 대한 사회의 규칙이나 금지율을 받아들이는 태도로써 공적인 권위의 정당성을 믿는 것[45]

40) • 발전이론은 범죄경력의 시작, 지속, 종료를 포함하여 범죄경력에 대한 광범위한 시각을 제공하며, 손베리(Thornberry), 샘슨(Sampson)과 라웁(Laub), 모피트(Moffitt) 등에 의해 주장되었다. 2009 기출
• 어렸을 때의 경험도 중요하지만 또 한편으로는 청소년으로의 성장기나 성인시기의 생활환경도 중요하다는 점을 강조한다. 발전이론에서는 범죄발전과 중단에 영향을 미치는 요인으로 기존 차별접촉/사회학습이론과 사회유대이론, 긴장이론이나 낙인이론에서 강조되었던 다양한 사회환경요인들을 강조했다는 점에 특징이 있다.

41) • 허쉬(Hirschi)의 사회통제이론에서 통제작용을 하는 사회유대요소로는 애착, 참여, 신념 등이 있다. 2004, 2007 기출
• 허쉬(Hirschi)의 사회통제이론에서 비행을 통제하는 요인은 신념(belief), 관여(commitment), 애착(attachment) 등이다. 2005 기출

42) • 기존의 연구에서는 선생님에의 애착이나 친구에의 애착은 비행과 미약한 관계만을 나타내지만, 부모와의 애착이 높은 아이들은 비행을 적게 한다는 결과를 제시하고 있다.
• "부모님께서 실망할까봐 비행을 망설이게 된다"는 것은 '애착'의 예이다. 2009 기출

43) 미래를 위해 공부하는 학생은 비행을 하면 자신에게 큰 손실이 있을 것으로 판단하기 때문에 비행을 하지 않게 된다. 즉, 모범학생은 자신의 미래에 대한 생활보장 등을 위해 투자하지만 불량학생은 전통적인 활동에 거의 투자를 하지 않으며, 이에 범죄행위에 가까워질 가능성이 높다.

44) 학교공부나 과외활동, 취미나 여가활동 등에 많은 시간을 보내는 아이들은 그만큼 시간적으로 너무 바빠서 비행을 할 시간이 없다.

45) 법을 지켜야 한다고 믿고 사회의 도덕을 잘 받아들이는 아이는 비행의 가능성이 낮지만 그렇지 않은 청소년들은 비행가능성이 높다.

〈사회적 자본의 개념〉46)

부르디외 (Bourdieu, 2003).	"지속적인 네트워크 혹은 상호 면식이나 인정이 제도화된 관계 즉, 특정한 집단의 구성원이 됨으로써 획득되는 실제적인 혹은 잠재적인 자원의 총합"
콜먼 (Coleman, 1990)	• 단일한 실재(single entity)가 아니라 개인적 그리고 집합적 행위를 조장하는 사회구조의 여러 다른 측면들을 포함하고 있다. • 사회적 자본을 물리적 자본(physical capital)이나 인적 자본(human capital)과 구분하고 있다. • 사회적 자본은 개인에게서 존재하는 것이 아니라 개인들 사이의 관계 속에 묻혀 있는 것 즉, 사회적 관계에 내재되어 있다.
린과 동료들(Lin, Cook, and Burt, 2001).	사회적 결속, 사회적 응집력, 연대, 그리고 사회해체와 같은 사회학적 개념의 유산들에 중심이 맞추어진다.
퍼트남 (Putnam, 1993)	"연결망, 규범, 그리고 신뢰와 같이 상호이익을 위한 행위와 협력을 촉진시키는 사회조직의 특성" 예 개인 상호 간에 신뢰(interpersonal trust)의 정도와 시민참여(civic engagement)의 수준

5. 깁스(Gibbs)의 억제이론

• 법률적 통제이론(억제이론, 제지이론, 예방이론)은 인간은 합리적이고 이기적이며, 범죄란 법규위반으로 인한 비용과 처벌을 합리적으로 계산한 결과로 본다.

• 범죄를 저지를 것인가의 여부는 전적으로 개인의 책임이지 사회의 책임이 아니며, 범죄는 처벌 즉, 사회적·외적 통제에 의해 억제되어야 하며 일반예방효과를 중시한다.

• Gibbs는 특정한 범죄의 발생률이 형벌내용의 공지, 형벌집행의 확실성, 형벌의 가혹성에 반비례한다고 하였다. 이는 만약 처벌이 불쾌하고 충분히 엄중하다면 사람들이 범죄에 가담하지 않을 것이라는 가정에 기초하고 있다.

46) 김상원, 사회적 자본과 범죄: 사회적 자본이 폭력범죄에 미치는 영향, 『한국치안행정논집』 제9권 제1호:1-25.

〈헤이건(Hagan)의 권력통제이론〉 2011 기출

1. 권력통제이론과 이론검증을 위한 측정들

- 헤이건과 그의 동료들(Hagan et al.)은 가족에서 부모의 권력관계가 어떻게 자녀들의 성별에 따른 차별적 통제로 이어지는지에 대한 설명을 권력통제이론을 통해서 제시하였다.
- 권력통제이론은 직장에서의 계급 구분을 가족 내의 부부권력관계로 연결시키고, 자녀의 성별에 따른 부모의 차별적 통제라는 기제를 통해 비행의 성차(性差)를 설명하려고 한다.
- '가정 내 사회통제 노동의 분업에서 나타나는 성 계층화'가 계급과 청소년비행을 연결할 수 있는 핵심적 인과고리라는 것이다.
- 남편과 아내가 직장에서 갖는 계급적 위치의 차이에 따라 가부장가족과 평등가족으로 구분할 수 있다고 본다.

가부장가족	• 직장에서 권위를 행사할 수 있는 직업을 아버지는 갖고 있는 반면 어머니는 그렇지 못한 경우 • 남편이 직장에서 권위를 갖는 지위에 있는 반면 아내는 가정 밖의 직장을 갖고 있지 않아서 소비와 생산의 영역이 성별에 따라 분리된 경우가 전형적인 가부장가족
평등가족	아버지와 어머니의 직업적 지위가 동등하여 소비와 생산의 성별 분리가 나타나지 않는 경우로 부부 간의 권력관계가 상대적으로 평등한 경우

- 권력통제이론에서는 가부장가족에서보다 평등가족에서 남자청소년과 여자청소년의 비행 정도의 차이가 덜할 것이라고 주장한다.

가부장가족	• 성별에 따른 생산 영역과 소비 영역의 분리가 자녀들에게도 사회적으로 재생산되는데, 아들은 생산의 영역(직장)에 맞게, 딸은 소비의 영역(가정)에 맞게 사회화되면서 그러한 성역할에 따라 딸에게 통제가 가해진다는 것이다. • '도구–대상(instrument–object) 관계'라는 도식에 의거하여 가부장가족에서 어머니는 아버지의 권력을 매개하는 도구가 되어 자식에 대한 통제를 수행하게 되고, 그 통제의 주된 대상은 아들이 아니라 딸이라고 주장한다. • 가부장가족의 딸들은 어머니의 엄격한 통제를 통해서 비행과 같은 위험하고 처벌의 우려가 있는 행동을 회피하고 조신하게 행동하도록 사회화된다고 본다.
평등가족	• 아버지의 권력이 위와 같은 방식으로 딸들에게 행사되지 못하기 때문에, 딸은 아들과 비슷한 정도의 통제를 받고 유사한 사회화 과정을 거치게 된다. • 딸은 아들과 마찬가지로 위험을 감수하는 행위에 대해서 허용적인 분위기에서 자라나게 될 것이라고 본다. 따라서 평등가족의 딸들은 비행의 가능성에 있어서 아들들과 큰 차이를 보이지 않게 된다는 것이다.

제4절 낙인이론(labelling theory)

1. 의의

1) 의의

- 낙인이론(labelling theory)은 미시 범죄환경론이다. 1938년 Tannenbaum의 『범죄와 지역사회』를 시작으로 1960년대 이후 본격적으로 논의된 낙인이론은 비행이 사회통제를 유발한다는 기존 이론과 달리 사회통제가 범죄를 유발한다는 정반대의 주장을 펼치고 있는데, 일탈행위와 사회적 낙인화의 동적 관계를 「사회적 상호작용」이라는 관점에서 파악하는 것으로, 「사회적 반작용이론」 또는 「사회반응이론」이라고도 한다.
- 낙인이론은 일탈행위와 사회적 낙인의 동태적 관계를 사회적 상호작용이라는 관점에서 파악하는 것으로써, 전통적·심리학적·다원적 범죄원인론을 배격하고 범죄원인의 전제인 범죄 자체가 형성되어 가는 사회적 통제과정에 초점을 두고 있다.
- 한 사람이 범죄자로 고착화되는 것은 초기의 일탈행위에 대해 사회적 통제를 체험한 결과라고 본다. 즉, 범죄가 범죄통제를 야기한다기보다는 범죄통제가 오히려 범죄를 야기한다는 명제로 압축된다.[47]
- 낙인이론에서는 범죄단계에 따라 범죄유발요인이 다를 수 있으며, 우발적·일시적 범행과 누적적·경력적 범행을 같은 원인에서 구할 수 없다고 본다.
- 범죄자를 교정하고 사회복귀하는 것을 목표로 내건 교정제도가 그 낙인효과로 인해 실제로는 사회복귀에 장애물을 조성한다는 것이다.

---

47) • 낙인이론은 범죄발생원인을 종래의 범죄원인론과 달리 파악하는 입장이다. 범죄는 일정한 원인에 의하여 발생하는 것이 아니라 오히려 일정한 통제기관 내지 사법기관의 낙인에 의하여 선별적으로 만들어지는 것이라고 한다. 낙인이론에 따르면 결국 범죄자로서 희생되는 자는 사회적 약자라고 한다. 2004 기출
• 낙인이론과 관련되는 학자로는 베커, 레머트, 탄넨바움 등이 있다. 2008 기출
• 낙인이론 및 갈등이론과 관련되는 사항에는 악의 극화, 법적 갈등, 주(主) 지위 등이 있다. 2008 기출
• 낙인이론의 출발점은 탄넨바움(Tannenbaum)의 '범죄와 지역사회', 태판(Tappan)의 '소년비행', 낙인이론의 아버지라 불리는 레머트(Lemert)의 '사회범죄학' 등에 있다.

• 탄넨바움(F. Tannenbaum)은 저서 『범죄와 지역사회(1938)』[48]에서, 범죄자를 만들어 내는 과정을 일탈강화의 악순환 즉, 꼬리표를 붙이고, 규정하고, 차별하고, 평가하고, 자의식을 심어주는 과정인 '악의 극화(Dramatization of Evil)'로 개념화하고 있다.[49]

2) 기본가정[50]

• 본질적으로 범죄적인 행위는 없으며, 범죄를 정의하는 것은 권력자들의 이해관계에 따른다.
• 어떤 사람이 법률을 위반했기 때문에 범죄자가 되는 것이 아니라, 형사사법기관에 의하여 범죄자로 규정되었기 때문에 범죄자가 된다.
• 모든 사람이 규범을 준수하고 규범을 일탈한다는 사실 때문에 범죄자와 비범죄자로 분류되어서는 안된다.
• 체포행위는 낙인과정의 시작이며, 체포와 형사사법기관의 결정은 범죄자가 범죄특성에 반하는 것으로 작용한다.
• 연령, 사회·경제적 계층, 인종 등은 형사사법기관의 결정을 차별적으로 만드는 주요한 범죄자의 특성이다.
• 형사사법제도는 범죄자로 인정된 자를 비난하고 거부하는 것을 허용하는 자유의지의 관점에서 형성된다.
• 낙인은 결국 비행적인 이미지와 하위문화로 판정되는 것을 만드는 과정이며, 그 결과 거부자들은 거부해 버린다.

48) F. Tannenbaum, Crime and the Community, New York : Columbia Univ. Press, 1938.
49) 사회에서 범죄자로 규정되는 과정은 일탈강화의 악순환으로 작용하여, 오히려 범죄로 비난받는 특성을 자극하여 강화시켜 주는 역할을 한다고 한다. 이것은 범죄가 원래 행위에 대한 평가에서 행위자에 대한 비난으로 바뀌면서 정상적인 행위까지도 의심받게 되는 상황에 그 원인이 있는데, 탄넨바움은 이를 '악(惡)의 극화(劇化)'라고 부른다. 이는 일단 자신에게 일탈자로서 낙인이 붙게 되면 스스로를 일탈자로 치부하는 것처럼 부정적인 자아관념을 갖게 되어 일탈행위를 계속하도록 만든다는 것이다. 2008 기출
50) 공정식, 살아있는 범죄학, 교육과학사, 2011:110.

2. 낙인이론의 특질

- 유전적 · 심리학적 · 다원론적 범죄원인론을 배척한다.
- 전통적 범죄학 이론에 있어서 비교적 등한시되어 온 낙인의 주체인 법집행기관이 자의성을 중요시한다.
- 일탈행위를 단순히 주어진 규칙에서 벗어난 행위라고만 보지 않고, 한 걸음 더 나아가 규칙 그 자체의 형성근거까지 문제로 삼는다.
- 일탈행위를 단순히 행위로만 분석하지 않고, 상호작용이라는 차원에서 분석한다.
- 일탈행위의 분석법으로서 공식통계에만 의존한 것이 아니라, 자기보고나 참여관찰의 병용 필요성을 강조한다.

3. 낙인의 효과와 형사정책[51)]

4D정책은 국가개입의 최소화와 사회 내 처우의 중요성을 강조하여 미국뿐만 아니라 유럽 각국에서도 1970년대의 지배적인 형사 사조가 되었다.[52)]

1) 비범죄화(decriminalization)

- 웬만한 범죄는 일탈로 규정하지 말자는 것이다. 사회적 일탈에 대한 섣부른 형사적 개입이 사태를 오히려 악화시킬 수 있음을 경고하고, 경미범죄, 합의적 범죄, 경미한 마약상용에 대한 형벌적 개입을 억제하는 데도 일정한 성과를 거두었다.
- 슈어는 국가의 급진적 불개입정책으로 표현하였다.[53)]

2) 비시설화(deinstitutionalization)

- 범죄자를 교도소와 같은 시설에서 처우하기보다는 '보호관찰제'와 같이 가능하면 사회 내에서의 처우를 통해 낙인을 덜 받고 사회에 보다 더 적응하기 쉽도록 하자는 것이다.

---

51) • 낙인이론이 형사정책에 미친 긍정적인 효과로는 다양한 전환제도의 도입, 비범죄화와 비형벌화의 확산, 소년범에 대한 보호처분적용 등이다. 2005 기출
- 전환처우(Diversion)의 이론적 근거가 되는 이론은 '낙인이론'이다. 2005 기출
- 낙인이론의 정책에는 비범죄화, 탈시설화, 전환처우(다이버전) 등이 있다. 2007 기출

52) 이만종, 범죄학개론, 학현사, 2005:103.

53) E. Schur, Radical Non-Rethinking the Delinquency Problem, Englewood Cliffs : Prentice-Hall, 1973.

- 교도소가 수형자를 교화 · 개선시키기보다는 범죄 학교화하는 폐단을 체계적으로 지적하면서, 시설 내 구금처우에 대한 대안으로 사회 내 처우(community treatment)의 필요성을 강조하였다.[54)]
- 시설 내 구금의 제한에는 구금처우에 소요되는 막대한 비용을 절감하려는 경제적 고려와 인도주의적 고려가 동시에 작용한 것이다.

3) 전환(다이버전: diversion)

- 범죄자를 체포, 기소, 처벌이라는 공식절차상에 두지 않고, 기소하기 전에 지역사회에서 일정한 처우를 받도록 함으로써 낙인을 가능한 한 줄이려는 것이다.
- 비형벌화(depenalization), 비형벌 우회절차(diversion)로써 일탈에 대한 사회적 관용을 확대하자는 주장이다.[55)]

4) 적법절차(due process)

계층 간에 차별 없이 공정하게 법이 집행되어야 한다는 것을 강조하면서 공정한 절차를 주장했다.

4. 학자들의 견해

1) 레머트(E. Lemert)와 낙인이론 2000 기출

(1) 의의

- 레머트(Edwin M. Lemert)는 저서 『사회병리학(Social Pathology)』과 『일탈 · 사회문제 및 통제(Human Deviance, Social Problems and Social Control)』에서 '1차적 일탈(primary deviance)'과 '2차적 일탈(secondary deviance)'을 설명하고 있다.[56)]

54) 정신질환의 경우, 낙인이론가들은 강제적 시설입원을 통한 치료는 실제로 정신질환자라는 오명을 씌우는 과정으로 파악하고, 강제적 입원 대신 외래치료와 지역사회 내 치료를 주장하였으며, 그 결과 구금형 정신병원을 폐지 · 제한하는 데 상당한 성과를 거두었다.

55) 1920년대 미국의 금주법의 실패, 미국 금주법(禁酒法)은 알코올의 판매를 새로이 범죄로 규정하여, 사람들의 금주습관을 함양하는 데 기여했다기보다는 밀주의 제조에 막대한 이윤을 보장함으로써 불법적 밀주업에 조직범죄의 관여를 유도하여, 조직범죄의 팽창을 야기시켰다.

56) • 전대양, 현대사회와 범죄, 형설출판사, 2002:107.

- 1차적 일탈이란 다양한 사회적 · 문화적 · 심리적 · 생리적 요인으로부터 야기되는데 때로는 우발적으로 일어날 수도 있고, 이러한 요인들의 결합에 의해 일어날 수도 있다. 그러나 이것은 개인의 자아에 대한 태도와 사회적 역할에 변화를 초래할 만큼의 대단한 것은 아니다.
- 2차적 일탈이란 1차적 일탈에 대한 사회적 반응에 의해 생성된 문제들을 방어하고 공격하거나 또는 그러한 문제에 적응하기 위한 수단으로써 나타난 일탈행동이나 사회적 역할들이다. 특히 2차적 일탈에 관심을 두었으며, 1차적 일탈이 반드시 2차적 일탈을 일으키는 것이 아니라고 주장한다.
- 1차적 일탈에 대한 부정적 사회반응과 그 결과로 인한 경제적 기회의 상실, 관습적 사회관계의 강화 등은 개인으로 하여금 자신의 태도와 사회적인 역할에 대한 상징적 재조직화(symbolic reorganization)와 부정적 자아관념(negative self-image)에 의한 행위를 촉진시켜 직업적 범죄자가 된다고 주장하고 있다.
- 종국적으로는 일탈자라는 외부의 낙인을 하나의 사회적 지위로써 수용하게 되어, 합법적 · 정체적 기회가 감소되고 정상인과의 대인적 관계가 줄어들며, 자기 자신을 일탈자로 자아규정하게 되어 계속해서 범죄행위를 저지르는 경력범죄자가 된다는 것이다.

[그림 3-2] 부정적 자아관념의 형성과 행태화과정

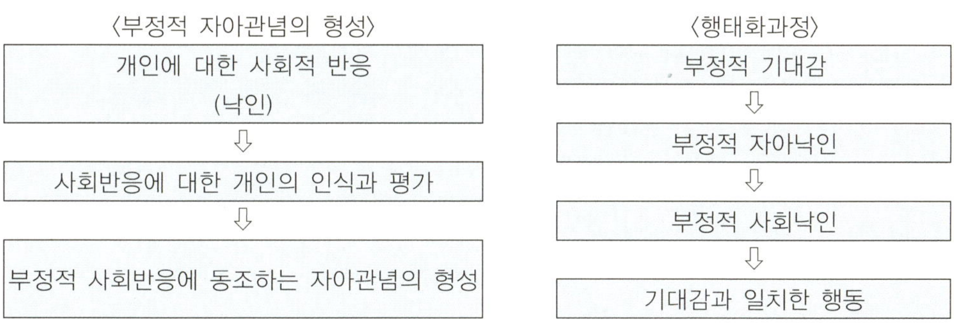

출처: 전대양, 현대사회와 범죄, 형설출판사, 2002:107.

- 일탈의 유형을 1차적 일탈과 2차적 일탈로 분류하여 2차적 일탈을 낙인의 과정으로 설명한 학자는 '레머트(E. Lemert)'이다. 2004 기출
- E. Lemert, Social Pathology, New York : McGraw-Hill, 1951; Human Deviance, Social Problems, and Social Control, Englewood Cliffs : Prentice-Hall, 1967.

(2) 형사사법기관의 공식적 반응에 의한 낙인효과

- 레머트는 2차적 일탈에 관심을 두어 사회적 반응의 종류를 '사회구성원에 의한 반응'과 '사법기관에 의한 공적인 반응'의 2가지로 나누고, 사법기관의 공식적인 반응이 가장 권위 있고 광범위한 영향력을 미친다는 것이다.
- 1차적 일탈자를 2차적 일탈자로 악화시키는 데 공식적인 반응이 미치는 낙인효과를 크게 5가지로 지적하였다.

낙인의 효과

① 오명 씌우기(signmatization)
형사사법기관의 공식적인 반응에 의해 1차적 일탈자에게는 '도덕적 열등'이라는 오명이 씌워지고, 공식처벌은 대중매체 등을 통하여 널리 알려지고 전과기록에 의해 장기적으로 기록됨으로써 1차적 일탈자는 사회복귀에 실패하게 되어 정상적인 사회성원으로서의 역할을 수행하지 못하고 2차적 일탈자로 발전하게 된다.

② 불공정의 자각(sense of injustice)
공식적인 처벌을 받는 과정에서 1차적 일탈자는 불공정한 사법집행의 여러 측면을 직접 경험함으로써 사법제도의 공정성에 대한 신뢰를 갖지 못할 뿐만 아니라 사회정의에 대한 신뢰감을 상실하게 된다.

③ 제도적 강제(institutional restraint)
공식처벌을 받게 되면 1차적 일탈자는 자신에 대한 사법기관의 판단을 받아들일 수밖에 없게 된다.

④ 일탈하위문화에 의한 사회화(socialization of deviant subculture)
공식처벌을 집행하는 시설특유의 일탈하위문화를 접함으로써 새로운 범죄기술이나 범죄행위를 옹호하는 가치관 등을 습득하게 된다.

⑤ 부정적 정체성의 긍정적 측면(positive side of negative identity)
형사사법기관이 부여하는 부정적 정체성을 일탈자가 수용함으로써 얻게 되는 이익 때문에 1차적 일탈자는 자신에 대한 부정적인 평가를 거부하지 않는 현상이다.
예 죄책감으로부터의 도피, 책임감에 대한 면책 등

2) 베커(H. Becker)와 낙인이론

- 저서 『국외자들(The Outsiders, 1963)』에서 일탈이론을 단계적 모델(sequential model)로 설명하면서, 일탈자 혹은 국외자라는 낙인이 일종의 사회적 지위(social status)와 같

은 효과를 준다는 것이다.[57]

- 일탈자는 자신에게 기대되는 사회적 역할을 마침내 받아들이고 그에 따라 행동하게 됨으로써, 그 결과 사회적 청중이 예측한 바대로 행동하게 되는, '자기성취적 예언(self-fulfilling prophecy)'이 이루어진다고 주장하였다.

5. 슈어(E. Schur)와 낙인이론

- 2차적 일탈자가 되는 과정이 단계적 경력의 특성을 갖는 것은 아니라고 주장한다.[58] 즉, 어떤 사람은 비난을 받고 낙인이 찍히는 반면, 어떤 사람들은 성공적인 변호와 협상을 통해 낙인을 벗어날 수 있다는 것이다.
- 사회적 낙인이 반드시 자아관념에 영향을 주는 것이 아닐 수도 있으며, 2차적 일탈은 사회적 낙인의 결과라기보다는 자아낙인(self-label)의 산물인 경우도 적지 않다는 것이다.

제5절 갈등론적 이론

1. 의의 2012 기출

- 갈등론적 이론은 모든 사회는 상충되는 이익집단 간의 갈등이 존재하며, 국가는 사회일반의 이익과 가치를 보호하기 위해서가 아니라 국가의 운영을 통제할 수 있는 충분한 힘을 가진 집단의 이익과 가치를 대변한다는 것이다. 2008, 2010, 2011 기출
- 법이란 지배계급의 가치와 신념의 표현이며, 형사사법기관은 그들의 사회통제기제에 불과할 따름이며, 범죄란 그 사회의 부와 권력의 불공정한 분배에 대한 반응으로

57) • '동시모델'은 최초의 일탈원인이 일탈행위의 전 과정에 작용한다고 보는 이론으로, 이는 기존이론들의 기본적 입장이다. 그러나 '단계적 모델'은 '동시모델'과 대치되는 개념으로서 일탈행위의 원인이 단계적으로 발전해 간다는 것을 내용으로 한다. 즉, 최초의 일탈행위에 대한 원인이 다음 단계의 일탈행위에 대한 원인으로는 타당하지 않게 된다는 것이다.
• 사회적 지위는 사회질서 속에서 개인이 차지하는 위치를 말한다. 주(主)지위(master status)와 보조적 지위(auxiliary status)로 구분되며, 주(主)지위는 일반적으로 상호작용의 과정과 유형에 결정적인 영향을 미침으로써 다른 지위를 능가하는 지위이다.

58) E. Schur, Labelling Deviant Behavior, New York : Harper & Row, 1971.

본다.

• 범죄의 원인보다는 법과 형사사법기관이 가지는 계급적 당파성을 규명하며, 갈등론적 이론의 뿌리는 마르크스와 엥겔스 이론이다.[59)]

2. 마르크스(Marx)의 계급투쟁과 범죄

• 자본주의하에서 프롤레타리아의 범죄는 생활조건에 대한 반응이며 생존수단으로 본다.

• 자본주의사회에서 노동자에 대한 지배는 경제・정치・문화・사회생활 등에 반영되어 자본가들의 이익을 보호하여 준다고 지적한다. 예 기업가들의 로비와 기업가들을 위한 법의 제정

3. 봉거(Bonger)의 자본주의와 타락

• 초기 갈등이론적 관점의 대표적인 학자로서, 마르크스(Marx)의 이론을 범죄학에 접목시켜 자본주의사회의 법은 부자들의 이기심을 채우기 위한 불법적 활동은 내버려둔 채 가난한 사람들의 이기심을 채우기 위한 행위들만 범죄로 규정지으며 처벌하려든다고 보았다.

• 범죄의 사회환경인 자본주의사회의 경제제도가 빈곤한 사람들의 개인적 불만족을 심화시키고 범죄성향을 더욱 증대시킨다는 경제적 결정론을 제시하였다.

• 자본주의사회의 구조가 파괴되고 사회주의의 이상이 실현되는 때에만 빈곤이 소멸되고 동시에 범죄의 동기도 없어진다고 주장하였다.

4. 퀴니(Quinney)의 범죄의 사회적 구성

1) 의의

• 마르크스(Marx)주의 범죄학의 거두로써, 형사사법제도는 사회통제기제를 합리화하기 위해 국가가 나서고 국가의 지원에 의해 행해지고 있다고 주장하면서, 형사사법제

---

59) • 급진주의 또는 갈등주의적 범죄이론은 사회적 소외를 중시한다. 2007 기출
• 사회갈등론적 관점과 관련된 학자로는 봉거, 볼드, 퀴니 등이 있다. 2008 기출

도의 가장 큰 목적은 서서히 쇠퇴해 가는 자본주의의 기존질서를 지탱하기 위한 마지막 기둥역할을 하는 것이라고 보았다.[60)]

- 형법을 국가와 지배계급이 기존의 사회·경제 질서를 유지하고 영구화시키기 위한 도구로 이해한다.[61)]

2) 노동자계급의 범죄[62)]

(1) 적응범죄(crime of accommodation)

자본주의에 의해 곤경에 빠진 사람들이 다른 사람의 수입과 재산을 탈취함으로써 보상받으려 하거나 혹은 자본주의에 의해 피해를 입은 사람들이 무력을 행사하여 다른 사람의 신체를 해하는 유형 등의 범죄를 말한다.

(2) 대항범죄(crime of resistance)

자본가들의 지배에 대항하는 범죄유형으로, Quinney는 비폭력적이거나 잠재적인 불법행위와 자본주의에 직접적으로 대항하는 혁명적인 행위들을 포함시켰다.

---

60) 퀴니(Richard Quinney)는 국가와 법 및 그에 의해 실행되는 범죄통제는 지배계급이 기존의 사회·경제질서를 유지하기 위해 사용하는 강압의 수단이며, 공식적인 범죄율은 그러한 강압 정도의 증거라고 한다. R. Miliband의 도구주의적 국가이론을 수용하면서, 초기에는 경제적 지배계급은 국가의 통치권력과 범죄통제기관의 주요 지위들을 직접 장악함으로써 자신들의 이해를 실현할 수 있게 된다고 주장하였다. 후기에는 범죄통제에 소요되는 국가경비(state expenditure)를 축으로 형성된 독점자본과 통제기관과의 연합을 밝히려고 하였다. 전대양, 현대사회와 범죄, 형설출판사, 2002:108.

61) 형사사법체계(criminal justice system)란 자본주의국가가 지배계급의 자본축적을 보호하고 잉여인구와 계급투쟁을 억압하기 위해 출현한 제도이며, 필요한 사회적 비용은 독점 자본부문에 의해 충당된다. 더욱이 형사사법체계의 기능이 확대되고 필요한 비용이 증대하게 됨에 따라, 형사사법체계에 대한 독점자본의 개입은 더욱 늘어나게 된다는 것이다. 따라서 '형사사법-산업복합체(criminal justice-industrial complex)'가 성립하게 되며 범죄통제 영역에서 국가와 독점산업간에 연합이 이루어진다는 것이다. 독점자본은 자본을 축적하기 위해 점차 국가에 의존하게 되고 국가는 사회적 비용을 충당하기 위해 독점자본에 더욱 의존하며, 범죄통제는 공존관계(symbiotic relationship)를 기반으로 지배계급의 이해를 옹호할 수밖에 없게 된다는 것이다. 전대양, 현대사회와 범죄, 형설출판사, 2002:108.

62) 자본주의의 물질적 상황하에서는 범죄란 필연적으로 발생할 수밖에 없으므로 자본주의의 포기를 통해서만 범죄를 예방할 수 있다고 주장하면서, 노동자계급의 범죄를 적응범죄와 대항범죄로 구분한 사람은 '퀴니(Quinney)'이다. 2005 기출

3) 자본가계급의 범죄

지배와 억압의 범죄(crime of domination & repression)로써, 자본가들이 자신의 이익을 보호하기 위해 저지르는 범죄이다.

(1) 기업범죄(corporate crime)로는 부당내부거래, 가격담합, 입찰담합 등 경제적 지배를 도모하기 위해 야기되는 범죄이다.

(2) 통제범죄(crime of control)는 불공정한 사법기관의 활동 등을 말한다.

(3) 정부범죄(crime of government)는 공무원들이나 정부관리들이 저지르는 정부부패 등을 말한다.

5. 셀린(Sellin)의 갈등이론

- 셀린(T. Sellin)은 저서 『문화갈등과 범죄(culture conflict and crime, 1938)』에서, '문화갈등'이란 사회적 가치에 대한 이해 및 규범의 충돌이라고 하였다.
- 1차적 문화갈등과 2차적 문화갈등이 있으며, 법규범이 다양한 가치를 반영하는 것이 어려울 때는 가장 지배적인 문화만이 반영되게 된다. 그 결과 반영되지 않은 문화의 행위규범을 따르는 경우 범죄로 인식되게 되는 것이다.[63)]
- 제1차 문화갈등은 상이한 이질문화 간의 충돌에 의한 횡적 문화갈등이다. 예 이민, 문화체계가 다른 국가 간의 병합 시 문화갈등
- 제2차 문화갈등은 동일문화 내에서 사회분화로 인한 규범의 갈등으로 종적 문화갈등이다. 예 신·구세대 간의 문화·가치관의 갈등, 도시민과 농촌사람들 간의 문화규범의 갈등 등

6. 볼드(Vold)의 집단갈등이론 2011 기출

- 갈등이론의 입장에서 범죄학을 발전시킨 학자로서, 법제정과 집행의 과정을 권력집단 간의 협상의 결과로 보고, 범죄를 개인적 법률위반이 아니라 비권력 소수계층의 집단투쟁으로 이해한다.

63) 셀린(T. Sellin)은 "범죄는 문화의 소산이다"라는 가설을 그 이론적 전제로 하고, 법규범에 위반하는 행위로 밀어넣는 것은 문화적 가치규범의 갈등이라고 주장한다.

• 이익집단의 이해관계가 다르기 때문에 갈등이 필연적이며, 결국 권력을 많이 가진 자가 경쟁에서 이기게 된다. 이는 공권력을 둘러싼 집단 간의 투쟁을 반영하는 것이라고 주장했다.

〈범죄환경론의 구분〉64)

1) 거시범죄환경론

거시범죄환경론은 사회적 상황 자체가 범죄를 유발시킨다는 견해이다. 즉, 개인별 차이에 관계없이 어떤 사람이라도 특정한 사회적 상황에 빠지면 상황이 미치는 영향에 의해 범죄를 저지를 가능성이 커진다고 본다. 따라서 사회적 상태, 경제구조, 문화 등과 같이 많은 사람들이 영향을 받는 광범위한 환경에 초점을 둔다.

<table>
<tr><td rowspan="5">거시범죄 환경론</td><td colspan="2">사회해체이론</td><td>Shaw & McKay, Bursik & Webb</td></tr>
<tr><td colspan="2">사회적 긴장이론</td><td>아노미이론(Merton), 제도적 아노미이론, 일반긴장이론</td></tr>
<tr><td colspan="2">범죄적 하위문화론</td><td>하위계급 주요 관심사론(Miller), 비행하위문화론(Cohen), 분화적 기회구조론(Cloward & Ohlin)</td></tr>
<tr><td rowspan="2">갈등론적 범죄론</td><td>보수적 갈등론</td><td>문화갈등이론(Sellin), 집단갈등이론(Vild), Turk의 범죄화론(권위에 의한 지배복종, 법률갈등)</td></tr>
<tr><td>급진적 갈등론</td><td>• 계급투쟁과 범죄(Marx), 자본주의와 탈도덕화(Bonger)
• 지배와 억압의 범죄, 화해와 저항의 범죄(Quinney)
• 후기 자본주의 갈등론(Spitzer)</td></tr>
</table>

2) 미시범죄환경론

미시범죄환경론은 개인이 처해 있는 주위상황에 주목하여 개인 상호 간에 이루어지는 대면접촉과정, 가정, 친구관계, 소속한 집단의 특성 등 개인에게 가까이 있는 환경들에 초점을 둔다.

<table>
<tr><td rowspan="3">미시범죄 환경론</td><td>사회학습이론</td><td>• 차별적 접촉이론(Sutherland)
• 학습이론의 발전 : 차별적 동일화이론(Glaser), 사회학습이론(Burgess & Akers)</td></tr>
<tr><td>통제이론</td><td>• 개인적 통제 : 자기관념 이론, 봉쇄이론, 동조성 집착이론, 중화기술이론
• 사회적 통제 : 사회유대(연대)이론
• 법률적 통제 : 억제이론</td></tr>
<tr><td>낙인이론</td><td>Lemert, Becker, Schur 등</td></tr>
</table>

64) 공정식, 살아있는 범죄학, 교육과학사, 2011:81-82.

〈범죄사회학적 접근방법에서 이루어진 범죄학의 통합시도〉[65)]

1) 의의

- 「인생경로(life course)」이론은 범죄의 요인은 각양각색이며 개개의 범죄요인의 영향의 크기도 사람에 따라 다르며, 한 사람의 범죄자가 범죄를 저지르게 된 요인은 성장함에 따라 변화한다는 것이다.
- 「인생경로(life course)」이론은 개개인의 인생경로의 차이에 영향을 미치는 요소에 사회학적 요소뿐만 아니라 생물학적 요소라든지 심리학적 요소도 포함시키고 있다.

2) 주요 연구

(1) 종단적 연구

- 무작위로 추출한 피검자집단(동일 연령의 자)을 대상으로 아동·소년기에서 성인 이후까지 장기간에 걸쳐 수년 주기로 자기조사와 심리테스트를 실시하여, 그중에서 범죄·비행을 저지른 자와 저지르지 않은 자의 차이가 어디에서 유래하는지 그 요인을 추출함으로써, 범죄·비행의 원인을 규명하고자 한 방대한 시도이다.
- 기원은 1950년대에 미국에서 이루어진 글뤽부부의 연구에서 비롯되었으며, 사회학적 요인뿐만 아니라 생물학적 요인이나 심리학적 요인도 중시하였다.

(2) 패린튼의 비행발전 연구

- 영국 케임브리지대학 범죄연구소가 중심이 되어 실시된 「비행발전(delinquent development)」 연구는 D. 패린튼 등이 1955년에 런던에서 태어난 500명(최종적으로는 403명)의 남성을 대상으로 10세에서 32세까지 사이에 8회에 걸쳐서 자기조사보고, 상세한 인터뷰, 심리 테스트 등을 실시하였고, 이를 토대로 상습범죄자가 범죄를 행하게 된 요인을 분석하였다.
- 인생경로 중에서의 다양한 경험이 행동선택의 방향이나 흐름을 결정하며, 특히 유년기의 경험이 이후의 범죄경력에 커다란 영향을 미친다는 사실을 강조하고 있다.

〈연구결과〉

1) 유년기에 다음과 같은 조건에 해당하는 자는 10대 시기에 반사회적 행동을 취할 가능성과 성인이 된 후에 범죄를 저지를 가능성이 높다.

---

65) 이만종, 최신 범죄학개론, 학현사, 2007:341-344.

① 가정이 경제적으로 빈곤하다. ② 부모나 형제 중에 범죄경력이 있다. ③ 자식에 대한 부모의 감시기능이 결여되어 있다	사회적 요인
④ 학업성적이 낮다. ⑤ 학업에 게으른 경향을 보인다. ⑥ 정직하지 않다. ⑦ 공격성이 강하다. ⑧ 다동성이 있다. ⑨ 충동성이 강하다. ⑩ 주의결함장애가 보인다.	개인적 요인

2) 범죄성을 지닌 아동에게는 흥분, 물건에 대한 소유욕, 동료 사이에서의 지위에 대한 욕구가 범죄의 동기를 유발하거나 촉진요소로 작용한다.

3) 일상생활의 다양한 일들이 아동의 행동에 영향을 미친다.[66]

4) 구체적인 상황하에서 범죄를 실행할지의 여부 판단은 비용과 이득의 비교 차이에 의거한다. 단, 비용이나 이득의 평가는 주관적인 것이어서 사람에 따라 다르다. [67]

5) 인생경로 중에서 어느 기간(시기)에서는 범죄를 촉진하는 요소로 작용한다 하더라도 다른 기간(시기)에서는 영향을 미치지 않는 경우도 있다.[68]

6) 성인범죄는 외적 요소(폭력적인 행위, 체포경력, 유죄경력 등)와 내적 요소(정신장애, 신경과민, 사회적 고립 등)에 따라 예측 가능하다.

3) 샘프슨과 롭의 단계적 성장이론

- 인생경로의 다양한 장면에 따라 범죄를 촉진하는 요소가 다르다는 주장은 미국의 R. 샘프슨과 J. 롭의 단계적 성장이론에서도 제기되고 있다.

66) 예 부모의 매우 세심한 가정교육이나 감시 등은 사회적 학습과정을 거치면서 범죄에 대한 아동의 자기억제를 고양시킨다. 반대로 반(反)사회적인 가정에서는 이와 동일한 과정을 통해 범죄경향을 고조시킨다.

67) 예 충동적인 소년은 근시안적인 이득밖에는 관심이 없기 때문에, 이후에 체포되어 형벌을 부과받을 가능성이 높다 하더라도 범죄를 일으키기 쉽다.

68) 예 신경과민(nervousness), 소극적 태도, 친구가 적은 것은 유년기나 소년기에는 마이너스(범죄를 촉진하는 방향)로 작용하지만, 성인이 된 후에는 플러스(범죄를 삼가는 방향)로 작용한다.

• 샘프슨과 롭은 1993년의 『범죄의 생성(Crime in the Making)』에서 비행경력이 있는 남성 500명과 비행경력이 없는 남성 500명을 대상으로, 유아기부터 40대에 이르기까지 장기간에 걸쳐 살펴본 글뤽부부와 셸던의 조사 데이터를 컴퓨터를 이용해 재(再)분석하여 다음과 같은 결론을 도출해 냈다.

1) 비행을 저지르는 아동들 중에는 가정, 학교, 동료 사이에서 트러블을 지니고 있는 경우가 많다. 이 점에서는 범죄의 원인을 사회적 통제결여에 있다고 하는 사회적 통제이론의 주장이 옳다.
2) 단, 범죄자가 성인이 될 때까지 상습적인 범죄경력을 쌓게 되면 이미 그것을 멈추게 할 수단이나 기술이 없다고 하는 사회적 통제이론의 주장은 잘못된 것이다. 성인상습범죄자를 범죄로부터 격리하는 것은 가능하다. 이를 위해서는 중요한 전환점이 2개(결혼과 취직)에 있다.
3) 과거의 경력을 아는 상태에서 이해해 주려는 배우자나 기회를 부여해 주려는 고용주의 존재는 사회자본(social capital)[69]을 쌓는 데 도움이 된다. 2012 기출
4) 비행소년이나 범죄자를 형사사법기관에서 처리함으로써 그들의 범죄성에 직접적인 영향은 주지 않는다. 하지만 그들이 형사사법기관에 의한 처리를 경험함으로써 결혼이나 취직의 가능성이 낮다고 한다면, 오히려 그들의 범죄경력을 촉진하는 방향으로 작용하게 된다.[70]

69) 사회자본이라 함은 생활을 유지해 나가기 위해 필요한 개인이나 사회제도와의 적극적인 관계를 가리키는데, 통제이론에서의 사회적 유대와 거의 비슷한 의미로 쓰인다.
70) 샘프슨과 롭의 주장은 다음과 같은 의문에 답변을 하지 못한다는 지적도 있다. ① 왜 소년기에 비행경력으로부터 벗어나는 자가 있는가? ② 결혼이나 취직에 성공하는 자와 성공하지 못하는 자의 차이는 어디에 있는 것인가? ③ 실제로는 사회자본이 결여되어 있음에도 불구하고 왜 범죄를 저지르지 않는 자가 있는가?

제 18 장 범죄학이론의 고찰

제1절 근대 이전의 범죄학

1. 의의

19세기 후반에 시작된 범죄 및 범죄자에 관한 '과학적 · 실증적 연구'[1] 이전의 범죄학을 말한다. 형사정책은 형벌이라는 고통부과의 방법이 범죄방지를 위한 형사정책의 기본수단이 되었다.

2. 복수주의시대

- 가해자인 범죄자에 대하여 피해자 측이 행하는 개인적 또는 집단적인 복수행위를 용납하는 것을 형사정책의 임무를 다하는 것으로 보았다.
- 바빌로니아시대부터, 초기에는 무자비한 '피의 복수(Blutrache)'를 인정하였으나, 후기에는 속죄금제도 및 '눈에는 눈, 이에는 이'라는 동해보복원칙(同害報復原則: lex talio)을 강제하였다.

1) • 김채영, "범죄학이론의 발전과 현대적 과제에 관한 연구", 호서대학교 행정대학원 석사학위논문, 2010:4-91.
• 롬브로조(Cesare Lombroso : 1836~1909)는 이탈리아의 법의학 · 정신의학자로서, 1870년경부터 이탈리아의 각 교도소에서 행한 범죄자의 두개골 등에 관한 연구의 결과를 정리하여, 1876년에 『범죄인론(L'uomo Delinquente)』을 저술하였으며, 과학적 범죄연구의 효시를 이루었다.

3. 위하주의(威嚇主義)시대

- 전제군주가 절대주의 체제를 유지하기 위해, 범죄행위를 군주에 대한 반역행위로 규정하고 형을 가혹하게 적용하는 위하적 억압을 하였다.
- 말엽에는 사형, 신체형, 장기유배 등의 가혹한 형벌방법을 더욱 널리 사용하여 당시 계몽사상의 발전을 억제하려 하였다.

4. 인도주의시대(periode humanitaire)[2]

- 전제군주에 의한 강력한 위하주의가 저항을 받고, 형의 완화 즉, 인도주의가 각 방면으로 강조되고 전개되던 시대이다.
- 2가지 방향 즉, 형량의 완화를 위한 '형법개혁운동'과 행형시설로서의 감옥의 개량을 위한 '감옥개량운동'이 전개되었다.

1) 형법개혁운동(Criminal Law Reform Movement) 2012 기출

- 베카리아(Cesare Beccaria: 1738~1794)에 의하여 처음 제창되었으며, 영국의 벤담(J. Bentham)[3], 독일의 포이에르바하(A. Feuerbach), 프랑스의 몽테스키외(C. L. Montesquieu) 등이 이에 동조하였다.
- 베카리아는 1764년, 저서『범죄와 형벌에 관하여(On Crimes and Punishment)』에서, 사람들은 자유의지를 가지고 자신들이 원하는 바를 선택하며 그 행위의 결과에 대해 책임을 진다는 가정 아래 여러 원칙을 제시하였다.
- 처벌은 쾌락과 고통의 원리에 근거하여야 하며, 형벌은 범죄자에게 근거하는 것이 아니라 범죄행위에 근거하여야 하며, 범죄에 따라 결정되어야 하며, 처벌은 신속하고 효과적이어야 하며, 고문과 사형은 폐지되어야 하며, 범죄를 처벌하는 것보다 범죄를 예방하는 것이 더욱 좋은 방안이라는 것이다.[4] 2011 기출

---

2) 인도주의시대 이후부터 즉, 18C에 태동한 범죄학을 고전주의 범죄학(classical criminology)이라고 한다.

3) 벤담(J. Bentham)은 범죄는 형법의 불비에서 생겨나며 범죄 없는 사회를 실현시키기 위해서는 형법개정이 필요하다고 하였다. 형벌의 목적은 개선, 격리, 피해자보호, 경제성에 있으며, 형벌은 인위적인 고통이기에 보다 큰 범죄의 해악이 있을 때에 한하여 정당화되며, 공리주의적 형벌관에 입각하여 '파놉티콘'이라는 감옥건축양식을 고안하기도 하였다.

- 형벌의 범죄방지효과는 형벌의 분량에 의하여 결정되는 것이 아니라 그 집행방법의 신속성, 정확성(필벌성) 및 공평성의 정도에 의하여서도 좌우됨을 주장하고, 형벌제도의 개혁 및 완화를 주장하였다.
- 1789년, 프랑스 인권선언과 1810년의 프랑스 형법전(나폴레옹 형법전)에 베카리아의 의견이 반영되었다.

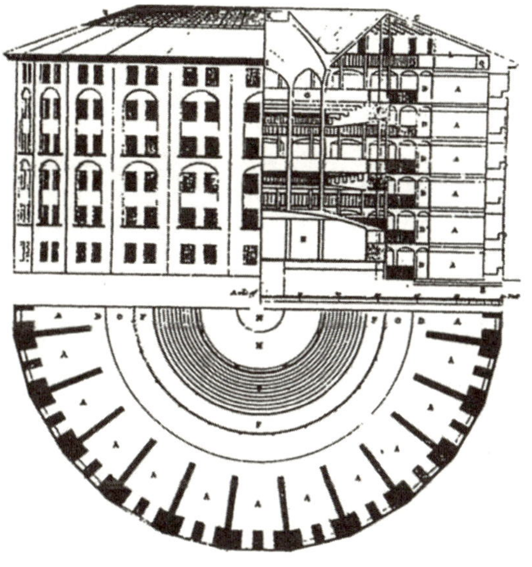

Although the panopticon is commonly associated with Jeremy Bentham it was originally his brother Samuel's invention. Jeremy got the idea during a visit to his brother in the 1780s and subsequently spent many years trying to put it into practice. Samuel Bentham was responsible for the construction of a panopticon in Russia in 1806, and saw the beginnings of its development before he left the country. His brother Jeremy never saw a panopticon built. See: http://www.ucl.ac.uk/Bentham-Project/journal/cpwpan.htm

출처: Tim Newburn, Criminology, Willan Publishing, 2007:325.

4) • 전대양, 현대사회와 범죄, 형설출판사, 2002:42-43.
- 범죄방지를 위한 수단으로서의 형벌은 어느 누구의 응보감정을 충족시키기 위한 수단으로 존재하는 것이 아니고, 어디까지나 사회 내의 범죄방지를 위하는 목적으로 존재하는 하나의 공리적 수단에 불과하기에, 형벌의 분량은 범죄방지의 목적에 필요한 최소한도에 그쳐야 하며, 그 이상의 것은 부당한 폭력이 되는 것이라고 주장하였다.

2) 감옥개량운동(Prison Reform Movement)

- 영국의 박애주의자 존 하워드(John Howard: 1726~1790)에 의하여 처음 제창되었다.
- 유럽 전역의 300여 개 감옥을 둘러보고, 1777년, 저서 『영국과 웨일스의 감옥의 상태(The State of Prisons in England and Wales)』에서 감옥은 징벌의 장소가 아니라 개선의 장소여야 하며, 죄수도 사람인 이상 사람답게 대접받아야 한다고 강조하면서 감옥개량방안을 제시하였다.

제2절 근대 이후의 범죄학

1. 롬브로조의 연구

- 격세유전설(atavistic heredity) 즉, 인간의 진화과정에서 이미 없어진 고대인간의 원시성이나 야만성과 관련된 유전적 특성이 알 수 없는 이유로 많은 세대를 뛰어넘어 나타난다는 것이다.
- 생래적 범죄인설(born criminal) 즉, 범죄자들 중 일부는 신체적 특징과 성향에 있어 격세유전적인 징후를 비범죄자들보다 더 많이 갖고 있어 범죄자로 운명지어진 존재로 태어난다고 하였다. 이러한 생래적 범죄자들은 두개골과 신체적 특징들을 5가지 이상 가지고 있다고 하였다.
- 롬브로즈가 '근대 범죄학의 아버지'라 불리는 것은 두개골을 수집하여 비교・분석함으로써 범죄의 원인을 검증하고자 한 새로운 연구방법 때문이다.[5)]

2. 근대 이후 형사정책 발전과정의 특징

- 형법・형소법・행형법 등 형사정책 각 분야에서 '교정주의'의 사상이 대거 진출하였다. 예 교정이념의 지배(dominance of the rehabilitative ideal), 소년법원제도의 발전, 집행유예 및 보호관찰제도의 발전 등

5) 전대양, 현대사회와 범죄, 형설출판사, 2002:48-50.

• 범죄 및 범죄자에 관한 과학적 연구체제가 크게 발전하면서 '형법의 몰락'이라는 현상이 나타났다.[6)]

3. 고전주의 범죄학의 평가[7)]

1) 의의

• 고전주의 범죄학자들은 자의적이고 혹독한 형사사법의 운용실태를 고발하고, 이를 지양하기 위해 법률에 따른 형벌의 집행, 효율적인 범죄방지를 위한 형벌부과방법 등을 주장하였는데 현대의 형사사법제도의 발전에 큰 영향을 미쳤다.

• 인간의 존엄성, 합리성, 공리주의 등을 추구함으로써 당시의 야만적인 형사사법제도를 개편하는 데 주도적인 역할을 하였으며, 형벌집행의 합리화와 형벌제도의 객관화에도 큰 기여를 하였다.

2) 고전주의에 대한 비판론

• 과연 법률이 공정하고 정의로운지에 대해 의문을 제기하지 않고 단지 법의 획일적인 집행만을 주장하였다.

• 범죄의 예방을 위해서는 적정한 처벌이 중요하다고 하였으나, 처벌보다는 범죄자에 맞는 처우와 교화개선이 필요하다는 주장에는 해답을 줄 수 없다.

• 인간의 본성을 너무 단순하게 보았다. 인간은 선악을 이성적으로 판단하고 자유로이 선택할 수 있는 존재라고 보았으나, 실제로 그런 존재인지를 논증하지는 못하였다.[8)]

---

6) 범죄 및 범죄자에 관한 각 방면의 연구를 시초로, 범죄를 예방・억제하기 위해서는 형법이라는 고유의 방법에 의하기보다 형법 이외의 방법에 의하여 그 목적을 추구하고자 하는 경향이 크게 나타났다.

7) 전대양, 현대사회와 범죄, 형설출판사, 2002:45-46.

8) 이에 따라 사람들의 행위가 개인의 자유의지보다는 외부적인 여러 가지 요인들에 의해 영향을 받는다는 실증주의 범죄학을 촉진시켰다. 그러나 실증주의에 입각한 재활과 교육이념, 부정기형 등과 같은 주장들로 범죄예방을 도모했으나, 그 성과가 기대에 미치지 못하고 범죄문제가 점점 더 악화되자 종래 고전주의 범죄학이 추구하였던 범죄억제에 관한 관심이 새롭게 제기되었다. 따라서 1960년대 후반기에 들어 고전주의는 새롭게 부활하여 억제이론과 범죄경제학으로 발전하며 오늘에 이르고 있다.

- 재량권 남용의 제거에 지나치게 매달리게 되어 형벌의 부과에 융통성을 결여하고 있다.

4. 실증주의 범죄학과의 비교[9)]

1) 의의

- 고전주의자들의 주장 즉, 선험적 자유의지가 더 이상 인정되지 않았으며, 인간도 생존하기 위해서는 주위환경에 적응해야 하므로 인간 외부에 존재하는 경제적 · 사회적 · 물리적 · 심리적 영향들에 의해 통제되고 결정된다는 결정론적 시각인 실증주의 범죄학(positivist criminology)이 대두되었다.
- 범죄에 대한 연구도 직관에서 증거로, 철학적 논의에서 과학적 인과관계의 해명(관찰과 실험을 통한 검증)으로 바뀌게 된 것이다.[10)]

2) 고전주의(비결정론) 2011, 2012 기출

- 고전주의 범죄학은 인간은 자신들의 자유로운 의사 또는 의지에 의하여 범죄행위를 저지른다고 보았다. 즉, 인간의 소질이나 환경은 사람의 범죄행동과는 무관한 것이며 자신들의 의지에 따라 합리적으로 범죄행위의 실행여부를 결정한다는 것이다.
- 사람들은 자유의지를 갖고 있다. 인간은 매우 합리적인 존재로 모든 행동을 자신이 결정하고 실행에 옮길 수 있는 존재이다.
- 인간의 본성은 항상 쾌락을 추구하기에 범죄행위에 이끌린다. 범죄행위는 매우 매력적인 것이며 범죄로 인한 이익은 사람들을 범죄행동으로 유혹한다.
- 범죄행동을 통제하고 사회를 평안하게 하기 위해서는 개인의 범죄행위에 대해 사회 전체가 대응하여 보복할 필요가 있다.
- 사회 전체의 보복이 형벌이며, 형벌의 부과로 잠재적으로 범죄행위를 저지르고자 하는 사람들로 하여금 욕망을 억제하도록 하여야 한다. 형벌이 효과적이기 위해서는 형벌의 부과가 정확하고, 확실하며, 신속해야 한다.

---

9) 전대양, 현대사회와 범죄, 형설출판사, 2002:62-64.
10) 전대양, 현대사회와 범죄, 형설출판사, 2002:47.

• 가장 효과적인 범죄예방은 사람들이 범죄를 선택하지 못하게 하는 형벌이다.

3) 실증주의(결정론)

• 실증주의자들은 범죄행위를 개인의 소질과 환경이 복합적으로 작용하여 표출된 것이라고 보았다.
• 인간은 자신의 의지에 따라 범죄행위의 실행여부를 결정할 수 있는 능력을 가진 존재는 아니고, 범죄자 자신이 출생 시부터 가지고 있던 생물학적 · 심리학적 특성이나 소질이 범죄자를 둘러싸고 있는 환경과 결합하여 범죄행위를 하도록 작용한다는 것이다.
• 인간의 행위는 개인이 통제할 수 없는 생물학적 · 심리학적 · 사회학적 특성의 작용이며, 범죄의 원인은 범죄자가 갖고 있는 신체적 · 심리적 · 사회적 열등성이나 요인이다.
• 개인이 저지른 범죄행위에 중점을 두기보다는 범죄자에게 중점이 두어져야 하며, 범죄문제의 원인 규명과 해결에는 과학적인 방법을 적용해야 한다.
• 범죄자에게 중점이 주어지므로 개개 범죄자가 갖고 있는 범죄요인을 제거하는 것이 범죄통제에 효과적이다.

4) 고전주의와 실증주의 비교

구분 / 학파	고전주의	실증주의
시대	• 18~19C	• 19~20C
학자	• 철학자, 작가, 법률가	• 생물학자, 수학자, 의사, 통계학자, 사회학자 등
전제	• 비결정론	• 결정론
범죄원인	• 자유의사	• 사회적 · 심리적 · 신체적 요인
관점	• 범죄행위	• 범죄자
수단	• 사법제도	• 과학적인 방법
목적	• 일반예방	• 특별예방

출처: 전대양, 현대사회와 범죄, 형설출판사, 2002:63.

제3절 유럽의 범죄사회학

1. 유럽 범죄사회학파의 형성

- 페리(E. Ferri)는 범죄학에 사회학적 방법론의 채택과 이론의 체계화를 시도하였다.
- 가로팔로(Garofalo)는 '자연범'설을 주장하였다.

2. 프랑스의 제도 · 환경학파

1) 제도학파

- 케틀레(Quetelet)는 1835년, 저서 『사회물리학(Physique Sociale)』에서, "사회는 범죄를 예비하고, 범죄자는 그것을 실천하는 수단에 불과하다"고 주장하였다.
- 모든 사회현상을 "대수의 법칙으로 파악하여 일정 사회에는 필연적으로 일정한 범죄가 발생하게 되므로, 우리는 매년 범죄의 예산(budget de Crime)을 세울 수 있다"고 주장하였다.
- 범죄는 개별적 사실로서의 의미를 가지는 것이 아니라 집단적 현상이며, 그 변동은 그때그때의 사회 · 경제적 상태와 함수관계가 있다고 주장하였다.
- 범죄학 연구에 통계학적 방법을 적용하였으며, 통계표를 통해 범죄현상의 규칙성이 존재한다고 주장하였다.

2) 환경학파(Ryon학파)

(1) 라카사뉴(Laccasagne)

- 라카사뉴(Laccasagne: 1843~1924), 타르드(J. G. Tarde: 1843~1904), 뒤르켐(E. Durkheim: 1858~1917) 등이 주요 학자이다.
- 롬브로조의 생물학적 결정론에 반대하였으며, 범죄에 개인적 요인의 존재를 부정할 수 없으나 사회적 요인을 더욱 중요한 것으로 보았다.
- 사회는 그 각각에 상응하는 범죄를 가지기 마련이며, 범죄자를 만드는 것은 사회이고 사람들을 유혹하여 범죄로 향하게 하는 것도 사회라고 하였다.

(2) 타르드(Tarde)

마르크스주의적 세계관에 입각하여 범죄원인을 사회제도 특히, 자본주의 경제질서의 제도적 모순에서 구하여 범죄자를 제외한 모든 사회에 책임이 있다는 극단론을 주장하였다.

(3) 뒤르켐(Durkheim)

자살, 범죄문제(Le Suicide, 1897)에서, 범죄는 사회문화구조상의 모순에 기인한다고 주장하였다.

3. 독일의 사회학적 이론

1) 리스트(Franz v. Liszt)

- 형벌은 법익보호에 있다는 보호형・목적형을 주장하였으며, 종래의 형법이 행위자를 고려하지 않고 행위만을 대상으로 한 점을 비판하고, 처벌되어야 할 것은 행위가 아니고 행위자이며(행위자주의), 행위자의 반사회적 성격을 형벌의 기초로 하였다.(주관주의・성격책임론)
- 범죄의 원인을 개인적 원인과 사회적 원인으로 구별하여, 형사정책 고유의 과제는 개인적 원인의 제거에 있고, 사회적 원인은 사회정책의 임무라고 주장하였다. 따라서 개선형주의에 따른 단기자유형 폐지, 집행유예와 부정기형의 도입, 행형제도의 개혁 등도 주장하였다.

2) 엑스너(Franz Exner)

『범죄생물학(1939)』에서 생물학적 견해에 사회학적 경향이 가미된 범죄사회학을 주장하였다.

제4절 미국의 범죄사회학

1. 미국 범죄사회학의 형성

미국의 범죄사회학은 사회학의 한 분과로서 발달하여, 사회주의적 실용주의가 그 기초이다. 사회학의 여러 이론의 범죄에의 적용이라는 방법으로 그 이론적 측면이 강조되면서 발전되었다.

2. 미국 범죄사회학의 제 이론

1) 문화전파를 중심으로 하는 이론

사회해체이론(Social Disorganization Theory), 문화전파이론(Cultural Transmission Theory), 분화적 접촉이론(Differential Association Theory), 이질적 동일화 이론(Differential Identification Theory) 등이 있다.

2) 문화갈등을 중심으로 하는 이론

문화갈등이론(Culture Conflict Theory), 하위계층문화이론(working-class culture theory) 등이 있다.

3) 사회구조를 중심으로 하는 이론

아노미이론(Anomic Theory), 비행부차문화이론(Theory of Delinquent Subculture), 차별적 기회이론(Differential Opportunity Theory) 등이 있다.

4) 사회심리를 중심으로 하는 이론

비행표류이론(Drift Theory), 중화기술이론(Techniques of Neutralization), 잠재적 가치이론(Theory of Subterranean Values), 자기관념이론(Self-Concept Theory), 견제이론(Containment Theory) 등이 있다.

5) 사회적 작용을 중심으로 하는 이론

사회적 작용을 중심으로 하는 이론에는 낙인이론(labelling theory)이 대표적이다.

6) 사회적 실패를 중심으로 하는 이론

(1) 신범죄학이론(New Criminology)

테일러(Ian Tayler)·월턴(Paul Walton)·영(Jock Young)의 저서 『신범죄학(The New Criminology)』[11] 등에서 주장하였다. 그중에서도 특히 "범죄의 정치경제(political economy of crime)"와 "범죄의 사회심리(social psychology of crime)"를 강조하였다.

(2) 비판적 범죄학이론(Critical Criminology)

- 사이커스는 저서 『비판적 범죄학의 대두』에서, 비판범죄학의 특징을 요약하고 있다.
- 개인에 초점을 맞추려는 범죄원인론에 대해서는 깊은 회의심을 가진다.
- 범죄를 다루는 여러 기관이 활동하는 배후에 있는 진정한 동기를 검토하는 방향으로 연구의 시점을 이행시키고자 하였다.
- 형법의 정당성 그 자체에 대하여 의문을 제기하고 재검토하려고 하였다.
- 범죄통계에 있어서 공식통계의 신뢰성을 문제시하면서 '암수범죄'의 존재와 그 중요성을 지적하고 있다.

(3) 급진적 범죄학이론(Radical Criminology)

플래트(Tony Platt)는 1974년 저서 『미국에 있어서 급진적 범죄학의 전망』[12]에서 주장하였다.

---

11) Talyer. Walton, and Youy, The New Criminology, New York : Harper and Rov. Publishers, 1973.

12) Platt. T., "Prospects of Radical Criminology in the United States", Crime and Social Justice, Vol. 1, Spring-Summer, 1974:2-9.

제5절 페미니스트 범죄학[13)]

1. 페미니스트 범죄학의 등장

페미니즘(feminism)이란 남녀동등권이나 여성해방을 지향하는 사상이라고 할 수 있으며, 1970년대부터 주장되었다.[14)]

〈표 3-17〉 심프슨의 페미니스트 범죄학의 분류

자유주의 페미니즘	• 성적 불평등은 제도적인 개선이 뒤따르지 않으면 쉽사리 없앨 수 없다.
사회주의 페미니즘	• 성적 차별이나 성적 억압은 자본주의 사회의 주요 특징이므로 새로운 사회구조를 건설해야만 극복할 수 있다.
급진적 페미니즘	• 가부장제도나 여성경시는 여성의 '성(性)'에 대한 남성의 침략행위 혹은 통제라고 보고, 성 침략이나 성적 통제를 완전히 소멸시킬 것을 주장하고 있다.

출처: 이만종, 범죄학개론, 학현사, 2005:143.

2. 여성범죄 연구에 대한 평가

1) 롬브로조의 여성범죄 연구

- 롬브로조와 페레로는 『여성범죄자와 매춘부(1895)』에서 여성은 "신체적 · 정신적으로 수동적이면서도 다른 한편으로 냉혹하고 계산 빠른 부도덕한 생물"이라고 하였다.
- 진화론적인 입장에서 보면 여성범죄자는 그러한 선조가 환생한 존재이므로 동물에 훨씬 가까운 존재이며, 형태학적으로 보면 보통여자에 비해 남성에 가까운 특징을 지니고 있다고 하였다.[15)]

---

13) 이만종, 범죄학개론, 학현사, 2005:142-155.

14) 관련연구로는 D. 크라인의 논문 "여성범죄의 원인론-관련문헌 리뷰"(1973), C. 스마트의 저서 『여성, 범죄 그리고 범죄학』(1976) 등이 있다. 페미니스트 범죄학자에는 영국의 경우 F. 하이덴존, L. 겔스솝, A. 모리스 등이 있으며, 미국의 경우에는 M. 체니스 린다, K. 데일리, J. 클레스, J. 멧산슈미트, S. 심프슨 등이 있다.

15) 여성범죄자는 체모가 많은데 이는 여성범죄자가 일반적인 여자보다 진화하였다는 것을 나타내는

- 범죄인류학상에서 나타난 신체적 특징을 지니는 비율이 남성범죄자보다 높으며, 여성범죄자는 정상인 자와 다를 뿐만 아니라 일반적인 여성과도 다른 특이한 존재로서의 이중적인 의미를 지닌 '괴물'이라고 결론지었다.

2) 기타 여성범죄 연구

(1) 토머스

- 『성과 사회(1907)』에서, 여성은 남성보다 덜 진화된 하층인류이므로 백인남성에 비해 난폭하고 현명하지도 않다고 주장했다.
- 『부적응소녀(1923)』에서, 소녀의 성(性) 비행을 조사하고 이를 토대로 여성은 남성에 비해 수동적이며 사회적 변화에 적응하는 능력이 결여되어 있으므로 비행을 저지르기 쉽다는 결론을 도출하였다.

(2) 폴락

- 『여성범죄(1950)』에서 여성범죄는 발각되기 어렵고 게다가 형사사법제도에서도 '기사도정신'에 입각하여 관대하게 취급되기 때문에 범죄수가 과소하게 집계되기 쉽다.
- 여성은 선천적으로 교활하고 감정적이며 복수심도 강하기 때문에 범죄성이 남성에 뒤지지 않으며, 『여성범죄(1961)』에서는 무릎 꿇은 남성을 묶어 올리는 마녀의 일러스트가 표지로 사용되기도 했다.
- 페미니스트 범죄학은 여성에 대한 편견에 기초한 것이며 여성차별에 직결되는 것이라고 강력하게 비판하였다.

(3) 아들러

- 『신여성 범죄자의 출현(1975)』에서, 여성해방과 범죄의 관계를 분석하였는데, 1970년대 중반에 나타난 여성해방・여성의 사회진출로 인해 여성이 남성화된 결과 여성범죄가 폭력화되고 양적으로도 증가하였다는 결론을 내렸다.

것이 아니라 이상 존재임을 의미한다는 것이다.

3. 여성취급에 대한 비판이론

- 페미니스트 범죄학은 종래의 범죄학이론이 남성을 주된 연구대상으로 삼았으며 여성의 존재는 무시되어 왔다고 비판하였다.
- 페미니스트 범죄학은 서덜랜드의 『범죄학 원리(제4판, 1947)』에 대해 여성을 고려하지 않은 상태에서 범죄원인론을 전개하였다고 주장한다.
- 마르크스나 엥겔은 범죄의 원인을 자본주의 사회구조에서 찾으려 했으나 자본주의 사회에서의 여성과 범죄의 관계에 대해 충분한 검토를 하지 못했다.
- 베커의 『아웃사이더들(1963)』에 대해 여성과 범죄의 문제에 대해 철저하게 조사할 필요가 있었음에도 불구하고 이를 행하지 않았다고 비판하고 있다.
- 신범죄학은 많은 전통적 범죄를 시민의 '체제에 대한 레지스탕스'로 보는 한편, 진정한 범죄는 전쟁이나 인종차별이며 이것이야말로 문제시해야 한다는 입장에서 종래 범죄학의 문제의식을 비판하였다.

4. 페미니스트 범죄학의 형사사법과정에 대한 비판

페미니스트 범죄학은 입법・행정・사법의 3권을 지금까지 남성이 지배해 왔기 때문에, 법의 제정・집행 및 적용 등 모든 단계에서 여성의 관점이 결여되어 있고 여성의 권리가 적절하게 보호되지 못했다고 지적한다.

1) 입법의 여성 멸시

입법기관은 여성에 대해 '성모(聖母)'의 이미지(강간의 피해자)와 '마녀'의 이미지(매춘부)를 구별하여 적용시켰으며, 동시에 '마녀'의 이미지에 대해서는 엄격한 대응을 해왔다는 것이다.

2) 수사와 재판의 불공정

- 하이덴존은 법원은 성적 행위에 대해 '이중적인 기준'을 적용하고 있으며,[16] 여성범

16) 미성년의 난잡한 교류나 성교에 대해, 여자에게는 과도하게 엄격한 태도를 취하면서 남자에게는 아무런 간섭도 하지 않는 경우가 많다.

죄 · 비행에 성적인 의미를 부여하여 특징지으려 하고 과잉으로 드라마화하려 한다고 비판하였다.

- 소녀는 반항적일수록 형량에서 부정적인 평가를 받아 낙인의 대상이 되며, 법원은 일반적으로 인정되고 있는 일부일처제나 동성애 금지규범을 받아들이지 않는 여성에 대해 엄격한 형량으로 처벌하는 경향이 있다는 것이다.

3) 여자수형자 차별

여자수형자를 사회에 대한 위험한 존재로 보는 것이 아니라 교육이나 지도가 필요한 '미성숙하며 연약한 여성'으로 파악하고 있으며, 중죄를 저지른 자는 '여성 고유의 악의나 부도덕성이 노출된 전형'으로 간주되어 남자수형자보다 엄격한 처우를 받고 있다는 것이다.

5. 페미니스트 범죄학의 주장

1) 강간죄

- 남성지배와 성적 불평등의 현실을 가장 상징적으로 나타내는 범죄로 페미니스트들은 강간죄를 들고 있다.[17)]
- 미국에서는 1970년대 후반부터 페미니스트 범죄학자의 주장을 고려하여 강간죄에 대하여 i) 진지한 동의 이외에는 동의의 존재를 인정하지 않으며 ii) 부부 간에도 강

---

17) • 종래에 미국에서는 강간죄가 성립되기 위해서는 피해자인 여성의 동의의 부존재가 요건이 되었었다. 그러나 실제로는 여성이 마음에 내키지는 않지만 어쩔 수 없이 동의한 경우나 일정시간 동안 저항한 후에 저항을 그만둔 경우까지도 동의의 존재를 긍정하는 식으로 취급되어 왔다. 이에 대해 페미니스트들은 가해자인 남성을 부당하게 보호하는 처사라는 비판을 하였던 것이다.
• 종래에는 부부 간에 이루어진 강간에 대해서는 i) 혼인 자체가 성교를 동의하는 의사표시이며, ii) 강간의 사실 입증이 곤란하며, iii) 가정 내의 문제에 형법은 개입하지 않는다는 3가지 이유에서 면책이 인정되어 왔다. 그러나 이러한 면책은 기혼여성의 자기결정권이나 프라이버시를 불합리하게 제한하는 것이 되므로 부부 간의 강간죄 성립도 인정해야만 한다고 주장하였다.
• 원래 강간죄의 가해자를 남성, 피해자를 여성으로 규정하는 점 자체가 성적 차별이라는 비판과 더불어 여성의 남성강간도 고려하여 범죄의 주체와 객체에 대한 규정이나 정의를 중성적인 것으로 개정해야 한다고 주장했다.
• 우리나라는 1970년 대법원이 정상적인 부부 사이에는 강간이 성립될 수 없다는 판결을 내렸다. 그러나 2004년 서울중앙지법이 부부 간 성폭력을 강제추행으로 단죄한 이후 2009년 부산지법은 최초로 부부강간을 인정하는 판결을 선고하였다. 하지만 대법원의 입장은 여전히 바뀌지 않아 그 귀추가 주목되고 있다.

간죄를 적용하며 iii) 법률상의 문구를 중성화한다는 등의 법개정이 추진되었다.

2) 낙태죄

여성의 중절 결정권(자기결정권)을 확장하며 기혼여성의 경우에는 인공임신중절의 요건이 되어온 '남편의 동의'를 삭제하여야 한다고 주장한다.[18)]

3) 매매춘 규제

페미니스트는 매매춘을 한편으로는 남성들에게 유리하도록 여성을 상품화하면서 다른 한편으로는 여성을 멸시하는 남성의 이기주의를 여실히 드러내는 '이중적인 기준'의 실례로 보고 그 근절을 목표로 삼고 있다.

〈표 3-18〉 비판범죄학[19)]과 주류범죄학의 비교

	비판범죄학	주류범죄학
범죄의 정의	• 뚜렷한 개념정의가 없으나 인간주의 범죄개념이 최소한의 합의를 이룸 • 범죄란 역사적으로 규정된 인권을 침해한 행위(Schlesinger) • 법적 범죄개념은 계급사회에서는 의문시 즉, 법은 지배계급의 이익과 합치되는 방향으로 집행된다. • 법적 범죄개념은 사회적으로 유해하지만 체계관리를 위해 도움이 되는 행위를 개념에서 제외 즉, 제국주의 성차별, 정부의 부패 등 국민에 대한 중요한 범죄 무시 • 법적 범죄개념은 계급지배를 강화시키는 방향으로 범죄학의 언어나 연구대상을 규정짓는 이데올로기적 도구로 작용 즉, 범죄연구는 국가정책에 예속	• 법적 범죄개념(Legal definition of crime) • 범죄란 형법을 위반한 행위, 형법을 기준으로 한 범죄개념이 가장 정확하고 객관적인 범죄개념(Tappan) • Sellin은 범죄란 집단이 있는 곳이면 언제 어디서나 존재하는 행위규범에 위반한 행위라 하고, Sutherland는 범죄란 사회적 해를 주는 행위로서 형법 및 민법을 다 포함하는 의미에서의 법적 대상이 되는 행위 • 비판범죄학은 형사학에서의 활용 여지가 거의 없다. • 비판범죄학은 법적 의미성을 결여하고 있다. • 비판범죄학은 범죄개념의 확정의 주류가 없다.

출처: 김채영, 범죄학이론의 발전과 현대적 과제에 관한 연구, 호서대학교 행정대학원 석사학위논문, 2010:63-64.

18) 미국의 경우, 인공임신중절의 자유화문제는 종교적・정치적 편향이 극명하다. 선거캠페인에서는 원칙적으로 공화당이 인공임신중절 규제를 지지한 반면, 민주당은 규제를 반대한다는 입장이 이미 공식화되어 있다고 한다.

19) 심영희, 비판범죄학의 문제점과 그 대안, 한국사회학, 제13집, 1974:15-22, 참조.

〈포스트모더니즘 범죄이론〉 2012 기출

- 포스트모더니즘 범죄개념은 사회적 소수집단에 대한 편견과 혐오, 그리고 차별을 유발하는 언어나 형사법체제상의 처벌조항은 물론이고 학문적으로 범죄화하는 언어를 해체하고 그것으로부터의 해방을 요구하는 것이라고 정의된다.
- 포스트모더니즘 범죄이론은 기존의 모더니즘 패러다임에 입각한 범죄학 이론을 비판하거나 부정한다. 또한 포스트모더니즘 범죄이론의 관점이 기존의 형사사법체계의 변화를 초래하거나 특정 범죄를 설명하는 데 있어서 상당한 설명력을 갖추고 있다고 본다.
- 범죄 그 자체나 관련된 법률의 제정이 권력자들의 담론에 의해 구성되는 산물이라고 보는 점에서 구성적 범죄이론과 아주 유사하다[20]. 범죄자가 범행을 하면 범죄자를 검거하고 사법처리를 하는 과정에서 범죄자, 법 집행기관(통제기관), 피해자 그리고 범죄학자의 담론적 언어에 의해 범죄가 구성되고 범죄자가 결정된다는 것이다.
- 특히 인종, 민족, 성별, 그리고 성적 지향 같은 특성을 이유로 차별과 억압을 받는 집단에 대한 범죄화와 합법화 과정을 설명할 수 있는 지식체계이다.
- 범죄원인을 경험적 검증과정에 의해 과학적 이론을 추구하는 현대의 실증주의적 연구정향에 대해 그와는 다른 비과학적이지만 지적인 방법을 지지하고, 특권이 없는 계층에 대한 우호적이고 진보적인 이론을 개발하기 위해 언어적 담론에 의해 경험적 검증이 필요 없는 현실적으로 자명한 관점을 제시하고자 하는 하나의 패러다임이다.

〈표 3-19〉 미국 범죄사회학과의 분류

중심	이론	학자
• 문화전파 중심이론	• 사회해체이론 • 문화전파이론 • 분화적 접촉이론 • 이질적 동일화이론	• Cooley • Shaw and McKay • Sutherland • D. Glaser
• 문화갈등중심 이론	• 문화갈등이론 • 하층계급문화이론	• Sellin • Miller
• 사회구조에 중심을 둔 이론	• 아노미이론 • 비행부차문화이론 • 이질적 사회구조이론	• Merton • Cohen • Cloward & Ohlin

20) 구성적 범죄학에 의하면, 범죄현상은 다양한 참여자들의 추론의 산물이며, 범죄에 대한 인과관계 분석은 결국은 힘없는 사람들을 범죄 원인제공자로 만드는 오류를 범하게 된다는 것이다.

• 사회심리를 중심으로 하는 이론	• 비행표류이론 • 비행중화기술이론 • 잠재적 가치이론 • 자기관념이론 • 견제이론	• Matza • Matza, Sykes • Matza, Sykes • Reckless, Dinitz • Reckless
• 사회적 상호작용 중심이론	• 낙인이론	• Becker, Gibbs, Schur • Kitsuse
• 사회적 실체중심이론	• 신범죄학이론 • 비판적 범죄학 • 급진적 범죄학	• Taylor, Waltony, Young • Sykes • Platt

출처: 김채영, 범죄학이론의 발전과 현대적 과제에 관한 연구, 호서대학교 행정대학원 석사학위논문, 2010:64.

〈각 학파들의 주요 학자〉

학파	학자	연도	주요 이론
• 이탈리아 범죄학파	• Lombroso • Garofalo • Ferri	• 1836~1909 • 1851~1934 • 1856~1929	• 생래적 범죄인설 • 범죄학 • 범죄사회학
• 프랑스 환경학파 (환경학파, 리옹학파)	• Lacassagne • Tarde • Durkheim	• 1843~1924 • 1848~1904 • 1858~1917	• 사회환경학설 • 모방의 법칙 • 범죄정상설
• 형사사회학파 (통계학파, 환경학파)	• Liszt • Hamel • Prins	• 1851~1919 • 1842~1917 • 1845~1919	• 형법학파 • 형법학파(실증주의 형법) • 형법학파
• 범죄생물학파 (신롬브로조학파)	• Kretschmer		• 체질유형학설
• 범죄사회학파	• Qutelet • Aschaffenburg • Bonger • Exner • Healy • Mezger	• 1896~1874 • 1866~1944 • 1876~1940 • 1881~1947 • 1869~1963 • 1884~1962	• 범죄항상설 • 범죄양식설 • 범죄학파 • 형법, 사회현상 • 정신의학자, 다인자분석 • 법학자, 동력학적 범죄설
• 현대범죄학 생태학	• Park, Burgess • Shaw, McKay • Mills		• 자연천이론 • 비행현상론 • 사회붕괴론
• 문화갈등	• Thomas • Sutherland • Wrirth		• 일상규범론 • 비행론 • 비행론

	• Sellin • Merton		• 행위규범론 • 아노미이론
	• Whyte		• 차별접촉이론
	• Akers • Skinner • Bandura		• 사회학습이론
• 사회심리학파	• Matza		• 비행중화, 표류이론
	• Hirschi		• 사회통제이론
	• Mead		• 낙인이론
	• Lemert		• 사회병리학
	• Tannenbaum		• 범죄와 지역사회
	• Goffmann		• Stigma의 사회학 (낙인찍기)

출처: 임상곤, 범죄심리학원론, 백산출판사, 2004:329.

제6절 발전범죄학(development criminology)

1. 의의[21)]

1) 의의

- 발전범죄학이란 범죄행위의 동태적 측면을 행위자의 성장단계별 상태나 발전과정 혹은 개인성향과 관련하여 설명하는 이론이다.

2) 발전범죄학의 특징

(1) 발전범죄학은 범죄현상의 분석에 있어서 행위자의 성장단계별 상태나 발전과정을 중요한 인과요인으로 고려한다.

- 발전범죄학에서 성장단계별 상태나 발전과정은 흔히 생애전이(life transition)나 생애궤적(life trajectory)으로 표현한다.[22)]

21) 이순래·박철현, 범죄현상에 대한 새로운 분석틀: 발전범죄학의 대두와 전개, 한국공안행정학회, 2000, pp. 81-125.

• 발전범죄학은 행위자가 성장단계별로 어떤 상태에 있으며 또한 지금까지 어떤 발전과정을 밟아왔는가를 범죄현상의 분석에 있어서 중요한 인과요인으로 고려한다.

(2) 범죄행위의 동태적 측면을 주요 분석 대상으로 한다.

• 발전범죄학은 과거범죄와 차후범죄와의 연계관계나 범죄단절현상 등 범죄행위의 동태적 측면을 주요 분석대상으로 한다.

2. 내용

1) 모피트(Moffitt)의 발전학습론

• 모피트는 연령과 범죄율과의 관계에 대해서 범죄자들을 생애지속범죄자(life-course persistent offender)와 청소년기 한정비행자(adolescence limited delinquents)로 구분하고, 이들의 작용으로 인하여 범죄율이 청소년연령대에 높고 성인연령대에는 감소하는 것으로 설명하였다.

생애지속범죄자	개인의 기본성향 면에서 결함이 있으며 어려서부터 범죄를 저지르기 시작하고 나이가 들어서도 범죄로부터 손을 씻지 못하고 만성적으로 범죄를 저지르는 사람들
청소년기 한정비행자 (한정범죄자)	기본성향의 면에서는 일반인들과 차이가 없지만 청소년이란 발전과정상의 특성과 학습이나 모방에 의해 청소년기에 국한하여 범죄를 저지르고 이후에는 그만두는 사람들

(1) 생애지속범죄자의 만성범죄행위

• 지속범죄자로서의 소질형성과 관련하여 모피트가 강조했던 사항은 정신심리적 기능(neuro-psychological function)의 장애와 어렸을 때의 부적절한 성장환경이다. 즉, 출생 전후에 모체나 태아의 이상으로 정신심리적 기능장애가 발생하고 부모의 무관심이나 양육방법의 잘못으로 이 같은 기능장애가 제대로 치유되지 못함으로써 지속범죄자로서의 성향이 형성된다는 것이다.

22) 생애전이란 행위자가 성장단계별로 어떤 상태에 있는가 즉, 성장과정에서 겪는 사건이나 단기적인 변화를 의미하며, 생애궤적이란 발전과정 즉, 가족생활, 교육경험, 직업생활, 범죄경력 등과 같이 중요한 사회적 사건에서 나타나는 장기적 발전형태를 뜻한다.

- 모피트는 생물학적 결정론을 넘어 생물학적 요인과 조기성장환경의 상호작용을 중요한 영향요인으로 고려했다.
- 모피트는 문제성향의 구체적 상태로 흥분성(irritability). 높은 활동성(high activity). 낮은 자아통제력 (low self-control), 낮은 인지능력(low cognitive ability) 등을 지적하였다.
- 지속범죄자들이 생애 전 과정에 걸쳐 정상적인 생활을 하지 못하고 반(反)사회적 행위에 빠지는 것은 바로 문제성향의 현시적 결과(contemporary outcomes)와 누적적 결과(cumulative outcomes)에 기인한다고 보았다.[23)]

현시적 결과	• 문제성향으로 말미암아 유발되는 부정적 결과이다. 예 높은 흥분성의 사람들은 성장과정의 여러 상황들에 있어서 그렇지 않은 사람에 비해서 감정적으로 대처하는 경향이 높고, 또한 낮은 인지능력의 사람들은 상황에 대해서 종합적인 판단을 하지 못하고 즉흥적으로 행동함으로써 여러 종류의 반(反)사회적 행위에 빠져들 수 있다. • 문제성향의 직접효과로 인하여 사회생활의 적응에 부정적 결과를 초래하는 경우이다.

23) 모피트는 누적적 결과가 초래되는 경우를 크게 3가지로 나누었다.
① 친(親)사회적 행위목록을 학습할 수 있는 기회가 제한되는 경우이다. 문제성향의 아동들은 높은 흥분성과 낮은 자아통제력 때문에 친구들이나 주위 사람들이 접촉을 회피하여 원만한 인간관계를 맺기 어렵다. 주위 사람들의 회피뿐만 아니라 문제아동 자신도 이들과의 관계를 기피함으로써 정상적인 아동의 경우는 친구관계나 주위 사람들과의 상호작용을 통하여 친(親)사회적 행위목록 즉 합법적인 문제해결방법을 학습할 수 있지만 문제아동들은 이 같은 학습기회를 갖지 못한다는 것이다.
② 어렸을 때의 비정상적 행위가 발전과정에서 덫으로 작용하는 경우이다. 낮은 자아통제력이나 충동성으로 문제아동들은 청소년기의 임신, 마약에의 탐닉, 중퇴, 범죄로 인한 상해 등의 사건을 겪을 가능성이 높다. 이러한 경험들은 미혼모의 경우처럼 이후에 해당아동이 정상적인 생활로 환원하고 싶어도 그럴 수 없게 하는 일생의 덫(snare)이 됨으로써 이들은 일생 동안 반사회적 생활양식을 버릴 수 없게 된다.
③ 사회적 낙인의 효과이다. 문제아동들의 행위에 가해지는 사회적 낙인은 좋은 직업, 고등교육, 원만한 결혼 등의 생활기회를 차단함으로써 문제아동들이 반사회적 생활양식을 지속하게 하는 누적적 이유로 작용할 수 있다. 이와 같이 모피트에 의하면 지속범죄자의 경우는 어렸을 때 형성된 문제성향이 주요한 원인이며, 문제성향의 현시적 결과와 누적적 결과로 인하여 이러한 성향의 사람들은 생애 전 과정에 걸쳐 범죄를 포함한 반(反)사회적 행위에 빠져들게 된다는 것이다.

누적적 결과	• 문제성향이 성장과정에서 누적적으로 부정적 영향을 미치는 즉, 문제성향의 간접효과에 의해 유발되는 결과들이다. 예 문제아동의 경우에 학교생활에 적응하기가 어려워 학업을 중도에 포기하고 이로 말미암아 어른이 되어서도 정상적인 취업기회를 갖지 못해 불법적인 수단으로 생계를 유지하는 경우 예 문제성향이 이후의 생활기회를 점차 제한함으로써 이들의 반(反)사회적 행위가 장기화되는 경우

(2) 청소년기 한정비행자의 범죄모방행위

- 한정범죄자들은 기본성향 면에서 정상인들과 별다른 차이가 없고, 한정범죄자의 최초범죄는 청소년기에 시작되며 성인기에 들면서 대부분 범죄로부터 손을 씻고 정상적인 생활로 환원한다는 것이다.
- 모피트는 청소년기에 범죄율이 급증하고 성인기에 감소하는 까닭은 청소년기에 한정범죄자들이 대규모로 출현하기 때문이며, 20대 이후에는 이들이 더 이상 범죄행위의 필요성을 느끼지 못하고 정상적인 생활로 환원하기 때문이라고 보았다.
- 청소년기에는 특유의 욕구가 있으며 비행이나 범죄는 이들의 욕구를 충족시켜 주기 때문에 대규모의 한정범죄자들이 출현한다고 설명하였다.
- 청소년기에 나타나는 특유의 욕구로 지적한 사항은 독립성(autonomy)의 추구와 성인역할(adult role)에 대한 갈망이었다.
- 청소년기에 한정범죄자가 대규모로 발생하는 이유는 욕구좌절을 겪는 일반소년들이 주위의 지속범죄소년들이 독자성이나 성인역할을 향유하는 것을 목격하고 이들의 행위를 모방하기 때문이라는 것이다.
- 모피트는 일반소년들이 지속범죄소년의 범죄를 모방하는 학습과정에서 찾아볼 수 있는 특이점들으로써 i) 학습과정에서 양자 간 감정적 애착이나 친밀한 의사소통이 필요 없으며 ii) 모방의 경우에 지속범죄소년과의 양적 관계가 질적 관계보다 중요하게 작용한다는 것이다.
- 모피트는 청소년기에 한정적으로 비행이 증가하는 이유를 비행의 상징적 가치부여기능과 신분강화기능의 측면에서 파악하였다.
- 모피트는 청소년기에 많은 비행을 저지른 한정범죄자들이 나이가 들면서 범죄를

그만두는 까닭은 상황변화, 인식의 변화, 낮은 현시적 불이익과 축적적 불이익 등 3가지 측면에서 범죄단절의 이유를 거론하면서, 한정범죄자들은 쉽게 범죄로부터 이탈할 수 있다고 보았다.

2) 애그뉴(Agnew)의 발전긴장론

(1) 의의

애그뉴는 일반긴장이론을 중심으로 소수의 만성범죄자가 일생 동안에 걸쳐 반복적으로 범죄를 저지르는 까닭과 일정시기에 급격히 증가하는 일시범죄자 문제에 관한 이론화를 시도하였다.

(2) 발전긴장론의 특징

- 발전긴장론은 개인의 소질 중에서 사회화의 영향을 비교적 많이 받는 문제해결능력을 범죄지속여부를 결정짓는 중요한 요인으로 고려하였다.
- 발전긴장론은 청소년들에 미치는 부정적 영향의 범위를 폭넓게 인정하였다.[24)]
- 부정적인 영향이 비행으로 연결되는 과정에서 인지능력의 차이나 청소년들의 권한이나 이들에 허용된 자원까지도 고려하였다.
- 비행이나 범죄를 청소년들이 부정적 감정을 회피 혹은 완화하기 위한 행위로 이해함으로써, 비행이나 범죄가 외부영향에 의해 결정된다는 단순도식을 회피하고, 행위자에 의해 제한적이지만 선택되는 행위라는 측면을 부각하였다.

3) 샘슨과 롭(Sampson & Laub)의 발전통제론 2011 기출

(1) 의의

- 샘슨과 롭은 비행이나 범죄발생을 통제하는 사회유대의 형태는 생애과정에 따라 다를 수 있다는 점에 주목하면서, 특정의 범죄자가 범죄를 지속하거나 그만두는 과정에 대한 생애과정별 사회유대의 영향에 관한 이론화를 시도하였다.

24) 발전학습론이나 발전통제론의 경우는 부모, 선생, 친구 등과의 관계에 치중하지만, 발전긴장론은 주위 이웃과의 관계나 일상생활의 다양한 상호작용형태까지 부정적 영향의 범위를 폭넓게 고려하였다.

- 사회통제이론을 반영하여, 샘슨과 롭의 발전통제론은 사회구성원들을 상호연관시키거나 개인을 보다 광범위한 사회제도에 연계시키는 구조에 반영되어 있는 사회유대의 역할을 중시하였다.
- 개인의 생애단계에 있어 중요한 사회유대의 형태는 단계별로 서로 다르며 특정개인의 범죄지속여부는 생애단계별 사회유대의 차이에 의해 설명할 수 있다고 보았다. 즉, 어렸을 때의 가족에 대한, 친구에 대한, 학교에 대한 사회유대와 성인기에 들어 직장에 대한, 결혼에 대한, 동료 등에 대한 사회유대의 차이를 살펴봄으로써 그 사람의 범죄지속현상을 설명할 수 있다는 것이다.
- 샘슨과 롭은 어렸을 때 형성된 범죄성향의 개인별 차이는 큰 문제가 되지 않으며 중요한 것은 그 사람이 성장하면서 맺게 되는 사회유대의 정도라고 주장하였다.
- 비록 어렸을 때 조기징후, 행동이상, 낮은 자아통제력 등을 보인 사람들이 만성범죄자로 발전하는 경우가 있더라도 이는 범죄성향이 성장단계에 결쳐 발현되어 그런 것이 아니라 조기비행에 의해 이후의 사회유대관계가 약화되었기 때문이라는 것이다.
- 발전통제론은 어렸을 때 형성된 개인성향이나 심리적 특성보다는 초기의 사회적 행동이 이후의 발전단계에서 맺게 될 가족관계, 학교생활, 동료관계, 직업선택 등에 유발시키는 문제들을 중요시하였다.

(2) 주요 특징

- 어렸을 때 형성된 문제성향 혹은 공격성향의 직접효과를 인정하지 않은 대신에, 샘슨과 롭은 전환점(turning point)과 누적적 불이익(cumulative disadvantage)의 역할을 강조하였다.

① 전환점의 역할

- 발전통제론은 한 사람이 성장하면서 접하게 되는 사회생활을 중시한다. 그중에서 전환점이 특정개인의 경우에 그 사람의 이후 발전방향에 중요한 영향을 미치는 사회생활경험을 지칭한다.[25)]

25) 전환점이란 한 개인의 생애 전 과정에 중요한 영향을 미치는 사회적 전이(social transition)이며, 전환점은 우연하게 대두될 수도 있지만 과거의 생활방식에 따라 어떤 규칙성을 가지고 대두한다는 것이다. 즉, 취업연령에 들어 직업을 갖는다든지 결혼적령기에 결혼을 하는 일과 같은 전환점

- 샘슨과 롭은 전환점은 이후 특정개인의 생애에 부정적일 수도 있고 긍정적일 수도 있다고 지적하였다.
- 샘슨과 롭은 전환점에 의하여 범죄발전의 경로가 수정될 수 있다고 주장했으며, 범죄자의 생애과정에서 특히 중요한 전환점으로 결혼과 직업경력을 지적하였다,
- 비록 어렸을 때 문제행동을 저질렀다고 하더라도 혼인이나 안정된 직업은 당사자들의 사회유대수준을 증진시킴으로써 정상적인 생활로의 환원시키는 전환점의 역할을 한다는 것이다.

② 누적적 불이익의 역할

- 샘슨과 롭은 차후범죄의 개연성은 과거범죄에 의해 주로 결정된다고 보았다.
- 과거범죄가 차후범죄를 유발하는 과정에서 이를 매개하는 것으로 누적적 불이익을 지적하였다. 즉, 과거범죄로 인하여 누적적 불이익이 생겨나며 이로 인하여 사회유대의 결손이 발생하고 차후 범죄의 개연성이 높아진다는 것이다.

〈누적적 불이익의 2가지 유형〉

누적적 연속성 (cumulative continuity)	과거범죄로 인하여 학교실패, 취업의 어려움 등과 같이 사회제도로부터 단절되는 현상
상호작용적 연속성 (interactional continuity)	상호작용과정에서 다른 사람들로부터 불이익을 경험하는 현상 예 어렸을 때 비행이나 범죄를 저지른 사람은 성장하면서 누적적 연속성이나 상호작용적 연속성으로 인하여 이후 성장과정에서 정상적인 사회유대관계를 형성하지 못해 성인기까지 지속적으로 범죄를 저지른다.

- 샘슨과 롭은 범죄적 소질이 중요한 것이 아니라 범죄를 저지르면 이로 인하여 사회유대관계가 영향을 받으며, 사회유대의 약화로 인하여 차후범죄의 개연성이 증가하는 것이라고 주장하였다.
- 조기비행으로 부모와의 관계가 악화되고, 학업에 실패하고, 동료로부터 배척을 당하고, 우울심리를 경험하고, 비행친구와 교제하는 등의 2차적 사회유대문제가 유발되며 이후의 반(反)사회적 행동은 이 같은 누적적 불이익에 의해 더욱 많은 영향을 받게 된다는 것이다.

들은 지금까지 그 사람의 발전궤적을 변화시킬 수 있으며, 범죄자들의 경우에 전환점은 이들이 범죄를 그만두고 정상적인 생활로 돌아오는 계기로 작용할 수 있다는 것이다.

제4편

범죄대책론

제19장 범죄예측론

제1절 범죄예측의 의의

1. 범죄예측의 의의

- 범죄예측(Crime Prediction)이란 범죄예방, 수사, 재판, 교정 등 형사처리의 각 단계에서 범죄자, 비행소년의 범죄, 재범위험성의 정도를 측정・판단하는 것을 말한다.
- 범죄예측은 소극적으로는 수형자의 재범위험성을 판단하여 가석방의 허가시기 등을 판단하는 목적으로 사용되며, 적극적으로는 치안공공재의 생산과 관련하여 범죄예방대책을 수립하는 데 있다.[1)]

2. 범죄예측의 기준

신뢰성	• 누가 해도 같은 결과를 가져오는 것
타당성	• 예측의 목적에 부합하는 내용으로 구성되는 것
단순성	• 예측조작이 간단할 것
효율성	• 적은 예측인자로 높은 효과를 가져올 것

1) • 박상기・손동권・이순래, 형사정책, 한국형사정책연구원, 1990:605.
• 천정환, 신범죄학, 백산출판사, 2006:452-460.
• 범죄예측(Crime Prediction)은 조기비행이나 재범행위를 저지르는 것을 미연에 측정・판단하는 것을 목적으로 하여 시작하였다. 이상현, 범죄심리학, 박영사, 2004:447-472.

3. 연혁[2)]

1) 미국

(1) 워너(Warner)

1923년, 최초로 '점수법'을 기초로 가석방 성공여부에 대한 사전판단의 자료를 마련하여 범죄예측을 연구하였으며[3)], 하트(Hart)의 비판을 거쳐 더욱 심화되었다.

(2) 버제스(Burgess)

1928년, 계량범죄학을 범죄예측연구에 도입하여, 최초로 '재범예측표'를 작성했으며 계량범죄학을 제창하였다.

(3) 글뤽(S. & E. T. Glueck)부부

1950년, 저서『소년비행의 해명』에서, 소년비행을 예측함에 있어서 '조기예측표'로 계량적 측정을 시도했는데, 형벌과 같은 일반예방기능이 비행소년을 갱생하는 것이 아니라 개인의 자기충동억제의 성숙발전이 소년의 갱생원인이 된다고 주장했다.[4)]

2) 독일

(1) 엑스너(Exner)

1935년, 미국을 방문한 후 버제스(Burgess)의 연구결과를 소개하고 예측의 필요성을 강조하였다.

---

2) 이상현, 범죄심리학, 박영사, 2004:454-457.

3) 미국의 범죄예측은 1923년 Warner가 매사추세츠 주(州) 교도소 수용자들의 가석방 전(前)의 기록에서 수용 중의 교정여부, 행상, 석방 후의 직업, 귀향지, 사실진술능력, 전과, 신병인수인 등 60개 항목을 조사한 후 점수법에 의해 가석방의 성공여부에 대한 사전판단을 한 것이 최초였다. 진계호, 형사정책, 대왕사, 2002:343.

4) 글뤽(Glueck)부부는 사회적 인자, 성격적 인자, 정신의학적 인자를 추출하여 아동의 장애비행을 예측하기 위한 목적에서 작성한 것으로 이 중에서 사회적 인자를 가장 중요한 예측인자로 보았다. 글뤽(Glueck)부부의 조기예측표는 Black, Glick, Tompson에 의해 검증되었고 스위스의 Fry에 영향을 주었다.

(2) 시트(Schiedt)

바바리아 교도소에서 범죄인의 15개 성격인자를 추출하여 '범죄예측표'를 작성해서 0~3점(교정가능), 4~9점(교정의문), 10점 이상(교정불능)으로 예측하였다.

3) 기타 국가

(1) 스위스의 프라이(Fry)

글뤽(Glueck)의 영향으로 사전예측, 사후예측 및 종국예측을 위한 예측요인을 찾아내어 예측표를 작성하였다.

(2) 영국의 만하임(H. Mannheim), 윌킨스(L. T. Willkins)

1960년대, Manheim, Wilkins 등은 회귀분석방법을 사용하여 재범예측표를 작성하였다.

(3) 위트(Witte)와 슈미트(Schimitt)의 생존분석

재범예측에 있어 범죄의 확률뿐만 아니라 그 시점까지도 예측하고자 하는 대표적인 연구로, '생존분석'이라는 통계적 방법을 사용하여 출소한 범죄자들이 범죄행위로 인하여 재수감되는 시기의 분포와 이에 영향을 미치는 요인을 밝히고자 하였다.

(4) 현대

- Hathaway & McKinly가 고안한 MMPI(다면성 인성검사법 : The Minnesota Multiphasic Personality Inventory)가 가장 표준화된 방법으로 쓰이고 있다.[5)]
- 1960년대에 들어 밥스트(Babst)의 형사분석(configurational method), 윌리암스(Williams)의 상관성분석(association analysis), 맥코튼(P. Smith MaCaugton)의 예측적 속성분석(predictive attribute analysis) 등 새로운 기법이 고안되어 다중회귀분석, 중판별분석 등의 다변량해석적 기법과 함께 보다 정밀한 것으로 개발되었다.

---

5) • 배종대, 형사정책, 홍문사, 2000:274.
• MMPI(다면성 인성검사법)는 문항수가 너무 많고, 피검자의 학력수준이 높아야 정확한 측정을 할 수 있는 단점이 있으며, 그 밖에도 범죄예측의 방법으로 CPL(캘리포니아 인성검사), 브리스톨 사회적응성지침, KD위험성 측정 등이 있다. 진계호, 형사정책, 대왕사, 2002:345.

4) 우리나라

- 우리나라에서는 미네소타 다항목 성격검사 즉, MMPI가 가장 널리 사용되고 있다. 이는 미국 미네소타대학교의 해서웨이(S. Hathaway)와 매킨리(J. Mckinley) 교수가 1940년에 개발한 것인데 이 검사의 기본원리와 이론을 채용하여 우리나라에서도 비행성 성격예측검사(delinquent personality prediction test)를 만들어 비행성 판별에 유용하도록 하기 위하여 소년경찰에서 사용하고 있다.
- 1960년 서울소년원에서 소년심판의 보조자료로 글뤽부부의 5개의 사회적 예측요인만을 사용하였다.

제2절 범죄예측의 방법

1. 예측대상에 따른 분류

1) 조기예측(early identification of potential)

조기예측은 유년기와 소년기의 시점에서 장래 대상자나 범죄나 비행에 빠져들 가능성을 예측하는 것이며, 범죄자로 되기 이전의 어느 시기에 예측방식의 이용목적상의 차이나 작성자의 이론에 따라서 행해지는 것이다.

2) 재범예측(prediction of recidivism)

재범예측은 이미 범죄나 비행을 일으킨 자가 장래 다시 범죄를 일으킬 가능성을 예측하는 것이다. 이는 판결 시 예측과 석방 시 예측으로 나누어진다.

2. 예측시점에 따른 분류

범죄예측은 예측시점을 기준으로, i) 형사사법 이전의 조기예측, ii) 수사단계에서의 예측, iii) 재판 시 행하는 재판 시 예측, iv) 가석방시 행하는 석방 시 예측으로 나눌 수 있다.[6)]

---

6) • 형사단계별로 범죄예측은 비행성을 미리 발견해 범죄를 미연에 방지하고자 하는 조기예측적 측

1) 조기예측

- 범죄의 사전예방을 위하여 범죄가능성을 예측하는 것으로써, 주로 잠재적 범죄자를 대상으로 하는 점에서 현실적 범죄자를 대상으로 하는 석방 시 예측이나 재판 시 예측과 다르다.
- 범죄경력이 없는 일반인을 대상으로 범죄위험성을 예측하는 것이 처음부터 범죄에 빠지지 않도록 미연에 예방할 수 있다는 점에서 의미가 있다.7)

2) 수사단계 예측

- 수사기관에서 비행자, 범죄자에 대한 수사를 종결하면서 내릴 처분을 결정할 때 사용하는 예측이다.
- 수사의 종결단계에서 경찰은 기소 또는 기소유예처분, 훈계방면을 할 것인가를 결정하는 데 있어서 범죄자에 대한 위험성 판정을 전제로 한다.

3) 재판단계 예측

- 재판단계에서 피고인의 개별처우를 위해 장래행동을 예측하는 것을 말한다.
- 특히 양형책임을 결정하는 중요한 수단으로 작용하며, 정확한 재판예측을 하기 위하여 판결 전 조사제도가 보완되어야 한다.

4) 석방단계 예측

- 석방할 때까지 얻은 자료를 토대로 가석방 후의 범죄 또는 비행의 여부를 예측하는 것

면인 '예방단계'(우리의 소년분류심사원에서의 비행예측, 톰슨과 글뤽부부의 조기예측연구)와 수사와 재판과 행형단계에서 이루어지는 '사법단계'에서의 범죄예측으로 나눌 수 있다.
- 범죄예측은 석방 시 예측 → 재판 시 예측 → 조기예측의 순서로 발전했다.
- 사법예측은 수사 시 예측, 재판 시 예측, 석방 시 예측으로 구분할 수 있다.
- 범죄예측은 시행주체를 기준으로 공적 기관에 의한 범죄예측과 사적 기관에 의한 범죄예측으로 나눌 수 있으며, 둘 간의 관계는 상호보완적으로 이용되어야 한다.

7) 범죄와 무관한 시민의 자유영역을 침해할 수 있으며, 대상설정에서 공평성과 경제성이 문제가 될 수 있는 한계가 있으며, 아무리 과학적 방법을 사용하더라도 어린 소년기에 미래의 비행을 미리 예측하는 것은 소년의 인격발전을 기계적으로 이해하지 않는 한 위험성이 너무 크며, 조기예측을 진지하게 생각하는 것은 매우 위험한 전체주의적 발상이라는 주장도 있다. 배종대, 형사정책, 박영사, 1998:313.

이다.

- 가석방 여부, 가석방의 최적시기 등을 판단하는 데 필요한 자료를 얻기 위해서 행하여진다.[8)]

3. 예측방법에 따른 분류

1) 전체적 관찰법

- 범죄자에 대하여 의학, 심리학, 사회학의 지식을 이용하여 예측대상자의 인격상태, 환경조건, 성장과정 등 인격과 관련된 사항의 전체를 분석한 결과를 바탕으로 범죄행동을 예측하는 방법이다.
- 임상적 경험에 의해 예측하므로 효율적인 결과를 기대할 수 있으나, 평가자의 주관이 개입하기 쉬우므로 객관적 기준을 확보하기 어렵다는 단점이 있다.[9)]

2) 통계적 예측법

- 일정한 사람의 비행이나 재범에 대한 위험성의 판정문제가 생길 때 범죄와 관련된 사항을 통계적 조사자료를 계량화한 예측표에 의해 범죄의 가능성을 예측하는 방법이다.
- 이미 만들어진 판정척도를 사용하므로 판정과정에 전문가의 개입을 요하지 않고 타당성을 가지나 개별범죄자마다 고유한 특성이나 개인의 편차를 예측과정에 충분히 반영할 수 없다는 단점이 있다.

---

8) 진계호, 형사정책, 대왕사, 2002:349.

9) • 전체적 평가법은 생물학적 범죄원인론의 관점에서 대상자의 인격을 연구분석하고 전체적으로 종합하여 대상자의 범죄행동을 논리적으로 예측하려고 하는 방법이다. 이를 전체적 관찰법, 진단적 방법, 임상적 예측법이라고도 하며, 종합적 지식을 응용하여 예측대상자의 인격관련사항 전체를 분석하는 방법이다. 이는 개인의 유전과 이상심리에 초점을 가지고 사례연구를 통해 직접적·임상적 예측을 하는 방법으로써, 유전성 범죄인에게 적용되고 직관적 예측법이라고 한다. 그러나 조사자의 개인적인 차이로 인하여 객관적이고 공정한 기준을 확보하기가 곤란하며, 개인의 특수성을 정밀진단할 수는 있으나 전문적인 것에 대한 견해차로 인해 객관적 기준의 확보가 곤란한 만큼 전문가의 도움이 있어야 사용가능하다는 단점이 있다.

• 점수법은 개인의 여러 기록과 여러 환경요인들에 점수를 부여하는 계량적 연구로 범죄를 예측하는 방법으로써 주로 환경성 범죄인에게 적용된다. 이는 객관성과 타당성이 높고 경제적이나 개인의 다양성을 단순화한 것이 단점이다. 진계호, 형사정책, 대왕사, 2002:347.

3) 통합적 예측법

- 직관적 예측방법과 통계적 예측방법을 일정한 방향으로 조합함으로써 각각의 예측방법의 단점을 보완하고자 하는 예측방법이다.
- 판단자가 먼저 직관적 예측을 하고 그 다음으로 예측표를 이용하여 그의 직관적 예측이 맞는지 검토하는 방식이다.[10]

4. 자료수집의 방법에 따른 분류[11]

1) 전망적(prospective) 방법

대상자의 선정 및 그 자료를 먼저 수집하고 대상자 선정 이후의 경과를 일정기간 추적하여 그 진전과정에 따라 성공・실패의 각 사례군을 기준으로 하여 예측방식을 작성하는 것이다.

2) 회고적(retrospective) 방법

결과가 판명되어 있는 시점에서 대상자를 선정하여 일정기간 소급하여 그 대상자의 자료를 수집하고 자료와 성공・실패와의 관계에서 예측방식을 작성하는 방법이다.

제3절 범죄예측의 효용과 한계

1. 범죄예측의 목적

- 개인의 처우결정을 위한 자료로써, 실제로 비행이 나타나지 않았다고 해도 장래 범죄나 비행에 결부될 가능성이 높은 성격을 가지고 있거나 그런 환경에 있는 사람들을 발견하여 적절한 예방활동을 통하여 그 가능성을 타진하는 작업에 이용될 수 있다.
- 처우방법의 효과측정을 위한 자료로써, 새롭게 개발된 처우의 효과 또는 적용한계를 파악하는 데 이용할 수 있다.

10) 배종대, 형사정책, 박영사, 1998:311.
11) 이상현, 범죄심리학, 박영사, 2004:458-472.

- 처우제도의 결정을 위한 자료로써, 몇 개의 처우과정을 포함한 처우제도의 효과성을 측정하여 처우결정을 위한 자료로 이용하는 데 있다.

2. 한계

1) 기술적 측면

범죄예측은 예측일 뿐이기 때문에 오류긍정과 오류부정의 2가지 잘못된 결과가 나타날 가능성이 존재한다. 오류긍정은 개인에게, 오류부정은 사회와 그 구성원에게 피해가 돌아가게 된다.[12)]

2) 윤리적 측면

- 조기예측의 결과 범죄를 행할 우려가 있다고 예측된 소년에게 특정한 예방조치를 가한다면 광의의 죄형법정주의에 위배되며 또 다른 인권문제를 야기할 수도 있다.
- 미취학아동이나 범죄를 행할 우려가 있는 아동들에게 범죄의 조기예측을 한다면 예측 그 자체로도 낙인의 효과가 발생할 수 있고, 범죄성이 없는 아동들에게 오히려 범죄성이 생기도록 하는 결과가 발생할 수도 있어 윤리적 문제가 제기될 수도 있다.

3) 정치적 측면

- 예측결과에 따라 이익 또는 손해를 볼 수 있는 관련집단들이 예측결과에 영향을 미칠 수 있는 문제점을 가진다.
- 특정집단이 자신들에게 유리한 자원을 확보하기 위하여 상징형성이나 상징조작 등을 행하게 된다.[13)]

---

12) 오류긍정(잘못된 긍정)은 A가 재범하리라고 예측했는데 실제로 재범하지 않은 경우를 말하며, 오류부정(잘못된 부정)은 A가 재범을 하지 않으리라고 예측했는데 실제로 재범을 한 경우로써, 오류부정(잘못된 긍정)의 경우가 가장 문제시된다.

13) • 특정국가의 경찰집단이나 교정기관이 경찰조직이나 교정조직의 확대를 위하여서는 앞으로 범죄가 증가될 것으로 예측하고 민간조사기구 또는 내부연구기관을 이용해 정치적 자원을 행사할 수 있다. 이런 현상은 특히 후진국에서 나타난다고 한다.
• 특정국가의 정치지도자가 자신의 특정한 목적을 달성하기 위하여 범죄예측이 높게 또는 낮게 나올 수 있도록 정치적 자원을 사용하고 특정한 상징조작이나 상징형성을 통해 자신의 정치적 목적을 달성하는 경우도 있다. 이런 정치적 측면의 문제점은 천정환 교수가 최초로 언급했다.

4) 교정복지적 측면

(1) 사전적 교정복지

우범자, 피해자, 준범죄인 등에 대하여 범죄가 장래에 발생하지 않도록 모든 자원을 동원하여 이루어지는 모든 역동적인 노력으로 예방적・적극적 교정복지와 관련되는 활동이다.

(2) 사후적 교정복지

이미 범죄를 행한 범죄인에 대하여 교정복지사 등이 재범방지와 올바른 재사회화, 정서적 지원을 위해 행하는 의도적이고 역동적인 노력으로 전통적 교정복지와 연결된다.[14)]

14) 천정환, 제1차 교정복지학술대회 자료집, p. 80.

제 20 장 범죄억제론

제1절 범죄의 예방

1. 범죄예방의 의의

- 범죄는 이미 발생한 경우 그 범죄에 대한 피해는 거의 회복이 불가능하고, 범죄자의 검거・교정 등에 많은 비용이 들며, 실질적인 교정 또한 어렵다.
- 범죄의 증가는 범죄자 및 피해자의 증가 및 사회적 관계에서의 불신과 불안, 두려움, 법의 권위추락 등 부정적인 환경을 조성하여 결국 사회해제(social disorganization) 현상을 불러온다.[1] 따라서 범죄의 발생을 미연에 방지하는 것이 최상의 대응방법이다.

〈표 4-1〉 범죄통제(crime control) 방법의 변천

근대 이전	응보와 복수[2]	사후 대응방법
고전주의 사상가들	형벌과 제재	
실증주의 사상가들	교정과 치료	
범죄사회학자들	범죄예방	사전 대응방법

1) • J. E. Conklin, The Impact of Crime, MacMillan Pub., 1975:356.
 • 경찰대학 교재편찬위원회, 경찰방범론, 경찰대학, 1998:22-24.

2) 탈리오법칙(lex talionis)은 피해자가 입은 피해와 같은 정도의 손해를 가해자에게 가한다는 보복의 법칙이다. 리온이라고도 하며, 반좌법(反坐法)・동해보복법(同害報復法)이라고도 번역된다. 성서에 "생명에는 생명으로써, 눈에는 눈으로써, 이[齒]에는 이[齒]로써"라는 표현이 이에 해당한다.

2. 범죄예방모델

1) C. R. Jeffery

C. R. Jeffery는 범죄통제의 모형을 ⅰ) 형벌을 통한 '범죄억제모델' ⅱ) 범죄자의 치료와 갱생정책을 통한 '사회복귀모델', ⅲ) 사회환경개선을 통한 '범죄예방모델'의 3가지로 구분하여 제시하였다.[3)]

(1) 범죄억제모델

형법 내지 형벌을 통하여 범죄를 방지하고 범죄인을 개선・교화하는 것으로 전통적인 방법이자 종래 형사정책의 주된 관심사였다.

(2) 사회복귀모델

임상적 개선방법, 지역활동, 교육・직업훈련, 복지정책 등을 통하여 범죄인을 재사회화하는 재범의 방지에 중점을 두어 행형론의 주요한 모델이 되고 있다.[4)]

(3) 범죄예방모델

- 도시정책, 환경정화, 인간관계의 개선, 정치・경제・사회 각 분야에서 갈등해소 즉, 환경개혁을 통하여 범죄를 예방하려는 것으로 근본적인 사회환경의 개선을 통하여 비로소 궁극적인 범죄방지가 가능하다고 보는 것이다.
- 범죄예방모델은 ⅰ) 범죄가 저질러지기 이전의 행동이며, ⅱ) 행동에 대한 직접적 통제이며, ⅲ) 범죄가 발생하는 환경과 환경에 대한 사람들의 상호작용에 초점을 두고, ⅳ) 사람의 행동을 연구하는 다양한 학문에 기초한 모형이다. 범죄예방은 "범죄가 발생하기 전에 이루어지는 직접적인 활동으로 주로 범죄환경에 초점이 두어지는 활동"으로 규정한다.

---

3) 정영석・신양균, 형사정책, 법문사, 1996:285; 이보령, 형사정책, 제일법규, 1996:355; 기광도, 범죄예방활동에 관한 이론, 형사정책연구소식, 26:21-31.

4) 범죄대책에 있어서 범죄인의 생물학적・심리학적 특성과 사회적 환경에 따라 그 효과가 차이가 난다는 비판을 받기도 하지만 임상적 개선, 지역활동, 교육・직업훈련, 복지정책 등을 통하여 범죄인의 재사회화에 중점을 두는 제퍼리가 제시한 모델은 '사회복귀모델'이다. 2005 기출

2) 미국 범죄예방연구소(NCPI)

- 미국 범죄예방연구소(National Crime Prevention Institute: NCPI)는 범죄예방을 "범죄적 기회를 감소시키려는 사전활동이며, 범죄에 관련된 환경적 기회를 제거하는 직접적 통제활동"으로 규정하고 있다.
- 범죄가 저질러지는 요소를 ⅰ) 범죄욕구, ⅱ) 범죄기술, ⅲ) 범죄기회로 구분할 경우, 범죄예방은 범죄욕구나 범죄기술에 대한 예방이 아니라 범죄기회를 감소시키려는 활동이라는 것이다.[5)]

3) S. P. Lab

- S. P. Lab은 범죄예방을 "실제의 범죄발생과 범죄에 대한 공중(公衆)의 두려움(perceived fear of crime)을 줄이는 사전활동"으로 규정하고 있다.[6)] 이는 실질적으로 범죄발생을 줄이려는 사전노력이기도 하고, 심리적인 측면에서 안전성의 확보, 범죄에 대한 두려움의 제거를 위한 노력이기도 하다.
- 범죄예방에서는 실제상의 범죄를 줄이는 것도 중요하지만, 공중(公衆)이 갖고 있는 범죄에 대한 불안과 공포를 제거하는 것도 매우 중요하기에, Lab은 범죄예방활동을 심리적 측면인 범죄에 대한 두려움의 제거활동까지 포함하는 것으로 규정하고 있다.

4) P. J. Brantingham과 F. L. Faust 2012 기출

P. J. Brantingham과 F. L. Faust는 질병예방의 공중보건모델과 유사한 3가지의 범죄예방 유형을 제시하였다.[7)] 그리고 범죄예방을 담당하는 주체는 크게 경찰을 비롯한 정부와 민간분야로 구분하였다.

5) National Crime Prevention Institute, Understanding Crime Prevention, Butterworths Publishers, 1986:27.
6) S. P. Lab, Crime Prevention : Approaches, Practices and Evaluation, Cincinnati, Ohio : Anderson Publishing Co., 1992:10-13.
7) 이상원, 방범론, 대명출판사, 2001:12, 참조.

〈표 4-2〉 범죄예방모델

1차적 범죄예방	일반대중	• 물리적·사회적 환경 중에서 범죄원인이 되는 조건들을 개선시키는 데 초점 • 환경설계, 이웃감시, 민간경비, 경찰방범활동, 형벌과 같은 일반예방, 방범교육 등과 형사사법기관의 활동 • 범죄행위를 야기할 가능성을 가진 문제들을 방지하는 것이 목적
2차적 범죄예방	우범자, 우범집단	• 잠재적 범죄자를 초기에 발견하고 범죄기회를 차단하여 범죄를 예방하고자 하는 것 • 우범지역에 초점, 범죄지역분석, 범죄예측 등 • 이미 존재하는 요인들과 일탈행위를 조장하는 요인들에 더 초점 • 우범환경이나 우범자를 대상으로 이들과 많이 접하는 지역사회지도자·교육자·부모에 의해 이루어짐
3차적 범죄예방	범죄자	• 실제 범죄자를 대상으로 범죄자들이 더 이상 범죄를 저지르지 않도록 하기 위한 활동 • 체포, 기소, 교도소구금, 치료, 사회복귀 • 민간단체나 지역사회의 교정프로그램 • 형사사법기관이 담당

5) 평가

- 범죄예방모델들을 종합하여 보면, 범죄예방활동은 i) 사전활동 즉, 범죄사건 이후에 대응하는 활동이 아니라 범죄가 발생하기 전에 수행되는 행위이고, ii) 실제의 범죄 및 공중(公衆)에게 인지된 범죄에 대한 두려움을 감소시키는 활동이며, iii) 범죄환경에 대한 직접적 통제뿐만 아니라 간접적인 활동도 포함한다.
- 범죄가 발생되는 상황적 기회를 제거하는 활동뿐만 아니라 범죄의 근본적 원인이 되는 사회적·경제적 환경을 개선시키는 활동, 실제 범죄자를 대상으로 하여 범죄자들이 더 이상 범죄를 저지르지 않도록 하기 위한 활동까지 포함하는 것이다.

3. 범죄예방의 제 이론

경찰이 수행하는 범죄예방활동은 주로 범죄욕구의 억제 및 상황적 범죄기회의 제거를 주 내용으로 하는 '억제이론(Deterrence Theory)' 및 '상황적 범죄예방론(Situational Crime Prevention)'과 최근 다양한 이론적 측면을 종합하여 대두한 '지역사회범죄예방론(Community Crime Prevention)'에 이론적 바탕을 두고 있다고 할 수 있다.[8)]

〈표 4-3〉 범죄이론과 예방이론

범죄이론	예방이론	내 용	비 판
고전학파	억제이론	• 범죄에 대한 국가의 강력하고 확실한 처벌	• 폭력과 같은 충동적 범죄에는 적용 한계
생물학적·심리학적 이론	치료 및 갱생이론	• 범죄자의 치료와 갱생, 교정을 통한 범죄예방	• 비용과다, 범죄자를 대상으로 하므로 일반예방효과에 한계
사회학적 이론	사회발전을 통한 예방이론	• 사회발전(사회적 환경개선)을 통한 범죄의 근본적 원인제거	• 범죄의 원인이 되는 사회적 환경을 개선할 능력이 있는가?
합리적 선택이론 범죄패턴이론 일상활동이론 생태학적 이론	상황적 예방이론	• 범죄기회의 제거 • 범죄환경 제거를 위한 도시계획 • 범죄행위의 이익감소	• 전이효과[9], 국가통제사회 가능성

1) 억제이론

(1) 의의

- 억제이론(Deterrence Theory)은 18세기 고전학파 이론을 바탕으로 하여 전개된 범죄예방이론이다.
- 범죄자에 대한 처벌은 범죄를 억제하는 효과가 있으므로 국가의 강력한 처벌을 통하여 범죄예방이 가능하며, 처벌의 억제효과를 극대화하기 위해서는 처벌의 신속성(Swiftness), 확실성(Certainty), 엄격성(Severity)이 보장되어야 한다고 주장한다.[10]

8) 기광도, "미국경찰의 범죄예방활동에 관한 연구", 한국형사정책연구원, 1995:28.

9) • 전이효과(displacement effect) : 범죄가 다른 곳으로 전이되어 전체 범죄는 줄지 않는다는 것이다. 즉, 전이효과(displacement effect)는 범죄목표물을 막는 행위는 결코 범죄를 예방하지 못하고 다른 유형이나 다른 시간, 다른 장소에서의 범죄행위로 전이된다는 것이다. Reppetto는 전이의 양상으로 ⅰ) 시간적 전이, ⅱ) 전술적 전이, ⅲ) 목적물의 전이, ⅳ) 지역적 전이, ⅴ) 기능적 전이를 지적하였다.
• 이익의 확산효과(diffusion of benefit): 클라크와 와이스버그(Clarke and Weisberg)의 이익의 확산효과(diffusion of benefit)는 전이효과와 반대로 상황적 범죄예방의 효과가 지역적으로 확산된다는 것이다. 한 지역의 범죄예방활동이 다른 지역의 범죄예방에도 긍정적 영향을 미치며, 다른 지역의 범죄감소에도 영향이 확산되는 이점이 있다는 견해이다.
• Ronald Clarke and David Weisberg, Diffusion of Crime Control Benefits, New York : Criminal Justice Press, 1994:25-32.

처벌의 신속성	• 즉각적인 처벌 즉, 법규를 위반하는 것과 처벌받는 시점 사이의 시간적 관계에 관한 것이다. • 보다 즉각적인 처벌이 시민들로 하여금 처벌에 대한 주관적 인식을 높여줄 것이다. • 신속성의 범죄억제효과를 지지하는 경험적 연구는 거의 없고, 단지 엄격성, 확실성과 상호작용할 때 효과가 있는 것으로 보인다.[11]
처벌의 확실성	• 처벌의 가능성에 관한 것이다. • 체포와 기소, 제재를 받을 가능성이 높을수록 법규위반율이 낮아질 것으로 가정한다.[12]
처벌의 엄격성	• 수감기간이나 벌금액의 정도와 같은 처벌의 가혹성 내지 강도에 관한 것이다. • 처벌이 엄하면 엄할수록 법규위반율은 낮아질 것으로 가정한다.[13]

(2) 경찰의 범죄예방활동

• 억제이론에 근거한 경찰의 범죄예방활동은 경찰력을 강화하여 범죄대응력을 높임으로써 신속한 현장출동 및 범죄자의 검거를 통한 범죄자 또는 잠재적 범죄자로 하여금 범죄를 저지르지 못하게 하는 방향으로 활동을 전개하게 된다.

• 경찰의 신속한 출동을 위하여 범죄의 인지로부터 현장도착시간에 이르기까지 원활한 통신체계와 범죄발생현장에 신속히 도착할 수 있는 교통체계를 확보하게 되며, 경찰의 자원과 활동이 강화될수록 범죄자의 체포가능성은 더욱 높아진다고 볼 수 있기 때문에 순찰인력 및 예산의 증원, 순찰경찰관의 자질향상, 각종 과학장비의 보강 등으로 경찰력을 강화하게 된다.[14]

---

10) 억제이론에서 범죄의 주요 설명은 신속성, 확실성, 엄격성이다. [2007 기출]

11) S. Klepper and D. Nagin, "The Deterrent Effect of Perceived Certainty and Severity of Punishment Revisited," Criminology 27, 1989:721–746.

12) 티틀과 로우(Tittle and Rowe)는 범죄율과 처벌의 확실성 간에 반비례의 관계가 있다는 연구를 발표하여 억제이론의 주장을 지지하였다. 예 음주운전의 경우 적발될 가능성이 높으면 높을수록 음주운전을 하지 않을 가능성이 높을 것이다. Charles Tittle and Alan Rowe, "Certainty of Arrest and Crime Rates : A Further Test of the Deterrence Hypothesis," Social Forces, 52, 1974:455–462.

13) • 예 음주운전을 할 경우 적발되면 면허취소나 구속 등의 처벌이 엄하면 엄할수록 음주운전의 확률은 줄어들 것이다. Larry J. Siegel, Criminology, St. Paul, MN : Wadsworth Publishing Company, 1998:115; Gary Green, "General Deterrence and Television Cable Crime : A Field Experiment in Social Crime," Criminology, 23, 1986:629–645.
• 미국 일부 주에서 삼진아웃제도(Three Strikes and You're Out)로 상습범죄자를 매우 엄하게 처벌하는 것은 엄격성의 예이다. [2009 기출]

(3) 억제이론의 한계 2011 기출

- 억제이론은 '합리적 선택이론'에 근거하고 있어, 절도 등 재산범죄에는 어느 정도 적용될 수 있으나, 개인의 합리적 선택보다 주변의 환경과 개인의 성향에 의하여 발생되는 폭력 등 충동적 범죄에는 적용하기 어렵다.
- 범죄자의 합리적인 선택을 위해서는 범죄행위에 대한 형벌의 내용을 미리 알고 있어야 하는데 현실적으로 대다수 국민들은 구체적인 형벌법규를 알지 못한다.
- 처벌을 통한 예방효과가 실패하였을 경우 이를 보완할 다른 대안의 제시가 없다.[15)]

---

14) 경찰력 강화를 통한 범죄예방활동 프로그램으로 시행되는 것으로는 경찰의 순찰, 시민의 범죄신고, 특별범죄신고전화 설치, 범죄분석, 몰래카메라 설치, 시가지 미행・잠복 수사팀 배치, 범죄예방교육 및 홍보, 첨단과학기술의 응용(순찰위치 자동확인체제, 차량번호자동판독장치, 자동차자료터미널장치, 금융전산망접속시스템 등), 지역자치방범대 활용, 기타(가옥번호지정, 방범설비설치지원, 현관불 점등 권장, 집보기의 중요성 계몽, 주민신고요원지정, 주민자동차 표시, 범죄신고 보상제도, 어린이지문 등록제도, 노약자경호원배치, 귀중품 등록 등) 등이 있다.

15) • 제지이론에 의하면 국가기관은 범죄에 대하여 범죄자를 확실하게 처벌하며, 죄질에 상당히 엄격한 처벌을 하여야 한다. 처벌에 의한 범죄억제는 2가지 유형 즉, 일반예방효과와 특별예방효과로 구분된다.
- 일반예방효과(general deterrence effect)는 범죄행위에 대한 국가의 확실한 처벌이 잠재적 범죄자로 하여금 범죄를 저지르지 못하게 하는 효과이다. 법을 위반하면 어김없이 처벌된다는 것을 일반시민에게 보여줌으로써 그들의 범죄를 예방하려는 것이다. 이는 경찰력의 증가, 경찰활동의 강화, 첨단장비의 도입 등이 범죄에 대한 체포 및 제재의 가능성을 높이고, 범죄의 비용을 증가시킴으로써 범죄를 억제하게 된다는 것이다.
- 기광도, "경찰과 범죄간의 관계분석 : 시계열분석을 중심으로", 한국경찰연구, 제6권 제2호, 한국경찰발전연구학회, 2007:255-287.
- Ehrlich, I., "Participation in Illegitimate Activities : A Theoretical and Empirical Investigation", Journal of Political Economics, 81(3), May/June, 1973; Phillips, L. & H. L. Votey, "An Economic Analysis of the Deterrent Effect of Law Enforcement on Criminal Activity", Journal of Criminal Law, Criminology and Police Science 63, 1972.
- 범죄자를 처벌함으로써 보통사람들의 범죄를 예방하는 일반적(general) 억제를 말한다. 2009 기출
- 특별예방효과(special deterrence effect)는 범죄를 저지른 자가 다시 범죄를 저지르지 못하게 하는 예방효과이다. 범죄자 개인으로 하여금 처벌기간과 이후의 생활에서 처벌의 두려움으로 범죄행위를 하지 못하게 하는 효과이다. 이러한 특별예방효과는 재범과 관련되어 있다. 특별예방효과는 범죄자가 다시 범죄를 저지르지 못하게 하려는 것이 그 목적이다. 무력화효과, 구금효과(incapacitative effect)로써, 경찰의 범죄자 체포활동의 결과로 발생하게 되는 범죄자에 대한 시설 내 구금으로 인한 격리가 범죄를 감소시킬 수 있다는 논리이다.
- 기광도, "경찰의 범죄억제력에 관한 고찰", 형사정책연구, 제12권 제4호(겨울호, 통권 제48호), 한국형사정책연구원, 2001:113-141; 이윤호, 범죄학개론, 박영사, 2002.

- 억제이론은 추론적 논의이기 때문에 처벌의 범죄억제효과를 경험적으로 연구하기 어렵다.[16)]

2) 치료 및 갱생이론

(1) 의의

- 치료 및 갱생이론은 19세기 베이컨(Francis Bacon)의 경험론, 다윈(Darwin)의 생물학적 진화론, 콩트(Conte)의 실증주의, 롬브로조(Lombroso) 등의 결정론적 인간관 및 범죄에 관한 생물학적 이론과 심리학적 이론에 바탕을 두고 전개된 이론이다.
- 치료 및 갱생이론에서는 인간의 행위는 자유의지가 아닌 생물학적 요인과 심리적 요인에 의하여 결정되며, 범죄자의 범죄행위는 기본적으로 생물학적 · 심리학적 · 내재적 결함을 가진 자의 행위이므로 범죄를 해결하되, 범죄자를 처벌하는 것보다는 치료와 갱생교육을 통하여 범죄예방을 시도해야 한다고 주장된다.
- 범죄행위보다 범죄자에 초점을 두고 범죄자의 속성에 대한 연구를 통해 치료에 중점을 두고 있으며, 사회단체 및 교도소, 갱생원, 교화원 등에서 치료 및 교육을 통한 범죄예방활동의 이론적 배경이 되고 있다.
- 범죄예방 프로그램은 병리현상의 치료와 도덕교육, 직업교육 등 사회에 적응할 수 있게 하는 치료와 갱생교육을 강조하게 된다.

(2) 한계[17)]

- 치료 및 갱생교육에는 비교적 비용이 많이 든다.
- 교도소 내에서의 치료 및 갱생교육은 부적절하게 이루어지는 경우가 많다.
- 수형자는 자유인으로 환경에 적응하는 것이 아니라 수형자의 환경에 더욱 잘 적응한다.
- 치료 및 갱생 프로그램은 대부분 범죄행위에 대한 간접적 통제활동이기 때문에 적극적인 범죄예방에는 한계가 있다.

16) 기광도, "범죄예방활동에 관한 이론", 형사정책연구소식, 한국형사정책연구원, 제26호, 1994:21-31.
17) 최근에는 치료 및 갱생교육에 의한 범죄예방효과에 대한 한계를 인식하고 새로운 형벌학이 연구되고 있는바, 새로운 형벌학에서는 수형자 교정, 보호관찰, 가석방, 청소년법원, 치료프로그램, 직업훈련프로그램, 지역사회에 기초한 교정프로그램 등이 시도되고 있다.

3) 사회발전을 통한 범죄예방이론(사회적 발전모델)

(1) 의의

- 20세기 초 특히 청소년의 범죄예방에 관한 새로운 전략의 일환으로 호킨스(Hawkins)와 웨이스(Weis)에 의하여 주장되었으며, 통제이론과 문화학습이론의 통합에 기초하고 있다.
- 청소년범죄는 사회적 유대감이나 통제가 강화될 때 감소하고, 사회적 통제가 약화될 때 증가하며, 동료나 지역사회로부터 학습한 문화의 영향을 받아 범행한다는 것이다.
- 인간은 자신의 주어진 환경에 의하여 개인의 태도 및 행위양식, 인성 등이 결정되는 것이므로, 범죄행위를 유발시키는 사회적 환경[18)]을 개선함으로써 근본적으로 범죄예방이 가능하다고 주장한다.

(2) 사회발전이론의 범죄예방프로그램

- 미국의 시카고 지역에서 오랜 기간 동안 전개되었던 시카고의 지역개발운동(CAP)과 영국의 안전도시운동(SCP)이 대표적이다.

범죄예방프로그램

〈시카고의 지역개발운동(Chicago Area Project: CAP)〉

시카고의 지역개발운동은 쇼(Shaw)가 '비행지역론(1929)'을 발표한 이후인 1932년부터 1957년까지 쇼와 매케이(McKay)를 비롯한 소년문제연구소의 회원(사회학자)들에 의하여 남부 시카고에 있는 러셀 광장지역을 중심으로 주로 청소년의 비행문제를 해결하기 위하여 시행된 것이다.

지역사회의 문제를 해결하기 위하여 지역사회의 지원자들과 지역사회의 각종 조직단체들로 하여금 지역사회의 활동 중에서 특히 레크리에이션, 순찰경계, 지역사회 재개발, 중재 등의 활동을 지원하도록 한 것이다. 그 결과 이상의 제 활동들은 성공을 거둔 것으로 평가되었다.

〈영국의 안전도시운동(Safer Cities Program: SCP)〉

영국의 안전도시운동은 1986년 영국 내무성의 후원 아래 볼턴 등 5개 도시를 중심으로 시작되어 현재까지 영국 내 20여 개 이상의 주요 도시지역에서 지역사회 범죄예방활동의 일환으로 실시되었다.

---

18) 특히 빈곤, 사회적 차별, 불평등 등이 그 예이다.

이는 지역사회와 여러 기관 및 이해집단(경찰, 보호관찰기관, 지역사회단체, 소수인종조직, 기업 및 경영주 등)이 협력하여 범죄를 줄이고 범죄에 대한 두려움을 줄여 보다 풍요로운 안전도시를 창조하자는 목표를 내걸고 추진하였다.

내무성은 각 지역조직에 대해 자금을 지원하고, 지역조직 간의 협력, 자문과 전문가의 조언을 제공하고 있으며, 안전도시운동은 각 지역의 특색에 따라 매우 다양하고 포괄적인 접근방법으로 범죄예방활동을 전개하였다.[19)]

(3) 한계

- 범죄의 원인이 되는 사회적 환경은 너무나 다양하기 때문에 모든 사회적 환경을 개선할 사회적 능력에는 한계가 있다.
- 전반적인 사회발전(정치 · 경제 · 사회 · 문화 등)이 이루어져야 하는데 그러기에는 막대한 인적 · 물적 자원이 필요하다.
- 사회발전을 통한 범죄예방프로그램의 시행이 실제로 그 지역의 범죄예방 및 감소에 기여하였는지는 불확실하다는 것이다.[20)]

---

19) • 일반적으로 실시하고 있는 안전도시운동 프로그램으로는 보안상태점검(가정, 점포, 공공건물), 가로조명개선, 청소년 선도활동, 인종차별감소를 위한 활동, 지역 내 범죄취약인구집단(여성, 노인 등) 지원, 약물의 오 · 남용방지활동, 범죄예방홍보 및 캠페인, 세미나 개최, 범죄예방기록 보존활동, 지역 내 집단 간의 협조관계 구축 지원 등이다.
• 특히 각 지역 내에서 가장 역점을 두고 있는 범죄예방의 대상범죄는 운송수단 관련범죄(car crimes)와 주거침입절도(burglary)로서 운송수단 관련범죄의 예방을 위해서는 자동차에 조향잠금장치 의무화, 거리의 조명확대, 거리와 주차장에서의 감시능력 향상, 자동차 내 범죄목표물 강화 등이 실시되고 있으며, 주거침입절도의 예방을 위해서는 환경설계를 통한 범죄예방전략, 이웃감시활동강화, 자동차순찰강화, 가정과 상점에 대한 보안점검, 경찰의 순찰강화, 피해가정의 이웃에 대한 감시조 편성 등이 실시되고 있다.

20) C. R. Jeffery, Crime Prevention Through Environment Design, Beverly Hills, 1977.

제2절 지역사회 경찰활동(community policing)

1. 개념과 의의

1) 지역사회 경찰활동의 개념

- 지역사회 경찰활동(community policing : COP)의 개념은 다의적이나, 그 핵심은 경찰이 발휘할 수 있는 역량과 지역사회의 잠재력을 유기적으로 결합시켜 범죄예방 및 질서유지 효과의 극대화를 도모한다는 데 있다.
- 경찰관들을 지역사회의 구성원으로 참여시키고 지역사회의 주민들을 경찰활동의 중심으로 초대하여 경영학에서 말하는 총체적 품질관리(Total Quality Management : TQM)를 도모한다는 것이다.[21)]
- 지역사회 경찰활동은 경찰의 진취적 자세와 경찰활동에 대한 주민의 참여가 중요한 요소로 간주되기에, Kelling은 지역사회 경찰활동의 확산을 '경찰활동의 조용한 혁명'으로 이해하였다.[22)]

2) 지역사회 경찰활동의 원리와 구조

- Trojanowicz는 지역사회 경찰활동의 10가지 기본원리와 지역사회 경찰활동의 9P를 제시하였다[23)].

21) 이황우 · 조병인 · 최응렬, 경찰학개론, 한국형사정책연구원, p. 363.
22) George Kelling, Police and Community: The Quiet Revolution, Washington D.C.: US Department of Justice, 1988; 이황우 외 2인, p. 363.
23) Robert Trojanowicz(1941~1994)는 미시건 주립대학 교수이면서 국립 지역사회 경찰활동본부(National Center for Community Policing)의 책임자로서 COP를 신앙처럼 여겼다. Rosert Trojanowicz and Bonnie Banqueroux, Community Policing : How to Get Started, 2nd ed. Cincinnati: Anderson Publishing Co., 1998, pp. 109-114; 이황우 외 2인, p. 363.

〈Trojanowicz의 지역사회 경찰활동의 10가지 기본 원리〉

10가지 기본 원리	① philosophy and Organizational Strategy ② Commitment to Community Empowerment ③ Decentralized and Personalized Policing ④ Immediate and Long-Term Proactive Problem Solving ⑤ Ethics, Legality, Responsibility and Trust ⑥ Expanding the Police Mandate ⑦ Helping Those with Special Needs ⑧ Grassroots Creativity and Support ⑨ Internal Change ⑩ Building for the Future
'9P'	또한 Trojanowicz는 ① philosophy ② personalized ③ policing ④ patrol ⑤ permanent ⑥ place ⑦ proactive ⑧ partnership ⑨ problem solving

• Eastern Kentucky University의 Cordner는 지역사회 경찰활동의 구조를 제시하면서, COP는 경찰과 지역주민이 상호협력을 중시하는 공동운명체로 간주하여 그 철학은 주민참여, 경찰기능활동, 인격적 봉사로 요약된다는 것이다.[24)]

〈표 4-4〉 Cordner의 지역사회 경찰활동의 구조

구분	공통요소
철학	주민참여, 경찰기능 확대, 인격적 봉사
절약	근무방식 개선, 예방노력 확대, 구역책임 강화
전술	민경제휴, 민경협력, 문제해결
관리	조직개편, 지침정비, 질적 평가

• 전통적 경찰활동은 범죄자를 검거하고 증거를 수집하고 공소유지가 가능하게 만드는 데 그치지만 지역사회 경찰활동은 범죄원인을 찾아내 이를 제거하는 단계까지 이어진다는 것이다.[25)]

24) Gray W. Cordner, "Community Policing: Elements and Effectiveness," Police Forum, No. 5, Vol. 3. pp. 1-8 ; Grary W. Cordner, "Community Policing : Principle and Elements," Summarized Note for the Special Lecture on Community Policing in Western Regional Institute for Community Oriented Public Safety (WRICOP), December, 2000.

2. 지역사회 경찰활동의 특징

1) 골드스타인(Goldstein)의 '지역사회 지향적 경찰활동(community-oriented policing)'의 특징[26]

- 지역사회 지향적 경찰활동에서 경찰은 스스로를 지역사회의 하나의 구성원으로 인식하고, 지역사회와 친밀한 관계를 유지하여 지역사회와의 신뢰관계를 형성하고, 적극적으로 지역사회의 문제를 파악하여 지역주민과 협력하여 해결하려는 것이다.
- 지역사회에 상주하는 소규모 파출소를 운영하거나, 도보나 자전거를 이용한 순찰제도를 실시하며, 범죄교육 및 범죄신고유도 등에 관심을 기울여 사전범죄예방 및 범죄진압에 힘쓰며, 지역사회의 주민 간 유대를 강화하여 범죄대응능력 및 비공식적 사회통제능력을 높이고, 경찰활동에 자발적으로 참여하는 것이다.

2) Skolnick과 Bayley

- Skolnick과 Bayley는 지역사회 경찰활동을 (1) 지역사회에 기초한 범죄예방의 강화, (2) 일반 공공서비스를 제공하기 위한 순찰체제의 개편, (3) 지역사회에 대한 경찰의 책임강화, (4) 분권화된 권한으로 제안하였다.[27]

(1) 지역사회에 기초한 범죄예방의 강화	• 지역사회에 기초한 범죄예방(community-based crime prevention)은 지역사회경찰활동의 가장 중요하고 궁극적인 목표이다. 예 이웃감시프로그램 • 공공감시, 재물표시(property marking), 주택안전 등을 통하여, 지역사회에 대한 책임을 부여하고, 이웃 간의 상호작용을 강화하여 지역사회의 비공식적 통제능력을 향상시키고, 경찰과의 협력 속에서 친밀한 지역사회와 경찰관계를 수립하게 한다.
(2) 일반 공공서비스를 제공하기 위한 순찰체제의 개편	• 지역사회 경찰활동에서 순찰체계는 기존의 자동차 순찰체제에서 도보에 의한 순찰로 전환한다. • 도보순찰은 시민들과 친밀하게 접촉할 수 있으며, 경찰의 존재를 인식시키고 원활한 정보의 교환을 가능케 한다.

25) 이황우 외 2인, p. 363.
26) Goldstein, 1986:6-30.
27) Skolnick and Bayley, 1988.

(3) 지역사회에 대한 경찰의 책임강화	• 지역주민과의 관계에 대해서 경찰의 책임을 강화하고, 경찰활동도 법규의 집행에서 지역사회에 지향된 활동으로 전환하며, 경찰의 직업만족도를 높여 경찰의 하위문화를 개선한다.
(4) 분권화된 권한	• 지역사회경찰활동에서는 경찰활동에 대한 명령체계를 중간관리층 중심으로 분권화하여 지역사회에 적절한 활동을 할 수 있게 한다.

3) Leighton의 '지역사회에 기초한 경찰활동(community-based policing)'의 특징[28)]

Leighton	• 경찰의 임무는 평화와 질서를 유지하며, 지역공동체에 공공서비스를 제공하고, 지역주민에게 안정감을 심어주는 것이다. 따라서 경찰의 주된 역할은 범죄진압자가 아니라 평화를 유지하는 공무원이다. • 경찰의 법적 권위는 민주주의 제도에 근거한다. • 경찰은 공공서비스를 제공하는 조직이다. • 범죄문제와 무질서에 대한 주요 전략은 사전적 접근방법과 문제해결적 접근방법이다. 이는 개별적 사건의 해결을 통하여 미래의 다른 사건까지 예방하려는 것이다. • 범죄문제에 대한 주된 정책은 범죄통제전략이 아니라 범죄예방전략 특히, 기회감소전략이다. 따라서 경찰의 활동은 지역사회의 환경과 요구에 맞도록 융통성을 지니고, 차별화된 사전적이고 적극적인 대응전략을 취한다. • 경찰활동의 평가하는 새로운 지표들은 범죄율과 검거율을 넘어서 범죄 및 무질서의 파악 및 해결능력, 공공서비스에 대한 공중의 만족도 개선, 경찰의 직업만족도의 향상, 지역사회의 문제에 대한 정보력, 범죄에 대한 두려움의 감소 등을 포함한다. • 조직구조에서는 분권화, 개방화, 통합적 구조의 특성을 갖는다. 일선경찰관에게 좀 더 많은 권한과 책임이 부여된다. • 경찰은 범죄전문가보다는 지역문제를 광범위하게 다룰 수 있는 경력 있는 일반인을 요구한다. • 지역사회와의 관계에서 지역주민을 고객, 동반자, 참여자로 인식하여, 범죄 및 무질서에 대하여 책임을 공유하며, 그러한 문제의 해결에서도 지역사회와 밀접한 협력관계 속에서 수행한다. • 지역문제를 해결하기 위하여 다른 국가기관 및 사회단체와의 협력을 강화한다. 경찰은 더 이상 고립되고 폐쇄된 조직이 아니라 서로 영향을 주고받는 개방된 조직으로 인식된다.

28) Leighton, 1991:485-522.

4) Friedmann의 '지역사회경찰활동(community policing)'의 특징[29]

지역사회경찰활동은 지역사회의 질서유지 및 범죄문제를 해결하려는 철학이며, 활동 전략이다. 지역사회경찰활동은 경찰-시민 간의 관계를 대립/적대에서 대등/협력관계의 전환이며, 경찰의 역할은 범죄진압자에서 공공서비스 제공자로, 경찰활동의 방향을 범죄진압/질서유지에서 범죄예방/공공서비스로, 소극적인 사후적 대응에서 적극적인 사전예방활동으로 전환하는 것이며, 소수자의 권리보호, 지역사회의 문제해결 등을 효과적으로 수행하려는 목적을 가지고 있다.[30]

<table>
<tr><td rowspan="2">Friedmann</td><td>• 지역사회경찰활동은 지역사회의 범죄문제, 범죄에 대한 두려움, 물리적 · 사회적 무질서 등을 경찰과 지역주민이 서로 긴밀히 협력하여 해결할 수 있게 하는 철학이며 전략이다.
• 지역사회경찰활동은 모든 경찰관의 적극적 참여를 필요로 한다.
• 지역사회경찰활동에는 경찰과 지역사회를 직접적으로 연결시킬 담당관(Community Policing Officer)이 필요하다. 이들은 정해진 담당구역의 주민들과 매일 직접적인 대면접촉을 하여야 한다.</td></tr>
<tr><td>• 지역사회 담당관은 지역주민과 함께 범죄문제, 범죄에 대한 두려움, 무질서 등의 상황을 파악하고 지역문제의 해결을 위한 방법을 찾아내는 역할을 한다.
• 지역사회경찰활동은 경찰과 지역주민 간의 상호신뢰에 입각하여 새로운 관계를 수립한다. 경찰은 시민의 삶을 향상시키는 촉매역할을 하며, 시민도 공공질서유지의 책임을 공유해야 한다.
• 지역사회경찰활동은 수동적인 사후활동이 아니라 적극적인 사전활동을 특징으로 한다. 또한 범죄문제 이외에도 다양한 영역에서 능동적인 공공서비스를 제공해야 한다.
• 지역사회경찰활동은 범죄피해에 취약한 청소년, 노인, 극빈자, 소수민족 등을 보호하는 데 노력해야 한다.
• 경찰활동에서 기술 및 장비의 혁신을 병행한다.
• 지역사회경찰활동은 경찰의 내부적 통합에 기초한다. 즉, 지역사회에 대한 정보의 제공과 지원, 내부의 원활한 의사교환을 통하여 지역문제의 해결에 협력하여야 한다.
• 지역사회 경찰활동은 분권화된 의사결정을 특징으로 한다.</td></tr>
</table>

29) Friedmann, 1992:11–39.
30) 기광도, 지역사회 경찰활동에 대한 비판적 고찰, 사회과학연구.

5) Trojanowicz와 Bucqueroux의 지역사회경찰활동의 특징

- Trojanowicz와 Bucqueroux는 지역사회경찰활동을 "지역사회경찰활동은 시민들과 경찰 간의 새로운 동반자 관계를 증진하기 위한 철학이며 조직적 전략이다"고 정의하고 있다.
- 지역사회경찰활동은 경찰과 지역사회가 그 사회의 문제들에 대하여 파악하고, 해결할 순위를 정하고, 해결하는 데 협력하여야 한다는 전제에서 시작한다.
- 지역에서의 전반적인 삶의 질을 개선할 목적을 가지고 범죄, 마약, 범죄에 대한 두려움, 사회적 또는 물리적 무질서, 이웃파괴 등의 문제에 대하여 서로 협력해야 한다.
- 지역사회경찰활동의 기본적 목적은 경찰과 지역사회 간의 갈등 및 긴장의 감소, 경찰의 효율성의 제고, 지역문제에 대한 효과적 해결, 경찰의 직업만족도의 제고, 지역사회에 대한 책임감을 높이는 것이다.
- 지역사회경찰활동은 범죄예방활동, 소수자 및 피해자(약물, 가정폭력)에 대한 보호, 시민의 참여 등을 위한 다양한 프로그램들을 개발하였다.
- 지역사회경찰활동의 활동전략으로는 범죄통제의 강화, 범죄에 대한 두려움 감소, 질서유지(무질서행위, 노숙자, 음주자, 무례한 행위, 파괴행위의 금지), 사회적 약자의 보호, 지역사회와의 관계개선 등이 있다.
- 지역사회경찰활동의 이념에 근거한 조직적 변화는 순찰조직의 미니파출소(mini-station) 및 경찰-지역사회 연계조직의 설립이다. 구체적인 프로그램의 경우에는 도보순찰(foot patrol), neighborhood based station, 이웃감시(neighborhood watch), 전문적 범죄예방단위(specialized crime prevention units), citizen advisory boards, meetings with community residents 등이 있다.

〈표 4-5〉 전통적 경찰활동과 지역사회 경찰활동의 비교

구 분	전통적 경찰활동	지역사회 경찰활동
경찰에 대한 시각	경찰이 범죄에 대한 전적책임	주민도 범죄방지에 대한 의무
역 할	범 죄 해 결	포괄적인 지역문제해결
업무평가방식	체포율, 범죄발생률, 수사율	범죄와 무질서에 대한 평가
업무우선순위	범죄와 폭력 퇴치	지역사회 문제해결
주된 업무	모든 사건	주민의 문제 및 관심사항
효율성 기준	반응시간	주민과의 협력 정도
조직구조	경직되고 집권화된 구조	분권화된 구조
타 기관과의 관계	갈등관계	협력관계
참여형태	수동적이고 소극적인 참여	능동적이고 자발적인 참여
의사소통	일방적(one-way) 의사전달	쌍방적(two-way) 의사전달
경찰과 지역사회 관계	공공관계(PR) 모형	주민참여모형, 공동참여모형

자료 : 김용한(1998), 지역사회 경찰활동의 구체적 활동모델 개발에 관한 연구, 연구보고서 98~15, 치안연구소, p. 20, 재작성.

3. 우리나라 지역경찰제

1) 의의

- 우리나라 경찰의 일선조직은 경찰서와 순찰지구대와 치안센터이다.[31)]
- 지역경찰이란 선택과 집중원리에 따라 경찰서 관내 행정구역과 치안상황을 고려해 책정한 "치안구역(policing District) 내 범죄의 예방 및 신속한 대응, 질서유지, 봉사활동 등 전반적인 치안수요를 책임지고 해결하는 경찰"[32)]을 말한다.

31) 경찰청 방범국에서는 2003.8.1부터 전국의 모든 경찰서를 대상으로 현 파출소를 순찰지구대와 치안센터로 전환한 "지역경찰제"를 실시하였다. 이는 파출소제도의 문제점을 개선하기 위하여 지역경찰제도, 즉 순찰지구대(2~3개 파출소의 통합), 치안센터체계로의 전환을 시도하였다. 지역경찰제는 파출소 운영체계를 효율화하기 위한 방안으로 경찰서 관할구역을 인구, 면적, 주민생활권, 교통망 등 지역실정을 종합적으로 고려, 3~5개 권역으로 나누고, 권역 내 파출소 인력, 장비를 집중하여 "순찰지구대"를 운영하여 집단폭력, 대형교통사고 등 효율적으로 대처하고, 현행 파출소에는 민원담당관을 배치, 치안서비스를 전문화시키는 "치안센터"를 운영하는 것이다. 순찰지구대는 도시형, 농촌형, 특수형 등 3가지 모델 중 예비 운영을 통해 지역특성, 치안수요에 따라 경찰서별로 적합한 방안을 시행하는 것이다.

〈지역경찰 조직 및 운영에 관한 규칙 제2조〉

지역경찰은 "관할지역의 실태를 파악하여 그에 알맞은 활동을 하고, 항상 즉응체제를 유지하여 경찰업무 전반에 걸쳐 초동조치를 함으로써 주민생활의 안전과 평온을 확보"하는 것을 주된 임무로 하고 있다.

2) 지역경찰제의 운영체계 및 실태

- 지역경찰제하에서는 경찰서 관할을 인구, 면적, 행정구역과 사건사고의 발생상황 등 지역설정에 맞게 3~5개 권역으로 구분해 권역 내 파출소 3~4개소의 인력과 장비를 통합해 순찰지구대를 설치해 순찰과 단속, 신고출동 등 현장치안활동을 중점 수행토록 한다.
- 경찰력의 선택과 집중을 통해 사건. 사고 발생 시 순찰차 3~5대, 경찰관 10여 명이 동시 출동하여 초기 제압능력을 증대하는 것이 지역경찰제 전환과 순찰지구대편성의 또 다른 목적이다.
- 순찰지구대는 지구대장과 3교대를 위한 3명의 사무소장, 2명의 관리요원, 3팀의 순찰요원으로 편성해 24시간 지휘, 감독체제를 유지하고 순찰전담으로 현장대응력을 극대화하는 데 그 편성 목적이 있다.

제3절 상황적 범죄예방이론

1. 상황적 범죄예방의 의의

1) 의의

- 상황적 범죄예방이론(Situational Crime Prevention)은 범죄가 발생하는 상황조건 및 범죄기회를 제거함으로써 범죄를 예방하려는 이론이다.[33]

32) 이창무, 경찰범죄예방활동의 질적 평가-지역경찰제를 중심으로-, 한국경찰학회보 제11호, p. 56.
33) • 상황적 범죄예방은 영국 내무부조사위원회(The British Government's Home Office Research Unit)에 의해 연구・개발된 것으로 내무부의 비행청소년에 대한 교정처우에서 시작되었다. 비행청소년들이 교정처우시설에 수용되어 있는 동안 일탈행위나 재범을 할 가능성은 그들의 배경이

• 범죄자는 고정된 성향을 가진 존재가 아니라 오히려 가변적인 상황적 요인에 따라 행동하는 역동적인 존재로 가정하고, 누구든지 범죄기회가 주어지면 범죄를 저지를 수 있는 잠재적 범죄자로 간주하며, 범죄를 예방하기 위해서는 범죄가 발생하는 상황적 조건 및 범죄기회를 제거하여야 한다고 주장한다.
• 억제이론과 마찬가지로 인간의 자유의지, 공리주의적 인간관에 입각한 합리적 선택이론(Rational Choice Theory) 및 일상활동이론(Routine Activity Theory)과 생태학적 범죄학(Ecological Criminology) 등에 기초를 두고 있다.[34)]

2) 특징

• 뉴만의 '예방공간(Defensible)' 개념과 제프리의 '환경설계를 통한 범죄예방(Crime Prevention Through Environmental Design)' 개념은 상황적 범죄예방과 일치하는 개념이다.[35)]
• 상황적 범죄예방은 범죄인보다는 환경을 중시한다. 범죄예방을 위해 개인보다는 그러한 환경에 초점을 둔다.
• 특정범죄에 초점을 두며, 이는 모든 범죄는 상황이 다르다는 가정에 근거를 두고 특정 범죄만을 대상으로 한다.[36)]

나 인성보다는 그 교정시설의 환경에 달려 있다고 보고 교정시설 내의 환경이 청소년들의 비행에 대단히 중요하다고 보았다. Clarke, R. V., Situational Crime Prevention–Successful Case Studies, Harrow and Heston, 1992:7–8.
• 상황적 범죄예방은 사물보다는 사람에 초점을 맞춘 것으로 범죄를 저지를 가능성이 있는 잠재적 범죄자들에게 나타난 행동양식, 가치관 등에 영향을 주는 거의 모든 활동을 포함한다. 주택정책, 보건정책, 교육・가족・노동정책 등과 같은 거의 모든 사회정책을 통해 이루어진다. Daniel Gilling, op. cit., 1997:5.

34) • R. V. Clarke, "Situational Crime Prevention: It's Theoretical Basis and Practical Scope," Crime and Justice, 4, 1983:225–256.
• 상황적 범죄예방론은 범죄가 저질러지는 상황에 초점을 맞추어 범죄자의 의사결정, 범죄사건의 시간 및 공간적 상황, 범죄피해자 및 감시상황 등을 고려하여 범죄를 예방하려는 이론이다. 이러한 상황적 범죄예방론의 형성에 가장 큰 영향을 준 이론은 '일상활동이론'이다. 2007 기출

35) Larry J. Siegel, Criminology, 5th ed., West Publishing Company, 1995:116.

36) 예 자동차를 가진 전문 절도범에 의해 자행되는 절도를 막기 위한 방법과 현금이나 귀금속을 터는 기회주의적 절도범을 막는 방법은 완전히 다른 것이어야 한다.

2. 상황적 범죄예방의 이론적 배경

1) 환경범죄학(environmental criminology)

- 이론의 기원은 19세기 케틀레(Quetelet), 게리(Guerry), 메이휴(Mayhew)나 2차 세계대전 전 미국의 시카고학파(Chicago School)에까지 거슬러 올라간다.
- 환경범죄학은 1970년대에 등장한 범죄의 환경적 결정요소에 관심을 보이던 각기 다른 범죄학을 모두 포괄하는 것이다.
- 브랜팅엄과 브랜팅엄(P. J. Brantingham & P. L. Brantingham)은 범죄는 기본적으로 법률(law), 범죄자(offender), 범죄표적(target), 범행장소(place)라고 하는 4가지의 결정요인을 갖고 있다고 한다.

〈생태학적 범죄학(Ecological criminology)〉

생태학적 이론에서 뉴만(Newman)은 '방어공간(defensible space)' 개념을 제시하면서 주택건축에 범죄예방을 고려할 것을 주장하였는데, 그는 공공주택의 건축에서 공동체의 익명성을 줄이고 범죄자의 침입 및 도주로를 차단하며, 순찰 및 감시를 용이하게 하는 주택설계를 통하여 범죄를 예방할 것을 제시하였다.[37] 또한 제퍼리(Jeffery, 1971)도 '환경설계를 통한 범죄예방(Crime Prevention Through Environment Design)' 개념을 제시하였는데, 그는 물리적 환경, 주택설계, 주민참여, 경찰활동 등의 요소를 종합적으로 고려하여 주택 및 도시설계를 함으로써, 지역사회, 우범지역, 주택지역, 교육기관 등을 범죄로부터 예방하고 범죄에 대한 두려움을 제거시킬 수 있다고 주장했다.[38] 이 관점에 따르면 경보장치, 밝은 가로등 설치, 이웃감시순찰 등과 같은 메커니즘은 범죄기회를 감소시킬 수 있다고 본다.[39] 이것은 범죄발생을 용이하게 하는 환경을 파악하고 개선하여 범죄발생을 줄이려는 시도이다.

2) 범죄기회이론(criminal opportunity theory)

- 범죄기회이론은 범죄발생의 기회요인이 무엇인가에 관심을 갖는 이론이다. 즉, 어떠한 상황이 다른 상황보다 범죄가 발생하기 쉬운가에 초점을 두고 그 상황요건을 발견

37) Oscar Newman, Defensible Space : Prevention Through Urban Design, New York : MacMillan, 1973:120–125.
38) C. Ray Jaffery, op. cit., pp. 75–83.
39) Pochara Theerthorn, "Architectural Style, Aesthetic Landscaping, Home Value, and Crime Prevention," International Journal of Comparative and Applied Criminal Justice, 12, 1988:269–277.

하려는 데에 관심을 둔다.

- 생활양식이론(lifestyle theory)과 일상활동이론(routine activity theory)이 있으며, 범죄피해조사를 통해 범죄피해의 발생원인을 밝힘으로써 범죄의 발생요건을 파악하려 했던 점에서 범죄피해이론이라 불린다.
- 범죄피해는 무작위적으로 발생하는 것이 아니라 어떠한 장소와 시간, 특정인구층에게서 주로 발생한다고 본다.
- 코헨(Cohen)과 펠슨(Felson)은 범죄발생의 요건 즉, 법위반에 동기화된 위반자(motivated offender), 범죄의 적합한 표적(suitable target), 범죄발생을 저지하는 감독의 부재(the absence of guardianship)를 제시하고 있다.

3. 범죄의 기회이론[40)]

1) 생활양식-노출이론(lifestyle-exposure theories)

- 개인의 직업적 활동과 여가활동을 포함한 일상적 활동의 생활양식이 그 사람의 범죄피해위험성을 결정하는 중요한 요인이 된다는 이론이다.
- 성별이나 소득수준의 차이가 그 사람의 생활유형의 차이를 가져오고 이는 결국 범죄피해의 위험성의 차이까지 초래하게 된다는 것이다.
- 폭력범죄의 피해자가 될 확률이 높은 사람들은 가족과 보내는 시간이 적고, 외부에서 보내는 시간과 하는 일이 많으며, 범죄자특성의 소유자와 빈번한 접촉을 하기 때문이다.[41)]

2) 일상활동이론(routine activity theory) 2012 기출

- 코헨과 펠슨이 주장한 범죄유발의 3가지 요소로는 ⅰ) 동기가 부여된 범죄자(motivated offender), ⅱ) 적합한 표적(suitable target), ⅲ) 보호할 수 있는 능력의 부재(absence of

---

40) 범죄피해의 원인을 설명하는 이론으로는 합리적 선택이론, 생활양식이론, 일상활동이론 등이 있다. 2010 기출

41) • 젊은 사람, 남자, 미혼자, 저소득층, 저학력층 등은 노년층, 여자, 기혼자, 고소득층, 그리고 고학력층보다 폭력범죄의 피해자가 될 확률이 높다고 할 수 있다.
• 여자보다 남자가 피해를 많이 당하며, 노인보다 젊은층이, 기혼자보다 미혼자가, 상류층보다 하류층이 피해를 많이 당한다. 2009 기출

capable guardianship)를 제시하였다.[42] 2009, 2011 기출

- 특정 범죄피해가 발생하기 위해서는 이 3가지 요소가 모두 일정한 시간과 공간에서 수렴되어야 한다고 주장하였다. 3가지 요소가 특정 시간・공간에서 수렴할 확률은 사람들의 일상활동이 갖는 성격에 달려 있다.
- 범죄자를 자극하거나 동기를 부여하는 구조적 조건이 변화되거나 증가되지 않더라도 매력적이고 무방비상태인 범죄표적이 늘어나는 한 범죄율의 증가는 얼마든지 가능하다고 한다.
- 실업률, 경제적 불평등, 인종차별 등 범인성을 증대시키는 구조적 조건이 저하됨에도 불구하고 범죄율이 지속적으로 증가하고 있는 이유를 설명할 수 있다.[43]

3) 합리적 선택이론(rational choice theory) 2011 기출

- 합리적 선택이론은 경제학적 가정을 토대로 하여 인간은 합리적이라는 명제에서 출발한다.
- 범죄행위는 범죄로 얻게 되는 이익과 범죄행위로 잃게 되는 손실에 대한 행위자의 합리적인 계산과정의 결과라 할 수 있다. 이는 인간은 누구나 쾌락을 추구하고 고통을 피하려 한다고 보는 고전주의 범죄학의 가정을 따른다.
- 범죄자의 범죄행위는 자신의 범죄행위에 있어서 체포위험(risk), 비용(cost), 이익(benefit)을 계산하여 자신에게 유리하다고 판단될 경우에 실행되며, 이러한 합리적 의사결정은 목표선정, 범죄행위시각, 범죄포기 등의 각 단계마다 이루어진다고 한다.

---

42) 일상활동이론에서 범죄피해에 영향을 미치는 요인은 동기가 부여된 범죄자, 적당한 범행대상, 보호나 감독할 수 있는 사람이다. 2007 기출

43) 구조적-선택모형(structural-choice model): ⅰ) 구조적-선택모형은 앞에서 언급된 Routine Activity와 Lifestyle-Exposure이론을 통합한 것이다. ⅱ) 동기부여된 잠재적 가해자와의 물리적 거리 즉, 근접성이 줄어들 때, 범죄의 위험성이 높은 환경에 노출될 때, 범죄표적이나 대상이 표적으로서의 매력성을 가질 때, 그리고 보호성이 결여(Absence of Guardianship)될 때를 범죄의 필요조건으로 제시하고 있다. ⅲ) 근접성과 노출은 그 사람의 사회적 상호작용의 특성을 유형화하며, 더 큰 위험성에 노출시키기 때문에 이 2가지를 범죄기회의 구조적 특징으로 고려할 수 있고, 반면에 매력성과 보호성은 특정한 범죄대상의 선택을 대변하기 때문에 선택요인이라고 말할 수 있다.

4. 상황적 범죄예방과 경찰활동

1) 의의

• 상황적 범죄예방이론에 입각한 경찰의 범죄예방활동 프로그램은 범죄발생의 상황적 조건을 통제하여 범죄기회를 줄이는 활동과 범죄피해를 감소시키는 활동으로 전개된다.44)
• 상황적 범죄예방이론이 일반화함에 따라 최근 경찰의 지역사회 범죄예방활동과 다기관적 협력체 구성에 의한 지역범죄 예방활동이 강화되는 경향을 보이고 있다.

2) 지역사회 범죄예방활동(community-crime prevention)

• 지역사회의 범죄는 범죄자의 범죄욕구와 그 지역의 환경과 주민에 의하여 제공되는 범죄기회의 상호관계 속에서 발생하기 때문에, 물리적 환경의 개선으로 공공(公共)감시의 증대 및 범죄취약성의 제거, 범죄예방활동에 시민참여, 범죄예방활동에 대한 경찰의 적극지원 등 그 지역의 환경과 지역주민에 의하여 제공되는 범죄기회를 줄임으로써 범죄를 감소시킬 수 있다고 전제한다.
• 경찰과 지역주민이 서로 협력하여 범죄예방프로그램을 수립하고, 재원을 마련하며, 지역사회의 범죄를 통제하고 예방하기 위한 종합적인 범죄예방활동을 강조한다.45)
• 지역사회 범죄예방활동은 상황적 범죄예방이론, 비공식적 사회통제이론46), 깨어진

---

44) • 상황적 범죄예방과 관련된 것으로는 방어공간, 목표물의 강화, 범죄기회 등이 있다. 2007 기출
• 기광도, "미국경찰의 범죄예방활동에 관한 연구", 한국형사정책연구원, 1995:10-11.

45) • 개인적 측면에서는 시민에 대한 범죄홍보활동을 통하여 범죄예방능력을 강화시키고, 순찰, 방범심방, 방범진단, 귀중품등록, 목표물보호강화, 목표물(범죄유발요인)의 제거, 목표물접근통제, 출입자 신원확인, 경비원 배치 등을 통하여 범죄기회를 사전에 제거하여 범죄발생을 감소시키는 활동으로 나타나며, 지역사회 측면에서는 범죄행위에 대한 시민감시, 체포의 가능성을 높이기 위한 시민순찰, 물리적 환경설계, 이웃감시, 폐쇄회로 텔레비전(CCTV)의 설치, 범죄촉진요인의 통제 등의 수단이 동원된다.
• 지역사회 경찰활동의 기본요소로는 경찰의 순찰활동은 범죄발샐 이전에 예방적 활동이 중요하다는 인식에서 출발한다. 경찰활동은 단순히 범죄인 검거뿐만 아니라 지역주민에 대한 일반서비스 제공을 위한 순찰활동이 강조된다. 선진국에서 실시하고 있는 이웃감시프로그램은 지역경찰활동의 이념을 기반으로 하고 있다. 2005 기출

46) 비공식적 범죄통제이론에서는 지역주민들 간의 활발한 상호작용으로 형성되는 지역사회의 규범 및 규칙을 준수케 하여 지역사회의 일탈 및 범죄의 발생을 예방하려는 활동이 제시되고 이러한

유리창 이론 등에 근거를 두고 있으며[47], 양호한 경찰과 지역사회관계(police-community Relations)를 중요시하는 지역사회 경찰활동(community-policing)[48]의 일환이라고 할 수 있다.[49]

3) 다기관적 협력체구성에 의한 지역범죄예방

- 지역 내 범죄예방관련기관 및 단체에게 범죄와 무질서 감축전략의 구체적 수행을 위한 법적 의무를 부과하여 지역범죄예방의 효과를 거두고자 하는 접근방법이다.
- 영국에서는 1981년 Brixton 폭동을 계기로 다기관적 협력의 중요성이 본격적으로 강조되기 시작하였으며, 1990년대 들어와 중앙정부의 다기관적 지역안전전략개발을 위한 예산제공이 이루어지면서 공식적인 활동이 개시되었다.
- 그 결과 후속조치로 '범죄 및 무질서법(Crime and Disorder Act 1998)'이 개정되어 지방자치정부와 경찰지역 내 관련기관들과 함께 범죄안전협력체를 구성하게 되었고, '범죄와 무질서법'상의 다기관적 협력체의 활동은 i) 협력체 내의 권한관계의 혼선, ii) 각 기관 간 업무를 조정할 주체적 기관의 부족, iii) 각 기관 단체의 이질적인 문화, iv) 실질적인 참여의 부족 등 시행상 여러 가지 한계와 문제점을 안고 있음에도 불구하고 매 3년을 주기로 지역 내 범죄와 무질서의 수준과 태양(態樣)의 진단 및 조사, 조사결과의 분석과 결과 발표, 문제해결을 위한 전략의 수립 및 발표 등을 하고 있다.

활동은 지역사회와 경찰과의 긴밀한 협력을 통하여 이루어진다는 점이 강조된다.

47) 최인섭, "지역사회범죄예방과 민간인 참여," 형사정책연구, 한국형사정책연구원, 1994:35.

48) • 최선우, 경찰과 커뮤니티, 대왕사, 2003:202-203.
- 전통적 경찰활동과 달리 지역사회 경찰활동이 중시하는 기준은 범죄의 두려움 감소, 범죄발생률의 감소, 경찰조직의 분권화 등이다. 2010 기출

49) • 경찰과 지역사회가 협력하여 수행하기 위한 대표적인 지역사회 범죄예방활동 프로그램에는 지역상주 출장소제도, 소집단 토론, 민원사건 개선프로그램, 유언비어 통제프로그램, 경찰대변인제도, 지역사회지원단 편성, 경찰주관 운동경기리그, 경찰의 위기개입활동, 갈등조정자제도, 경찰학교 연락경찰관제도, 청소년 전문가제도, 이웃감시 프로그램(Neighborhood Watch Program: NWP), 지역봉사단, 경찰·성직자연대 프로그램 등을 들 수 있다. 이러한 프로그램들의 시행을 통하여 단순한 범죄기회 감소의 차원을 넘어서 지역주민들 간 사회적 상호작용을 증대시키고 공동체의식을 형성케 하여 지역사회의 비공식적 사회통제를 강화하는 기능을 담당하게 하는 것이다.
- 지역사회 범죄예방활동으로는 이웃감시, 시민순찰, 지역사회경찰활동 등이 있다. 2009 기출

지역사회 경찰활동과 깨어진 창이론[50)]

1) 지역사회 경찰활동

- 전통적인 경찰활동이 범죄대응적 범죄투쟁자로서의 역할을 수행하였다고 한다면 지역사회 경찰활동은 범죄예방적 문제해결사로서의 역할을 중시하고 모든 경찰활동은 범죄예방과 질서유지에 초점을 맞추어야 한다는 것이다.[51)]
- 지역사회경찰활동은 시민들의 삶의 질에 대한 관심부족과 중앙집권적인 경찰관료조직으로 인하여 범죄와 무질서의 예방효과가 없는 것으로 평가되었다. 이에 따라 1990년대에 접어들어 지역사회의 범죄와 무질서를 보다 근원적으로 차단하기 위해서 1994년 William Bratton이 미국 뉴욕경찰국장으로 취임하여 "깨어진 창이론(broken window theory)"과 이를 응용한 "무관용경찰활동(zero tolerance policing)"을 채택, 경이적인 범죄감소를 경험하여 국제적인 관심을 불러일으킨 바가 있다.[52)]

2) 깨어진 창 가설(The Broken Windows Hypothesis) 2012 기출

- '깨어진 창 가설'이란 낙서나 유리창 파손 등 경미한 범죄를 방치하면 결국 큰 범죄로 이어지게 된다는 범죄심리학 이론이다.
- 지역사회의 무질서가 범죄의 직접적 원인으로서 지역사회 내의 기초질서 위반행위의 방치가 심각한 범죄를 야기하기 때문에 기초질서의 단속을 강조하고 있다.
- 1982년, 윌슨(James Q. Wilson)과 켈링(George L. Kelling)은 "Atlantic Monthly"라는 평론잡지에, '깨어진 창(Broken Windows)'이라는 논문을 실었다.
- 깨어진 창[53)]이란 사소한 사회규칙위반에 대해 징벌이 잘 이루어지지 않는 공동체를 상

---

50) 1982년, 윌슨(James Q. Wilson)과 켈링(George L. Kelling)은 Atlantic Monthly라는 평론잡지에, "깨어진 창(Broken Windows)"이라는 논문을 실었다. James Q. Wilson and George L. Kelling, "Broken Windows : The Police and Neighborhood Safety", Atlantic Monthly, March 1982:249; 정진환, 비교경찰제도, 백산출판사, 2006:231-232.

51) • 지역사회의 무질서는 범죄의 직접적인 원인이다. 지역사회 내의 기초질서 위반행위의 방치가 문제이다. 지역사회 내의 통제와 법의식은 범죄발생에 영향을 준다. 2007 기출
• 깨진 유리창이론은 건물의 파손이나 낙서, 쓰레기의 방치 등 물리적 퇴락이 범죄증가의 중요한 발단이 되며, 물리적 퇴락에 대한 조치나 대처가 이루어지지 않으면 공공장소의 질서유지에 어려움을 겪게 되며, 물리적 퇴락과 사회적 무질서를 지역의 통제력 결여로 인지한다. 2010 기출

52) 스코간(Wesley Skogan)은 무질서(disorder)의 개념을 설명하면서, 무질서를 인간적(Human)인 것과 물리적(Physical)인 것으로 분류하였다. 인간적(Human)인 무질서에는 공공장소에서의 폭음, 거리의 갱이나 행패, 거리에서의 마약거래나 흡음, 소란, 매춘행위 등이 있으며, 물리적(Physical)인 무질서에는 예술·문화의 파괴, 빌딩의 폐허, 쓰레기 등이 있다. Wesley G. Skogan, Disorder and Decline : Crime and Spiral of Decay in American Neighborhood, New York : Free Press, 1990:21-50.

53) 공격적 구걸인, 주취자, 약물중독자, 무차별폭력성향을 가진 청소년들, 성매매자, 부랑자, 정신병

징하며, 주민들은 이러한 위반에 무관심해지고 태연히 받아들이게 된다. 즉, 사회질서에 생긴 작은 균열 하나가 큰 후속결과를 초래할 수도 있다는 것이다.

- 지역주민들의 장래 범죄피해에 관한 공포나 사회질서유지에 대한 무관심과 같은 결과를 초래하지 않기 위해서는 사소한 사회규칙의 위반 내지 주민다수를 불쾌하게 하는 행동이 법으로 범죄로 성립하든 아니든 상관없이 경찰에 의해 예방되거나 진압되어야 함을 강조한다.
- '깨어진 창'으로 인해 지역사회의 규범기준이 쇠퇴되고 결국에는 건전한 지역공동체의 삶의 질이 저해됨으로 인해 도시 내부가 황폐해짐으로써 잃어버린 지역주민들의 안전감정을 회복하기 위하여 결연히 대처하여야 한다는 것이다.
- 1990년대 초반, 뉴욕시 지하철에서의 질서회복을 강조한 뉴욕시장 R. Giuliani와 1990년대 중반 뉴욕시의 범죄율 감소를 위해 뉴욕시 경찰청장 W. Bratton이 정책으로 반영하였다.

〈깨어진 창 가설〉
무질서(Disorder) → 시민공포(Citizen Fear) → 철수(물리적 · 사회적) → 증가된 약탈행위(Increased Predatory Behavior) → 범죄증가(Increased Crime) → 황폐의 심화(Spiral of Decline)

출처: George Kelling and William Bratton, "Declining Crime Rates : Insiders' View of the New York City Story," The Journal of Criminal Law & Criminology, 88, No. 4, 1988:1217–1231.

4) 무관용 경찰활동

- 무관용 경찰활동(zero-tolerance policing)이란 경찰이 사회적 반문화행위의 부분집합에 불과한 질서위반행위자나 주취자, 폭력청소년, 구걸행위자, 노숙자 등에게 초점을 맞추고, 그들이 거리에서 자취를 감추게 하기 위해서는 적극적으로 범죄통제활동을 전개하는 것이다.
- 경찰은 범죄에 대하여 강경하고 엄격하게 대응해야 하며, 재량권을 행사하지 말고 법집행을 해야 하며, 중범죄뿐만 아니라 사소한 무질서나 경미한 범죄에 엄격히 대응해야 한다.

자 등과 무임승차자, 노상방뇨자, 소음에 의한 생활방해자, 벽에 페인트나 스프레이 등으로 낙서하는 자, 벤치나 가옥입구 등에서 잠자는 자들로부터 대중공간을 되찾아오고, 사소한 무질서행위로부터 방치되고 있는 공동체를 암시하는 말.

5. 범죄대체(crime displacement)

1) 의의

- 범죄대체(crime displacement)란 잠재적인 목표로부터 다른 목표로 범죄가 이동하는 것을 말한다. 범죄누수(crime spillover)로 불리기도 한다.
- 한 지역이나 표적에 대해 범죄를 감소시키거나 예방하려는 활동은 다른 지역이나 다른 잠재적 표적에게로 범죄가 '흘러 넘어가는 결과'를 가져온다는 것이다. 즉, 다양한 범죄예방활동이 범죄의 총 발생 건수를 감소시키기보다는 범죄가 옮겨가도록 만드는 것이다.[54)]

2) 범죄대체현상의 분류

〈범죄대체(crime displacement)〉 2012 기출

구분	내용
유익한 대체	범죄예방 조치를 실시함으로써 중범죄가 포기되고 사소한 범죄로 옮겨가는 것
유해한 대체	범죄예방조치를 통해 일단 저지된 범죄가 더욱 심각한 범죄 또는 범죄피해율이 높은 장소나 표적들로 굴절되는 것
(1) 공간적 대체현상	• 범죄가 지리적 위치를 옮겨가는 것 • 일정 지역에 대한 특정범죄예방대책들을 시행함으로써 인근 지역에서 그 범죄가 증가하는 현상
(2) 시간적 대체현상	같은 지역 내에서 범죄가 일어나고 있지만 다른 시기로 범죄가 이동하는 것 예 절도범죄 발생시간이 저녁 늦은 시간에서 이른 아침으로 이동하는 것
(3) 전술적 대체현상	범죄자가 동일한 범죄행위를 저지르는 데 있어 새로운 범죄수단을 활용하는 것. 예 잠기지 않은 문을 출입수단으로 삼던 침입절도범이 유리창을 깨는 방법으로 사용하는 것
(4) 표적(대상)대체	미혼 여성회사원들의 방어무기사용이 증가함에 따라 강도들이 방어능력이 떨어지는 노쇠한 보행자를 표적으로 범죄를 저지르는 행위

54) '예방이득의 확산(diffusion of benefits)' 일정한 범죄를 예방하기 위하여 어떤 조치를 취했을 때 의도하지 않았던 다른 범죄를 예방하게 된다는 것이다. 즉, 범죄예방조치를 취함으로써 직접적인 범죄예방뿐만 아니라 간접적인 범죄예방효과가 나타난다는 것이다. 임창주, "상황적 범죄예방에 관한 연구", 전남대학교 석사학위논문, 1999:57-58.

(5) 기능적(functional) 대체현상	• 범죄자가 새로운 형태의 범죄행위를 저지르는 것. 예 단순절도범이 침입절도범으로, 침입절도범이 강도로 • 범죄예방효과의 소멸(extinction) 즉, 범죄예방 프로그램이 단기적으로는 예방효과를 보지만 범죄자들이 새로운 범죄상황에 적응함으로써 그러한 예방효과는 소멸되게 됨. 예 모든 주택에 침입절도를 위한 경보 시스템을 설치한 경우 잠재적인 범죄자들은 단순 침입절도에서 무장한 강도로 바뀌어 더욱 위험한 범죄를 저지르게 되는 것

3) 범죄대체와 경찰활동

- 범죄대체현상은 특정지역의 방범체제가 확고하여 범죄행위가 어려워질 경우 범죄자가 다른 지역으로 이동하여 범행을 저지르게 되는 현상으로써[55], 경찰활동의 증가에 따라 늘어난 것은 실제 범죄가 아니라 경찰활동에 의해 높아진 범죄에 대한 인지능력 향상이 공식범죄통계상의 범죄율을 증가시켰다는 설명이다.[56]
- 경찰의 활동은 범죄동기 자체를 제거하지는 못하기 때문에 경찰활동의 강화는 단지 범죄의 장소와 대상 등의 대체효과만을 야기할 뿐이라는 것이다. 체포될 위험이 높은 상황에 직면한 범죄자는 덜 위험한 범죄유형과 방법, 대상으로 전환할 가능성이 높아지며, 그렇게 될 경우 덜 위험한 범죄대상은 그만큼 범죄수익 역시 적어질 가능성이 높아질 것이기 때문에 범죄자는 일정 수준의 소득을 유지하기 위해 더 많은 범죄를 저질러야 할 수도 있게 된다.[57]

---

55) Gober, T., "The Crime Displacement Hypothesis : An Empirical Examination", Crime Delinquency, 26, 1981:390-404.

56) • Jacob, H. & M. J. Rich, "The Effects of the Police on Crime : A Rejointer", Law and Society, 16, 1981.
• 경찰의 생산성효과(police productive effect)라고도 한다(기광도, 2001). 경찰력이 증가하면 시민들은 범죄 검거 가능성이 높다고 인지하게 되어 범죄신고를 더 많이 하게 될 수 있고, 경찰 자체로서도 충원된 인력 및 자원을 통하여 자체 범죄인지능력을 향상시키고 신고된 사건을 보다 철저하게 파악할 가능성이 높아(신고된 사건을 공식적으로 처리하지 않을 가능성의 감소)진다. 그 때문에 경찰력 증가는 '가시적'(숨은 범죄를 제외한 범죄라는 의미로 해석) 범죄발생률을 증가시키기도 한다. Swimmer, G., "The Relationship of Police and Crime : Some Methodological and Empirical Results", Criminology, 12, 1974; Wilson, J. Q. & B. Boland, "The Effect of the Police on Crime", Law and Society, 12, 1978:367-390.

57) 'backfire effect'라고 하는데, 우리말로는 '맞불효과'로 번역(기광도, 2007)된 바 있다.

- 공식범죄통계는 오로지 형사법기관에 의해 인지되고 처리된 범죄들만의 통계이다.[58] 따라서 신고 등에 의해 인지되고 경찰과 검찰에 의해 공식적으로 처리된 범죄만 증가하여도 즉, 범죄암수가 줄어들기만 하여도 실제 범죄와는 무관하게 공식범죄통계상의 범죄율은 증가하게 된다.[59]

제4절 환경설계를 통한 범죄예방(CPTED)

1. 의의

- CPTED(Crime Prevention Through Environmental Design)란 물리적 설계・주민참여・경찰활동 등의 3요소를 종합적・계획적으로 연계시켜 지역사회 전체・특정구역・교육기관・교통수단 등을 범죄로부터 안전하게 보호하고 범죄에 대한 공포를 제거하는 방범기법을 말한다.[60]
- 범죄를 유발하는 물리적인 환경개선을 통하여 적절한 설계와 물리적 환경을 효과적으로 사용함으로써 범죄와 범죄에의 공포를 감소시키는 범죄통제전략이라 할 수 있다.

2. CPTED의 내용 2011 기출

1) 접근통제(Access Control)	자물쇠, 장애물, 경보장치 등의 범죄예방장치들을 설치하고 범죄예방표어(Sticker), 표시(Sign), 도로설계, 도시계획과 같이 범죄인에게 심리적인 부담감을 줌으로써 권한 없이 주거지나 사업장에 출입하는 것을 막는 것을 말한다.

---

58) Savitz, 1982; O'Brien, 1985; Schneider & Wiersema, 1990; 김준호・이동원, 1991; 황지태, 2009.
59) 황지태, 한국의 치안인력과 범죄율에 관한 소고, 형사정책연구, Korean Criminological Review, 제21권 제1호(통권 제81호, 2010년 봄호):121-148.
60) • 환경설계를 통한 범죄예방에서 강조하는 것은 '건축물 구조변경'이다. 2004 기출
• 범죄피해방지 전략에는 문제지향적 경찰활동, 방범설계, 범죄방어공간 등이 있다. 2005 기출
• 최근에 대두된 범죄억제전략으로 환경설계를 통하여 범죄예방을 도모하고자 하는 것은 CPTED이다. 2005 기출
• 환경설계라고 말할 때의 '환경'이란 인간적・물리적・사회적 환경을 두루 포괄하는 개념이다. 환경설계를 통한 범죄예방전략을 적용하기에 가장 적합한 범죄유형은 절도범죄이다. 2010 기출

2) 감시(Surveillance)	의심스러운 사람・침입자를 감시하는 환경과 범죄를 저지하거나 또는 진행 중인 범죄를 간파하는 환경의 합법적인 사용자의 감시역량을 강화시키는 것을 말한다.
3) 행사지원(Activity Support)	주민들이 자신의 주거환경이 범죄에 취약화되지 않도록 환경조성활동을 촉진시키는 것을 말한다.
4) 동기강화(Motivation Reinforcement)	• 범행의 위험이 증가하는 것과 범행의 대가(代價)가 감소했다는 것을 범죄인들이 깨닫게 함으로써 범인들의 범행에 대한 동기를 소멸시키는 것을 말한다. • OTREP는 범죄기회(opportunity), 범죄표적(target), 범행의 위험(risk), 범행을 위한 노력(effort), 범죄를 통한 수익(Payoff)을 말한다.

3. CPTED 예방공간의 물리적 요소 2011 기출

1) 영역설정 (Territoriality)	• 자기 집이나 부지(敷地)에 대해 느끼는 것과 같이 근린 사이의 공용공간에 대해서도 "나의 것이라는 의식" 또는 "관할구역의식"을 갖고 동시에 그 공용공간에 대해서도 주민끼리 책임지는 것을 말한다. • 영역설정이란 어떤 지역에 대한 합법적인 이용을 의미하며, 사적(私的) 영역(private space), 반사적(半私的) 영역(semi private space), 반공적(半公的) 영역(semi public space), 공적(公的) 영역(public space) 등 4개의 영역이 있을 수 있다.
2) 자연적 감시(Natural Surveillance)	• 합법적인 이용자들에게 이웃과 외부인의 활동을 부여할 수 있도록 영역을 설계하는 것이라고 한다. • 거주자가 일상의 생활을 영위하면서 특히 반공적(半公的) 영역을 침범하는 자를 배제할 목적으로 그곳을 시각적・청각적으로 자연스럽게 감시하는 것을 말한다. 예 시선(Gazing), 조명(Lighting), 공용공간의 위치, 접근로의 위치
3) 표현(Image)	• 범죄에 취약하게 보이지 않고 주변 지역사회로부터 고립되지 않도록 지역사회를 조성하는 것을 의미한다. • 사람들에게 일정하게 부각되는 단지의 인상과 주변환경의 이미지로써, 잠재적인 범죄자가 범죄를 실행하기에 용이하다고 인상지워지는 이미지가 되지 않도록 환경을 설계한다.
4) 주변지역보호(Safe Area and Street)	단지 주변지구를 구성하고 있는 주택가, 기타 건축・토목・조경시설의 성격을 말한다. 건물군의 형태나 배치에 유의하고 주거단지를 안정성이 높은 지역에 배치하도록 배려한다.

영역설정
(1) 사적(私的) 영역: 주택・주호(住戶, dwelling unit)로서 이를 전용(專用)하고 있는 가족에게 귀속되어 있고, 그 가족구성원 이외의 어느 누구라도 그들의 허가 없이 무단으로 출입할 수 없는 영역을 말한다. (2) 반사적(半私的) 영역: 주택・주호(住戶, dwelling unit)의 직접적인 연장지역으로 개인정원과 현관입구 등을 가리키고, 사적 영역만큼은 아니지만 그곳에 출입하는 것 역시 가족구성원으로부터 엄격하게 그 근거를 밝혀야 출입이 가능한 영역이다. 반사적 영역은 사적 영역에서만 접근할 수 있도록 되어 있다. (3) 반공적(半公的) 영역: 일반주택지의 좁은 도로, 소규모 아동공원, 중층주택의 복도와 계단, 동간(棟間)공간을 가리킨다. 이 영역에 출입하는 낯선 자는 거기에 출입하는 용건을 명시적으로나 묵시적으로 명확하게 밝히지 않는 한 출입을 제지당하게 된다. (4) 공적(公的) 영역: 주요 가로(街路), 큰 도시공원 등을 가리키고 반드시 특정한 거주집단에 귀속해 있지 않아서 법으로 금지되어 있지 않은 행위는 상당히 자유롭게 행할 수 있는 영역이다.

4. 상황적 범죄예방의 대책 2011 기출

클라크(R. V. Clarke)는 상황적 범죄예방의 12가지 전략을 제시했다.[61)]

1) 범죄비용을 증가시키는 전략(increasing the effort)

(1) **범죄표적의 견고화** (target hardening)	물리적 장애물을 설치함으로써 잠재적인 범죄자들의 범행을 막는 것이다. 예 출입문 잠금장치, 창문창살의 설치, 이중잠금장치, 금고, 서비스 종사자들에 대한 보호시설로서 안전망 설치 등[62)]
(2) **접근통제전략** (access control)	잠재적인 범죄자들이 물리적이나 실제적으로 범죄현장에 들어가게 하는 것을 더욱 어렵게 하는 것이다. 예 고층집합주택의 관리인 배치, 자동시정장치(autolock system)의 설치, 자동차에 부착된 번호판[63)], 개인 또는 공공건물의 출입문에 접수처 설치, 비밀번호나 고객번호로 건물출입을 제한

61) Clarke, R. V., op. cit., 1992:3-36.
62) 개인적 수준의 범죄예방대책 중 휴가철 빈집털이를 예방하기 위하여 전자식 잠금장치를 설치하는 것은 '대상강화'이다. 2008 기출
63) 미국에서 주민자동차 표시(Auto Bumper Decal)전략을 지역주민들의 차량 범퍼에 문양을 부착하

(3) **범행의지의 굴절** (deflecting offenders)	범죄의 가능성이 있는 이들이 범행의 기회를 갖지 못하게 하는 것이다. 예 사람들이 대중에게 뭔가를 말하고 싶어 하는 곳에 '낙서판' 설치, 경쟁팀의 관중들을 따로따로 분리해 놓은 경기장을 설계함으로써 폭력사고의 위험감소
(4) **범행도구의 통제** (controlling facilitators)	총기단속법은 범행에 사용될 수 있는 특정형태의 총기의 사용을 제한하는 것이다. 예 일부 도시는 마약거래자들이 사용하기 쉬운 지점에 위치한 공중전화의 위치를 이동

2) 범행위험을 증가시키는 전략(increasing the risk)

(1) **출입감시**(entry/exit screening)	특정 물건을 일정장소로 이동, 운반을 곤란케 하는 것이다. 예 공항의 금속탐지기로 비행기에 총이나 폭탄을 갖고 탑승하는 것을 방지, 가게, 도서관 등에서 도난방지장치
(2) **공식적 감시**(formal surveillance)	범행의 우려가 있는 범죄인을 막기 위한 정복차림의 경관이나 감시장치를 사용하는 것이다. 보안카메라와 다른 보안 전자장치들은 경찰의 공식적 감시능력을 확대시키기 위한 것이다. 예 차량절도방지를 위하여 자동차의 엔진 내부에 위치추적장치 설치
(3) **고용인에 의한 감시**(employee surveillance)	지하철역에서 매표원, 호텔의 도어맨 등을 활용한다.
(4) **자연적 감시**(natural surveillance)	일정한 지역을 감시하는 인력과 장비의 능력을 증가시키는 모든 방법을 말한다. 예 가로등 설치, 주택의 울타리나 담장 허물기

3) 범죄의 이득을 감소시키는 전략(reducing the risk)

(1) **범죄표적의 제거** (target removal)	예 대중교통을 이용할 때 거액의 금전지참 금지, 편의점에 시간잠금장치를 갖춘 금전출납기를 설치
(2) **재물의 소속 확인** (identifying property)	주거침입 범죄인들의 범행 표적이 되는 재산에 인식표를 부착함으로써 예방 예 소, 돼지, 말 등에 소유주의 낙인, 귀중품에 소유주 표시프로그램

는 방법이다. 자동차 범퍼에 문양을 부착하는 이유는 순찰 중인 경찰관과 지역사회의 주민들로 하여금 지역 거주자의 소유가 아닌 차량이 눈에 띄면 유심히 살펴보고 의심스러울 경우에는 적절한 조치를 취할 수 있게 하기 위해서이다. 조병인, 범죄대책론, 한림원, 1993:217.

(3) **범행유인의 제거** (removing inducement)	예 낙서된 벽면 청소
(4) **규범 제정**(rule setting)	규범이 정착되어 있으면 만약 자신이 범행을 저지르면 비싼 대가를 치러야 한다는 것을 잠재적인 범죄자들에게 분명하게 인식시켜 줄 수 있다. 예 성폭력 관련 법령의 주지 및 엄격한 적용

제 21 장 범죄피해자론

제1절 범죄피해자론의 의의

1. 범죄피해자의 개념[1)]

1) 최협의의 개념

범죄로 인하여 법익이 침해 또는 위협된 자를 말한다.

2) 협의의 개념

사회적으로 유해한 행위를 통해 법익을 침해당한 사람을 말한다.

3) 광의의 개념

직접 법익을 침해당한 피해자뿐만 아니라 그와 밀접한 관련이 있는 자(가족)들까지 포함한다.

4) 최광의의 개념

'범죄피해자'를 '피해자'로 파악하고, 범죄뿐만 아니라 범죄와 관련이 없는 자연재해나 사고 등에 의해서 피해를 입은 자까지를 포함한다.

---

1) 김용준, 범죄피해자학, 백산출판사, 2009:27-30.

〈피해자학이론에 필요한 주요 개념〉 2011 기출

범죄와의 근접성(proximity to crime)	• 범죄와의 물리적 근접성 • 범죄다발지역에 가까울수록 피해 위험성이 증대된다. • 범죄의 잠재적 표적이 사는 곳과 상대적으로 많은 수의 범죄자가 발견된 지역과의 물리적 거리로 나타낼 수 있다. • 범죄다발지역에 거주하는 사람일수록 범죄피해자가 될 위험성이 더 많은 이유는 범죄자와의 빈번한 접촉가능성을 증대시키기 때문이다.
범죄에의 노출(exposure to crime)	• 범죄에 대한 취약성(vulnerability)을 나타낸다. • 외진 지역에 위치한 건물이나 가옥은 침입절도에 그만큼 많이 노출되는 것이며, 위험한 시간에 위험한 지역에 처한 사람은 당연히 강도나 폭행의 위험성을 더 많이 안고 있다. • 대체로 개인의 일상적 활동(routine activity)과 생활양식(life-style)에 기인하는 바가 크다.
표적의 매력성(target attractiveness)	• 범죄에 있어서 특정한 표적이 범죄자에게 상징적·경제적 가치가 있기 때문에 선택된다는 논리에 기초하고 있다. • 범죄의 표적으로서 매력은 가치뿐만 아니라 물리적 저항이 적을수록 매력적인 표적이라고 할 수 있다. • 범죄피해의 구조적-선택모형에 의하면, 표적의 결정 시 중요한 것은 표적과 관련된 상이한 가치와 주관적 유용성이라고 한다. • 표적의 매력성은 고가(高價)이거나 이동이 용이한 재화의 소지여부, 공공장소에서의 보석 패용 여부, 사회경제적 지위나 가족의 소득 등을 이용해서 측정되고 있다.
보호능력(capable guardianship)	• 피해의 대상이 될 수 있는 사람이나 물건의 범죄발생을 미연에 방지할 수 있는 능력을 일컫는다. • 보호능력이란 대인적 또는 사회적인 면과 물리적 차원을 공히 내포하고 있다. 사회적 보호능력이란 가족구성원, 이웃 주민과의 친분 또는 협조와 같은 것을 들 수 있고, 물리적 차원의 보호성은 방범시설이나 장치를 통해서 이루어질 수 있다. 또한 가로등이나 보호등의 설치 및 기타 방범에 관한 집단활동에 참여하는 것 등도 포함한다.

2. 범죄피해자구조법

• 「범죄피해자보호법」 제1조는 "범죄피해자 보호·지원의 기본 정책 등을 정하고 타인의 범죄행위로 인하여 생명·신체에 피해를 받은 사람을 구조(救助)함으로써 범죄피해자의 복지 증진에 기여함을 목적으로 한다"고 규정하고 있다.

- 「범죄피해자법」 제3조는 "범죄피해자"란 타인의 범죄행위로 피해를 당한 사람과 그 배우자(사실상의 혼인관계를 포함한다), 직계친족 및 형제자매 및 범죄피해 방지 및 범죄피해자 구조 활동으로 피해를 당한 사람도 범죄피해자로 본다고 규정하고 있다.[2)]

1) 직접피해를 입은 개인 또는 집단

범죄피해자란 범죄로 인하여 육체적・정신적 상처와 고통, 재산상의 손실을 입거나 기본권을 침해당한 개인 또는 집단을 의미한다.

2) 간접적 피해자

- 피해방지를 위해서 노력하는 과정에서 피해를 당한 사람을 말한다.
- UN의 「사법의 기본원칙」 제2조는 "직접피해를 당한 자뿐만 아니라 그 가족, 피부양자 및 피해자지원 또는 후속적 피해방지를 위해 노력하는 과정에서 피해를 당한 사람도 피해자에 포함된다."고 하여 간접피해를 인정하고 있다.
- 헨티히(Hentig)는 1941년, "행위자와 피해자 사이의 상호작용에 관한 연구"라는 논문에서, "범죄피해자는 단순한 수동적 객체에 불과한 것이 아니라 범죄화과정의 적극적 주체가 된다"고 주장하였다. 2010 기출

「범죄피해자보호법」 [시행 2011.10.26] [법률 제10898호, 2011.7.25, 타법개정]
제1조(목적) 이 법은 범죄피해자 보호・지원의 기본 정책 등을 정하고 타인의 범죄행위로 인하여 생명・신체에 피해를 받은 사람을 구조(救助)함으로써 범죄피해자의 복지 증진에 기여함을 목적으로 한다. **제2조(기본이념)** ① 범죄피해자는 범죄피해 상황에서 빨리 벗어나 인간의 존엄성을 보장받을 권리가 있다.

2) • "타인의 범죄행위로 피해를 당한 사람과 생계를 같이 하는 사람"은 해당되지 않는다. 2010 기출
• 구 「범죄피해자구조법」은 생명 또는 신체를 해하는 범죄행위에 의한 피해이더라도 정당방위와 정당행위로 인한 경우와 과실범의 경우는 제외한다. 피해자와 가해자 간에 친족관계에 있는 경우 구조금 지급의 결격사유가 된다. 생명 또는 신체를 해하는 타인의 범죄행위로 인해 피해가 발생한 경우에 한한다. 2004 기출

② 범죄피해자의 명예와 사생활의 평온은 보호되어야 한다.

③ 범죄피해자는 해당 사건과 관련하여 각종 법적 절차에 참여할 권리가 있다.

제3조(정의) ① 이 법에서 사용하는 용어의 뜻은 다음과 같다.

1. "범죄피해자"란 타인의 범죄행위로 피해를 당한 사람과 그 배우자(사실상의 혼인관계를 포함한다), 직계친족 및 형제자매를 말한다.
2. "범죄피해자 보호·지원"이란 범죄피해자의 손실 복구, 정당한 권리 행사 및 복지 증진에 기여하는 행위를 말한다. 다만, 수사·변호 또는 재판에 부당한 영향을 미치는 행위는 포함되지 아니한다.
3. "범죄피해자 지원법인"이란 범죄피해자 보호·지원을 주된 목적으로 설립된 비영리법인을 말한다.
4. "구조대상 범죄피해"란 대한민국의 영역 안에서 또는 대한민국의 영역 밖에 있는 대한민국의 선박이나 항공기 안에서 행하여진 사람의 생명 또는 신체를 해치는 죄에 해당하는 행위(「형법」 제9조, 제10조제1항, 제12조, 제22조제1항에 따라 처벌되지 아니하는 행위를 포함하며, 같은 법 제20조 또는 제21조제1항에 따라 처벌되지 아니하는 행위 및 과실에 의한 행위는 제외한다)로 인하여 사망하거나 장해 또는 중상해를 입은 것을 말한다.
5. "장해"란 범죄행위로 입은 부상이나 질병이 치료(그 증상이 고정된 때를 포함한다)된 후에 남은 신체의 장해로서 대통령령으로 정하는 경우를 말한다.
6. "중상해"란 범죄행위로 인하여 신체나 그 생리적 기능에 손상을 입은 것으로서 대통령령으로 정하는 경우를 말한다.

② 제1항제1호에 해당하는 사람 외에 범죄피해 방지 및 범죄피해자 구조 활동으로 피해를 당한 사람도 범죄피해자로 본다.

제2절 범죄피해자의 분류[3)]

1. 헨티히(Hans von Hentig)의 분류[4)]

1) 일반적 피해자

연소자, 노인, 정신박약자 또는 정신장애자, 이민자, 소수민족, 평균능력 이하자(둔감한 자, 알코올 중독자) 등으로, 육체적·정신적 행동특성이나 사회적 지위가 열악하다는 점 때문에 일반적으로 피해자가 될 소지가 큰 피해자를 말한다.

2) 심리학적 피해자

무기력한 자, 의기소침한 자, 탐욕자, 품행이 방정하지 못한 자, 호색가, 고립되어 외로운 자, 실연자, 독선적인 자, 남을 괴롭히기 좋아하는 자, 궁박한 상황에 있는 자 등 심리학적 관점에서 볼 때 피해자가 되기 쉬운 자를 말한다.

3) 저항하는 피해자(activating victim)

활동적인·저항하는 피해자란 스스로가 범죄자로 전락하는 피해자를 말한다. 원래 자신에게 피해를 야기하였다고 생각되는 사회제도 등에 반항함으로써 스스로 범죄를 자초하여 범죄자가 되는 경우를 말한다. 즉, 이는 2차·3차 피해현상의 역작용을 범죄라는 형태로 극복하는 피해자를 말한다.

2. 엘렌베르거(Ellenberger)의 분류

1) 일반적·현실적 피해자

외형적으로 특정한 요인 즉, 연령, 직업, 정신병적·사회적·신체적 상황 등 때문에 피해를 당하는 사람을 말한다.

---

3) 김용준, 범죄피해자학, 백산출판사, 2009:30-32.
4) 미국으로 망명한 독일의 범죄학자 헨티히(Hans von Hentig)는 피해자학의 선구자이며, 1948년에 저서 『범죄자와 그의 피해자(The Criminal and His Victim)』에서 분류하고 있다.

2) 잠재적 피해자

실제적으로는 범죄피해를 당하지 않았지만 자기혐오 경향, 우울증 및 아벨증후군과 같은 특징을 가지고 있어 범죄피해자가 될 가능성이 높은 자를 말한다.

3. 멘델존(Benjamin Mendelsohn)의 분류[5)]

1) 전혀 잘못이 없는 피해자 : 영아살해의 피해대상인 영아나 약취유인의 피해대상인 유아같이 아무런 자각 없이 피해를 입는 자
2) 책임이 매우 적거나 조금 인정되는 피해자: 무지로 낙태를 감행하다가 사망한 임신부와 같이 책임이 매우 적거나 조금 인정되는 피해자
3) 가해자와 똑같은 정도의 책임이 있는 피해자: 동반자살자, 자발적인 피해자, 살인을 촉탁하거나 승낙한 자, 매춘과 같은 피해자 없는 범죄로 인한 피해자 등
4) 가해자보다 더 책임이 있는 피해자: 화를 돋워 범죄를 촉발한 피해자
5) 책임이 아주 많은 피해자: 공격적 피해자나 정당방위의 상대방, 예컨대 침입절도를 시도하다 집주인의 총에 맞은 자와 같은 경우[6)]
6) 기만적 또는 상상적 피해자: 범죄피해를 가장하고 타인을 무고한 자, 피해 망상자 · 히스테리 발작자 · 병적 거짓말쟁이와 같은 경우

4. 피해자화 단계에 따른 분류

1) 1차 피해자화

범죄나 불법행위, 기타 개인, 단체 · 집단이 사회생활 중 부당한 사건에 의해 육체적 · 물질적 · 심리적 피해를 직접적으로 받게 되는 것을 말한다.

2) 2차 피해자화 2008, 2012 기출

- 형사사법기관에 종사하는 공무원이 범죄사건을 처리하는 과정에서 잘못 대응함으로써 범죄피해자가 사건 그 자체로 인한 피해 이외에 새롭게 입게 되는 피해를 말한다.

---

5) 이스라엘의 변호사로서 흔히 피해자학의 '아버지'라고 하며, 피해발생에 대한 피해자의 책임의 정도(피해자의 유책성)에 따라 분류하였다.
6) 범죄자에 대한 유책성이 가장 큰 피해자의 유형은 '정당방위의 상대방'이다. 2005 기출

• 최초의 범죄피해에 대하여 사건을 처리하는 과정에서 파생되는 피해자가 받게 되는 피해를 말하며, 주로 수사기관이나 재판기관에서 발생하는 피해자 본인이나 그 가족 등의 고통이 주가 된다.

3) 3차 피해자화

1, 2차 범죄피해에서 적절한 피해자 지원이나 대책을 받지 못한 경우 반사회적 · 비사회적 반응을 보이고 그에 관련된 피해를 말하는 것이다. 예 강간범죄 피해자가 수사과정에서 수모를 느껴 자살에 이르는 경우

제3절 회복적 사법

1. 회복적 사법(restorative justice)의 개념[7] 2011 기출

회복적 사법이란 피해자와 가해자 및 지역사회구성원 등 범죄사건 관련자들이 능동적으로 참여하여 피해자 또는 지역사회의 손실을 복구하고 관련 당사자들의 재통합을 추구하는 범죄피해 처리 및 대응방식을 말한다.[8]

2. 회복사법의 유형 2012 기출

(1) 배상명령	징벌적인 의미가 있는 것으로 법원이 가해자로 하여금 자신의 행위로 인해 발생한 피해를 배상하도록 명령하는 대신에 그에게 부과된 형벌을 완화해 주는 제도이다. "피해회복"이란 가해자가 진심어린 사죄와 가능한 범위에서 최선을 기울인 배상을 통해 피해자를 납득시킴으로써 가해자와 피해자 서로 간의 갈등을 극복하고 법적 평화를 회복하는 것을 말한다.
(2) 형사화해	주로 민간인 중재나 중재기관을 통해서 조정과 대화를 통해 피해자와 가해자 그리고 지역사회가 가해자의 범죄행위로 인하여 발생한 손실을 복구하고 그들 사이의 갈등을 극복하여 화해를 이루어내어 법적 평화와 사회의 재통합을 이루는 것을 말한다.

7) 김용준, 범죄피해자학, 백산출판사, 2009:351-352.
8) 회복적 사법제도는 사법처리 과정에서 형사사법기관이 가해자와 피해자 간의 조정과 합의를 강조하며, 피해자와 가해자 또는 지역사회 등 범죄사건 관련자들이 사건의 해결과정에 능동적으로 참여하고, 피해자 또는 지역사회의 손실을 복구하고 관련 당사자들의 재통합을 추구하는 일체의 범죄대응방식이다. 2009, 2010 기출

〈표 4-6〉 응보적 사법정의와 회복적 사법정의의 개념

	응보적 사법정의	회복적 사법정의
1. 범죄에 대한 이해	• 범죄는 위법행위로써 국가를 거역한 것임 • 위법행위가 법 규정을 따라 기술적(technical) 용어로 한정됨	• 범죄는 개인을 거역한 것이며 또한 관계를 파괴시킨 것 • 위법행위는 윤리적·사회적·경제적·정치적인 전체 맥락에서 이해됨
2. 정의에 대한 개념	• 범죄자와 국가 사이의 상호경쟁적 관계에서 법에 의하여 죄를 결정하여 이에 따르는 고통을 부과하는 것	• 범죄피해자, 범죄자, 그리고 지역사회가 범죄로 인한 상처를 고치고 화해를 가져올 수 있는 해결책을 강구하는 데 참여케 함
3. 정의에 대한 여러 측면들	• 죄의 대가를 치르는 것이 중심 • 과거에 초점을 둠 • 범죄에 관계된 사람들의 욕구는 부차적임 • 서로 간에 적극적으로 싸우는 모델 • 서로 간에 차이점들이 강조됨 • 범죄자가 저지른 해(harm)를 정정하도록 규정 • 범죄자에 초점, 피해자는 무시됨 • 국가와 범죄자가 핵심 • 손해배상이 거의 이뤄지지 않음 • 국가가 범죄자에게 조치를 취함 • 범죄자는 피동적임 • 범죄자와 지역사회의 관계가 악화됨 • 반성과 용서를 못하게 함 • 경쟁적이고 개인주의적인 가치가 격려됨	• 문제해결이 중심 • 미래에 초점을 둠 • 욕구가 우선적임 • 대화하는 모델 • 서로 간의 공유점을 추구함 • 상응하는 해를 부과 • 피해자의 욕구가 중요시됨 • 피해자와 범죄자가 핵심 • 손해배상이 이뤄지는 것이 정상적임 • 범죄자가 문제해결의 일익 담당 • 피해자, 범죄자, 지역사회가 문제해결에 참여할 수 있는 역할 인정 • 범죄자는 문제를 해결해야 할 책임 있음 • 지역사회로의 범죄자 통합이 증가됨 • 반성과 용서가 격려됨 • 상호성과 협력이 격려됨

주) 배임호, "회복적 사법정의의 배경, 발전과정, 주요 프로그램 그리고 선진교정복지", 교정연구, 통권 3호, 2007:151. Howard Zehr R. J., Changing Lenses: A New Focus on Crime and Justice, Scottdale, PA : Herald Press, 1990:181,185.

출처: 김용준, 범죄피해자학, 백산출판사, 2009:428-429.

3. 회복적 사법의 장 · 단점

회복적 사법의 장점	• 직접 가해자를 만나지 않고 합의에 도달할 수 있을 뿐만 아니라 피해자가 범죄의 영향을 판사나 가해자에 알리는 등 많은 피해자들이 자신들의 능동적 역할과 감정적 치유로 만족하게 된다.[9] • 회복적 사법은 사건의 처리과정이나 결과에 대한 더 많은 정보를 피해자에게 제공해 준다. • 피해자에게 참여의 기회를 넓혀주는 것이다. • 회복적 사법이 피해자에게 공정하고 존중의 처우를 제공하여 준다. • 회복적 사법이 물질적 회복을 가져다준다. • 회복적 사법은 피해자에게 사과와 감정적 회복을 가져다준다.
회복적 사법의 단점	• 강력사건과 같은 일부의 피해자는 회복적 사법의 결과로 더 두려워할 수 있다. • 피해자들이 회복적 사법의 결과로 권한 불균형을 초래할 수 있다. • 회복적 사법의 핵심쟁점은 재피해자화의 위험으로 인하여 피해자가 참여의 이점을 볼 수 있어야 하지만, 오히려 '이용'될 수 있다. • 회복적 사법이 지나치게 피해자에 대한 손상(harm)에 초점을 맞추고 강력범죄에서 핵심적 요소인 범법자의 정신태도를 경시하고 있다. • 회복적 사법이 공익보다는 사적 잘못(private wrong)에 지나치게 초점을 맞춘다. • 회복적 사법은 피해자와 가해자를 회복과정에 참여시킴으로써 처분의 불균형을 초래할 수 있는 것이다. 이러한 불균형은 법 앞에 동등한 보호를 받을 권리를 침해할 수 있다.[10]

9) 회복적 사법의 중심은 피해자의 사법과정에의 직접적인 개입을 통하여 사건을 종결할 수 있으며, 피해자가 추구하는 공식적 과정이 덜한 사법과정을 제공한다.

10) J. M. Balboni, "Balanced and Restorative Justice: Reengaging the Victim in the Justice Process," in Sgarzi and McDevitt(eds.), op. cit., pp. 369-382.

제 22 장 형벌과 범죄

제1절 형법과 범죄

1. 형법의 의의

1) 형법의 개념

형법이란 어떤 행위가 범죄이고 이에 대한 법률효과인 형벌 또는 보안처분을 규정한 법규범의 총체라고 할 수 있다.

2) 형법의 기능

(1) 규제적 기능

- 형법의 가장 근원적 기능으로써 행위규범 및 재판규범으로서의 기능으로써 일반국민과 법관을 규제한다.
- 형법은 범죄에 대한 국가형벌권의 행사를 명백히 함으로써 일반국민으로 하여금 형법의 준수를 명하는 동시에 사법관계자에 대해서는 범죄의 인정과 형벌적용의 지표로 삼도록 한다.

(2) 보호적 기능

- 법익보호와 사회윤리적 행위가치의 보호라는 사회질서의 기본가치를 보호하는 기능을 말한다.
- 법익보호의 기능은 보호적 기능의 핵심이다. 즉, 형법은 일정한 행위를 범죄로 하고 이에 대하여 형벌을 과할 것을 규정함으로써 범죄로부터 개인적 · 사회적 · 국가적

법익을 보호하는 기능을 한다.

- 사회윤리적 행위가치의 보호기능이란 사회공동체의 일원으로서 개인이 실천해야 할 행위의 가치를 보호하는 기능을 한다.
- 형법은 그 개입이 필요 불가결하다고 판단될 경우에 최후의 수단으로 시민의 자유에 개입할 수 있어야 한다는 보충성의 원칙이 적용된다.[1)]

(3) 보장적 기능

국가형벌권의 발동한계를 분명히 함으로써 국가형벌권의 자의적 행사로부터 시민(일반시민, 범죄인)의 자유와 권리를 보장하는 기능을 말한다.[2)]

(4) 사회보호적 기능

- 형벌과 보안처분이라는 수단에 의하여 범죄로부터 사회질서를 유지하고 보호하는 형법의 기능을 말한다.
- 범죄에 대하여 형벌, 보안처분을 예고함으로써 일반인의 범죄를 억제하도록 하는 일반예방기능과 범죄인의 재범의 위험성을 제거하여 사회복귀를 촉진하는 특별예방기능이 있다.

---

1) 국가형벌권의 행사는 겸허하게 억제되어야 한다는 의미에서 형법의 '겸억성'이라 부르기도 한다. 따라서 국가가 질서유지, 법익보호의 목적을 달성하기 위하여는 민법적·행정법적 제재수단을 우선적용하고 이에 의해서 목적을 달성할 수 없을 때 마지막 수단으로 형사제재를 적용하게 된다. 형사제재는 마지막 수단이라는 점에서 형법은 극히 미미한 일부분에만 적용되므로 이를 형법의 '단편성'이라고 한다.

2) • 일반국민에 대한 효과로써 형법은 일반국민에 대하여 형법에 규정되어 있는 범죄 이외에는 어떤 행위를 하더라도 범죄자로서 처벌받지 않는다는 것을 보장한다는 의미에서 국민에게 무한한 행동의 자유를 보장한다.
   • 범죄인에 대한 효과로써 비록 범죄인이라도 형법에 정해진 형벌의 범위 내에서만 처벌되고 그 이외의 부당한 처벌을 받지 아니할 것을 보장한다.

〈표 4-7〉 형법의 발전

구분	시기	주요 내용
복수시대 (사형(私刑))	• 원시시대~고대국가 형성 이전	• 사적 복수 • 종교적 · 미신적 사회규범 • 동해보복(同害報復)
위하시대 (형벌의 국가화)	• 고대국가~17세기	• 왕권강화와 공(公)형벌(刑罰) • 잔혹한 형벌제도 • 16세기 카톨리나 형법전 및 교회법 • 규문주의(죄형전단주의) • 일반예방주의의 강조
박애시대 (형벌의 법률화)	• 18세기 초~19세기 중엽	• 계몽주의 · 합리주의 · 민주주의 · 법치주의 • 개인의 자유와 인권의 중시 • 죄형법정주의의 확립 • 응보형주의의 강조 • 인도적 형벌제도 • Beccaria, Feuerbach, Kant, Hegel
과학시대 (형벌의 개별화)	• 19세기 후반~현대	• 범죄의 격증, 상습범, 소년범 • 특별예방주의의 강조 • 범죄인의 재사회화(특별예방주의) • 범죄인과 범죄원인에 대한 실증적 연구 • Lombroso, Ferri, Garofalo, Liszt

제2절 형벌과 범죄

1. 의의

- 형법의 기본관념에 대한 지도이념이 되는 법철학적 이론을 형법이론이라고 하며, 형벌이론과 범죄이론이 있다.
- 형벌이론에는 응보형주의와 목적형주의가 있으며, 목적형주의는 다시 일반예방주의와 특별예방주의로 나누어진다. 범죄이론에는 객관주의와 주관주의의 대립이 있다.

2. 형벌이론

1) 응보형주의

- 인간의 자기결정능력을 신뢰하고 국가의 사명을 개인적 자유의 보호에 제한하는 이상주의적·개인주의적·자유주의적 사상의 산물로, 형벌의 본질은 범죄에 대한 정당한 응보에 있다고 하는 사상이다.
- 응보형주의는 책임과 일치할 것을 요구함에 의하여 형벌권의 행사를 책임주의에 의해 제한하고자 한다.

2) 목적형주의

(1) 의의

형벌은 그 자체가 목적이 아니라 범죄를 방지하기 위한 예방의 수단에 지나지 않는다는 입장이다.

(2) 일반예방주의

- 일반예방주의는 형벌을 사회에 대한 위하적 작용으로 이해하여, 형벌의 목적은 일반인 즉, 잠재적 범죄인의 위하에 의한 범죄예방에 있다고 본다.
- 소극적 일반예방이란 범죄를 결심한 행위자가 그 행위로 인하여 받게 될 형벌을 생각하여 범죄를 단념하게 되는 효과를 말한다.
- 적극적 일반예방이란 형벌을 통하여 적극적으로 일반인의 규범의식을 강화하고 법규범에의 자발적인 복종을 가능케 함으로써 규범의 안정화를 가져오는 효과를 말한다.

(3) 특별예방주의

- 특별예방주의란 형벌의 목적을 범죄인에 대한 위하와 범죄인의 사회복귀 또는 격리를 통하여 바로 그 범죄인이 다시 죄를 범하는 것을 방지하는 데 있다고 본다.
- 집행유예, 선고유예, 가석방, 단기자유형의 제한, 상습범의 특별취급, 상대적 부정기형제도 등은 특별예방주의의 표현이다.

제3절 형벌의 종류

1. 형벌의 종류와 의의

1) 의의

- 형벌은 국가가 범죄에 대한 법률상의 효과로서 범죄자에 대하며 책임을 전제로 하여 과하는 법익의 박탈을 말한다. 형벌은 책임을 기초로 과하여지는 제재인 점에서, 범죄인의 위험성을 기초로 하는 보안처분과 구별된다.
- 형법이 규정하고 있는 형벌에는 생명형인 사형, 자유형인 징역 · 금고 · 구류, 명예형인 자격상실 · 자격정지, 재산형인 벌금 · 과료 · 몰수의 9종이 있다(제41조).

> **제41조(형의 종류)** 형의 종류는 다음과 같다.
> 1. 사형 2. 징역 3. 금고 4. 자격상실 5. 자격정지 6. 벌금
> 7. 구류 8. 과료 9. 몰수

- 과태료(행정질서벌)나 추징은 형법상 형벌이 아니다.

〈표 4-8〉 현행 형법상 형벌의 종류 2008, 2009, 2010 기출

생명형		사형(교수형, 군형법상 총살형)
자유형	징역	• 수형자를 교정시설에 구치하여 정역에 복무
	금고	• 징역과 유사하나 정역에 복무하지 않음
	구류	• 수형기간이 짧다는 점(1일 이상 30일 미만)에서 징역이나 금고와 구별
명예형	자격상실	• 일정한 자격이 상실
	자격정지	• 일정한 기간 동안 일정한 자격의 전부 또는 일부 정지
재산형	벌금	• 50,000원 이상으로 하며 상한은 무제한
	과료	• 2,000원 이상 50,000원 미만
	몰수	• 범죄반복의 방지나 범죄에 대한 이득의 금지를 목적으로 범죄행위와 관련된 재산박탈(다른 형에 부가하는 부가형이 원칙)

2) 사형

(1) 사형제도의 의의

수형자의 생명을 박탈하는 것을 내용으로 하는 형벌이다. 그 집행방법으로 형법은 교수형을 채택하고 있으며(제66조), 군형법에서는 총살형을 인정하고 있다(군형법 제3조).3)

(2) 사형존폐론

(가) 사형폐지론 2009 기출

사형의 폐지를 주장하는 입장으로써 Beccaria에 의하여 처음 주장되었다. i) 사형은 인간의 존엄과 가치를 보장하고 있는 헌법과 일치할 수 없고, ii) 오판에 의하여 집행된 때에는 그 잘못을 회복할 수 없으며, iii) 위하적 효과가 기대만큼 크지 않으며, 개선과 교육이라는 형벌의 목적을 전혀 달성할 수 없다는 점을 근거로 한다.

(나) 사형존치론

i) 사형의 위하적 효과를 부정할 수 없고, ii) 형벌의 본질이 응보에 있는 이상 극악한 범죄인에게는 사형을 선고하지 않을 수 없으며, iii) 일반인의 법의식을 근거로 하여 사형을 존치하여야 한다고 한다.4)

3) 자유형

(1) 자유형의 의의

수형자의 신체적 자유를 박탈하는 것을 내용으로 하는 형벌로서, 형법은 징역・금고・구류의 3종을 규정하고 있다.

> **제42조(징역 또는 금고의 기간)** 징역 또는 금고는 무기 또는 유기로 하고 유기는 1개월 이상 30년 이하로 한다. 단, 유기징역 또는 유기금고에 대하여 형을 가중하는 때에는 50년까지로 한다. 〈개정 2010.4.15〉
> **제67조(징역)** 징역은 형무소 내에 구치하여 정역에 복무하게 한다.
> **제68조(금고와 구류)** 금고와 구류는 형무소에 구치한다.

3) 사형제도를 통해 얻고자 하는 형벌의 목적은 응보・억제・무능력화이며, 교화가 아니다. 2010 기출
4) 다수설은 현실에 비추어 사형의 폐지는 아직 시기상조라는 태도를 취하고 있으며, 대법원도 사형은 헌법에 반하지 않는다고 판시하고 있다.

(2) 형법상의 자유형

(가) 징역

수형자를 교도소 내에 구치하여 정역에 복무하게 하는 것을 내용으로 하는 형벌이다(제67조). 무기와 유기의 2종이 있다. 유기는 1개월 이상 30년 이하이나, 형을 가중하는 때에는 50년까지로 한다(제42조).

(나) 금고

수형자를 교도소 내에 구치하여 자유를 박탈하는 것을 내용으로 하는 형벌로서(제68조), 정역에 복무하지 않는 점에서 징역과 구별된다. 금고에도 무기와 유기가 있으며, 그 형기는 징역의 경우와 같다.

(다) 구류

수형자를 교도소 내에 구치하지만, 그 기간이 1일 이상 30일 미만인 점에서 징역이나 금고와 구별된다(제46조).[5)]

> **제46조(구류)** 구류는 1일 이상 30일 미만으로 한다.

4) 재산형

(1) 재산형의 의의

범인으로부터 일정한 재산을 박탈하는 것을 내용으로 하는 형벌이다. 형법에는 벌금과 과료 및 몰수의 3종이 있다.

(2) 벌금과 과료

• 벌금은 일신전속적 성질을 가지므로 제3자의 대납이나 국가에 대한 채권과의 상계,

---

5) 자유형의 개선방안으로는 1) 자유형의 단일화 : 징역·금고·구류의 구별을 폐지하고 자유형을 단일화해야 한다는 견해이다. 징역·금고의 구별기준인 파렴치성의 판단이 그리 쉽지 않고, 형벌의 목적을 개선과 재사회화에 둔다면 우선 교정행정정책의 일관성을 유지하기 위해서도 단일화가 필요하며, 징역과 금고를 구별하는 것은 노동천시사상에 지나지 않고 실제로 금고수형자의 대부분이 신청에 의하여 정역에 종사하고 있는 점 등을 논거로 한다. 2) 단기자유형의 폐지 : 6월 이하의 단기자유형은 폐지 내지 제한되어야 한다는 주장이다. 단기자유형을 집행할 경우 수형자의 개선에 적합하지 않고, 범죄인은 이른바 지하문화 또는 부차문화(sub-culture)를 학습하여 범죄성을 강화하게 되고 범죄 배양효과·낙인효과가 심각하다는 역효과가 발생한다는 점을 논거로 한다.

제3자와의 연대책임, 상속 등은 원칙적으로 인정되지 않는다.[6)]

- 과료도 벌금형과 동일하나, 경미한 범죄에 대하여 적은 금액이 부과된다는 점에서 구별된다.

제45조(벌금) 벌금은 5만원 이상으로 한다. 다만, 감경하는 경우에는 5만원 미만으로 할 수 있다. 〈개정 1995.12.29〉

제47조(과료) 과료는 2천원 이상 5만원 미만으로 한다. 〈개정 1995.12.29〉

제69조(벌금과 과료) ① 벌금과 과료는 판결확정일로부터 30일 내에 납입하여야 한다. 단, 벌금을 선고할 때에는 동시에 그 금액을 완납할 때까지 노역장에 유치할 것을 명할 수 있다.
② 벌금을 납입하지 아니한 자는 1일 이상 3년 이하, 과료를 납입하지 아니한 자는 1일 이상 30일 미만의 기간 노역장에 유치하여 작업에 복무하게 한다.

제70조(노역장유치) 벌금 또는 과료를 선고할 때에는 납입하지 아니하는 경우의 유치기간을 정하여 동시에 선고하여야 한다.

제71조(유치일수의 공제) 벌금 또는 과료의 선고를 받은 자가 그 일부를 납입한 때에는 벌금 또는 과료액과 유치기간의 일수에 비례하여 납입금액에 상당한 일수를 제한다.

〈벌금형의 장 · 단점〉[7)] 2012 기출

구분	내용
장점	• 자유형보다는 형 집행비용이 적게 든다. • 수감으로 인한 실업 · 가정파탄 · 범죄오염 등의 위험성을 제거할 수 있다. • 주로 도박, 뇌물, 조세법위반, 경제사범 등의 이욕적인 범죄자에게 효과적이다. • 국고의 수입을 늘릴 수 있다. • 벌금형을 탄력적으로 운영하면 빈부에 따른 정상참작이 가능하다. • 단체 즉, 법인(法人)에 대한 적절한 형벌수단이 된다. • 오판 시 회복이 가능하고 신속한 업무처리를 할 수 있다. • 피해자와 범죄인의 명예보호적 측면도 있다. • 단기자유형의 대체방안으로써 형사정책상 비시설화의 도모로 인한 범죄자의 사회화에 기여한다.
단점	• 범죄자를 방치함으로써 공공의 안전을 해친다. • 경제적 능력이 있는 사람에게는 일반예방이나 특별예방효과를 거두기 어렵다. • 벌금납부를 위하여 새로운 범죄행위를 유발할 수 있다. • 현재 벌금미납자의 노역집행을 위한 별도의 시설이 없고, 대체로 노역수들이 건강상 문제가 많아 교정시설에서 실제적인 노역집행을 할 수 없는 경우가 허다하다. • 거액의 벌금미납자도 3년 이하의 노역으로 벌금을 대체할 수 있어서 형평성에 어긋난다.[8)] • 벌금의 징수가 어렵고 사법행정에 추가부담을 준다.

6) 벌금형의 개선책으로는 총액벌금제도 대신 일수벌금형제도와 벌금의 분납제도 등이 제시되고 있다.
7) 이윤호, 범죄학, 박영사, 2007:545-546.

(3) 몰수

(가) 의의

범죄반복의 방지나 범죄에 의한 이득의 금지를 목적으로 범죄행위와 관련된 재산을 박탈하는 것을 내용으로 하는 재산형이다.

> **제48조(몰수의 대상과 추징)** ① 범인 이외의 자의 소유에 속하지 아니하거나 범죄 후 범인 이외의 자가 정을 알면서 취득한 다음 기재의 물건은 전부 또는 일부를 몰수할 수 있다.
> 1. 범죄행위에 제공하였거나 제공하려고 한 물건
> 2. 범죄행위로 인하여 생하였거나 이로 인하여 취득한 물건
> 3. 전2호의 대가로 취득한 물건
>
> ② 전항에 기재한 물건을 몰수하기 불능한 때에는 그 가액을 추징한다.
> ③ 문서, 도화, 전자기록 등 특수매체기록 또는 유가증권의 일부가 몰수에 해당하는 때에는 그 부분을 폐기한다. 〈개정 1995.12.29〉

(나) 성질

① 부가형

> **제49조(몰수의 부가성)** 몰수는 타형에 부가하여 과한다. 단, 행위자에게 유죄의 재판을 아니할 때에도 몰수의 요건이 있는 때에는 몰수만을 선고할 수 있다.

② 대물적 보안처분 : 몰수는 형식적으로는 일종의 형벌이지만 실질적으로는 대물적 보안처분에 속한다(통설).

(4) 추징 · 폐기

추징은 몰수에 갈음하여 그 가액의 납부를 명령하는 사법처분이나, 몰수의 취지를 관철하기 위하여 인정된 제도하는 측면에서 부가형으로서의 성질을 갖는다.

> **제48조(몰수의 대상과 추징)** ② 전항에 기재한 물건을 몰수하기 불능한 때에는 그 가액을 추징한다.
> ③ 문서, 도화, 전자기록 등 특수매체기록 또는 유가증권의 일부가 몰수에 해당하는 때에는 그 부분을 폐기한다. 〈개정 1995.12.29〉

---

8) **제69조(벌금과 과료)** ① 벌금과 과료는 판결확정일로부터 30일 내에 납입하여야 한다. 단, 벌금을 선고할 때에는 동시에 그 금액을 완납할 때까지 노역장에 유치할 것을 명할 수 있다. ② 벌금을 납입하지 아니한 자는 1일 이상 3년 이하, 과료를 납입하지 아니한 자는 1일 이상 30일 미만의 기간 노역장에 유치하여 작업에 복무하게 한다.

5) 명예형

(1) 명예형의 의의

범인의 명예 또는 자격을 박탈하는 것을 내용으로 하는 형벌로서, 형법은 자격상실과 자격정지를 규정하고 있다.

(2) 자격상실

> **제43조(형의 선고와 자격상실, 자격정지)** ① 사형, 무기징역 또는 무기금고의 판결을 받은 자는 다음에 기재한 자격을 상실한다.
> 1. 공무원이 되는 자격
> 2. 공법상의 선거권과 피선거권
> 3. 법률로 요건을 정한 공법상의 업무에 관한 자격
> 4. 법인의 이사, 감사 또는 지배인 기타 법인의 업무에 관한 검사역이나 재산관리인이 되는 자격

(3) 자격정지

일정한 기간 동안 일정한 자격의 전부 또는 일부를 정지시키는 것을 내용으로 하는 형벌이다.

> **제43조(형의 선고와 자격상실, 자격정지)** ② 유기징역 또는 유기금고의 판결을 받은 자는 그 형의 집행이 종료하거나 면제될 때까지 전항 제1호 내지 제3호에 기재된 자격이 정지된다.

2. 형벌의 양정(量定)

1) 의의

- 법관이 구체적인 행위자에 대하여 선고할 형을 정하는 것을 형의 양정 또는 형의 적용이라고 한다.
- 협의로는 구체적인 사건에 적용될 형의 종류와 양을 정하는 것을 의미하고, 광의로는 그 형의 선고와 집행여부를 결정하는 것을 포함한다.

2) 형의 양정의 단계

법정형	처단형	선고형
• 개개의 구성요건에 규정되어 있는 형벌 • 형법은 상대적 법정형을 원칙으로 하고 있고, 여적죄(제93조)에 관하여만 절대적 법정형(사형)을 규정하고 있다.	• 법정형이 처단의 범위로 구체화된 형 즉, 법정형에 선택할 형종이 있는 경우에는 먼저 형종을 선택하고 그 형에 필요한 가중 감경을 한 형이 처단형이다. • 선고형의 최종적 기준이 된다.	• 법원이 처단형의 범위 내에서 구체적으로 형을 양정하여 당해 피고인에게 선고하는 형 • 선고형은 정기형이 원칙이나 소년범에 대해서는 상대적 부정기형을 인정하고 있다(소년법 제60조).
예 살인죄의 중지미수 사형, 무기, 5년 이상	예 법관이 유기징역 선택 2년 6월 이상 30년 이하	예 4년 선고

3. 양형(量刑)

1) 양형의 의의

법정형에 법률상의 가중・감경 또는 작량감경(酌量減輕)을 한 처단형의 범위에서 구체적으로 선고할 형을 정하는 것을 말한다.

2) 양형의 기준

양형은 형벌의 목적에 따라 결정되어야 한다. 따라서 양형에 있어서는 행위자의 책임뿐만 아니라 예방의 목적이 고려되어야 한다.

3) 양형의 조건

제51조(양형의 조건) 형을 정함에 있어서는 다음 사항을 참작하여야 한다.

1. 범인의 연령, 성행, 지능과 환경
2. 피해자에 대한 관계
3. 범행의 동기, 수단과 결과
4. 범행 후의 정황

4. 선고유예

1) 의의

- 선고유예란 범정(犯情)이 경미한 범죄에 대하여 일정한 기간 동안 형의 선고를 유예하고 그 유예기간을 경과한 때에는 면소(免訴)된 것으로 간주하는 제도이다.
- 선고유예의 취지는 장차 피고인의 사회복귀를 용이하게 하여 특별예방의 목적을 달성하기 위함이다.

2) 선고유예의 요건

- 1년 이하의 징역이나 금고, 자격정지 또는 벌금의 형을 선고할 경우일 것
- 개전(改悛)의 정상이 현저할 것
- 자격정지 이상의 형을 받은 전과가 없을 것

제59조(선고유예의 요건) ① 1년 이하의 징역이나 금고, 자격정지 또는 벌금의 형을 선고할 경우에 제51조의 사항을 참작하여 개전의 정상이 현저한 때에는 그 선고를 유예할 수 있다. 단, 자격정지 이상의 형을 받은 전과가 있는 자에 대하여는 예외로 한다.
② 형을 병과할 경우에도 형의 전부 또는 일부에 대하여 그 선고를 유예할 수 있다.

3) 선고유예와 보호관찰

제59조의2(보호관찰) ① 형의 선고를 유예하는 경우에 재범방지를 위하여 지도 및 원호가 필요한 때에는 보호관찰을 받을 것을 명할 수 있다.
② 제1항의 규정에 의한 보호관찰의 기간은 1년으로 한다. [본조신설 1995.12.29]

4) 선고유예의 효과

- 선고유예의 판결을 할 것인가는 법원의 재량에 속하나, 선고유예의 판결을 하는 경우에는 범죄사실과 선고할 형을 결정하여야 한다.
- 형의 선고유예를 받은 날로부터 2년을 경과한 때에는 면소된 것으로 간주한다(제60조). 즉, 유예기간은 언제나 2년이다.

> **제60조(선고유예의 효과)** 형의 선고유예를 받은 날로부터 2년을 경과한 때에는 면소된 것으로 간주한다.

5. 집행유예

1) 의의

- 형을 선고함에 있어서 일정한 기간 동안 형의 집행을 유예하고 그 유예기간을 경과한 때에는 형의 선고의 효력을 잃게 하는 제도를 말한다.
- 단기자유형의 피해방지와 범죄인의 조속한 사회복귀를 위한 특별예방의 관점에서 인정되는 제도이다.

2) 집행유예의 요건

- 3년 이하의 징역 또는 금고의 형을 선고할 경우일 것
- 정상에 참작할 만한 사유가 있을 것
- 금고 이상의 형을 선고한 판결이 확정된 때부터 그 집행을 종료하거나 면제된 후 3년까지의 기간에 범한 죄가 아닐 것

> **제62조(집행유예의 요건)** ① 3년 이하의 징역 또는 금고의 형을 선고할 경우에 제51조의 사항을 참작하여 그 정상에 참작할 만한 사유가 있는 때에는 1년 이상 5년 이하의 기간 형의 집행을 유예할 수 있다. 다만, 금고 이상의 형을 선고한 판결이 확정된 때부터 그 집행을 종료하거나 면제된 후 3년까지의 기간에 범한 죄에 대하여 형을 선고하는 경우에는 그러하지 아니하다. 〈개정 2005.7.29〉
> ② 형을 병과할 경우에는 그 형의 일부에 대하여 집행을 유예할 수 있다.

3) 집행유예와 보호관찰, 사회봉사명령 및 수강명령

- 형의 집행을 유예하는 경우에는 보호관찰을 받을 것을 명하거나 사회봉사 또는 수강을 명할 수 있다(제62조의2 제1항).
- 집행유예가 그 본래의 형사정책적 목표를 달성하기 위하여는 보호관찰에 의한 범죄

인의 생활형성에 대한 지도와 감독이 필요하기 때문이다.

- 보호관찰의 기간은 집행을 유예한 기간으로 한다. 다만, 법원은 유예기간의 범위 내에서 보호관찰기간을 정할 수 있다(동조 제2항).
- 사회봉사명령 또는 수강명령은 집행유예기간 내에 이를 집행한다(동조 제3항). 사회봉사명령은 유죄가 인정된 범죄자를 일정한 기간 내에 지정된 시간 동안 무보수로 근로에 종사하도록 하는 제도이며, 수강명령은 일정한 시간 동안 지정된 장소에 출석하여 강의, 훈련 또는 상담 등을 받도록 하는 제도이다.
- 보호관찰과 사회봉사명령을 동시에 명할 수 있다(판례).

제62조의2(보호관찰, 사회봉사 · 수강명령) ① 형의 집행을 유예하는 경우에는 보호관찰을 받을 것을 명하거나 사회봉사 또는 수강을 명할 수 있다.
② 제1항의 규정에 의한 보호관찰의 기간은 집행을 유예한 기간으로 한다. 다만, 법원은 유예기간의 범위 내에서 보호관찰기간을 정할 수 있다.
③ 사회봉사명령 또는 수강명령은 집행유예기간 내에 이를 집행한다.
[본조신설 1995.12.29]

6. 가석방

1) 의의

- 가석방이란 자유형을 집행받고 있는 자가 개전의 정이 현저하다고 인정되는 때 형기만료 전에 조건부로 수형자를 석방하고 일정한 기간을 경과한 때에는 형의집행을 종료한 것으로 간주하는 제도를 말한다.
- 가석방은 수형자의 사회복귀촉진이라는 특별예방사상과 정기형제도의 보완에 그 취지가 있고, 행정처분으로 형집행의 일부를 포기하는 형집행작용이다.

2) 가석방의 요건

- 징역 또는 금고의 집행 중에 있는 자가 무기에 있어서는 20년, 유기에 있어서는 형기의 3분의 1을 경과한 후일 것

- 행상이 양호하여 개전의 정이 현저할 것
- 벌금 또는 과료의 병과가 있는 때에는 그 금액을 완납할 것

> **제72조(가석방의 요건)** ① 징역 또는 금고의 집행 중에 있는 자가 그 행상이 양호하여 개전의 정이 현저한 때에는 무기에 있어서는 20년, 유기에 있어서는 형기의 3분의 1을 경과한 후 행정처분으로 가석방을 할 수 있다. 〈개정 2010.4.15〉
> ② 전항의 경우에 벌금 또는 과료의 병과가 있는 때에는 그 금액을 완납하여야 한다.
> **제73조(판결선고 전 구금과 가석방)** ① 형기에 산입된 판결선고 전 구금의 일수는 가석방에 있어서 집행을 경과한 기간에 산입한다.
> ② 벌금 또는 과료에 관한 유치기간에 산입된 판결선고 전 구금일수는 전조 제2항의 경우에 있어서 그에 해당하는 금액이 납입된 것으로 간주한다.

3) 가석방의 기간과 보호관찰

가석방된 자는 가석방기간 중 보호관찰을 받는다(동조 제2항). 가석방기간 동안에는 당연히 보호관찰이 개시된다(필요적 사항). 다만, 가석방을 허가한 행정관청이 필요가 없다고 인정한 때에는 그러하지 아니하다(동조 단서). 불필요한 보호관찰을 강제할 필요는 없기 때문이다.

> **제73조의2(가석방의 기간 및 보호관찰)** ① 가석방의 기간은 무기형에 있어서는 10년으로 하고, 유기형에 있어서는 남은 형기로 하되, 그 기간은 10년을 초과할 수 없다.
> ② 가석방된 자는 가석방기간 중 보호관찰을 받는다. 다만, 가석방을 허가한 행정관청이 필요가 없다고 인정한 때에는 그러하지 아니하다. [본조신설 1995.12.29]

4) 가석방의 효과

- 집행유예와 같이 형의 선고의 효력이 없어지는 것은 아니다.
- 가석방기간은 형의 집행이 종료된 것이 아니므로 이 기간 중 다시 죄를 범하여도 누범이 되지 않는다(판례).

> **제76조(가석방의 효과)** ① 가석방의 처분을 받은 후 그 처분이 실효 또는 취소되지 아니하고 가석방기간을 경과한 때에는 형의 집행을 종료한 것으로 본다. 〈개정 1995.12.29〉
> ② 전2조의 경우에는 가석방 중의 일수는 형기에 산입하지 아니한다.

7. 보안처분

1) 의의

- 형벌로는 행위자의 사회복귀와 범죄의 예방이 불가능하거나 행위자의 특수한 위험성으로 인하여 형벌의 목적을 달성할 수 없는 경우에 형벌을 대체하거나 보완하기 위한 예방적 성질의 목적적 조치를 말한다.[9)]
- 보안처분은 행위자의 사회적 위험성을 전제로 하여 특별예방의 관점에서 선고되는 것이라는 점에서 책임을 전제로 한 형벌과 구별된다. 형벌은 책임주의에 의하여 제한되나, 보안처분은 비례성의 원칙에 의하여 제한된다.

2) 보안처분의 종류와 성질

(1) 보안처분의 정당성

- 헌법 제12조 제1항은 '누구든지 법률과 적법한 절차에 의하지 않고는 보안처분을 받지 아니한다'고 규정하여 보안처분에 대한 헌법적 근거를 마련하고 있다.
- 보안처분에는 책임주의가 적용되지 않지만 일반적인 법원칙으로서의 비례성의 원칙이 적용되는 범위에서만 정당화될 수 있다.

(2) 보안처분의 종류

(가) 대인적 보안처분과 대물적 보안처분

- 대인적 보안처분 : 장래의 범죄행위를 방지하기 위하여 특정인에게 선고되는 보안처분을 말한다. 예 치료감호처분, 교정처분, 보호관찰 등

---

9) E. F. Klein에 의하여 최초로 주장된 보안처분은 Franz v. Liszt의 보안형벌을 거쳐 현대적 의미의 보안처분으로 실현되었다.

• 대물적 보안처분 : 범죄와 법익침해의 방지를 목적으로 하는 물건에 대한 보안처분을 말한다. 예 몰수, 영업소 폐쇄

(나) 자유박탈 보안처분과 자유제한 보안처분

구 분		종 류
대인적 보안처분	자유박탈 보안처분	• 치료감호처분 : 형벌의 효과를 기대하기 어렵거나 재범의 우려가 있는 책임능력결함에 대한 처분 • 교정처분 : 교정소 또는 금주시설 수용처분, 약물 등 중독성범인에 대한 수용처분 • 보호감호처분 : 사상범 · 상습범 · 누범의 위험이 있는 강력범에 대한 자유형집행 후의 수용처분 • 노동시설수용처분 : 상습적인 부랑자 · 걸인 · 매춘부 등 노동혐기자에 대한 노동소 수용처분 • 사회치료처분 : 인격장애가 있는 누범자, 성적 충동범인 등 범죄성 정신병질자에 대한 사회치료시설 수용처분
	자유제한 보안처분	• 보호관찰 : 형벌집행 없이 사회생활을 하면서 보호관찰기관의 지도 · 감독 · 보도를 받게 하는 처분 • 선행보증 : 집행유예나 가석방의 경우 보증금제공 또는 보증인을 내세워 선행을 확보하는 처분 • 직업금지 : 직업상 또는 업무상의 의무에 위배되는 행위를 하거나 할 위험이 있는 자에 대한 당해 직업이나 영업금지 처분 • 기타 : 주거제한, 국외추방, 단종 · 거세, 주점출입금지, 운전면허 박탈
대물적 보안처분		• 몰수, 영업소 폐쇄, 법인 해산

(3) 현행법상 보안처분

학 설	내 용
치료감호법	• 치료감호처분 • 보호관찰처분
기타 법률	• 형법상의 보호관찰 · 사회봉사명령 · 수강명령 (제59조의2, 제62조의2, 제73조의2 제2항) • 소년법상의 보호처분 및 사회봉사명령 · 수강명령(제23조) • 보호관찰 등에 관한 법률상의 보호관찰처분(제3, 29, 30조) • 보안관찰법(구 사회안전법 대체입법)상의 보안관찰처분 • 성폭력범죄의 처벌 등에 관한 특례법상의 보호관찰(제16조) • 마약류관리에 관한 법률상의 중독자에 대한 치료보호 (마약류관리에 관한 법률 제40조 등) • 감염병의 예방 및 관리에 관한 법률상의 일정한 감염병환자의 강제처분 (제42조) • 국가보안법상의 공소보류자에 대한 감시 · 보도(제20조) • 성매매알선 등 행위의 처벌에 관한 법률상의 윤락녀의 보호지도소 수용 (제4조) • 출입국관리법상의 국외강제퇴거처분(제46조)

제 23 장 교정과 범죄

제1절 교정이론

1. 행형목적에 관한 이론[1)]

1) 응보형주의

- 응보형주의는 절대국가에 대응한 죄형균형의 원칙에서 나온 것으로, 범죄에 대해 동일한 처벌인 응보를 부과함으로써 사회질서가 유지된다고 보았다.
- 행형을 형벌 그 자체로만 파악하였으며, 칸트, 헤겔, 슈탈 등이 주장하였고, 19세기 중반까지 중시된 교정이념이다.
- 응보형주의는 책임주의로, 책임 있는 자만을 처벌하므로 책임무능력자의 존재를 인정한다.

2) 목적형주의

- 목적형주의는 자유의사론이 아닌 인간의 의사는 환경 등에 의해 결정된다는 의사결정론을 전제로 한다.
- 범죄의 행함과 행하지 않음은 오직 인간의 개인적 자유의사에 의해서 결정되는 것이 아니라 그의 성격과 그를 둘러싼 여러 사회적 환경 때문에 발생된다고 본다.
- 리스트가 주장한 것으로써 형벌을 수단으로 하여 개선 · 교화하려는 목적지향성을

1) • 천정환, 신범죄학, 백산출판사, 2006:511-517.
• 교정이념에는 사회복귀, 무력화, 응보 등이 있다. 2007 기출

인정하는 것이다. 즉, 범죄는 그의 의지로 생기는 것이 아니고 환경에 적응치 못하는 성격에 의해 발생하므로, 책임여부와 관계없이 그 성격을 교정하는 것이 형벌의 목적이고, 따로 책임무능력자를 구별할 필요가 없어 책임무능력자의 존재를 부정하며, 나아가 교화와 개선을 통해 범죄인을 재사회화시킬 것을 강조했다.

3) 교육형주의

- "형벌은 교육이다"를 바탕으로 교정 · 교화를 통해 재범을 막는 데 형벌의 목적을 두었다. 즉, 재사회화의 방법으로 교육수단을 강조했다.
- 범죄원인과 범죄인의 성격을 조사해 그에 맞는 교육적인 행형관리를 행형의 본질로 본다.
- 교육형주의는 목적형주의를 발전적으로 승화한 이론으로 리스트의 제자인 Lanza, Saldana, Liepmann이 주장했다. 교정교육프로그램의 개발을 중요시하게 된다.

2. 교정처우의 원리

교정처우란 법원의 재판에 의해 자유형이 확정된 범죄인에 대하여 법원이 정한 교정재(correction service)의 생산기간 내에 교정시설 내에서 교정공무원, 교정위원 등과 수형자의 쌍방적 협동 또는 일방적 지도[2)]로써 행해지는 각종 처우라고 정의할 수 있다.[3)]

1) 인도주의

- 재소자를 처우할 때 인도적 · 인간적 방법으로 처우하자는 입장이다.
- 비인간적인 수용(남녀혼합 구금)상태의 폐단을 지적하고 감옥개량운동을 전개한 Howard의 감옥상태론, '범죄와 형벌'에서 형벌은 목적을 위한 최소한의 수단으로 해야 되고 비인간적인 사형폐지를 주장한 Beccaria, 열악한 수용상태에 놓인 죄수들을 돕기 위해 필라델피아 수인(囚人)구호협회(1776)를 결성한 Wister, 누진제에 점수제를 결합한 가석방제도를 실시한 마코노키 등이 관계된다.

---

2) 미성숙된 수형자에게는 교정공무원 등이 교정재를 주도적 지위에서 생산해야 한다.
3) 최근 우리나라 교정처우의 변화로는 민영교도소 도입, 지역기반 교정확대, 수형자의 인권에 대한 관심 확대, 전자감시 등의 도입 등이 있다. 2007 기출

2) 법률주의

수형자를 처우할 때 법률에 의해 처우하라는 것이다. 행형법은 수형자의 마그나카르타이다.

3) 과학주의

범죄인 처우와 기술에 각종 과학적 방법 즉, 범죄인의 과학적 분류와 처우 및 범죄예측에도 과학적 방법이 도입되었다.

4) 처우의 개별화

- 수행자는 인성과 환경 등이 제각기 다르므로 교화를 위한 처우는 개별적으로 적용시켜야 한다는 것으로 실증주의적 관점에서 강조되고 있다.
- 처우의 개별화의 전제는 과학적인 분류심사제의 개발, 분류심사 전문요원의 확보, 시설의 다양화, 재량권의 확대 등이 요구된다.[4)]
- 처우의 개별화는 실무에서 운용을 잘못하면 처우의 불평등과 형벌의 공평성이 침해될 수도 있다.

5) 처우의 사회화

- 교정시설 내에서의 죄수들의 생활은 가능한 일반사회의 생활상태와 비슷하게 하자는 유사화 원칙으로써 사회접근주의라고도 한다. 예 부부접견제도
- 교정재의 생산은 과거처럼 완전히 폐쇄된 격리된 공간에서보다는 교정시설 내의 교도소 사회도 가능한 일반사회와 유사하게 꾸며 놓을 때 교정재의 생산성이 훨씬 높고 생산된 교정재도 내구성이 오래 간다는 전제하에서 나온 교정처우의 지도원리이다.[5)]

---

4) 처우의 개별화는 처우의 단일화에 반대되는 개념이다. 즉, 각 개인에게 맞는 교육과 작업, 교화를 통해 사회복귀를 도모하자는 것이다.

5) 천정환 박사는 처우의 사회화를 중시하여 교도소 내의 교정공무원 중 여성공무원의 비율을 높일 것과 수형자에게 완전한 Sex권의 보장, 흡연권의 보장, 장애인도 교정공무원으로 임용시킬 것, 일정요건하에서의 음주권의 보장 등을 주장하고 있다.

제2절 소년보호처분

1. 소년보호의 원칙 2010 기출

소년법상 보호처분규정은 보호사건에 대한 일반법적 성격을 가지고 있고, 형사사건에 대한 규정은 형사법에 대한 특별법적 성격을 가지고 있고, 실체법과 절차법의 성격을 모두 가지고 있다.[6]

1) 실체법적 성격

(1) 보호주의

소년의 건전한 육성을 위해 보호사건에는 보호처분을, 형사처분에는 특칙을 적용한다.

(2) 교육주의

소년보호의 절차에 보호활동의 모든 과정에서 교육적 정신이 관철되어야 한다. 따라서 소년범죄에 대해서는 처벌을 위주로 할 것이 아니라 치료・개선을 우선적으로 해야 한다.

(3) 인격주의와 규범주의

소년보호는 소년의 인격에 내재하는 범죄적 위험성을 제거하여 소년의 건전한 육성을 목적으로 하여야 한다. 이를 위해서는 소년의 행위・태도에 나타난 개성과 환경을 중시하여 소년의 인격과 관련된 개인적 범죄특성도 함께 고려하여야 한다.

(4) 예방주의

소년보호는 이미 죄를 범한 소년의 처벌이 아니라 그 소년이 더 이상 범죄를 범하지 않도록 하고, 우범소년도 그 대상으로 하여 소년이 사회에 적응하지 못하는 상태에 빠지지 않도록 보호・육성하여야 한다.

6) 소년사법제도의 기본이념은 국친주의, 예방주의, 교육주의이다. 2008 기출

2) 절차법적 성격

(1) 개별주의

소년 개개인을 1건으로 독립해서 취급하고, 그 개성을 중시하여 범죄인에게 알맞은 처우를 전개하여야 한다.

(2) 직권주의

법원이 적극적・지도적인 입장에서 심리를 진행하는데, 이는 국가의 후견적 역할이 강조되는 소년법상의 원칙의 표현이다.

(3) 과학주의

소년범죄인의 처우를 단지 법률에만 의뢰하지 말고 정신의학・심리학・사회학・ 교육학 등의 전문가의 협력을 얻어 그들의 진단과 의견을 참작하여야 한다.

(4) 밀행주의

인권보장이나 재범방지의 측면에서 어느 나라의 소년법이든 소년심판의 비공개와 함께 기사게재・방송 등의 보도를 금지 또는 제한하는 규정을 두고 있다.

(5) 통고주의

전 국민의 협력으로 요보호성이 있는 소년을 조기에 발견하자는 데 취지가 있다. 소년법은 보호자 또는 학교와 사회복지시설의 장(長)도 범죄・촉법・우범소년을 관할하는 소년부에 통고할 수 있도록 하고 있다.

「소년업무 처리규칙」

[시행 2009.11.19] [경찰청예규 제413호, 2009.11.19, 타법개정]

제7조(소년경찰의 기본정신) 소년경찰활동은 다음 각 호의 사항을 기본정신으로 한다.

1. 건전육성의 정신 : 소년경찰활동은 소년을 건전하게 지도・육성・보호함을 근본으로 한다.
2. 소년의 특성 이해 : 소년의 심리・생리, 기타의 특성을 깊이 이해하고 선도를 행한다.
3. 처우의 개별화 : 소년범죄 등 비행은 구성요건을 규명하기보다는 소년의 성행 및 환경, 기타 비행의 원인을 정확히 파악하여 개별적으로 타당한 선도 및 처우를 행한다.

4. 처우의 과학화 : 소년의 선도와 처우는 과학적 지식과 방법으로 조사·분석, 검토하여 결정한다.
5. 비밀의 보장 : 소년의 선도와 처우는 소년의 인격과 자주성을 존중하고, 비밀을 보장하여 소년 및 관계자가 불안을 갖지 않도록 한다.
6. 관계자의 존경과 신뢰의 획득 : 인격의 향상과 식견의 함양에 힘써 소년 및 관계자로부터 존경과 신뢰를 얻는다.

2. 소년범 대책

1) 소년범의 분류 2008, 2011 기출

소년법 및 소년업무처리규칙(경찰청예규)에서는 소년을 비행소년, 불량행위소년, 요보호소년으로 나누고 있으며, 비행소년은 다시 범죄소년, 촉법소년, 우범소년으로 나뉜다.

〈표 4-9〉 소년업무처리규칙상 소년의 분류

비행소년	• 범죄소년, 촉법소년, 우범소년 중 어느 하나에 해당되는 자
불량행위소년	• 비행소년은 아니지만 음주, 흡연, 싸움, 기타 자기 또는 타인의 덕성을 해하는 행위를 하는 소년
요보호소년	• 비행소년은 아니지만 학대, 혹사, 방임된 소년 또는 보호자로부터 유기·이탈되었거나 그 보호자가 양육할 수 없는 경우나, 기타 경찰관직무집행법 제4조 또는 아동복지법에 따른 보호를 필요로 하는 자

분 류		연 령	행 위
요보호소년	범죄소년	14세 이상 19세 미만	• 형벌법령에 저촉되는 행위 • 범죄를 저지른 범죄소년은 보호처분의 대상
	촉법소년[7]	10세 이상 14세 미만	• 형벌법령에 저촉되는 행위 • 형사미성년자로서 범죄를 저지른 촉법소년은 보호처분의 대상

	우범 소년	10세 이상 19세 미만	• 법에 저촉되는 행위는 하지 않았으나 우범소년에 해당하는 소년은 보호처분의 대상 • 다음에 해당하는 사유가 있고 그의 성격이나 환경에 비추어 앞으로 형벌 법령에 저촉되는 행위를 할 우려가 있는 10세 이상인 소년 i) 집단적으로 몰려다니며 주위 사람들에게 불안감을 조성하는 성벽이 있는 것 ii) 정당한 이유 없이 가출하는 것 iii) 술을 마시고 소란을 피우거나 유해환경에 접하는 성벽이 있는 것

소년법 제1조(목적) 이 법은 반사회성(反社會性)이 있는 소년의 환경 조정과 품행 교정(矯正)을 위한 보호처분 등의 필요한 조치를 하고, 형사처분에 관한 특별조치를 함으로써 소년이 건전하게 성장하도록 돕는 것을 목적으로 한다. [전문개정 2007.12.21]

제2조(소년 및 보호자) 이 법에서 "소년"이란 19세 미만인 자를 말하며, "보호자"란 법률상 감호교육(監護教育)을 할 의무가 있는 자 또는 현재 감호하는 자를 말한다.
[전문개정 2007.12.21]

제3조(관할 및 직능) ① 소년 보호사건의 관할은 소년의 행위지, 거주지 또는 현재지로 한다.
② 소년 보호사건은 가정법원소년부 또는 지방법원소년부[이하 "소년부(少年部)"라 한다]에 속한다.
③ 소년 보호사건의 심리(審理)와 처분 결정은 소년부 단독판사가 한다.
[전문개정 2007.12.21]

제4조(보호의 대상과 송치 및 통고) ① 다음 각 호의 어느 하나에 해당하는 소년은 소년부의 보호사건으로 심리한다.
1. 죄를 범한 소년
2. 형벌 법령에 저촉되는 행위를 한 10세 이상 14세 미만인 소년
3. 다음 각 목에 해당하는 사유가 있고 그의 성격이나 환경에 비추어 앞으로 형벌 법령에 저촉되는 행위를 할 우려가 있는 10세 이상인 소년
가. 집단적으로 몰려다니며 주위 사람들에게 불안감을 조성하는 성벽(性癖)이 있는 것
나. 정당한 이유 없이 가출하는 것
다. 술을 마시고 소란을 피우거나 유해환경에 접하는 성벽이 있는 것
② 제1항제2호 및 제3호에 해당하는 소년이 있을 때에는 경찰서장은 직접 관할 소년부에

---

7) • 10세 이상 14세 미만의 자가 저지른 형사처벌 대상이 되는 행위는 '촉법행위'이다. 2004 기출
• 소년법에서 형벌법령에 저촉되는 행위를 한 만 10세 이상 만 14세 미만의 청소년들은 '촉법소년'이다. 2007 기출
• 2007년 12월 21일에 개정된 소년법에 의하여 촉법소년의 적용연령은 '10세 이상 14세 미만'이다. 2007.12.21. 개정 소년법, 참조. 2008 기출

송치(送致)하여야 한다.

③ 제1항 각 호의 어느 하나에 해당하는 소년을 발견한 보호자 또는 학교·사회복리시설·보호관찰소(보호관찰지소를 포함한다. 이하 같다)의 장은 이를 관할 소년부에 통고할 수 있다. [전문개정 2007.12.21]

「소년업무 처리규칙」

[시행 2009.11.19] [경찰청예규 제413호, 2009.11.19, 타법개정]

제1장 총칙

제1절 통칙

제1조(목적) ① 이 규칙은 소년을 과학적으로 선도·보호하고 유해환경을 정화하며, 비행을 방지하고 비행소년을 합리적으로 처우함으로써 소년을 건전하게 지도육성하기 위하여 소년업무 처리의 지침을 정함을 목적으로 한다.

② 소년업무 처리에 관하여는 「경찰관직무집행법」, 「소년법」, 「형사소송법」, 「아동복지법」, 「청소년보호법」, 「사법경찰관리집무규칙」, 「범죄수사규칙」 등 기타 법령에 특별한 규정이 있는 경우를 제외하고는 이 규칙이 정하는 바에 따른다.

제2조(정의) 이 규칙에서 사용하는 용어의 정의는 다음과 같다.

1. “소년”이란 소년법(이하 “법”이라 한다) 제2조의 규정에 해당되는 자를 말한다.
2. “범죄소년”이란 법 제4조제1항제1호의 규정에 해당되는 자를 말한다.
3. “촉법소년”이란 법 제4조제1항제2호의 규정에 해당되는 자를 말한다.
4. “우범소년”이란 법 제4조제1항제3호의 규정에 해당되는 자를 말한다.
5. “비행소년”이란 범죄소년, 촉법소년, 우범소년 중 어느 하나에 해당되는 자를 말한다.
6. “불량행위소년”이란 비행소년은 아니지만 음주·흡연·싸움 기타 자기 또는 타인의 덕성을 해하는 행위를 하는 소년을 말한다.
7. “요보호소년”이란 비행소년은 아니지만 학대·혹사·방임된 소년 또는 보호자로부터 유기·이탈되었거나 그 보호자가 양육할 수 없는 경우나 기타 「경찰관직무집행법」 제4조 또는 「아동복지법」에 따른 보호를 필요로 하는 자를 말한다.
8. “보호자”란 친권자, 후견인, 법정대리인, 재학하는 학교의 장, 담임교사, 기숙사의 사감, 아동복지시설의 장, 고용주 또는 대리인 등 소년을 직접 보호 감독하는 자를 말한다.
9. “관계자”란 보호자 및 피해자, 고소인 또는 고발인, 증인 기타 소년의 선도 또는 소년사건 처리에 직·간접으로 관계있는 자를 말한다.

2) 소년보호처분의 종류 및 기간[8] 2011, 2012 기출

소년보호처분의 종류	소년보호처분의 기간
• 보호자 또는 보호자를 대신하여 소년을 보호할 수 있는 자에게 감호 위탁	• 6개월(6개월 범위에서 1차 연장가능)
• 수강명령	• 100시간 이하
• 사회봉사명령	• 200시간 이하
• 보호관찰관의 단기보호관찰	• 1년
• 보호관찰관의 장기보호관찰	• 2년(1년의 범위에서 1차 연장가능)
• 아동복지시설이나 그 밖의 소년보호시설에 감호 위탁	• 6개월(6개월 범위에서 1차 연장가능)
• 병원, 요양소, 또는 소년의료보호시설에 위탁	• 6개월(6개월 범위에서 1차 연장가능)
• 1개월 이내의 소년원 송치	–
• 단기 소년원 송치	• 6개월 이하
• 장기 소년원 송치	• 2년 이하

3) 형사처분의 특칙 2009 기출

(1) 대상자

형사처분의 대상은 비행소년 중 범죄소년에게만 해당된다.

(2) 조사 · 심리상의 배려

법원은 소년형사사건에 관하여 그 필요한 사항을 조사하도록 조사관에게 위촉할 수 있으며, 사건심리에 있어서도 관련 피의사건과 그 절차를 분리해야 한다.

(3) 사형과 무기형의 완화

행위 시 18세 미만인 소년에 대해서는 사형 또는 무기형을 과할 경우, 15년의 유기징역에 처해야 한다.[9]

8) 소년보호처분의 유형에는 보호자 또는 보호자를 대신하여 소년을 보호할 수 있는 자에게 감호위탁, 사회봉사명령, 1개월 이내의 소년원 송치 등이 있으나, '병영훈련캠프'는 해당되지 않는다. 2010 기출
9) 형사사건이라도 소년에 대해서는 사형을 선고하지 않으며, 교정성적이 양호한 소년원생은 가퇴원할 수 있다.

(4) 상대적 부정기형의 인정

소년이 법정형 장기 2년 이상의 유기형에 해당하는 죄를 범한 때에는, 장기 10년, 단기 5년 내의 범위에서 부정기형을 선고한다.

(5) 분리 · 분계주의

소년의 유기형 집행은 소년교도소 또는 일반교도소의 분계된 장소에서 집행한다.

제3절 비범죄화

1. 의의 2011, 2012 기출

Naucke는 비범죄화(decriminalization)[10]란 지금까지의 가벌적인 행위가 처벌되지 않게 되는 과정이며, 이미 범죄로 처벌하고 있던 행위에 대한 형벌권의 폐지나 철회, 형벌의 경감조치 등을 포함하기에, 비범죄화(delegalization), 비형벌화(depenalization), 다이버전(diversion)[11][12] 등으로 구분하기도 한다.

2. 우리나라 비범죄화 논의의 전개

1) 1988년 제2차 형법개정

형법 제104조의 2의 국가모독죄[13] 조항이 삭제되었다. 이는 군부독재 청산작업의 일환으로 이루어졌다.

---

10) Ancel이 1966년, '신사회 방위론'에서 최초로 주장하였다.

11) 다이버전(Diversion)이란 범죄인의 자연스런 사회복귀와 재범방지를 위해서 사법처리 대신에 지역사회의 보호와 관찰 등을 실시해야 한다는 제도를 말한다. 이는 형사사법의 탈제도화라는 의미에서 낙인이론의 산물이라고 할 수 있다. 2009 기출

12) 전환제도(Diversion)의 장점은 형사사법절차의 과중한 부담을 해소할 수 있는 방법이 되며, 형사사법제도로부터 조기에 이탈시킴으로써 낙인효과를 억제할 수 있으며, 범죄자에 대한 인도적 처우 등 인도주의적 형사사법제도의 형성에 기여할 수 있다. 2004 기출

13) 국가모독죄는 정권안보의 차원에서 반대세력들의 비판을 차단하기 위해서 1975년 제1차 개정형법에서 신설한 것이었다.

2) 1995년 제3차 형법개정

공연음란죄, 도박죄, 혼인빙자간음죄, 간통죄,[14] 혼인목적약취유인죄 등 경미한 범죄가 논의되었다.

3) 2009년, 헌법재판소는 혼인빙자간음죄에 대해 위헌결정을 내렸다.[15]

3. 비범죄화의 분류

1) 입법단계에서의 비범죄화(법률상의 비범죄화)

(1) 형벌폐지입법에 의한 비범죄화

- 입법작용에 의하여 형벌법규가 무효화됨으로써 이루어지는 비범죄화로써, 실정법상의 형벌법규 자체가 대체입법 없이 무조건 삭제되는 경우는 순수한 형태의 비범죄화이다.
- Naucke는 선언적 비범죄화와 실질적 비범죄화로 구분하고 있다.[16][17]

---

14) • 간통행위는 단순히 도덕적·윤리적 비난의 대상에 불과하므로 처벌대상에서 제외해야 한다고 주장하는 것은 '비범죄화'이다. 2008 기출
- 간통죄 폐지의 논거는 간통행위의 불벌(不罰)은 세계적으로 입법추세하는 점(1964년 제9회 국제형법회의에서 간통을 처벌하지 않기로 결의하였고, 현재 간통처벌국가는 중국과 우리나라뿐이다), 헌법상의 인간의 존엄과 행복추구권의 보장은 개인의 성적 자기결정권을 존중함을 요청한다(개인적 자유주의 사상)는 점, 형법은 개인의 사생활 질서, 특히 성(性)에 관계된 사적 윤리에는 간섭해서는 안 된다는 점, 동의하는 간통행위에는 원칙적으로 피해자가 없다는 점, 암수(暗數)가 많고 법의 실효성이 거의 없다는 점, 형사정책적으로 볼 때 형벌의 범죄억지효과나 재사회화의 효과는 거의 없다는 점, 간통죄를 존치시킴으로써 범죄의 예방적 효과가 있을 것으로 생각하는 것은 우리의 고정관념에서만 유지되고 있는 생각이지 아무런 실증적 근거가 없다는 점 등 총 11가지 이유를 제시하고 있다. 법무부, 형사법개정공청회 자료집, 형사법개정자료(XII), 1992:411-412. 하지만 여론조사 결과 3분의 2 이상이 간통행위 처벌의 찬성을 원한다는 이유로 간통죄는 그대로 존치되었다.

15) 형법 제304호의 「혼인빙자간음죄」에 대한 위헌결정 선고, 헌법재판소가 결정한 형법조항에 대한 최초의 단순위헌판결이며, 형법조항에 대한 법률상의 비범죄화를 이끌어내기 위한 시도이다. 그러나 입법기관의 역할을 사법기관이 대신 행함으로써, 헌법재판소의 형사처벌조항 위헌결정의 소급효에 따라 수많은 재심과 국가에 대한 손해배상 청구사건을 조장하였다.

16) • 선언적 비범죄화 : 잠재적 피해자로부터의 사회적 저항도 없이 형벌을 대체할 다른 수단이 강구되지도 않은 상태에서 그대로 사라지는 것.
- 실질적 비범죄화: 잠재적 피해자로부터의 사회적 저항이 있음에도 불구하고 형벌을 대체할 다

(2) 형벌조정입법에 의한 비범죄화

• 일정한 행위유형을 범죄로 규정하되 그에 대한 법률효과인 법정형의 조정을 통한 비범죄화와 법정(法定)형의 하향조정과 대체 형벌의 신설에 의한 비범죄화가 있다.

예 사형만을 규정하고 있는 조항에 자유형을 선택형으로 추가하거나, 사형을 삭제하고 무기징역형을 두는 방법, 자유형만을 규정하고 있는 조항에 벌금형을 선택형으로 추가하거나, 자유형의 형기를 낮추는 방법

(3) 형법대체입법에 의한 비범죄화

여전히 일탈행위로 규정되어야 하는 행위에 대하여 기존의 좁은 의미에서의 형벌규정은 삭제하되 다른 형태의 제재를 부과하는 비범죄화이다.

① 제3의 형사제재로의 대체

i) 보안처분으로의 대체

• 보안처분은 범죄로부터 사회를 방위하고 범죄자를 재사회화하기 위한 방법으로서, 특정범죄자에 대하여 형벌부과만으로는 형사제재로서의 목적달성이 부적합하거나 혹은 법적 관점에서 형벌이 허용되지 않는 경우에 시행하는 처분이다.

• 대인적 보안처분인 치료감호, 선행보증, 주거제한, 전자감시와 대물적 보안처분인 영업장 폐쇄, 법인의 해산명령이 있다.

ii) 보호관찰, 사회봉사변경, 수강명령으로의 대체 예 성구매자 재범방지 교육(존스쿨제도) : 형벌이 선고되지 않고 검찰단계에서 기소유예의 조건으로 부과되는 처분

② 행정제재로의 대체

형사처벌 대신 행정질서벌을 확대하여 각종 행정법규 위반자에 대하여는 행정벌을 가하는 형태의 비범죄화 유형으로써, 경미범죄, 행정범의 성격이 강한 범죄영역에서 볼 수 있다. 예 독일, 성매매행위를 비범죄화하였지만, 학교·병원 등 금지구역에서 행할 경우에는 질서

른 수단이 강구되지 않은 상태에서 그대로 사라지는 것으로써, 사회가 일정한 행위에 대한 처벌상의 이익을 완전히 상실하여, 비범죄화와 동시에 해당행위가 법적·사회적으로 완전히 승인되는 경우. 예 일본·독일 등에서의 간통죄 폐지입법, 독일, 1969년, 수간(獸姦), 성인 간의 동성애에 대한 처벌규정 삭제.

17) 최협의의 비범죄화, 가장 완벽한 형태의 비범죄화, 진정한 의미의 비범죄화, 순수한 의미의 비범죄화, 비범죄화의 정도(正道)라고도 한다.

위반법에 위반되어 질서위반금을 부과하게 된다. 그러나 집요하게 금지구역에서 성매매행위를 할 경우에는 형법상의 문제로 되어 경죄(輕罪)로 처벌받게 된다.

③ 사회법으로의 대체

형법상의 '낙태죄'를 특정한 경우에 있어서 비범죄화하였다. 예 모자보건법(2010.1.18. 개정, 법률 제9932호) 제14조(인공임신중절수술의 허용한계)

④ 보험법으로의 대체

헌법재판소는 2009년, 교통사고처리특례법 본문 중 업무상 과실 또는 중대한 과실로 인한 교통사고로 말미암아 피해자로 하여금 중상해에 이르게 한 경우에 공소를 제기할 수 없도록 규정한 부분이 헌법에 위반된다고 선고하여 위헌결정을 하였다.

⑤ 민사제재로의 대체

i) 민사금전벌로의 대체

- 행정관청 또는 법원이 행정상의 의무확보수단으로써 의무위반행위를 한 자에게 민사절차에 의하여 금전벌을 부과하는 제도이다.
- 화해와 용서를 통해 갈등을 해소하고자 하는 이론으로서 미국의 민사금전벌제도(civil money penalties)와 같은 회복적 사법이론에 따른 것이다.

ii) 민사적 원상회복으로의 대체

가해자에게 피해자에 대한 원상회복을 위한 이행급부를 부과하고 형벌을 포기하는 제도이며, 피해자와 가해자 사이의 화해와 연대성 회복에 중점을 두고자 하는 새로운 시도이다.

iii) 징벌적 손해배상(punitive damages)으로의 대체

가해자의 행위가 폭력적(violent), 억압적(oppressive), 악의(malice), 기망(fraud), 의도적인 무시(wanton) 등으로 특별히 그 사정이 가중될 만한 사유를 수반하는 때에는 피해자가 현실로 입은 손해를 초과한 손해배상액의 지급을 명할 수가 있다.

2) 집행단계에서의 비범죄화[18]

(1) 의의

- 형사제재규정이 입법적으로 그대로 존속함에도 불구하고 일정한 행위 또는 상황에 대한 형사사법기관활동의 점진적인 변화로 형법의 적용범위가 축소되는 비범죄화를 말한다.
- 형법투입의 사회적인 비용이 너무 높은 경우, 형법 이외의 다른 사회통제수단에 의한 규율들이 더 적합한 경우, 형벌법규와 국민의 법감정 사이에 현저한 차이가 있는 경우, 사회변화와 함께 처벌의 필요성이 없어졌으나 아직 법률이 폐지되지 않은 경우 등에 적용된다.

(2) 수사단계에서의 비범죄화

① 경찰의 무혐의처리(훈방)

- 훈방권은 검사만이 수사종결권을 갖는 우리나라 형사소송법 구조하에서 경찰서장 또는 지구대장이 '범죄사실이 경미하고 뉘우치는 정이 뚜렷하며 피해회복된 자로서, 60세 이상 고령자 또는 미성년자인 초범자, 정신박약, 보행불구, 질병자, 주거 및 신원이 확실하고 정상을 참작할 만한 부득이한 사유가 있는 자, 상습범이 아닌 자, 기타 경찰서장이 특히 훈방할 사유가 있다고 인정하는 자'에 대하여 적발현장에서 방면할 수 있는 권한을 말한다.
- 「즉결심판에 관한 절차법」 제3조 제1항에 규정한 경찰서장의 즉결심판청구권과 동법 제19조(형사소송법의 준용)에 근거하여 훈방권을 인정한다.

② 형사조정제도의 활용

형사조정제도는 재산범죄의 고소사건(사기, 횡령, 배임 등)과 소년, 의료, 명예훼손 등 일정한 형사사건에 대하여 피해자와 피의자가 화해에 이를 수 있도록 형사조정위원회에서 분쟁을 조정하는 제도를 말한다.

18) 사실상의 비범죄화, 광의의 비범죄화이다.

③ 검찰의 기소편의주의, 소추요건의 상향조정 등이 있다.

(3) 재판단계에서의 비범죄화

재판단계에서의 비범죄화란 판례를 변경하여 형벌법규의 해석・적용을 수정하거나 처벌근거규정과 처벌강화규정의 축소해석 내지 처벌완화규정과 처벌면제규정의 확장해석을 통하여 종래 처벌하던 행위를 처벌하지 않는 것을 말한다.

① 판례의 변경을 통한 비범죄화

예 2004년, 서울남부지방법원의 한 판사가 양심적 병역거부자에 대하여 기존의 유죄판결을 깨고 무죄판결을 선고한 것

② 법문의 해석을 통한 비범죄화

법문의 해석과 관련하여 비범죄화를 추구하는 유형으로는 i) 명확성의 원칙 위반 사안, ii) 종래 처벌의 반성적 고려에 의한 사안, iii) 피고인에게 유리한 해석 사안 등으로 나누어 볼 수 있다.

③ 법원의 각종 유예선고를 통한 비범죄화가 있다.

제4절 구금제도

1. 의의

구금제도란 범죄인을 교정시설에 구금하여 자유를 박탈하여 형벌을 집행하는 제도를 말하며 “시설내처우”이다.[19)]

19) 1595년 네덜란드 암스테르담 노역장은 현대적 교도소제도 발전의 효시이며, 현대적 교정시설이 대두된 것은 영국 하워드(J. Howard)의 독거제에서 비롯되었다.

2. 전통적인 시설내처우인 구금방식

1) 혼거제

(1) 의의

혼거제 · 잡거제란 여러 명의 수용자를 동일한 거실에 구금하는 가장 오래된 제도이다.

(2) 장점

- 관리가 편리하고, 형벌의 통일을 도모할 수 있으며, 비용이 저렴하고, 수용자의 상호 감시로 자살을 방지할 수 있다.
- 작업시행이 편리하고, 사회적 적응훈련에 용이하고, 수용자의 심신단련을 도모할 수 있다.

(3) 단점

- 악풍(惡風)의 감염과 탈옥가능성이 많아지며, 사적 감정을 해침으로써 인격의 개발을 저해한다.
- 수형자 상호 간에 갈등이 유발되며, 교도관의 계호[20]상 감시와 규율유지가 곤란하다.
- 출소 후 재범가능성이 많으며, 개별처우가 곤란하며, 독거제에 비해 비위생적이며, 동성애의 폐해 우려가 있고, 거실 내 생활상의 책임감이 희박하여 관급품 · 대여품 등의 관리가 곤란하다.

2) 독거제 2012 기출

(1) 의의

- "펜실베이니아제", "필라델피아제"라고도 하고 범죄자의 정신적 개선에 중점을 둔 제도이다.
- 범죄자의 개선을 위한 최선의 방법은 독거구금상태에서 절대의 침묵 · 정숙 · 고독을

---

20) 교도소 등의 교정시설의 안전과 질서를 유지하기 위하여 수용자를 경계 · 감시 및 지도 · 명령하고, 안전 및 질서가 침해되거나 침해될 우려가 있는 경우에는 이를 진압하고, 원상회복을 위하여 강제력을 행사하는 것은 '계호(戒護)'이다. 2004 기출

유지하며, 회오(悔悟) · 반성 · 속죄하게 하여 정신적 개선을 도모하는 제도이다. 먹고, 자고, 일하고, 종교지도를 받는 등 모든 것을 자신의 거실에서 행한다.

(2) 장점

- 수용자 간의 통모(通謀)를 방지하고, 동료 간의 불량성의 감염을 회피할 수 있으며, 반성 · 회오의 기회를 제공한다.
- 개별처우에 편리하고, 구금형의 고통을 절실하게 하고, 수형자의 명예를 보호한다.
- 질병발견에 용이하고, 전염병예방에 기여하고, 미결수의 증거인멸과 공모위증을 방지할 수 있다.
- 수형자의 계호상 유리하고, 직원의 감시가 용이하며 난동방지에 유리하다.

(3) 단점

- 수형자의 자치활용이 불가능하므로 행형목적과 상충되며, 고독상태에 의한 심리적 · 생리적 장애로 자살 등을 초래할 위험이 있다.
- 수형자의 상호감시가 불편하며, 운동과 의료가 불편하고, 집단교육 · 집단작업이 불편하다.
- 재정상 경비가 과다하며, 독거생활은 인간본능을 박탈하며, 구금성 정신질환을 유발할 수 있다.

3) 오번(Auburn)제

(1) 의의

1823년 뉴욕 주 오번감옥에서 본격적으로 실시된 것으로서, 엄정독거제의 단점을 보완하면서 혼거제의 단점인 수형자 상호 간의 악풍감염 및 도주 · 증거인멸을 방지하여 교도소 내의 질서유지를 도모하려는 데 있다.[21]

(2) 장점

- 엄정독거제에 비해 인간적이며, 작업시행에 적합하다.

---

21) 주간작업 시에 대화(교담)를 금하고 침묵을 강요하므로 '침묵제'라고도 하며, 주간에 작업장에서 혼자 작업하고 야간에는 독거시킨다는 의미에서 '절충제' 또는 '야간독거제'라고도 한다.

- 상호 간의 악풍감염을 방지할 수 있으며, 공모에 의한 도주와 반항을 방지할 수 있다.
- 집단생활하에서 사회적 훈련이 가능하며, 주야독거제도의 심신허약 등 여러 폐해를 방지할 수 있다.

(3) 단점

- 수형자 상호 간의 의사소통이 금지되어, 인간 본연의 사회성 훈련이 불완전하다.
- 상호의사소통의 두절로 작업능력이 저하되며, 개별처우가 곤란하다.
- 계호・감시・규율유지가 곤란하며, 독거제에 비해 비위생적이며 방역이 곤란하다.
- 은밀한 부정행위나 출소 후 동료수형자와의 교제로 재범가능성이 많다.
- 인간의 본성인 공동생활의 습성을 박탈함으로써 정신적・생리적인 장애를 초래할 수 있다.

3. 개방처우

1) 의의

- 개방처우란 행형(교정)의 사회화를 위하여 시설내처우에 있어서 요구되는 격리와 엄격한 규율 등을 완화하여, 가능한 한 교정시설 내의 생활을 일반사회생활과 접근시켜 수행자를 일반사회와 교통케 함으로써, 시설화에 따른 악영향과 인격의 파괴를 피하고 사회에의 재적응을 용이케 하는 처우방법이다.[22]

2) 개방처우의 형태

- 시설 내 기반을 둔 중간처우로는 개방교도소, 외부통근・통학제, 주말구금제, 귀휴제, 부부 및 가족접근제, 외부전문가 상담제 등이 있다.
- 사회 내 기반을 둔 중간처우로는 중간처우의 집, 석방 전 보도제도, 다목적센터, 집단처우센터 등이 있다.

---

22) • 전통적인 폐쇄처우와 사회내처우의 중간단계에 위치하므로 '중간처우'라고도 하며, 처우의 사회화를 추구한다는 점에서 '사회적 처우'라고도 한다.
• 개방시설제도는 수형자의 사회재적응에 도움이 되며, 사회내처우와 시설내처우의 중간형태로써 보안기능을 최소화한 시설이며 응보보다는 재통합에 중점을 둔 처우이다. 2006 기출

3) 시설내 기반을 둔 중간처우

(1) 개방교도소

- 유형적 · 물리적 도주방지조치가 없고, 피수용자의 자율 및 책임감에 기반을 두고 운영되는 교정시설이다.[23)]
- 교정의 인도화(人道化)와 사회화에 기여하며, 단기자유형의 폐해를 보완하며, 교정경비의 절감이 가능하다.
- 수용의 부정적인 폐해를 경감하며, 수형자와 교도관과의 인간관계 개선으로 수형자의 교정교화 및 재사회화에 공헌한다.
- 시민의 법감정에 배치되어 수용하기 어려우며, 지역사회의 반대로 인한 설치의 어려움이 있다.

(2) 외부통근제도(Work Release)

야간과 휴일에는 시설에 구금하고 주간은 직장에 통근하는 것을 허용하는 제도로써, 반구금처우 내지 반자유처우의 성격을 지닌다.[24)]

(3) 외부통학제도

재소자가 주간에 시설 외의 지역사회에서 교육을 받을 수 있게 하는 일종의 교정교육제도이다.

(4) 주말구금제도

- 주말에 수형자를 시설에 구금하고 평일에는 자유를 허용하는 것으로 형의 분할집행의 한 형태이다.
- 휴일에만 집행하는 "휴일구금", 주말 이외의 연말연시 · 휴가 등 비교적 장기의 휴가시간에 구금생활을 하게 하는 "단속구금", 야간과 휴일에만 구금하는 "반구금제(반자유제)"가 있다.

23) 우리나라의 유일한 개방시설인 천안개방교도소는 종래 생활관으로서의 기능을 폐지하고 현재는 교통 · 과실범죄자 등에게 개방처우를 실시하고 있다.

24) 우리나라의 수용자처우법 제68조 및 제69조에 의거하여, 교정시설 안에 설치된 외부기업체의 작업장에서 작업할 수 있는 근거를 마련하였으며, 외부통근 작업대상자의 선정기준 등에 관하여 필요한 사항은 법무부령으로 정하도록 하고 있다. 또한 외부통근제도는 행정형을 채택하고 있다.

(5) 귀휴제(歸休制)

- 수형자에 대하여 일정한 사유로 단기간 행선지를 정하여 외출 또는 외박을 허용하는 제도로써 "형벌휴가제", "외출・외박제"라고도 한다.
- 수형자의 사회적응력을 배양하는 방법으로서 접견, 서신 등과 함께 외부와의 교통을 중요한 작용으로 하는 반자유처우의 한 형태이다.
- 석방 후 원활한 사회복귀 및 취업준비를 가능케 하고, 근친자의 위독 시 방문 또는 사망 등과 같은 중요 가족사에의 참여를 가능케 한다.
- 특정작업에의 취업자 및 모범수형자에 대한 포상이며, 부부 간의 면회 등 가족관계의 유지를 가능케 한다.
- 우리나라의 귀휴제도는 수용자처우법 제77조에 근거하고 시행령은 법무부령이다.
- 허가요건은 "6개월 이상 복역하고 형기를 1/3 이상 지난 자,[25] 교정성적(행상)이 우수한 자"이다.
- 허가사유는 "㉠ 가족 또는 배우자의 직계존속이 위독한 때 ㉡ 질병이나 사고로 외부의료시설에의 입원이 필요한 때 ㉢ 천재지변이나 그 밖의 재해로 가족, 배우자의 직계존속 또는 수형자 본인에게 회복할 수 없는 중대한 재산상의 손해가 발생하였거나 발생할 우려가 있는 때 ㉣ 그 밖에 교화 또는 건전한 사회복귀를 위하여 법무부령으로 정하는 사유가 있는 때"이다.

(6) 부부 및 가족 접견

부부면회제도는 접견의 한 형태로서 부부 간의 접견 시 교도관의 입회를 생략하고 그에 상당한 행동의 자유를 부여하거나 또는 특별한 면회실에서 접견을 하도록 함으로써 부부 간에 애정의 자유를 보호하는 제도이다.[26]

4. 사회내처우인 중간처우 2012 기출

1) 전통적 중간교도소

출소기일이 임박한 수형자 즉, 만기석방 또는 가석방대상자에 대하여 석방 전 상당기간

25) 21년 이상의 유기형 또는 무기형의 경우에는 7년이다.

26) 우리나라에서는 1999년 5월부터 대전교도소 등 4개 시설에 침실・부엌 등이 갖춰진 주택형태인 '부부만남의 집'이 설치되었다. 2003년부터는 '가족만남의 집'으로 확대・개편되어 시행되고 있다.

을 지역사회와 가까운 곳에 위치한 중간교도소로 이송하여 주로 개방처우의 여러 방법으로 처우를 받게 하여 출소준비를 온전하게 하여 정상적이고 원활한 사회복귀를 도모하는 제도를 말한다.

2) 현대의 중간처우의 집(Halfway House)

중간처우의 집이란 교도소도 구치소도 아니면서 완전한 구금시설과 완전한 자유시설의 중간에 있는 시설을 총칭하는 개념이다.

3) 사회내처우센터

사회내처우센터(Community Treatment Center)는 중간처우의 집과 유사한 시설이다. 이에는 석방 전 보도센터, 가석방 호스텔(Parole Hostel), 보호관찰 호스텔(Probation Hostel), 다목적센터 등이 있다.

4) 수용자 합동접견

교도소 내 특별구역에서 주로 모범수형자를 선정하여, 그들의 가족과 보안시설물이 없는 상태에서 직접 대면하면서 일반접견보다 장시간 동안 더욱 자유롭게 접촉하도록 하는 제도이다.

5) 사회견학

견학장소로는 주로 유적지, 애국지사 발자취, 종교시설, 사회복지시설, 사회교육시설 등 국민정신을 함양하기에 적합한 장소 및 각종 산업시설이 이용되고 있다.

6) 외부전문가 상담제

시설 내에서의 처우를 유지하면서도 시설 내에서의 생활을 일반사회의 전문가들과 활발하게 접촉시켜 석방 후 사회적응을 용이하게 하기 위한 시설내처우의 사회화를 확대한 것이다.

참고문헌

국내문헌

공정식, 살아있는 범죄학, 교육과학사, 2011.
강동범, "사이버범죄와 형사법적 대책", 한국형사정책연구원, 형사정책연구, 제11권 제2호, 2000.
강숙자, 한국 여성운동 이념정립을 위한 시론", 이화여자대학교 박사학위논문, 2004.
경찰대학 교재편찬위원회, 경찰방범론, 경찰대학, 1998.
경찰수사보안연수원, 컴퓨터범죄수사, 2000.2.
경찰청, 2011 경찰백서, 2011년 10월.
고건호, "폭력조직의 활동영역과 대책", 강력검사연구논문집(Ⅳ), 대검찰청, 1994.
기광도, "미국경찰의 범죄예방활동에 관한 연구", 한국형사정책연구원, 1995.
기광도, "경찰과 범죄간의 관계분석 : 시계열분석을 중심으로", 한국경찰연구, 제6권 제2호, 한국경찰발전연구학회, 2007.
기광도, "경찰의 범죄억제력에 관한 고찰", 형사정책연구, 제12권 제4호, 한국형사정책연구원, 2001.
기광도, "범죄예방활동에 관한 이론", 형사정책연구소식, 제26호, 한국형사정책연구원, 1994.
기광도, "미국경찰의 범죄예방활동에 관한 연구", 한국형사정책연구원, 1995.
김용준, 범죄피해자학, 백산출판사, 2009.
김재중, "집행유예에 관한 동향과 개선방안", 법학연구, 제19권 제1호, 충북대학교 법학연구소, 2008.
김주현, "조직범죄수사에 필요한 제도개선방향에 관한 소고", 강력검사연구논문집(Ⅳ), 대검찰청, 1994.
김채영, 범죄학이론의 발전과 현대적 과제에 관한 연구, 호서대학교 행정대학원 석사학위논문, 2010.
김한균・강은영, "범죄의 양형분석 및 재범방지를 위한 성폭력 범죄자 사후관리방안", 법무연수원, 2006.
대검찰청, 범죄분석, 1983(1/4-4/4).
대검찰청, 마약류범죄백서, 대검찰청, 2001.
대법원, 1976.4.13 선고 76도 340 판결.
대법원, 1977.1.27 선고 77도 3469 판결.
문영호・정진수, "조직폭력의 실태와 대책", 한국형사정책연구보고서, 한국형사정책연구원, 1993.
박기석, "부부강간행위의 강간죄 성립여부", 형사정책연구, 제15권 제4호, 한국형사정책연구원, 2004.
박상기・손동권・이순래, 형사정책, 한국형사정책연구원, 1990.
박재오, "조직폭력의 문제점과 근절방안", 강력검사연구논문집(Ⅳ), 대검찰청, 1994.
배임호, "회복적 사법정의의 배경, 발전과정, 주요 프로그램 그리고 선진교정복지", 교정연구, 통권 3호, 2007.
배종대, 형사정책, 홍문사, 2000.
양근원, 사이버범죄의 특징과 수사방향, 수사연구, 수사연구사, 2000년 6월.
양근원・장윤식, 사이버범죄수사론, 경찰대학, 2008.
여성부, "성매매방지를 위한 국외사례연구", 정책자료 2001-18, 2001.
연합뉴스, 2008.12.12.
이만종, 범죄학개론, 학현사, 2002.
이보령, 형사정책, 제일법규, 1996.
이상원, 방범론, 대명출판사, 2001.

이상현, 범죄심리학, 박영사, 2004(3판).
이윤호, 범죄학, 박영사, 2007.
임상곤, 범죄심리학원론, 백산출판사, 2004.
장다혜, "단순강간의 형사법상 판단기준에 관한 여성주의적 연구", 이화여자대학교 대학원 박사학위 논문, 2004.
전대양, 현대사회와 범죄, 형설출판사, 2002.
전대양, "연쇄 강간범의 범죄심리학적 특성", 한국범죄심리연구, 한국범죄심리학회, 제2권 제1호, 2006.
전대양 · 송병호, 조직범죄론, 형설출판사, 2004.
정신교, 범죄학개론, 형설출판사, 2005.
정영석 · 신양균, 형사정책, 법문사, 1996.
조병인, 현대사회와 범죄, 법문사, 2000(제3판).
조병인, "하이테크 범죄의 실태와 대책", 1999년도 한국공안행정학회 국제범죄 학술세미나 자료집.
조병인, 범죄대책론, 한림원, 1993.
조은경, "강간피해의 심리적 반응에 대한 고찰", 피해자학연구, 제3호, 한국피해자학회, 1994.
지광준, 형사정책, 경인, 1998.
진계호, 형사정책, 대왕사, 2002.
천정환, 신범죄학, 백산출판사, 2006.
최선우, 경찰과 커뮤니티, 대왕사, 2003.
최응렬, "환경설계를 통한 범죄예방", 동국대학교 대학원 박사학위논문, 1984.
최인섭, "조직범죄의 특성과 실태", 제12회 형사정책 세미나자료, 한국형사정책연구원, 1994.
최인섭, "지역사회범죄예방과 민간인 참여", 형사정책연구, 한국형사정책연구원, 1994.
최인섭 · 전영실, "강간범죄의 실태에 관한 연구", 한국형사정책연구원, 1992.
최정호, 마약범죄수사론, 경찰대학, 2008.
한국정보보호센타, "정보보호 통계자료", 정보보호뉴스, 제14호, 1999년 8월.
헌법재판소, 1990.9.10. 89헌마82 전원합의부.
헌법재판소, 2010.10.25. 2000헌바60 전원합의부.
헌법재판소, 2008.10.30. 2007헌가17 · 21, 2008헌가7 · 26, 2008헌바21 · 47(병합) 전원합의부.
황지태, "한국의 치안인력과 범죄율에 관한 소고", 형사정책연구, 제21권 제1호, 2010.

국외문헌

Sutherland Edwin & Cressey Donald, Principle of Criminology, 6th ed., Philadelphia : Lippincott, 1960.
Albanese Jay, Organized Crime in America, Cincinnati : Anderson, 1989.
Block Alan & Chambliss William, Organized Crime, Elsevier Science, 1982.
Carter D. L., "Computer Crime Categories", FBI Law Enforcement Bulletin, 64, No. 7, 1995.
Champion Dean John, The American Dictionary of Criminal Justice : Key Terms and Major Court Cases, L.A. California : Roxbury Publishing Company, 2005.
Charles, P. Pfleeger, Security in Computing, U.S. : Prentice-Hall PTR, 1997.
Clarke, R. V., "Situational Crime Prevention: It's Theoretical Basis and Practical Scope", Crime

and Justice, 4, 1983.
Clarke Ronald & Weisberg David, Diffusion of Crime Control Benefits, New York : Criminal Justice Press, 1994.
Clarke. R. V., Situational Crime Prevention : Successful Case Studies, Harrow and Huston, 1992.
Conklin, J. E., The Impact of Crime, MacMillan Pub., 1975.
Cressey Donald, Theft of the Nations, Harper Torchbooks, 1977.
Denner, W. G. & Lab. S. P., Victimology, 2nd ed., Cincinnati, OH : Anderson Publishing Co., 1998.
Ehrlich, I., "Participation in Illegitimate Activities : A Theoretical and Empirical Investigation", Journal of Political Economics, 81(3), May/June, 1973.
Gober, T., "The Crime Displacement Hypothesis : An Empirical Examination", Crime Delinquency, 26, 1981.
Green Gary, "General Deterrence and Television Cable Crime : A Field Experiment in Social Crime", Criminology, 23, 1986.
Groth, A. N., Burgess, A. W. & Holstom, L. L., "Rape : Power, Anger and Sexuality", American Journal of Psychiatry, 1977.
Hagan, Frank E., "The Organized Crime Continuum : A Further Specification of a New Conceptual", Criminal Justice Review, 8, 1983.
Howard Zehr R. J., Changing Lenses : A New Focus on Crime and Justice, Scottdale, PA : Herald Press, 1990.
Jacob, H. & Rich M. J., "The Effects of th Police on Crime : A Rejointer", Law and Society, 16, 1981.
Jeffery C. R., Crime Prevention Through Environment Design, Beverly Hills, 1977.
Karmen Andrew, Crime Victims : An Introduction to Victimology, Belmont : Thomson Wadsworth, 2006.
Kelling George & Bratton William, "Declining Crime Rates : Insiders' View of the New York City Story", The Journal of Criminal Law & Criminology, 88, No. 4, 1988.
Kenny Dennis J. & Finckenauer James O., Organized Crime in America, Belmont, CA : Wadsworth Publishing Company, 1995.
Klepper S. & Nagin D., "The Deterrent Effect of Perceived Certainty and Severity of Punishment Revisited", Criminology, 27, 1989.
Lab, S. P., Crime Prevention : Approaches, Practices and Evaluation, Cincinnati, Ohio : Anderson Publishing Co., 1992.
Lemert, E., Social Pathology, New York : McGraw-Hill, 1951.
Lemert, E., Human Deviance, Social Problems, and Social Control, Englewood Cliffs : Prentice-Hall, 1967.
Lester, D. & Lester, G., Crime of Passion, Chicago : Nelson Hall, 1975.
Mack, John A., "The Organized and Professional Labels Criticized", International Journal of Crime and Penology, 1, 1973.
Merton Robert K., Social Theory and Social Structure, New York : The Free Press, 1957.
National Crime Prevention Institute, Understanding Crime Prevention, Butterworths : Publishers, 1986.
Newburn Tim, Criminology, William Publishing, 2007.
Newman Oscar, Defensible Space : Prevention Through Urban Design, New York : MacMillan, 1973.

Phillips, L. & Votey H. L., “An Economic Analysis of the Deterrent Effect of Law Enforcement on Criminal Activity”, Journal of Criminal Law, Criminology and Police Science, 63, 1972.

Platt, T., “Prospects of Radical Criminology in the United States”, Crime and Social Justice, Vol. I, Spring-Summer, 1974.

Reckless W. C., “A New Theory of Delinquency and Crime”, Federal Probation, Vol. 25, 1961.

Reckless Walter C., Dinitz Simon & Murry Ellen, E., Self Concept as Insulator Against Delinquency ASR., Vol. 21, 1956.

Schur, E., Radical Non-Rethinking the Delinquency Problem, Englewood Cliffs : Prentice-Hall, 1973.

Schur, E., Labelling Deviant Behavior, New York : Harper & Row, 1971.

Siegel, L. J. & Senna J. J., Essentials of Criminal Justice, Thomson Wadsworth, 2007.

Siegel, Larry J., Criminology, St. Paul: Wadsworth Publishing Company, 1998.

Siegel, Larry J., Criminology, 5th ed., West Publishing Company, 1995.

Simon L. M. J., “Do Criminal Offenders Specialize in Crime Types”, Applied and Preventive Psychol., 6, 1977.

Skogan Wesley G., Disorder and Decline : Crime and Spiral of Decay in American Neighborhood, New York: Free Press, 1990.

Sutherland Edwin H., White Collar Crime, N.Y. : Dryden Press, 1969.

Svalastoga Kaare, “Homicide and Social Contact in Denmark,” American Journal of Sociology, Vol. 62, 1966.

Swimmer, G., “The Relationship of Police and Crime : Some Methodological and Empirical Results”, Criminology, 12, 1974.

Talyer, Walton & Young, The New Criminology, New York : Harper and Row Publishers, 1973.

Tannenbaum, F., Crime and the Community, New York : Columbia Univ. Press, 1938.

Theerthorn Pochara, “Architectural Style, Aesthetic Landscaping, Home Value, and Crime Prevention”, International Journal of Comparative and Applied Criminal Justice, 12, 1988.

Tittle Charles & Rowe Alan, “Certainty of Arrest and Crime Rates : A Further Test of the Deterrence Hypothesis”, Social Forces, 52, 1974.

U. S. Organized Crime Control Act of 1970.

Williams, J. E., Criminology and Criminal Justice, London, 1982.

Wilson James, Q. & Kelling George L., “Broken Windows : The Police and Neighborhood Safety”, Atlantic Monthly, March, 1982.

Wilson, J. Q. & Boland B., “The Effect of the Police on Crime”, Law and Society, 12, 1978.

저자약력

양원규(梁元奎)

영남대학교 법정대학 행정학과(행정학 학사)
경북대학교 일반대학원 행정학과(행정학 석사)
경북대학교, 경일대학교 일반대학원 행정학과(행정학 박사)
현) 대경대학교 경찰행정학과 교수 · 학과장
공무원 시험문제 검증위원
한국직업능력개발원 심사위원
경북지방경찰청 경찰공무원 징계위원회 위원
대구지방경찰청 · 경북지방경찰청 경찰학교 외래교수
한국치안행정학회 운영위원회 영남지회 회장
한국정부학회 섭외홍보위원회 집행이사 · 학회 간 교류협력위원회 위원
대한지방자치학회 부회장 · 총무위원장 · 감사
대구경실련 경제정의연구소 운영위원
전) 현대행정문제연구소 소장
대구광역시 지방공무원교육원 외래교수
대구광역시 · 영천시 시험출제위원

〈저서〉

민간경비론 제대로 알기(백산출판사, 2013)
경찰관리론 제대로 알기(2판, 백산출판사, 2013)
경찰관리론 제대로 알기(백산출판사, 2012)
조직이론 제대로 알기(대왕사, 2012)
범죄학 제대로 알기(백산출판사, 2012)
행정학 제대로 알기(6판, 백산출판사, 2011)
경찰조직관리론 제대로 알기(백산출판사, 2010)
행정학 제대로 알기(개정신판, 백산출판사, 2010)
경찰행정법 제대로 알기(2판, 한올출판사, 2009)
경찰학총론 I 제대로 알기(백산출판사, 2009)
경찰학총론 II 제대로 알기(백산출판사, 2009)
경찰학총론 제대로 알기(도서출판 한영, 2007)
경찰행정법 제대로 알기(한올출판사, 2006)
경찰행정법(2003), 지방자치경찰론(2003), 행정학 제대로 알기(2003)
실패와 성공학(2002), 조직과 인간(2002), 공직윤리론(1999)
행정학연습(1999), 환경행정론(1998), 행정학개론(1997)
신체계 도시 · 지방행정론(1996), 승진 행정학연구(1994), 신체계 행정학(1991)
현대지역사회개발론(1990), 행정학(1985), 객관식 문제중심 행정학(1984)
주관식 문제중심 행정학(1982) 외 다수

〈논문〉

- "The Effects of Police Organizational Culture to the Organizational Commitment through the Job Satisfaction", 경찰조직문화가 직무만족과 조직몰입에 미치는 영향, 한국지방자치학회, 2011년도 동계학술대회, pp. 683-702
- 방범용 CCTV의 효율적 운영방안, 대한지방자치학회 2010년 추계학술대회논문집, pp. 173-181
- "Implication of Conflicts on Inspector's Promotion Process", 경위근속승진제에 대한 갈등의 함의, 한국치안행정논집, 제4권 제1호:21-38
- "Perspectives on Characteristic of Police Culture", 경찰문화의 특징에 관한 고찰, 한국치안행정논집, 제4권 제1호:191-210
- "Theoretical Perspectives on Police Culture : In Concepts, Characteristics, and Research Trend of Police Culture", 경찰문화에 대한 이론적 고찰 -경찰문화의 개념과 특징 및 연구동향을 중심으로, 영남정치학회보 제17권, 2006:25-45
- "A Theoretical Study of the Korean Bureaucracy Culture", 한국관료문화의 이론적 고찰, 영남정치학회보 제16호, 2005:55-75
- "A Study on the Concept of Political Rationality in Policy-Making", 정책결정에 있어서 정치적 합리성 외 다수

저자약력

배철효(裵哲孝)

영남대학교 행정대학원 졸업(행정학 석사)
경남대학교 대학원 졸업(행정학 박사)
현) 수성대학교 경찰행정과 학과장
전) 수성대학교 학사운영처장
수성대학교 민간경비교육센터장
대구과학대학교 경찰행정과 교수
한국치안행정학회 회장
한국민간경비학회 회장
(사)한국행정학회 공공안전연구회 회장
한국경찰학회 부회장
한국경찰연구학회 부회장
(사)대한지방자치학회 부회장
공인 경비지도사 시험출제위원 및 검토위원
공인 신변보호사 시험출제위원 및 검정위원
공인 행정관리사 시험출제위원
충청북도 7급 지방공무원 공개채용시험출제위원
청원경찰시험출제위원
경찰청 고객만족평가단 위원
대구지방경찰청 정책평가단 위원
동부경찰서 경찰발전위원회 위원
법무부 범죄예방 소년선도 분과위원회 위원
대구지방검찰청 서부지청 형사조정위원회 위원
대구지방경찰청 집회시위시민감시단 위원장
대구구치소 교정자문위원회 위원장
민주평화통일자문회의 자문위원
한국전문대학교육협의회 학과평가위원

〈논저〉
신사무관리론(학문사, 2004)
경찰인사관리론(남두도서, 2004)
현대행정관리론(도서출판 대영문화사, 2004)
공인행정사 문제연구(도서출판 대영문화사, 2005)
경비지도사 민간경비론(엑스퍼트, 2006)
경찰학개론(도서출판 대영문화사, 2007)
경호학개론(도서출판 대영문화사, 2009)
범죄학 제대로 알기(백산출판사, 2012)
경찰서비스 기능의 향상방안에 관한 연구 외 다수

저자약력

정우열(鄭祐烈)

경희대학교 대학원(행정학 석사)
영남대학교 대학원(행정학 박사)
현) 경운대학교 경찰행정학부 교수
한국행정사학회회장(지역)
경상북도 의회의정비심의위원장
대한지방자치학회회장
행정고등고시 및 5급 승진시험 출제위원
경상북도 산하기관·단체 경영평가위원
경상북도 지방경찰청 인권위원회위원

〈저서〉
현대행정학(공저, 삼우사, 2006)
경찰조직관리론(공저, 형설출판사, 2009)
민간경비론 제대로 알기(공저, 백산출판사, 2013)

〈논문〉
지방자치단체의 친환경 정보기술산업의 육성방안(공저, 2011)
한국 지역경찰 체제의 발전과정에 관한 연구(공저, 2009)
경찰조직의 학습구축이 조직유효성에 미치는 영향관계분석(공저, 2008) 등 다수

저자약력

장철영(張哲榮)

영남대학교 행정학과 및 동 대학원 졸업(행정학 박사)
현) 대구외국어대학교 경찰행정학과 교수
한국행정학회 편집위원
대한지방자치학회 편집이사
한국정부학회 총무위원장
한국치안행정학회 경찰행정연구위원장
한국민간경비학회 국제이사
한국정치발전연구원 행정분과 위원장
경상북도 경산시 정책자문위원
한국공안행정학회 정회원
경북지방경찰청 평가위원

〈저서〉
민간경비론(백산출판사, 2013)
현대사회와 범죄(지식인, 2013)
신편 경찰학객론(21세기사, 2013)
경찰학총론 제대로 알기(2판, 백산출판사, 2013)
〈SPSS 사회현상 조사분석 및 연구논문 작성을 위한〉 알기 쉬운 통계기법의 활용(대명출판사, 2011)
경찰조직관리론(형설출판사, 2009)
Focus 행정학(한울기획, 2003)

〈논문〉
- A Study on the Status of Cyberbullying and Countermeasures for the Solutions(한국치안행정논집, 2013)
- 경찰공무원의 직무특성과 조직효과성 관계에 있어 조직공정성의 조절효과에 관한 연구: Ping의 2단계 접근법을 중심으로(공저, 한국공안행정학회보, 2013)
- 해양경찰의 효율적 정책집행체계 구축 방안에 관한 연구: 불법어로를 중심으로(위기관리 이론과 실천, 2013)
- 해사안전관리 효율화를 위한 조직 기능 수행체계 진단: 해상교통안전 분야를 중심으로(공저, 한국치안행정학회, 2013)
- 선박안전관리 효율화를 위한 관리체계 개선에 관한 연구(공저, 한국민간경비학회, 2013)
- 유해물질 사고 예방과 대응을 위한 경찰조직 및 기능 수행체계에 관한 정책적 함의(공저, 치안정책연구, 2013)
- 한국 경찰공무원의 부패유형 탐색 및 함의: KINDS를 통한 언어네트워크 분석(한국치안행정논집, 2012) 등 다수

행정학 제대로 알기(제6판)

제 1 장 행정학 일반이론

제1절 행정의 개념 / 제2절 공행정과 사행정 / 제3절 행정학의 발달 / 제4절 현대행정의 특징 / 제5절 행정과정 / 제6절 행정이념 / 제7절 과학적 관리론 / 제8절 인간관계론 / 제9절 행정행태론 / 제10절 행정문화 / 제11절 행정생태론 / 제12절 행정체제론 / 제13절 비교행정론 / 제14절 발전행정론 / 제15절 신행정론

제 2 장 정책 및 기획론

제1절 공익 / 제2절 행정목표 / 제3절 목표관리(MBO) / 제4절 정책결정 / 제5절 기획 / 제6절 사회지표 / 제7절 갈등 / 제8절 권위

제 3 장 조직이론

제1절 조직의 의의 / 제2절 공식적 조직과 비공식적 조직 / 제3절 관료제 / 제4절 조직의 원리 / 제5절 위원회 / 제6절 계선기관과 참모기관 / 제7절 공기업 / 제8절 조직과 개인 / 제9절 동기부여이론 / 제10절 조직과 환경 / 제11절 집권과 분권 / 제12절 중앙집권과 지방분권 / 제13절 일선기관 / 제14절 광역행정 / 제15절 행정상의 관리계층 / 제16절 리더십 / 제17절 의사전달 / 제18절 조직혁신 / 제19절 조직발전

제 4 장 인사행정론

제1절 인사행정의 발전 / 제2절 인사행정기관 / 제3절 공직의 분류 / 제4절 계급제와 직위분류제 / 제5절 직업공무원제 / 제6절 임 용 / 제7절 능력발전 / 제8절 사기 / 제9절 근무규율

제 5 장 재무행정론

제1절 재무행정의 의의 / 제2절 재무행정기관 / 제3절 재무행정의 법적 기초 / 제4절 예산의 의의와 원칙 / 제5절 예산의 종류 / 제6절 예산의 분류 / 제7절 예산제도의 발달 / 제8절 계획과 예산 / 제9절 자본예산 / 제10절 예산과정 / 제11절 구매행정

제 6 장 행정통제론

제1절 행정책임 / 제2절 행정통제 / 제3절 옴부즈만제도 / 제4절 행정개혁

■ 책 소개

경찰조직관리론 제대로 알기

제1장 경찰조직의 의의
제1절 경찰조직의 의의 / 제2절 경찰조직의 기본요소 / 제3절 경찰조직의 특징

제2장 경찰조직의 원리
제1절 조직원리의 의의 / 제2절 경찰조직의 제 원리 / 제3절 경찰관료제

제3장 경찰조직의 이념
제1절 의의 / 제2절 내용

제4장 경찰조직관리의 이론
제1절 경찰조직관리의 의의 / 제2절 Classical Approach / 제3절 Human Relative Approach / 제4절 Behavioral Science Approach / 제5절 Contemporary Approach

제5장 경찰조직의 목표와 기획
제1절 경찰조직의 목표 / 제2절 경찰기획

제6장 경찰관리자의 역할과 Motivation
제1절 경찰관리자 / 제2절 경찰기관장의 역할과 유형 / 제3절 동기부여이론

제7장 경찰 Leadership
제1절 의의 / 제2절 경찰 Leadership 이론의 변천 / 제3절 경찰 Leadership의 유형 / 제4절 경찰 Leadership의 분류

제8장 경찰조직의 Communication
제1절 의의 / 제2절 조직 Communication의 유형 / 제3절 Johari Window 모형 / 제4절 경찰 Communication의 장애요인과 극복방안

제9장 경찰조직에서의 갈등관리
제1절 갈등관리의 의의 / 제2절 경찰조직내 갈등관리의 상황과 전략

경찰학총론 제대로 알기(제2판)

제 1 편 경찰과 경찰학

제 1 장 경찰의 개념
제1절 경찰개념의 의의 / 제2절 경찰개념의 역사적 변천

제 2 장 경찰의 분류
제1절 실질적 의미의 경찰과 형식적 의미의 경찰 / 제2절 경찰의 분류

제 3 장 경찰의 목적과 수단
제1절 의의 / 제2절 경찰의 목적 / 제3절 경찰의 수단

제 2 편 경찰의 이념과 윤리

제 1 장 경찰행정의 이념
제1절 경찰행정이념의 의의 / 제2절 경찰행정이념의 내용 / 제3절 고객지향과 경찰서비스 / 제4절 고객지향의 경찰서비스 개선전략 / 제5절 시민헌장제도

제 2 장 경찰의 철학
제1절 경찰의 사상적 기초 / 제2절 코헨과 펠드버그(Cohen & Feldberg)의 경찰활동의 기준

제 3 장 경찰의 윤리
제1절 경찰윤리의 필요성 / 제2절 경찰역할모델과 작은 호의에 대한 찬반론 / 제3절 Kleinig의 경찰윤리교육의 목적 / 제4절 경찰의 다짐 / 제5절 경찰윤리와 법적 강제

제 4 장 경찰부패와 내부고발
제1절 경찰부패의 의의 / 제2절 내부고발

제 5 장 경찰문화
제1절 조직문화 / 제2절 경찰문화

제 3 편 경찰권

제 1 장 경찰행정의 법원
제1절 경찰행정의 법원 / 제2절 성문법원(成文法源) / 제3절 불문법원(不文法源) / 제4절 법원(法源) 간의 충돌과 경합

제 2 장 경찰권
제1절 경찰권의 의의 / 제2절 경찰권의 근거 / 제3절 경찰권의 한계

제 3 장 경찰개입청구권
제1절 의의 / 제2절 인정근거

제 4 장 경찰의 관할
제1절 의의 / 제2절 경찰의 관할

제 4 편 외국경찰의 역사와 제도

제 1 장 영국경찰
제1절 영국경찰의 역사 / 제2절 영국경찰의 제도

제 2 장 프랑스 경찰
제1절 프랑스경찰의 역사 / 제2절 프랑스의 경찰제도

제 3 장 독일경찰
제1절 독일경찰의 역사 / 제2절 독일의 경찰제도

제 4 장 스페인경찰
제1절 스페인경찰의 역사 / 제2절 스페인의 경찰제도

제 5 장 미국경찰
제1절 미국경찰의 역사 / 제2절 미국의 경찰제도

제 6 장 일본의 경찰
제1절 일본경찰의 역사 / 제2절 일본경찰의 조직

제 7 장 중국의 경찰
제1절 중국경찰의 역사 / 제2절 중국경찰의 조직

제 5 편 한국경찰의 역사와 제도

제 1 장 전근대적 경찰제도
제1절 부족국가시대의 경찰제도 / 제2절 삼국시대의 경찰제도 / 제3절 통일신라시대의 경찰제도 / 제4절 고려시대의 경찰제도 / 제5절 조선시대(갑오경장 이전)의 경찰제도

제 2 장 근대적 경찰제도
제1절 갑오경장부터 한일합병 이전까지의 경찰제도 / 제2절 식민지기의 경찰제도

제 3 장 현대적 경찰제도
제1절 미군정기의 경찰제도 / 제2절 정부수립 이후 1991년 이전의 경찰제도 / 제3절 1991년 경찰법 이후의 경찰제도

경찰관리론 제대로 알기(제2판)

제1장 경찰인사관리론

제1절 경찰인사관리의 의의와 목적 / 제2절 엽관주의와 실적주의 / 제3절 직업공무원제도 / 제4절 경찰공무원의 분류 / 제5절 인사관리기관 / 제6절 경찰공무원의 외부임용 / 제7절 경찰공무원의 내부임용 / 제8절 교육훈련제도 / 제9절 근무성적평정제도 / 제10절 다면평가 / 제11절 경력평정 / 제12절 기타 인사운영제도 / 제13절 경찰공무원의 권리/ 제14절 경찰공무원의 의무 / 제15절 경찰공무원의 책임

제2장 경찰재무관리론

제1절 경찰예산의 의의 / 제2절 예산과정 / 제3절 예산제도의 발달

제3장 경찰장비 및 물품관리론

제1절 경찰장비관리 / 제2절 무기 · 탄약관리 / 제3절 기동장비관리 / 제4절 진압장비 / 제5절 물품관리

제4장 경찰보안관리론

제1절 보안의 의의 / 제2절 비밀의 보호 / 제3절 보안감사

제5장 경찰홍보관리론

제1절 경찰홍보의 의의 / 제2절 경찰홍보의 전략과 유형 / 제3절 경찰홍보의 문제점

제6장 경찰통제관리론

제1절 경찰통제의 의의 / 제2절 경찰통제의 유형

제7장 경찰혁신관리론

제1절 행정개혁 / 제2절 경찰혁신

민간경비론 제대로 알기

제 1 장 민간경비총론

제1절 민간경비의 의의 / 1. Security의 개념 / 2. Private Security(Industry)의 개념 / 3. 민간경비(산)업의 분류 / 4. 민간경비의 역할과 임무

제2절 민간경비와 공경비의 관계 / 1. 민간경비와 공경비의 의의 / 2. 민간경비와 공경비의 유사점 / 3. 민간경비와 공경비의 차이점 / 4. 민간경비와 공경비의 제휴

제3절 민간경비의 성장이론 / 1. 의의 / 2. 민간경비의 성장이론

제 2 장 민간경비의 발전과정

제1절 고대의 민간경비 / 1. 의의 / 2. 시대별 민간경비

제2절 영국의 민간경비 / 1. 민간경비의 시작 / 2. 규환제도(함성제도: 喊聲制度, Hue and Cry) / 3. 헨리 국왕의 법령(Legis Henrici) / 4. 주야 감시시대 / 5. 보우가의 주자 / 6. 현대적 의미의 방범활동의 시작

제3절 미국의 민간경비 / 1. 미국 민간경비의 발달 / 2. 미국 민간경비의 특징

제4절 독일의 민간경비 / 1. 민간경비업체의 현황과 구조 / 2. 민간경비업무의 영역확대

제5절 일본의 민간경비 / 1. 발달과정과 역사적 배경 / 2. 일본의 경비서비스 / 3. 일본민간경비의 특징과 활동영역

제6절 우리나라의 민간경비 / 1. 민간경비의 발달 / 2. 한국의 민간경비제도

제 3 장 민간경비의 환경

제1절 국내치안환경의 변화 / 1. 2011년 주요범죄 발생동향 및 특징 / 2. 국내치안환경의 변화

제2절 경찰의 임무와 수단 / 1. 경찰의 임무와 수단 / 2. 경찰의 목적 / 3. 경찰의 수단

제3절 경찰과 민간경비의 방범활동 / 1. 방범경찰 / 2. 경찰의 범죄예방활동

제 4 장 민간경비의 조직과 업무

제1절 민간경비의 유형 / 1. 주체에 따른 분류 / 2. 목적에 따른 분류 / 3. 성격에 따른 분류

제2절 자체경비와 계약경비 / 1. 의의 / 2. 자체경비(상주경비: 常住警備) / 3. 계약경비

제3절 민간경비의 실시과정 / 1. 의의 / 2. 경비진단활동 / 3. 경비계획 / 4. 경비조직화 / 5. 경비인력의 수요와 경비원의 고용

제 5 장 민간경비의 운용

제1절 시설경비 / 1. 시설경비 / 2. 외곽경비 / 3. 내부경비 / 4. 경보시스템 / 5. 경비조명
제2절 화재예방경비 / 1. 화재의 의의 / 2. 화재경비 / 3. 화재안전교육과 진압
제3절 재난관리경비 / 1. 테러경비 / 2. 노사분규관리 / 3. 비상계획의 수립
제4절 혼잡경비 / 1. 혼잡경비의 의의 / 2. 혼잡경비의 실시 절차 / 3. 군중의 정리의 원칙 / 4. 혼잡경비 활동상의 주의사항 / 5. 사고발생 시 처리
제5절 특수경비업무(중요시설경비) / 1. 중요시설 / 2. 중요시설경비 /
제6절 기타 경비 / 1. 주거시설경비 / 2. 고층빌딩경비 / 3. 은행 등 금융기관의 경비 / 4. 의료 및 건강관리 기관의 경비 / 5. 숙박시설의 경비 / 6. 판매시설경비 / 7. 내부절도 및 산업스파이 / 8. 교육시설의 경비
제7절 환경설계를 통한 범죄예방(CPTED) / 1. 의의 / 2. CPTED의 내용 / 3. 예방공간의 물리적 요소

제 6 장 컴퓨터범죄 및 안전관리

제1절 사이버범죄 / 1. 사이버범죄의 의의 / 2. 사이버범죄의 분류 / 3. 사이버범죄의 일반적인 특징
제2절 컴퓨터범죄론 / 1. 컴퓨터범죄의 의의 / 2. 컴퓨터범죄의 수법과 유형
제3절 컴퓨터 안전대책 / 1. 컴퓨터범죄대책의 의의 / 2. 컴퓨터범죄의 동향 / 3. 컴퓨터 안전장치 / 4. 시스템의 안전장치

제 7 장 민간경비의 법적 지위와 관계 법령

제1절 민간경비의 법적 지위 / 1. 미국 민간경비의 법적 지위 / 2. 일본 민간경비의 법적 지위 / 3. 독일의 민간경비의 법적 지위 / 4. 우리나라 민간경비의 법적 지위
제2절 경비업법 / 1. 의의 / 2. 경비업법의 내용
제3절 청원경찰법 / 1. 의의 / 2. 내용
제4절 우리나라 민간경비산업의 개선방안과 전망 / 1. 우리나라 민간경비의 문제점 / 2. 우리나라 민간경비의 개선방안 / 3. 우리나라 민간경비의 전망

범죄학 제대로 알기

2012년 3월 10일 초판 1쇄 발행
2014년 2월 20일 2판 1쇄 발행

저 자 양 원 규·배 철 효
정 우 열·장 철 영

발행인 진 욱 상·진 성 원

발행처 백산출판사

서울시 성북구 정릉로 157(백산빌딩 4층)
등록 : 1974. 1. 9. 제 1-72호
전화 : 914-1621, 917-6240
FAX : 912-4438
http://www.ibaeksan.kr
editbsp@naver.com

이 책의 무단복사 및 전재는
저작권법에 저촉됩니다.

값 25,000원
ISBN 978-89-6183-878-8